MECHANICS-
MERCANTILE
LIBRARY.

A Nation of Outsiders

A Nation of Outsiders

How the White Middle Class Fell in Love
with Rebellion in Postwar America

GRACE ELIZABETH HALE

OXFORD
UNIVERSITY PRESS

2011

Oxford University Press, Inc., publishes works that further
Oxford University's objective of excellence
in research, scholarship, and education.

Oxford New York
Auckland Cape Town Dar es Salaam Hong Kong Karachi
Kuala Lumpur Madrid Melbourne Mexico City Nairobi
New Delhi Shanghai Taipei Toronto

With offices in
Argentina Austria Brazil Chile Czech Republic France Greece
Guatemala Hungary Italy Japan Poland Portugal Singapore
South Korea Switzerland Thailand Turkey Ukraine Vietnam

Published by Oxford University Press, Inc.
198 Madison Avenue, New York, NY 10016

www.oup.com

Oxford is a registered trademark of Oxford University Press

Library of Congress Cataloging-in-Publication Data
Hale, Grace Elizabeth.
A nation of outsiders : how the white middle class fell in love
with rebellion in postwar America / Grace Elizabeth Hale.
    p. cm.
Includes bibliographical references and index.
ISBN 978-0-19-539313-2
1. Popular culture—United States—History—20th century.
2. Whites—United States—Social conditions—20th century.
3. Middle class—United States—History—20th century.
4. Dissenters—United States—History—20th century.
5. Counterculture—United States—History—20th century.
6. Social psychology—United States—History—20th century.
7. United States—Social life and customs—20th century. I. Title.
E169.12.H338   2011
306.0973—dc22   2010018091

9 8 7 6 5 4 3 2 1

Printed in the United States of America
on acid-free paper

**For Sarah and Emma,
for always asking questions**

Contents

Acknowledgments

For financial support, I am grateful to a number of institutions and programs. The University of Virginia's College of Arts and Sciences awarded me multiple summer and other research grants and a sesquicentennial fellowship. Deans Ed Ayers and Meredith Woo, Associate Dean Bruce Holsinger, History Department chairs Chuck McCurdy and Brian Owensby, and American Studies chairs Maurie McInnis and Sandhya Shukla enabled me to take outside fellowships as well as an essential family leave. The National Humanities Center, the Virginia Foundation for the Humanities, and the Institute for Historical Studies at the University of Texas at Austin have all supported various stages of the research for and writing and editing of this book, and all of these institutions are amazing places to work. I want especially to thank Kent Mullikin and Lois Whittington at NHC for bearing with me during a year in which my dad was sick and dying, Ann White Spencer and Roberta Culbertson at VFH for their support and willingness to reschedule my fellowship, Julie Hardwick and Courtney Meador at the IHS, and Erika Bsumek for helping make Texas home this year. I also received a summer research grant from the Gilder Lehrman Foundation.

Over the last decade, I have presented pieces of this work at Vanderbilt University, the University of California–Santa Barbara, Emory University, the University of Virginia, New York University, the University of North Carolina–Chapel Hill, the University of South Carolina, Rutgers University, Virginia Tech, West Virginia Wesleyan, Purchase College–SUNY, the Southern Historical Association, and the American Studies Association. I want to thank all the commentators in these venues for their constructive criticisms. Jeremy Varon deserves a special acknowledgment for making sharp and yet also generous comments at the right moment and helping me to finish.

My agent, Geri Thoma, found a wonderful home for my project. Susan Ferber at Oxford University Press has been the perfect editor, reading every page more than once and pushing me exactly the right amount. I am grateful to both of these amazing women for their hard work on behalf of my book.

For intellectual community at UVA, I thank Brian Balogh, Reginald Butler, Alon Confino, Claudrena Harold, Chuck McCurdy, Tom Klubock, all my wonderful American Studies colleagues, graduate student members of the UVA Southern Seminar over the decade 1997–2007, and other UVA people thanked elsewhere in this list. Graduate students Scott Matthews and Megan Stubbendeck provided essential research help with this book. Scott and Lisa Goff have been more like colleagues than graduate students in the ways they have challenged my thinking and commented on my work over the years. I am also grateful to the following UVA undergraduate students for inspiring me: Horace Ballard, Veronika Bath, Aaron Carico, Whitney Gruenloh, Emily Hagan, Taylor Harris, Anna Rakes Isley, Erin Levin, Elizabeth Alabama Mills, Molly Minturn, Nora Nunn, Morgan Saxby, Kevin Simowitz, Terri Taylor, Lauren Tilton, Meg Weckstein, Shannon Wendling, Emily Westkaemper, and Ruthie Yow.

The following people have my deep gratitude for their friendship, intellectual generosity, editing help, and unwavering support for this project: Ed Ayers, Peter Dimock, Nelson Lichtenstein, Bryant Simon, and Lauren Winner. The following friends have sustained me and my daughters in ways small and large but always essential: Cindy Aron, Steve Arrata, Majida Bargach, Eileen Boris, Kathryn Burns, Scott Casper, Deborah Cohn, Nancy Corwith, Chad Dodson, Amy Halliday, Paul Halliday, Paul Harvey, Bob Jackson, Cindi Katz, Ann Lane, Eric Lott, Manuel Lerdau, Vicki Olwell, John Pepper, Kamalini Ramdas, Ann Marie Reardon, Elizabeth Thompson, Heather Thompson, David Waldner, Ann Hill Williams, and Lisa Woolfork. For nurturing my daughters through a very difficult time, I am grateful to all the folks at University Montessori School. For friendship, old and rich and deep, I thank Margaret Hall, Jessica Hunt, Eliza McFeely, and Lynn Ponce de Leon. Mandy Hoy has shared great books, long runs, her parenting skills, and her wonderful cooking for years. David Holton helped me discover my love of theater and all things Canadian. For conversations about history, cooking with kids, midnight pharmacy runs, and funerals, I am grateful to Kristin Celello and Carl Bon Tempo. I am indebted to Franny Nudelman for more than a decade of beautiful friendship, shared children, the example of her teaching and writing, and our intellectual collaboration, and to Cori Field for her grace and generosity and for our shared quest to be good historians and parents simultaneously. In the last two years of this book project, Brooke Bostic shared his love, serenity, and sense of adventure, and I am deeply thankful. My gratitude to the amazing group of women who are my Charlottesville "family," Lawrie Balfour, Anna Brickhouse, Bonnie Gordon, and Liz Witner, is literally immeasurable. Without the running, advice, child care, love and support, intellectual community, and the all-essential "book summit," I would never have been able to keep going.

For their support, I am grateful to my family: Joan Berry Hale, Trace Hale, Joanna Hale Prior, Jim Fisher, and Mark Prior. My father, Lester C. Hale, did not live to see this book finished, but he was my rock and remains a model for me in infinite ways. My last debt is to my daughters, Sarah Ellen Innis Hale and Emma Chandler Innis Hale, born just before I started this book, for their bottomless love, their passion for learning, and for teaching me what is important.

C

A Nation of Outsiders

Introduction: Outsiders and Rebels

[We have become] a nation of outsiders, a country in which the mainstream, however mythic, [has] lost its compelling energy and its magnetic attraction.
Peter Schraf, *Harper's* (1970)

This book begins with two simple questions. Why did so many white middle-class people see themselves as outsiders in the second half of the twentieth century? And what effect did this vision have on American culture and society? Answering these questions requires tracing the history of a knot of desire, fantasy, and identification I call the romance of the outsider, the belief that people somehow marginal to society possess cultural resources and values missing among other Americans. To tell this story, I follow this romance at work in the novels, memoirs, musical recordings, photographs, films, cultural criticism, political organizing efforts, and other pieces of the expressive culture of the period, and examine how individuals used this romance, how it channeled their creativity and actions and produced new ways of thinking about history and the agency of individuals.

In the 1950s and early 1960s, the romance of the outsider began to appear among self-conscious white bohemians and in books, music, and movies made for white youth. It often started with longing, desire, what we might call love. In the 1953 film *The Wild One*, it sparkled in the way the small-town teenaged girl smiled in reaction to Marlon Brando's bad boy character, the leader of a motorcycle gang in the city, who answered her question "What are you rebelling against?" by snarling, "Whaddaya got?" It danced in the voice of Sal

Paradise, Beat writer Jack Kerouac's fictionalized stand-in in his 1957 novel *On the Road*:

> At lilac evening I walked with every muscle aching among the lights of 27th and Welton in the Denver colored section, wishing I were a Negro, feeling that the best the white world had offered was not enough ecstasy for me, not enough life, joy, kicks, darkness, music, not enough night . . . I wished I were a Denver Mexican, or even a poor overworked Jap, anything but what I was so drearily, a "white man" disillusioned.

It hit readers like a sledgehammer in Norman Mailer's 1957 essay "The White Negro":

> And in the wedding of white and black it was the Negro who brought the cultural dowry . . . he kept for his survival the art of the primitive, he lived in the enormous present, he subsisted for his Saturday night kicks . . . the pleasures of the body . . . and in his music he gave voice to . . . his rage and the infinite variations of joy, lust, languor, growl, cramp, pinch, scream and despair of his orgasm.

It animated campus journalist and Kerouac fan Tom Hayden's description of hearing participants in the southern sit-in movement speak in 1960. These black and white activists "lived on a fuller level of feeling than any people I'd ever seen," he wrote. "Here were the models of charismatic commitment I was seeking. I wanted to live like them."[1]

Popular music—postwar jazz, rock and roll, and especially folk music—served as a key medium for this romance. It sang in New York City painter, photographer, and musician John Cohen's account of meeting Roscoe Holcomb, a banjo player and impoverished former coal miner, in eastern Kentucky in 1959 and listening to him play a song he had written: "My hair stood up on end. I couldn't tell whether I was hearing something ancient, like a Gregorian Chant, or something very contemporary and avant-garde. It was the most moving, touching, dynamic, powerful song I'd ever experienced." It moved within a critic and fan's description of the people who made folk music: "There are beautiful, relatively uncomplicated people living in the country close to the soil, who have their own identities, their own backgrounds. They know who they are, and they know what their culture is because they make it themselves . . . mostly in their singing." It rang in music collector Larry Cohn's description of hearing blues musician Son House sing in New York City in 1965: "I had never seen nor imagined that anyone could sing with such intensity and not drop dead on the spot. Because every song was a complete catharsis. I mean it was so emotional." It danced through future musician Janis Joplin's first encounter with the blues: "They were playing that fifties crap on the radio. It seemed so shallow, all oop-boop. It had nothing. Then I heard Leadbelly, and it was like a flash. It *mattered* to me."[2]

By the mid-1960s, it was hard to imagine youth culture without this romance. It echoed through the hippie counterculture, into the back-to-the-land movement, and everywhere young Americans self-consciously created new communities. It flourished in the Jesus People movement, as hippies rebelled against not just the lifestyle but also the liberal religion of middle-class America and took up conservative forms of Christianity. And it thrived among young political conservatives who followed William F. Buckley in seeing themselves as rebels in an era dominated by liberalism. By the end of the seventies, it had even worked its way into fundamentalist and Pentecostal strands of Christianity, where rejuvenated believers used the romance of the outsider to transform their isolation and separatism into strengths, markers of difference reworked into sources of power.

White middle-class Americans imagined people living on the margins, without economic or political or social privilege, as possessing something vital, some essential quality that had somehow been lost from their own lives. They often found this depth of meaning and feeling in what they took to be the expressive culture of black people, but other outsiders served as well. However the margins and center were defined, the key imaginative act was the "discovery" of difference. These encounters with outsiders enabled some middle-class whites to cut themselves free of their own social origins and their own histories and in identifying with these others to imaginatively regain what they understood as previously lost values and feelings. They remade themselves. They became outsiders too. The romance of the outsider spread throughout American culture because it provided an imaginary resolution for an intractable mid-century cultural and political conflict, the contradiction between the desire for self-determination and autonomy and the desire for a grounded, morally and emotionally meaningful life. Politically supple, it registered people's conflicting longings for affective, aesthetic, and social freedoms and yet also for social and historical connections.

By the end of the twentieth century, the romance of the outsider had become so pervasive that few scholars questioned how odd and uncanny it was, how historically unprecedented, to understand politically and economically enfranchised people as marginal and alienated. A critical mass of white middle-class Americans had developed alternative measures of the relationship of the individual to society, geographies mapped not with class, race, gender, and citizenship but according to less material measures of value like depth of feeling and belief. In the process, they changed the very meaning of ideas like authenticity and community. This book traces the history and consequences of this romance.[3]

Images of and stories about outsiders did not appear suddenly in the aftermath of World War II. The postwar white middle-class's attraction to outsiders and rebels (their self-conscious cousins) was not new. It had deep roots in earlier oppositional modes and expressive traditions. Historical precedents fill entire genres of literature, for example, from picaresque fiction to Romantic poetry and travel writing. In the late 1820s and 1830s, white working-class interest in and identification with African Americans generated new forms of theater as white entertainers painted their faces black, danced, and sang. Minstrelsy, or "acting black," wildly popular through the early twentieth century, powerfully shaped America's emerging popular culture and future forms of white rebellion.[4]

In the late nineteenth century, interest in outsiders inspired "song catching," or the study of Appalachian music and the collection of American Indian artifacts. It produced new fields of academic research, from anthropology and folklore studies to ethnomusicology. And it sparked new kinds of art. Fascination with outsiders was crucial to modernism as an artistic movement as visual artists in retreat from realism embraced "primitivism," modes of representation imagined as belonging to people living "outside" Western culture. As America's first self-conscious bohemias emerged, members took up the Romanticism that had inspired earlier European communities of artists, writers, and others fleeing the constraints of middle-class respectability. In the 1930s, the American left welded these ideas about outsiders together to create a cultural politics that positioned a culture of the folk, understood as a particularly American counterpart to the proletariat, against a commercialized and compromised popular culture.[5]

Equally as important as these secular sources, faith taught many middle-class Americans to see outsiders—people who opposed received wisdom and accepted behavior—as morally superior. In the Second Great Awakening, for example, believers followed itinerant preachers and joined upstart denominations in opposition to more established churches and learned to value their own individual, interior relationships with God. Across the nineteenth century, evangelical Christians increasingly focused on their inner lives and embraced what their critics saw as excessive emotional displays, rather than good works, as symbols of their salvation. Some believers formed utopian communities like the Shakers' Hancock Village in Massachusetts and the Perfectionists' Oneida Community in upstate New York to achieve godliness by self-consciously separating themselves from the fallen world. In the early twentieth century, some evangelical Christians followed yet another set of rebellious ministers and lay leaders into self-conscious opposition to a powerful and liberalizing Protestantism they believed had gone too far in accommodating modernity. Their answer, announced in a series of books called *The Fundamentals*, was to return to a Bible-centered faith, shun the larger world, and emphasize the difference and separateness of true believers. Across the twentieth century, conservative Christians cultivated their self-consciously oppositional culture and their own romance of the outsider.

After World War II, broad historical changes long under way—migration to cities and suburbs, the rise of white-collar corporate employment, the growth of government and corporate bureaucracies, and the changing nature of family life—continued to erode middle-class whites' sense of control over their lives and their feelings of rootedness in place and community. The emergence of the cold war and the possibility of nuclear annihilation as well as African Americans' growing demand for greater rights only increased middle-class white fears. Organic community (grounding in time and place and a web of human relationships) and individualism (white male self-determination disguised as a universal ideal) may have always been more myths than realities, but the existence and compatibility of these ideals lay at the core of middle-class whites' conception of citizenship. Could they be reconciled? Could they survive?

What was new in this postwar period was the way historical trends coalesced to make the figure of the outsider seem like a solution to the conflict between these ideals. The rapid expansion of photographic journalism, television, radio, and leisure tourism put the lives of people who were not white or not middle-class or not American increasingly on display. Middle-class Americans after 1945 had easier and more varied access to people who seemed marginal, exotic, or primitive than they had possessed before this period. *Life* magazine, the television news, and the songs on rapidly diversifying radio stations enabled middle-class people to eavesdrop on and peer into other people's lives, to hear their music and their stories, and to see where and how they lived, from the comfort and safety of their middle-class homes. In this context, people understood as outsiders seemed readily available as resources for white middle-class needs and desires.

The convergence of these historical trends spread a love for outsiders from self-consciously oppositional enclaves into the very unlikely arena of mass culture, the commercialized ideas, values, visions of the good life, and expressive forms that dominated the nation at mid-century. Mass culture, allegedly breeding conformity and destroying more authentic "folk" cultures, seemed to be part of the problem. But in this historical moment, beginning in the 1950s, it also seemed to become part of the solution, adeptly spreading knowledge of people not living middle-class suburban lives. Romanticizing outsiders enabled some middle-class whites to see themselves as different and alienated too. They learned to use mass culture—understood as the American way of life and as their culture—to critique mass culture. By the end of the twentieth century, the outsider romance had become an essential characteristic of white middle-class subjectivity.

At the level of imagination and identification, the romance of the outsider reconciled incompatible yearnings for self-determination and emotional and social connection in three related and often overlapping ways. First, middle-class whites often displaced these contradictions onto their fantasies of outsiders and remade themselves through identification with these marginal figures. Second, middle-class whites sometimes split conflicts between individual autonomy and social grounding into two different spaces. Separation from a space imagined as the arena of the dominant culture appeared, then, as an act of self-determination, and social connection became possible in a separate place imagined as existing on the margins. Third, middle-class whites sometimes dissolved the contradictions in ecstatic, mystical experiences that radically altered consciousness and intensified both emotional and physical sensations. Listening to or playing music, dancing, taking drugs, meditating, chanting, or praying, some participants experienced an alternative place without physically traveling at all, a space free of alienation. With increasing frequency across the half century after 1945, white middle-class Americans used these strategies to balance individual autonomy and social grounding at the symbolic level.

All of these ways of wielding the romance of the outsider worked within a left-to-right political continuum and an earnest-to-ironic emotional range. Yet observers have persisted in describing the process in dualistic terms, as either good or bad, as resisting or strengthening the political order. For many scholars who came of age in the 1950s and 1960s, rebellion was subversive and transgressive and therefore good. In the work of Wini Breines, George Lipsitz, and other scholars, as well as sixties activists turned writers like Tom Hayden, Constance Curry, and Bill Ayers, outsiders and rebels created the spaces where political resistance emerged and left emancipatory politics began.[6]

Yet the romance of the outsider proved as useful in building the New Right as in building the New Left. William F. Buckley and others grasped this fact and used it to rebuild American conservatism. Always politically promiscuous, rebellion can work for any kind of oppositional politics, but it can also be an essential part of how a particular political and social order maintains its hegemony. Recent scholars, however, have erred too far in this direction, seeing the romance of the outsider and white middle-class love of rebellion as a new kind of opiate of the masses. For Leerom Medovoi, Thomas Frank, Sean McCann, and Michael Szalay, cultural rebellion works in the interests of U.S. capitalism and the nation-state, co-opting any radical potential that might lie within American popular culture. This book argues that just as the romance of the outsider is inherently neither right nor left, it is also neither completely separate from nor completely a tool of the U.S. political economy. Its power in fact derives from precisely this slipperiness, the fact that it can be simultaneously both inside and outside. Dancing between the established political and social categories, the outsider romance upends and redefines these social and political geographies even as it momentarily reconciles individual autonomy and the collective good.[7]

Part I, "Learning to Love Outsiders," surveys historical movements, figures, novels, films, and songs through which middle-class whites learned to love outsiders and their use of that identification to fuel their own rebellion. Chapter 1, "Lost Children of Plenty: Growing Up as Rebellion," begins with an examination of J. D. Salinger's *The Catcher in the Rye*, the best-selling 1951 novel that simultaneously represented and also helped create the idea of white middle-class teenage alienation. Holden Caulfield managed to exist both inside and outside the privileged life he found so "phony" and became the first in a string of iconic and popular fictional rebels. Salinger's novel offered one of the first important and widely read critiques of what critics increasingly called mass culture—commercialized forms of cultural expression that reached (or tried to reach) large audiences—from within mass culture. Yet the love for outsiders and rebellion on display in *Catcher* also redeemed mass culture, seemingly opening a space within for difference, opposition, and individualism. The chapter concludes with an exploration of the complicated ways in which white middle-class teenage girls and young women embraced the romance of the outsider and yet faced particular hardships when they tried to move beyond their love for male rebels and remake themselves as outsiders.

Chapter 2, "Rebel Music: Minstrelsy, Rock and Roll, and Beat Writing," explores the emergence of the outsider romance in the white youth culture of the 1950s. "Black" sounds, from the music of Elvis Presley and the jazzy prose of Jack Kerouac to the bebop that formed the soundtrack for beatnik life, taught middle-class whites to love blackness. Young whites learned to use forms of expression understood as black as emotional and aesthetic resources for expressing their own needs and desires. Chapter 3, "Black as Folk: The Folk Music Revival, the Civil Rights Movement, and Bob Dylan," traces how a surging interest in folk music taught white middle-class young people to love poor rural people, especially in the South, as "the folk." The folk music revival played a crucial role in democratizing bohemian rebellion and spreading knowledge about and interest in leftist politics and the civil rights movement. For a moment in the mid-sixties, Bob Dylan embodied the fantasy that middle-class whites and poor blacks could create a new politics out of a shared sense of alienation from American society.

Chapter 4, "Rebels on the Right: Conservatives as Outsiders in Liberal America," examines William F. Buckley, Young Americans for Freedom (the group of young conservatives he helped organize), the growth of libertarianism, and Hunter S. Thompson. In the 1950s, Buckley built a career as a conservative journalist, journal editor, and scholar by arguing that conservatives were the real outsiders in liberal America. Inspired by Buckley's rebel persona and Ayn Rand's libertarian novels, young middle-class whites created a conservative youth movement that challenged the New Left. By the end of the sixties, the libertarian-leaning, gun-loving, self-proclaimed Democrat Hunter S. Thompson made clear just how much white middle-class rebels on the right and left actually shared.

Part II, "Romance in Action," traces the role of the romance of the outsider in postwar politics. Chapter 5, "The New White Negroes in Action: Students for a Democratic Society, the Economic Research and Action Project, and Freedom Summer," examines white middle-class romanticism at work in New Left political organizing. SDS built its organization by linking politically minded white students outside the South with news of the black civil rights rebels within the region. By 1964, however, a faction of SDS's leadership wanted to move the student organization into the kind of community organizing in the North that the Student Nonviolent Coordinating Committee was creating in the South. ERAP, which mostly floundered on its organizers' romanticism, was the result. The chapter ends with an examination of the 1964 Mississippi Summer Project as a high point in the left's mobilization of the romance of the outsider. Chapter 6, "Too Much Love: Black Power and the Search for Other Outsiders," traces what happened when African Americans explicitly rejected white "love." Many white activists retained their romanticism by shifting their fantasies to other outsiders, like the Vietnamese resistance fighters. Others responded to African Americans' demand that they work in their own communities. Defining exactly what constituted their communities then became a form of activism, as white college students, white women, and white draftees organized to fight their own oppression. Still other white activists like the Weather faction of SDS and the White Panther Party took up a new romantic image of black militants and their revolutionary authenticity in place of the old image of blacks as the folk.

Chapter 7, "The Making of Christian Countercultures: God's Outsiders from the Jesus People to Jerry Falwell and the Moral Majority," examines how the Jesus People movement and Christian fundamentalists in the 1970s and 1980s romanticized outsiders and acts of rebellion. In the 1970s, Jesus "freaks" braided together theologically conservative Christianity with countercultural attitudes toward music, dress, and emotional expression and built the basis for the explosion of mega-churches in the next decade. Many Christian fundamentalists, having chosen separatism from modern society since the Scopes trial, missed these cultural developments. At the end of the seventies, Jerry Falwell began to use the romance of the outsider to push these fundamentalists to see their marginality as an asset. Most fundamentalists believed their moral authority grew out of their religious practices. Yet in the aftermath of the civil rights movement, oppressed outsiders possessed broad cultural authority. Falwell used the romance of the outsider to bring his oppressed "majority"—"Bible-believing Christians"—back into politics. Chapter 8, "Rescue: Christian Outsiders in Action in the Anti-Abortion Movement," explores what happened when Randall Terry took this call for Christian rebellion all the way into civil disobedience. In the late 1980s and early 1990s, Terry and his organization Operation Rescue positioned their work as the civil rights movement of the day and transformed the anti-abortion fight into the right's mass protest movement.

In the present, the romance of the outsider continues to influence how middle-class whites understand the overlapping relationships between culture and politics, individuals and the larger society. Love of outsiders enables many middle-class whites to imagine these links as matters of individual choice in which history and social structures do not matter. In this way, white middle-class romanticism remakes individualism (with its elite, white, male privilege) for white middle-class men and, to a more limited degree, women, in an age in which it cannot work structurally but can work psychologically and emotionally. The outsider romance also shapes contemporary life by perpetuating inequalities under the guise of identification and love. Legitimating a destructive refusal to acknowledge limits and to discuss the trade-offs necessary to make a good life for the most people, it reconstitutes privileges by rejecting them and creates agency out of the disavowal of power. At the level of social thought, white middle-class love for outsiders and rebellion makes the connection between culture and politics appear transparent and direct. Under this assumption, increasing people's ability to represent themselves culturally—a kind of representational self-determination—increases their political power as well. In practice, however, political and cultural agency have proved to be not so clearly or easily linked.

Because the reconciliation of the contradiction between autonomy and connection is always threatening to come undone in the material world, love of outsiders mediates and undermines at the same time and generates an increasing obsession with authenticity. As the belief that people's individual feelings and perceptions, their interior lives, are the most important gauges of reality and truth grows, however, the meaning of authenticity changes. Instead of a way of testing an artifact or person's fidelity to some external material or historical standard, it has become an emotional measure, a fantasy that can reconcile contradictory desires and make the impossible seem true. As a result, we live in an age when illusions—the idea that black culture is more authentic and middle-class whites are outsiders—rule. The romance of the outsider perpetuates a disavowal of power that damages us all.

PART I

Learning to Love Outsiders

CHAPTER 1

Lost Children of Plenty: Growing Up as Rebellion

When I was all set to go, when I had my bags and all, I stood for a while next to the stairs and took a last look down the goddam corridor. I was sort of crying. I don't know why. I put my red hunting hat on, and turned the peak around to the back, the way I liked it, and then I yelled at the top of my goddam voice, "Sleep tight, ya morons!" I'll bet I woke up every bastard on the whole floor. Then I got the hell out.

J. D. Salinger, *The Catcher in the Rye*

After 1951, if a person wanted to be a rebel she could just read the book. Later there would be other things to read—Jack Kerouac's *On the Road*, Eldridge Cleaver's *Soul on Ice*, and Sylvia Plath's *The Bell Jar*. But J. D. Salinger's *The Catcher in the Rye* was the first best seller to imagine a striking shift in the meaning of alienation in the postwar period, a sense that something besides Europe still needed saving. The success of this book and the many other novels, autobiographies, and films that followed its pattern made the concept of adolescent alienation commonplace, but in the postwar era the very idea shocked many Americans. Adults who had lived through depression and war believed that children growing up in peace and prosperity—*Life* named them "the luckiest generation"—should be happy. Salinger's antihero Holden Caulfield was a particularly unlikely rebel. He lived unconstrained by poverty, racism, or anti-Semitism, and he did not face the narrow options available for ambitious girls.

Instead, Holden's alienation was personal, psychological, and spiritual. Salinger's novel helped create a model for the rebel of the future by popularizing the problem of middle-class adolescent alienation.[1]

In *The Catcher in the Rye*'s first line, Holden Caulfield shuns his parents and his own audience and, at least in terms of his readers, reels many of them in forever instead:

> If you really want to hear about it, the first thing you'll probably
> want to know is where I was born, and what my lousy childhood
> was like, and how my parents were occupied and all before they had
> me, and all that David Copperfield kind of crap, but I don' feel like
> going into it, if you want to know the truth.

This, Holden tells us right off, is not going to be a story that grounds its young character in the warm nest of the family.

> In the first place, that stuff bores me, and in the second place, my
> parents would have about two hemorrhages apiece if I told anything
> pretty personal about them . . . They're nice and all—I'm not saying
> that—but they're touchy as hell. Besides, I'm not going to tell you my
> whole goddam autobiography or anything. I'll just tell you about
> this madman stuff that happened to me around last Christmas.

If none of the normal connections can be assumed, however, Holden admits in the very act of telling that he has not given up on the search.[2]

By the end of the novel, Holden has found something to mourn and regret and even love, something that will last, past his own and his sister Phoebe's childhood, past his sudden happiness at Phoebe's looking "so damn nice . . . going around and around, in her blue coat and all" on the carousel: "All I know is, I sort of *miss* everybody I told about . . . It's funny. Don't ever tell anybody anything. If you do, you start missing everybody." If meaning is absent in the larger world, Holden makes it in the act of telling. He falls in love with the story he has created out of and about his own alienation. Readers are invited to share this love, for Holden's own tale but also for the stories they can think or write or play or sing about their own alienation and for the redemption they might find there too. In *Catcher*, Salinger pushes the romance of the outsider out of the marginal minstrel fantasies of bohemia and popular culture and into upper-middle-class adolescence, the seemingly idyllic center of white postwar America. There, lodged on high school reading lists—despite off-and-on attempts to ban it because Salinger uses the word "fuck"—both the book and the romance have remained.[3]

Holden Caulfield becomes a rebel that both intellectuals and young middle-class Americans can bond with and even love. These readers feel connected to Holden and sometimes in turn to other *Catcher* fans in a kind of pop cultural community of outsiders. The act of telling, Holden's expression of his own alienation, helps create both a new model of the white well-off adolescent as outsider and a new kind of belonging. In this way, *Catcher* satisfies contradictory feelings, the urge to be self-determining through resisting social rules and conventions, and the urge to be a part of a community. And despite Caulfield's gender, this reconciliation of contradictory desires through identifying with outsiders and rebels seems to work for some female as well as male readers. A first-person narrative about a person who is neither an adult nor a child, the novel displaces the incompatibility of these desires into the borderlands of adolescence.

Like Mark Twain's *The Adventures of Huckleberry Finn*, published in 1884, *Catcher* is a radical portrayal of disillusionment with America disguised by its author as a tale of childhood adventure. Critics and scholars have remarked on the connections between the two coming-of-age novels with their white boy protagonists since soon after *Catcher* was published. Huck's running away with the slave Jim is the equivalent of Holden's screaming, "*Sleep tight, ya morons!*" as he leaves Pencey Prep. Their upthrust fingers in the faces of their worlds, their attacks on what their societies most value—slave property and a secure, upper-middle-class future—in both cases, rebellion preserves the boys' innocence and dramatizes their refusal to conform, to accept the compromises adults make with their respective societies. Each novel became a part of the popular culture of its era even as it offered a serious comment on the limits of that culture.[4]

In Holden, critics and reviewers found a character acutely sensitive to the conformity and spiritual numbness that modern life generates in the world imagined in the novel. One fictional character's experience of alienation, of course, mattered little historically. *Catcher* became a powerful model of adolescent alienation across the postwar era because of the intersection of broad historical trends with Salinger's skill as a writer and changes in the publishing industry. In the 1950s, the paperback revolution transformed book publishing and made novels almost as cheap as magazines. At the same time, the postwar economic boom gave white middle-class teenagers more money to spend and more leisure time in which to enjoy their purchases. Paradoxically, the novel also got a boost from journalists' and intellectuals' anxiety about "mass culture"; *Catcher* sold 1.5 million copies in paperback in its first decade. *Catcher in the Rye* offered a model for rebellion against mass culture even as it was also a very profitable part of mass culture.[5]

Though the novel predates the invention of two new popular culture genres aimed at the same white middle-class youth market, *Catcher*, rock and roll music, and teenpics (films made for teenagers) all shared an oppositional stance toward conventions and norms imagined as central to American life. In fact, the very idea of white middle-class adolescent alienation became increasingly powerful because older observers like journalists and white middle-class adolescent fans themselves connected their rebellion to the oppositional positions of other groups: the "plague" of juvenile delinquency among working-class urban youth, the self-conscious rebellions of bohemians and artists, and, even more importantly, African Americans' historic position as outsiders in America.[6]

It also helped that the adolescents in those homes lay on their twin beds flipping the radio dial and the pages of magazines looking for something different. No one used mass culture to resist mass culture better than middle-class white teenagers. For the first time, in the postwar period, a critical mass of adolescents had the money and the leisure time to cultivate their own cultural tastes. Their parents saw this prosperity and could not understand how these kids could have any problems. Businesses like radio stations, record companies, and Hollywood saw this prosperity and thought about how to reach these new consumers. Radio and the movies, in particular, needed new markets, as television became the family entertainment of choice in the growing suburbs. As *Esquire* argued in 1965 in an article entitled "In the Time It Takes You to Read These Lines the American Teenager Will Have Spent $2,378.22," "this vague no-man's-land of adolescence" had become "a subculture rather than a transition."[7]

What many of these teenagers wanted was separation, something, anything to distinguish and distance them from their parents and other adults. With help from the music, movie, and radio industries, they created a new teen culture grounded in a mood of opposition to their parents and their plenty. In contrast to a more respectable emotional repression, white teenagers increasingly valued the expression of passion and desire. In place of their parents' controlled and polished forms of entertainment, they sought the raw and frenetic. And in defiance of the white norms of middle-class America, they embraced popular black music and fantasies of African American life. For teenagers and college students, mass culture was not just a problem, as many intellectuals argued in the mid-twentieth century. It was a solution. It was not just the space of a conformity that killed American individualism. It was a space of resistance. It was not just the household of the organization man. It was the home of the rebel. Most importantly, it gave white teenagers a window, however smudged, on black cultural expression.

In the 1950s and 1960s, mass culture gave some young white Americans a glimpse of redemption. Rebels and outsiders were out there. Other possibilities existed. A novel or rock and roll song or a film could be a vehicle for expressing feelings of alienation, for thinking about a different kind of life. The fact that many outsider characters were male did not stop young white women from seeking alternatives too, although rebellion was always more dangerous for them. Holden Caulfield may not have had the answers, but he suggested how some white middle-class white kids could start asking the questions.

The Alienation of Holden Caulfield

By the end of the decade, marketing experts and advice columnists, ministers and law enforcement officials, politicians and academics had all discovered adolescent rebellion. In 1951, however, J. D. Salinger walked Holden Caulfield right into the middle of a time when most white kids at least were supposed to be happy. Sure, American troops were fighting and losing in Korea. A book called *How to Survive an Atomic Bomb* seriously advised people in danger to drop to the ground and shield their eyes and keep their heads. But these kids lived in a nation of growing prosperity and unchallenged economic power. Their parents and their president and the products for sale everywhere promised them a world free from the hardships adults had so recently endured. With a little preparation and the right stuff, they were told, even a nuclear holocaust would be easier to survive than the Great Depression. Before the Beats and Jack Kerouac's *On the Road* (1957), before movies like *Rebel Without a Cause* (1955), *Blackboard Jungle* (1955), and *West Side Story* (1961), before Elvis Presley's first hits and the invention of rock and roll, before comic books could make people crazy, before gangs and knife fights, greased-back hair, and black leather jackets became part of popular culture, before most people had even heard of juvenile delinquency, the adolescent antihero of *The Catcher in the Rye* got kicked out of Pencey Prep.[8]

Pencey Prep is not Holden Caulfield's first school. He has been expelled before, from Whooton and Elkton Hills. None of these places are public high schools. Holden is middle-class, upper-middle-class more precisely. His parents and his younger sister, Phoebe, live in a spacious if not elegant apartment on the Upper East Side of Manhattan. His father, a lawyer, makes "dough" and buys cars, plays golf and bridge, drinks martinis and misses school plays because of work. He looks "like a hot shot." And Holden, despite his failures, expects to be successful too. He tells Sally Hayes, a girl he sort of dates, about his future, what he imagines as a typical grown-up American life: "After I went to college and all . . . I'd be working in some office, making a lot of dough, and riding to work in cabs and Madison Avenue buses, reading newspapers, and playing bridge all the time, and going to the movies." But Holden has stepped into a mess. Even more than the white kids, upper-middle-class white adults are supposed to be happy. The middle-class lifestyle, "the American way of life," after all, is the United States' best weapon against the Communists, the highest achievement of postwar American life. Holden's slangy sketch of WASP security skewers everything many postwar Americans were hoping to achieve.[9]

What exactly is it, then, that alienates Holden Caulfield? With his name and credentials, he is not black or ethnic or newly arrived. Holden is not even, despite some literary critics' references to Salinger's hiding in his writing the traces of his own half-Jewish ancestry, a Jew. He is not a young woman facing a world of restricted choices. He is not poor and never expects to be without his parents' money or, in later life, his own well-paying white-collar job. Holden's sense of prosperity, in fact, is so secure, a decade after World War II wiped away the last of the Great Depression, that his fear as he wanders alone in New York City after leaving Pencey Prep before the end of the term and even the fact that he spends one night in a train station only add to the romantic aura of his rebellion. He has by then already slipped back into the family apartment once. The reader knows he can just go home. He has the key.

Still, Holden is alienated, estranged from what his parents, teachers, and acquaintances—he does not seem to have any friends—expect of him. And *Catcher* is about more than the teenage angst the novel helped invent. At the start of the 1950s, few Americans were articulating this new mood of discontent, what the poet Allen Ginsberg, the writer Norman Mailer, the theorist Paul Goodman, the critic Susan Sontag, and others would later call the new consciousness, the great refusal, the new sensibility. C. Wright Mills, an academic sociologist, came closest at the time to describing a form of psychological and cultural alienation remarkable like Holden's but not limited to teenagers. Mills's *White Collar*, a sociological investigation of contemporary middle-class life, and *Catcher*, both begun before the war, worried over for a decade, and published in the same year, have more than a little in common despite differences of genre and tone. Mills's letters to friends and family about what he thought he was doing in *White Collar* describe *Catcher* as well: "It's all about the little man and how he lives and what he suffers and what his chances are going to be; and it is also about the world he lives in, has to live [in], doesn't want to live in." Everybody, Mills insisted, denying that class distinctions make much difference in the experience of alienation, is "a little man." Mills wanted to put all of America in *White Collar*: "the alienation, and apathy and dry rot and immensity and razzle dazzle and bullshit and wonderfulness and how lonesome it is, really, how terribly lonesome and rich and vulgar." "To be politically conscious," Mills argued in *White Collar*, "is to see a political meaning in one's own insecurities and desires."[10]

In Holden's teenage idiom, Salinger actually employs a more accessible language for making this point, "the great refusal," than Mills's own sociological abstractions. When Phoebe asks her big brother to name something he likes, something he would like to be, and suggests a lawyer, he replies, "Lawyers are all right, I guess—but it doesn't appeal to me. I mean they're all right if they go around saving innocent guys' lives all the time, and like that, but you don't *do* that kind of stuff if you're a lawyer." To be successful in any then current meaning of the term, to have money, dates, friends, to have a purpose even, a person has to be a phony. For Holden, being a phony is the very definition of failure. Then Holden breaks through to an answer:

> Even if you did go around saving guys' lives and all, how would you know if you did it because you really *wanted* to save guys' lives, or because you did it because what you *really* wanted to do was to be a terrific lawyer, with everybody slapping you on the back and congratulating you in court when the goddam trial was over, the reporters and everybody, the way it is in the dirty movies? How would you know you weren't being a phony? The trouble is, you *wouldn't.*

In the movie-saturated world of mid-twentieth-century America, Holden suggests, self-consciousness and reflexivity abound. When people are able to imagine watching themselves like characters on a screen, to be both inside and outside themselves simultaneously, how can they separate pure guiding purpose from reaction and effect? Negotiating this dilemma, trying to live with the "rot" and the "razzle dazzle," will become an essential part of the postwar rebellion that *Catcher* helps shape.[11]

Holden, narrating his story of "madman stuff that happened to me," first uses the word "phony" on page 3. Even Pencey's headmaster's daughter, he insists, knows her father, "old Thurmer," is a "phony slob." When Holden goes to say good-bye to the one teacher at Pencey he likes, "old Spencer" recalls meeting Holden's parents and calls them "grand people." Stopping the scene, Holden says to his readers: "There's a word I really hate. It's a phony. I could puke every time I hear it." Holden tells Mr. Spencer he left another school, Elkton Hills, "because I was surrounded by phonies . . . They were coming in the goddam window." Of a pious and wealthy alum who started a national chain of discount "undertaking parlors" and prayed in his car, Holden tells us, his audience, "I can just see the big phony bastard shifting into first gear and asking Jesus to send him a few more stiffs." Ward Stradlater, Holden's room-mate at Pencey, is a "phony kind of friendly." In New York and lonely, Holden thinks of calling "this girl I used to go around with quite frequently, Sally Hayes," who had written him "this long phony letter inviting me over to help her trim the Christmas tree." Holden tells his audience in another aside that he was almost in a movie once, "but I changed my mind at the last minute. I fig-ured that anybody that hates the movies as much as I do, I'd be a phony if I let them stick me in a movie short." At a jazz club, the phonies in the audience solicit "a very phony, *humble* bow" from "old Ernie" the piano player, who is really "a big snob." "People always clap for the wrong things," Holden snaps. "If I were a piano player, I'd play in the goddam closet."[12]

To Holden, his classmates, teachers, advisors, parents, and his brother D. B., who has given up his short stories to write for the movies, are all phonies. Lies, hypocrisy, and untruth are everywhere, and almost everyone occasion-ally succumbs. The word "phony" so saturates Holden's language that it becomes a mantra, a chant that somehow provides him with a thread of meaning in an otherwise empty world. The one thing Holden knows he wants is what he does not want, to be a phony. The irony is that as Holden sets off from his prep school to find something real, he cannot avoid phoniness him-self. He lies to his classmate Ernie Morrow's mother on the train. He lies in bars to buy drinks. He lies to the prostitute he hires and then is too scared to sleep with when she comes to his hotel room. "I'm the most terrific liar you ever saw in your life," he tells us.[13]

In *Catcher*'s urban picaresque, Holden tours the liminal spaces of the city—downtown hotels, jazz clubs, bars, and Central Park and Penn Station at night, places where different kinds of people collide, places on the margins of his white upper-middle-class world—looking for that opposite of phoniness, authenticity, but he does not find it. His hotel is full of "perverts and morons," "screwballs all over the place!" He watches a gray-haired "distinguished look-ing guy" wearing only his shorts "dress up in real women's clothes—silk stock-ings, high-heeled shoes, brassiere, and one of those corsets with the straps hanging down and all," and then "a very tight black evening dress." The hotel bellboy Maurice, pimping the young prostitute named Sunny that Holden hires, smacks him when he refuses to pay a jacked-up rate. In Central Park at night, a place he knows "like the back of my hand," Holden gets lost in the spooky dark looking for the duck pond. No one and no place is what it seems to be.[14]

Visiting the best teacher he ever had, "old Antolini," at a very "swanky apartment" on Sutton Place, Holden seems poised at last to find some meaning. Antolini cautions him against his romantic fatalism, against "dying nobly" for an unworthy cause. "You'll find that you're not the first person who was ever confused or frightened and even sickened by human behavior," Antolini insists. "Many, many men have been just as troubled morally and spiritually as you are right now." But after Holden falls asleep on the couch, Mr. Antolini makes a pass at him. He wakes up in the dark to find his former teacher "petting" or "patting" his head. Scared, Holden leaves. Yet another potential guide has failed him.[15]

In his travels, Holden finds phoniness—that contradiction between appearance and reality—everywhere, even in himself. "I'm some sort of an atheist," he insists, but "I feel like Jesus and all." "I'm an illiterate," he argues elsewhere, "but I read a lot." If there is ever another war, he will not fight, Holden explains, but he is glad "they've got the atomic bomb invented." But nothing for Holden is more contradictory than sex. "In my mind," Holden confesses, "I'm probably the biggest sex maniac you ever saw"; he even fantasizes about "very crumby stuff," "perverty" stuff, with a girl. The problem is that Holden believes he should not have sex or even "horse around" with girls he does not like, but with girls he does like, he wants to be careful. "Sex," Holden admits, "is something I just don't understand." Even his appearance is contradictory: "I act quite young for my age sometimes. I was sixteen then . . . and sometimes I act like I'm about thirteen. It's really ironical, because I'm six foot two and a half and I have gray hair." Others, especially his father, think he is immature: "It's pretty true, too, but it isn't *all* true. People always think something's *all* true." Holden even contradicts himself here. Truths that are all true are exactly what he is looking for, truths that, unlike the adults he encounters, stand firm. Like echoes, like the repetition of the word "phony," the partial truths in *Catcher* emphasize the tension between Holden's rebellion and his deep desire for connection and meaning.[16]

With no one to guide him, Holden refuses to grow up and remains a mass of contradictions. Getting kicked out of school means he never has to graduate. Being a virgin means he never has to think about his interactions with women like Sally, that girl Jane Gallagher that he really liked who keeps her kings in the back row when she plays checkers, or anyone else in more complicated terms. Old Spencer tells him that life is a game and a person has to play by the rules. Holden's adventures, his explorations of the margins of middle-class propriety, never change his answer: "Game my ass. Some game. If you get on the side where all the hot-shots are, then it's a game, all right—I admit that. But if you get on the *other* side, where there aren't any hot-shots, then what's a game about it. Nothing. No game." Why grow up when life, Holden insists, like a million teenagers after him, is just not fair.[17]

But the game that Holden cannot see the point of playing here is not just adulthood. It is adult manhood. At Pencey, Holden fails at sports as well as his classes. He could not care less about the big football game, and his attempt to participate, as the manager of the fencing team, ends in debacle when on the way to a meet he leaves the foils on the subway. He fails at fighting too. Aiming at Stradlater while he is brushing his teeth, Holden tries to "split his goddam throat open" with the brush but grazes the side of his head instead. He has lost, Holden confesses, the only two fights he has been in: "I'm not tough. I'm a pacifist, if you want to know the truth." Later, he does not even duck as Maurice the bellboy pimp punches him in the stomach. Holden is still a virgin, he tells us, because he listens to girls: "Most of the time when you're coming pretty close to doing it with a girl . . . she keeps telling you to stop. The trouble with me is, I stop." He has "trouble just *finding* what I'm looking for," he confesses, knowing what and where and how to touch a woman. And when he notices that the prostitute Sunny is almost a kid herself, he cannot go through with it. Sex seems too much like taking something from or harming a girl—and Holden really likes both women and girls: his classmates' mother on the train, the tourist he dances with in the bar, even the phony Sally Hayes that he fights with, his old friend Jane Gallagher, and his sister, Phoebe. "You don't always have to get too sexy to get to know a girl," he tells us. "Every time they do something pretty, even if they're not too much to look at, or even if they're sort of stupid, you fall half in love with them, and then you never know *where* the hell you are."[18]

Growing up, becoming a man, means accepting limits, the fact that bad things happen, especially the greatest fraud, the seeming security of white middle-class life and the fact that people die. Three years earlier, Holden's younger brother, Allie, only eleven, died of leukemia. Allie was smart and sensitive and lyrical. He wrote poetry all over his baseball mitt to have something to read while he stood in the outfield. The one aggressive act Holden admits to in his tale occurred when he smashed the windows in the garage with his fists the night Allie died, breaking his hand, which still hurts when it rains. The suicide of Holden's classmate at Elkton Hills, James Castle, "a skinny little weak-looking guy with wrists about as big as pencils," only aggravates the wound. Holden cannot get over it, cannot go on with life like his father and his older brother, D. B. He senses that his mother, distracted and suffering from frequent headaches, cannot get over Allie's death either. She is not even good at faking it. At least she is more like Holden, even if she cannot help him.[19]

As Phoebe pushes him to name something he loves, something besides the dead Allie, something besides the lawyer that he would like to be, Holden replies, mangling a poem by Robert Burns:

> You know that song, "If a body catch a body comin' through the rye"? I keep picturing all these little kids playing some game in this big field of rye and all. Thousands of little kids, and nobody's around—nobody big, I mean—except me. And I'm standing on the edge of some crazy cliff. What I have to do, I have to catch every-body if they start to go over the cliff—I mean if they're running and they don't want to look where they're going I have to come out from somewhere and *catch* them. That's all I'd do all day. I'd just be the catcher in the rye and all.

He will be the adult, the parent who can actually protect the children, the one who makes the seeming security of middle-class life real. He will erase the gap that generates phoniness; he will eliminate the consequences of the limits of life and thus the limits themselves; he will catch and save not just Allie and the other children but childhood itself as a space of innocence.[20]

Phoniness is not the only thread that winds through Holden's wanderings. Again and again, Holden wonders where the ducks in Central Park go when the lagoon is frozen. He asks taxicab drivers, who think he is crazy. Does the city come and get them and haul them to a warm home? Do they fly south, migrating out of the winter like retirees? Do they bed down and tough it out in the woods and brush, along the shore? Later, investigating the lagoon himself, he tromps along its frozen messy edges in the dark. Wondering about the ducks is a child's way of dealing with death, of hoping that the missing will return. Is a dead person like the snow that melts and then falls again or the sun that sets and then rises the next day? Holden wants the world to be like this childish vision. Allie and even James Castle will not have to die then. And Holden, who calls out, "Allie don't let me disappear. Allie don't let me disap-pear," will be able to save his own dissolving self.[21]

When Maurice the pimp hits Holden as Sunny takes his money, he falls to the bathroom floor and thinks he is dying. Then he starts pretending that he has a bullet in his guts. Holden "pictures himself" drinking a shot of bourbon and getting his gun. In his life as a movie scene, he will hunt old Maurice down and "plug" "six shots right through his fat hairy belly." He will be a man of action. As the end of the film in his mind slaps the reel, he thinks about the gap between this movie fantasy and reality. Then he crawls into bed and contemplates killing himself. Only his fear that no one will cover him up, that bystanders will see him "all gory," keeps him off the window ledge. The melodrama and the spectacle, the heightened emotions lent the scene by a thousand pulp novels, plays, and films, would fill even his own desperate last act with phoniness. And so Holden, like a million middle-class teenagers after him, survives. Rebellion against the world's compromises, Holden Caulfield tells us, is the only way to the fight the phoniness, the only way to act morally, the only way, at last, to live.[22]

For all its intensity, its insistence that every gesture and emotion is significant, *The Catcher in the Rye* is not the kind of realist novel that grounds its character development in descriptions of goods or clothing or landscapes, in the fully fleshed-out texture of the material world. No contemporary events appear in *Catcher*—no details of a year around 1949 or 1950, no political events like the Soviet Union's successful testing of its own atomic bomb, the end of the Berlin airlift, or Truman's Fair Deal, and no cultural markers like fashion's "New Look," a turn toward fuller skirts, or the release of *Pinky*, a hit film about racial conflict. External events that are mentioned, like the Radio City Rockettes' Christmas show, occur every year. The jazz pianist Ernie could be playing in a bar anytime in the forties or fifties. The world that Holden cannot live in is not located precisely in historical time, in either cultural or political history. The history on display here is instead more abstract, more difficult to date precisely but nevertheless powerful.[23]

In *Catcher*, Salinger offers his readers a survey of the ways people have rebelled in the past and a model for how they might rebel in the future. Collectively, Holden's stories about the people he meets suggest many of the possibilities for understanding the relationship of the individual to society available in twentieth-century America. The novel presents not so much a distinct historical period as an account of the critical moment when media images' colonization of peoples' emotions and even their sense of their own most individual and intimate experiences reach some sort of saturation point. In particular, motion pictures—a stand-in for the whole vast world of popular culture—generate a great deal of Holden's feelings of alienation even as they also provide a model of emotional reality. How could Holden feel at home and figure out what was meaningful in a world in which "real" life could never live up to life as imagined in the movies?[24]

Paradoxically, then, given his obsession with phoniness, Holden borrows his most revealing moments from movie scenes. In the dorm at Pencey, for example, he imitates decades of film melodramas as he pulls his red hunting hat down over his eyes and says in a "very hoarse voice," "I think I'm going blind. Mother darling, everything's getting so *dark* in here . . . Mother darling, give me your *hand*. Why won't you give me your *hand*?" Horsing around for his classmate is the closest Holden ever comes to asking his mother to help him, to come back out of her grief. Later, after Maurice the pimp punches him, Holden again escapes from his inability to act in his life into a film scene, into his ability to act for an audience. When suicidal despair later breaks through this fantasy, the fact that his death will not be neat like a movie keeps Holden alive until dawn. The next night, sick and lost and unable to find the ducks in the dark, Holden sits on a bench with ice in his hair and imagines his death: "I started picturing millions of jerks coming to my funeral and all . . . What a mob'd be there. They all came when Allie died, the whole goddam stupid bunch of them." Holden, in the hospital with his broken hand, missed Allie's funeral, but in his mind he lives through his own.[25]

There are many of these movie-like scenes in *Catcher*, places where Holden confesses he is playacting his life and more subtle passages when he leaves his borrowed stories—the stock plots of a hundred pulp novels, cheap plays, and popular movies—for his readers to find. "If there's one thing I hate, it's the movies," he tells us, even as he imitates them. Holden craves the audience—"I'm an exhibitionist"—that this borrowed drama at least potentially provides, people who might care about him. But he also turns to the movies when he does not want to probe too deeply, when he does not really want to feel.[26]

Holden's one actual trip to the movies makes the novel's most direct historical reference: to war, the history, of course, that haunts adults in the late forties and early fifties. The film Holden sees, the 1942 World War I film *Random Harvest*, sentimentalizes wartime sacrifice, turning loss and pain into a romance. An injured soldier, an amnesiac, falls in love with a music hall star and writes a best seller, only to discover his lost past of aristocratic privilege and almost lose his new love. The movies create false emotions, Holden warns us, describing how he wanted to "puke" while watching the film. The woman next to him, he offers as an example, cried the whole time and yet did not care enough for her child to take him to the bathroom. Films produce feelings that cannot be trusted in the world outside the screen.[27]

Still, war movies not surprisingly make Holden think about war. Like Salinger, Holden's brother D. B., now a "prostitute" working in Hollywood instead of being a "real" writer, landed in Normandy on D-day. D. B. hates the army. After the war, he tells Allie and Holden "the Army was practically as full of bastards as the Nazis were." When Allie asked him if being a soldier was not good for a writer, D. B. answers by asking whether Rupert Brooke or Emily Dickinson is the better war poet. Allie replies Dickinson. Salinger here, intentionally or not, offers a critique of novelists like Norman Mailer who talked about the war and other horrors as great experiences for writers and paraded their own presence in battle as the source of their works' authenticity and truth. "Real" life can be all too romantic, and people can know, like Dickinson, what they do not directly take part in or witness. The invented and imagined can be the "real." D. B. can hate the war and the army and yet love *A Farewell to Arms*, which Holden feels is full of phonies. Representations, poetry and novels and movies by and about people who were not there, can generate deep insight. How, then, Holden needs to know, can a young man tell which phonies—which fictions or fakes—are indeed true?[28]

Waiting for Phoebe to leave school at lunch and meet him the next day, Holden unwinds a final film in his head. His vague plan is to escape out west and live in a cabin, and he imagines his return home at long last at the ripe old age of thirty-five.

> I knew my mother'd get nervous as hell and start to cry and beg me
> to stay home and not go back to my cabin, but I'd go anyway. I'd be
> casual as hell. I'd ask them all to visit me sometime if they wanted to,
> but I wouldn't insist or anything. What I'd do, I'd let old Phoebe
> come out and visit me in the summertime and on Christmas
> vacation and Easter vacation. And I'd let D. B. come . . . but he
> couldn't write any movies in my cabin, only stories and books. I'd
> have this rule that nobody could do anything phony when they
> visited me. If anybody tried to do anything phony, they couldn't stay.

The problem, of course, is that the scene itself is false, a movie melodrama that Holden will never live. He has already sneaked into his home like a thief. He does not recount his actual homecoming in that "madman" time. Yet he must have ended up at his parents' apartment, sometime after watching Phoebe in all her radiant innocence going around and around on the carousel. He admits he writes from a mental hospital. And that is all.[29]

There are two sources of the golden age, then, of the good life before the fall, in *The Catcher in the Rye*: One is the innocent world of childhood as embodied in Allie and Phoebe and the children playing in Holden's field on the edge of the cliff; the other, despite what Holden claims, is the world of the movies. Of course, Allie is dead, and Phoebe, in her almost-parental role, reminds him that he has to like something. Betraying Holden's vision of childhood, she demands to go out west with him. When he says no, she responds by chucking his prized red hunting hat, worn bill-backward like a catcher's cap, at him. She refuses to go back to school and then tells Holden to shut up. It is Holden's, not Phoebe's, fantasy that she lives a beautiful, easy life. He needs her to stay put, to play her role in the school play, to play her role in his life, but Phoebe too wants to be someone else, trying on middle names (this week it is Weatherfield) and alter egos in her journal. The movies provide an image of emotional reality that for Holden is an alternative to childhood. Then again, they are not real. "The goddam movies," he tells us, are just like the children. "They can ruin you. I'm not kidding." Holden cannot be a child again, though, and his life is not a movie.[30]

The minor characters in *Catcher* suggest some of the other meanings of alienation circulating in *Catcher*'s historical moment. As Holden encounters Carl Luce, Mr. Antolini, James Castle, and Dick Slagle, he discovers that these men and boys cannot help him. None of them has the answer. Romanticism, Marxism, Freudian theory, and existentialism, and a growing faith in art as the source of salvation and the anchor of individualism—all of these ways of thinking may offer insight and understanding, but none of them is, in Holden's words, "*all* true."

Holden's adolescent alienation owes a deep debt to the Romantic poets and their attempt to turn life into art. In the late eighteenth and early nineteenth centuries, the British writers William Wordsworth, Samuel Taylor Coleridge, John Keats, and Lord Byron radically transformed the nature of art and, along with Goethe and other German writers, helped initiate what would become a literary movement by inventing a new kind of poetry, a lyric of the self.[31]

As a young Cambridge student, Wordsworth discovered that his own experiences and emotions were a rich source for his poetry. But the revelation of personal experience was too radical to embrace directly. Instead, he explored as a kind of proxy what he imagined to be the feelings and experiences of the rural people he observed all around him. Wordsworth and Coleridge collaborated on a volume of poems, published as *Lyrical Ballads*, about these people on the margins—children and the elderly, miners and peddlers, the mad and others outside the boundaries of polite society. Their poems, they argued, "were written chiefly with a view to ascertain how far the language of conversation in the middle and lower classes of society is adapted to the purposes of poetic pleasure," whether despite its "strangeness and awkwardness" it "contains a natural delineation of human passions, human characters, and human incidents." "Humble and rustic life was generally chosen," they wrote, "because in that condition, the essential passions of the heart find a better soil in which they can attain their maturity . . . and speak a plainer and more emphatic language." Together, the two poets helped create a whole new group of poetic subjects.[32]

They also helped establish an aesthetic pattern followed by many artists and writers ever since, using outsiders as a route back into the self. For the "humble" folk the poets wrote about gave them something in return, a plainness of form and simplicity of language. It was a short series of steps from empathy for people on the margins through this new language to an emphasis on the poet himself. "Such a holy calm/ Would overspread my soul, that bodily eyes/ were utterly forgotten, and what I saw/ Appeared like something in myself, a dream/ A prospect in the mind," Wordsworth wrote in *The Prelude*. "I was often unable to think of external things as having external existence," he later recalled, "and I communed with all that I saw as something not apart from, but inherent in, my own immaterial nature. Many times while going to school have I grasped a wall or a tree to recall myself from this abyss of idealism to the reality." Keats was "certain of nothing" but "the heart's affection and the truth of the imagination." Confusing insides and outsides, trying to make life into art, the Romantic poets helped create a new and more secular and personal form of transcendence.[33]

Catcher revisits the legacy of the Romantic poets and their attempt to turn life into art. Holden's wanderings in the city are a middle-class adolescent's version of the Romantic poet's travels, his explorations of the margins of his sheltered New York City childhood. As in Romantic poetry, the outer landscape in *Catcher* blinks quickly into Holden's inner landscape and back. When Holden goes to Central Park to see if the ducks are there in winter, he gets lost. He cannot find the lagoon, even though he has been going there all his life. At last he sees the water: "What it was, it was partly frozen and partly not frozen. But I didn't see any ducks around. I walked all around the whole damn lake— I damn near fell *in* once, in fact—but I didn't see a single duck." Discovering the margins—both people on the border of middle-class white urban life and places like the edge of the water—very quickly becomes both a metaphor for and a means of discovering the self.[34]

Over the course of the nineteenth century, the Romantic poets' interest in nature and peasant life, in anything outside of respectable society, became bohemian painters' interest in art, urban workers, and the East, in anything outside middle-class life. As the historian Jerrold Seigel has argued, "bohemia" originated in mid-nineteenth-century France, in Paris, along with the bourgeoisie way of life it opposed. Bohemians are "all those who, driven by an unstinting sense of calling, enter into art with no other means of existence than art itself," one participant wrote in 1851. "Their everyday existence" was "a work of genius." They turned their life into art. By the mid-nineteenth century, bohemians had already acquired a set of characteristics often adopted by rebels after them: odd dress and long hair, living for the moment, makeshift and transient lodging, sexual freedom and radical politics, heavy drinking and drug use, uneven work habits, and a community based in bars and coffeehouses. Later, self-consciously avant-garde artists took up many features of this bohemian way of life, particularly its insistence on the artist's persona and lifestyle as works of art.[35]

Nothing was as marginal, as outside respectable society, as sexual freedom, even in the mid-twentieth century. In *Catcher*, Holden's old student advisor Carl Luce, with his preference for Eastern philosophy and his interest in sex as "both a physical and a spiritual experience," takes up a bohemian-style life and attempts to turn his existence into art. Holden had known Luce as an older student at the Whooten School, one of the places Holden went before Pencey. Luce had moved to the city after he graduated to study at Columbia. Holden did not like him much at school, but alone in the city, he called him up anyway. Luce, he recalled, had given these terrific sex talks in the dorm. He could be "very enlightening sometimes." Waiting for Luce in a "swanky" hotel, he noticed "the other end of the bar was full of flits." And Luce, Holden remembered, was kind of "flitty himself, in a way. He was always saying, 'Try this for size,' and then he'd goose the hell out of you while you were going down the corridor. And whenever he went to the can, he always left the goddam door open and *talked* to you while you were brushing your teeth." Holden, of course, cannot help asking Luce about his sex life when he does arrive. Luce keeps telling him to change the subject even as he reveals he is dating a sculptress, recently arrived from China and in her late thirties, who lives in the Village. Holden, he advises, should go to see a psychoanalyst like Luce's dad. Luce, even though his name means "light," can offer Holden no insight. His artsy life is too far from the childhood innocence Holden is trying desperately to save.[36]

Holden's former teacher Mr. Antolini offers another romantic, bohemian spin on Holden's own alienation. When Holden goes to spend the night with "old Antolini" and his wife (Holden guesses she is sixty years older than her husband), his ex-teacher lectures him late into the night. "You're a student—whether the idea appeals to you or not. You're in love with knowledge." Other people have made art out of "their troubles": "You'll learn from them—if you want to. Just as someday, if you have something to offer, someone will learn something from you. It's a beautiful reciprocal arrangement. It isn't education," Antolini insists. "It's history. It's poetry." Holden, tired and more than a little confused, just yawns. Art, the novel suggests when Holden wakes up to find his ex-teacher touching him, is not even enough for Mr. Antolini. And poetry has not saved Allie or even D. B., who is also in his own way dead, abusing his talent for cash in Hollywood. A romantic sense of art as the rarified expression of spiritual alienation and also its cure is simply not going to work for Holden or many other adolescent boys.[37]

Catcher finds even less to use in the Marxist understanding of alienation as the separation of a person's work from her sense of self. Writing during the postwar Red Scare, Salinger creates a fictional landscape in which there is no ideological left. Alienation exists, but it is not a political and economic problem. Unlike some of the Beat poets, who were then already living their soon to be infamous vision of cultural rebellion, the fictional Holden does not even gesture in the direction of radical politics. None of the characters in *Catcher* suggests any act aimed at transforming America's political economy. Sure, people are alienated from their work in *Catcher*—crabby taxi drivers, corrupt bellhops, martini-drinking lawyers like Holden's dad, and even his brother D. B. But this alienation is presented as an individual and psychological problem. Holden remembers a former roommate at Elkton Hills, Dick Slagle, who coveted Holden's nice Mark Cross suitcases even as he branded them "new and bourgeois." In fact, "bourgeois" is Slagle's favorite word. Everything Holden has is "bourgeois as hell," even his fountain pen, which Slagle of course borrows. After two months, they both ask for a room change. "It's really hard to be roommates with people," Holden confesses, admitting that he liked the boy, "if your suitcases are much better than theirs." Class difference exists, and it affects friendships. But in an America where even the nuns whom Holden has just seen and who trigger his memory of Slagle have at least cheap suitcases, everything is already bourgeois. Politics are nonexistent. People don't kill themselves over class.[38]

They do, however, kill themselves to make a point about the irrationality of the universe. Salinger wrote *Catcher* over a ten-year period in which existentialism emerged as one of the most important trends in postwar thought. The philosopher Jean-Paul Sartre published *Existentialism and Human Emotions*, an adaptation of his wildly popular 1945 Paris lecture, in English in 1946.

For Sartre, there was no essential human essence, no universal characteristics of humanity that preceded human existence. People defined their own realities. They created whatever meaning existed. For philosopher Albert Camus, whose influential text *The Rebel* appeared in English in 1954, humans made reality in the act of opposition: "What is a rebel? A man who says no: but whose refusal does not imply a renunciation. He is also a man who says yes as soon as he begins to think for himself." Broadly popularized in America in the years after *Catcher*'s publication, existentialism shaped the reception of *Catcher* and Salinger's later books. It did not take much imagination to add Salinger to Camus's list of writers and artists challenging the cherished beliefs of their societies.[39]

Catcher, however, is not a book that celebrates the act of rebellion. It is not acting but narrating, expressing individual feelings, that gives life meaning in Salinger's novel. James Castle is *Catcher*'s existentialist, jumping out of a window to escape humiliation—Holden will not describe the repulsive act—at the hands of a crowd of classmates. Castle has refused to take back his comment that one of these bullies is a very conceited guy. Still, he proves that he can make his own choice, that he can act, at least, as if there is meaning, that he can be free. Even in the shower, Holden hears him hit the ground. Castle had been wearing Holden's turtleneck when he jumped, and "his teeth and blood were all over the place." No one would touch him until Mr. Antolini came, covered him up, and carried his body off to the infirmary. Suicide is certainly a symbolic act, but the meaning conveyed does not much matter to the maker. The actor may be right and true, but he is also dead.[40]

Holden does not go this way, and the best answer others can give him about the meaning of life is Freud. For many educated Americans at mid-century, Freudian thought returned a sense of destiny, of sweep and drama and tragedy, to individual lives, previously provided by religion and history. Holden never tells us why his parents did not send him for psychoanalysis after Allie died and he broke the windows and his hand. They wanted him to go, but somehow he did not. Carl Luce too offers him this advice. And Mr. Antolini tries to give him the answer he is seeking by quoting a psychoanalyst. But since Holden starts his story from "this crumby place" in California that is obviously a mental hospital, it is always clear that analysis is where Holden will end up. Telling the "madman stuff" is part of Holden's time on the couch. Freud the scientist is also Romantic in this sense—he too teaches individuals to read their own lives like a book or a film, to see their own experience as full of telling symbols and metaphors and moments that reveal the plot. The entire novel is Holden's own psychoanalytic reading, a fact that the self-conscious movie scenes make clear.

Art, then, is not the answer in Mr. Antolini's Romantic sense, but art, or more democratically self-expression, enables a person to shape the meaning of her life in a way that suicide, a solitary act of refusal, cannot. In front of an audience, self-expression becomes a larger, less individual and more social act. Salinger turns existentialism's emphasis on action, its acts of refusal, into the act of representing acts of refusal, into autobiography. The actor in life becomes instead an actor in representing that life. And this difference—that the seeker can salvage meaning not just through acting in the world but also by expressing his feelings to the world—will be one of the most important characteristics of postwar rebellion. The idea that to express feelings of alienation, to protest, is to live is not new in 1951. It has deep roots among working-class blacks—the blues—and self-consciously bohemian members of urban artistic enclaves. *Catcher's* accomplishment is to repackage these ideas about self-expression for a young, more affluent audience. Holden is not black or working-class or bohemian, and he does not break the law. If he is richer than most, he is otherwise a fit enough model for every white boy's and more than a few white girls' middle-class angst. And this is mostly how *The Catcher in the Rye* has been and continues to be read. *Catcher's* first reviewers, writing long before the book acquired its cult status, worried over this issue of identification. Taking up Holden's adolescent idiom to re-create a conversation between a teenage boy narrator and "this girl Helga," the *New York Times Book Review* gave the novel a fairly positive review. Some readers, the reviewer suggested in his faux-Holden voice, would love this boy: "You needn't swear, Helga, I said. Know what? This Holden, he's just like you. He finds the whole world's full of people who say one thing and mean another and he doesn't like it." A reviewer who panned the novel feared the appeal of a character like Holden: "He is alive, human, preposterous, profane and pathetic beyond belief . . . Fortunately, there cannot be many of him yet," the reviewer assured readers, "but one fears that a book like this given a wide circulation may multiply his kind." Ernest Jones, a psychoanalyst who had studied with Freud, reviewed *Catcher* for the *Nation*. He was also troubled by the potential popularity of "the unpretentious, mildly affecting chronicle." Readers who should have known better loved the novel, he suggested, because "the book is a mirror . . . It reflects something not at all rich and strange but what every sensitive sixteen-year-old since Rousseau has felt, and of course what each one of us is certain he has felt." *Catcher*, he argued, was "a case history of us all."[41]

Reviewers who loved the novel believed Salinger got the speech and feelings of the American teenager exactly right. The Book of the Month Club—*Catcher* was its July selection—raved that the word "brilliant is an unsatisfactory adjective. That rare miracle of fiction has again come to pass: a human being has been created out of ink, paper and images . . . One can actually hear it [Holden's voice] speaking," the review continued, and "what it has to say is uncannily true, perceptive and compassionate." The daily *New York Times* also praised *Catcher* as a brilliant first novel. "Holden's mercurial moods, his stubborn refusal to admit his own sensitiveness and emotions, his cheerful disregard of what is sometimes known as reality," its reviewer argued, "are typically and heartwarmingly adolescent." He and his friends, a later critic confessed, identified completely with Holden. Another wrote that there were "millions of young Americans who feel closer to Salinger than to any other writer" because "he not only speaks [their language]; he shapes it." And "he expresses their rebellion" as well. Alfred Kazin, one of the most important literary critics at the time, stressed that this identification was at the heart of *Catcher*'s appeal. Salinger "is a favorite with that audience of students, intellectuals, instructors, generally literary, sensitive, and sophisticated young people" who believe "that he speaks for them and virtually to them." Holden became a fictional model of rebellion so powerful that he deeply affected the way many readers understood their own lives.[42]

What Holden offered readers, with his slangy language and his not-exactly-going-anywhere life, was a way for them—for everyone—to be an artist. Rebellion here is not an act. It is not political, in an ideological sense. It is an expression of the inner life. It is a feeling. For Holden, self-expression is enough, and self-expression, the democratization of the modern idea of what it means to be an artist, is the flip side of the problem of mass culture. Sure, mass culture's ever-present images and stories haunt people's imaginations, coloring how they act and feel and experience even their own lives. But people in turn get to craft their own stories. In Holden, Salinger created a seductive character, an artifact of mass culture that critiqued mass culture, a fictional person that in turn shaped how real people think and feel and love.[43]

None of this magic works, however, without an audience. The connection is through the telling, not the living. Holden has an audience, and he knows it. He speaks directly to his readers, recounting events that are in fact months in the past. "Some things are hard to remember," he confesses. "You'd like her," he says of Phoebe. Of Allie, he assures us, "If you'd known him, you'd know what I mean." The connections Holden makes here occur outside the flow of his fictional life, at a remove, as he is representing it. Telling his story gives the alienated Holden an entirely new set of connections, with his readers whom he addresses directly, with the people who know what he means.[44]

If, as Holden believes, modern life alienates all sensitive, feeling people, then the answer, the only way to live, is to love other outsiders. Holden is lost. He never quite manages to find and connect with any other rebels, despite his New York City wanderings. But he finds them in his readers. And *Catcher* casts childhood as the space of innocence, free of the compromises and failures of adult life, as a place available to us all. This is why Allie's death is such a tragedy, and why Holden, an adolescent on the cusp of manhood (its own kind of margin) yet fighting the beast all the way, is such a good, if not a reliable, narrator. It does not matter if Holden is completely right. It only matters that he tries to maintain his innocence. Resisting the romance of the center, the desire to belong to the adult world all around him, Holden makes many readers love him and also love themselves. In their own self-expression, they can create themselves anew. They can rediscover truth and innocence. They can connect with other rebels. And they can create a new community and even perhaps a different world.

Mass Culture and the Rebel

If mass culture was a problem for some, it was also a solution for many. It was the place people went to live with the Bomb, singing along with "Atom and Evil," drinking "Atomic" cocktails, sending off box tops for "Atomic Bomb Rings," and lusting over a cover girl called "the Anatomic Bomb." It was the place industrial workers looked for relief as many unions traded away workplace democracy for higher wages and benefits for those lucky enough to keep their jobs in the face of automation. It was the place young mothers alone in the suburbs turned to try to hold on to themselves under an ocean of laundry and a tidal wave of toddlers' demands. It was the place scared ex-Communists and their friends imagined to escape McCarthyism, turning their dreams of a working-class democracy into pulp novels and B movies about gangsters who beat the bosses, disguised now as policemen and politicians, and still got the girl. It was the place war couples went flush with pent-up desire and war-salary savings to build a life different from their parents, beyond the old urban neighborhoods, off the failing farms, and outside the sprawling fear of depression and war. It was the place southern blacks traveled to find the shiny new Ford or the stylish new dress that showed up the crackers and shouted "We are not inferior" above the din of segregation's daily humiliations. It was a business that sold meanings and emotions and yet also a medium in which people did not just find but also made a sense of self and a sense of community. It was the medium both real and imagined that people used to ease the contradictions between their dreams and their realities, literally having it all at last, a world without limits, amen. It was the cause of postwar conformity and also the cure.

For many American intellectuals, especially former leftists who had retained the form if not the content of their past Marxism, contradictions did not simply exist. They aroused people to political action and resolution, unless something intervened to mask the truth. At mid-century, many intellectuals decided that this new opiate of the masses was something they called "mass culture," commercialized, mass-produced forms of expression from popular music and film to clothing and paperback fiction. While mass culture certainly existed before World War II—Tin Pan Alley songs and Hollywood films, for example—these scholars and critics anxiously charted its expansion in the late 1940s and 1950s. With higher wages and greater leisure time, they lamented, Americans rushed to purchase televisions and transistor radios, refrigerators and washing machines, rock and roll 45s and cheap paperbacks, and inexpensive copies of everything from fashion's New Look to Colonial furniture and abstract art. All this consumption, in turn, eroded American individualism. Mass culture alienated Americans from the ideas and artifacts that should be at the center of their culture.

In the 1950s, the ideas of these intellectuals powerfully shaped the romance of the outsider by defining the center as culturally flawed. In their thinking, Americans' problems were increasingly aesthetic, philosophical, and moral rather than economic and political. Their critiques also raised the issue of representation, not in the explicitly political sense of who made decisions for people within the government but in the cultural terms of who created and distributed the words and images and sounds that determined life's meaning. The concept of mass culture enabled intellectuals to think about the relationship of the individual and the larger society without explicitly referencing political ideology at all. It was not a coincidence that the concept of mass culture emerged and spread into broad use in the midst of the cold war.[45]

As intellectuals increasingly defined the culture at the center—mass culture—as the problem, it became a small step to see cultures understood as existing at the margins—the creative expression of outsiders—as part of the solution. In this kind of thinking, opposition, like conformity, took place in cultural terms, on cultural grounds. The mid-twentieth-century rebel figure differed from earlier visions of individuals who opposed their societies. Earlier rebels were people who fought for the Confederacy in the Civil War or for the independence of the Philippines or the Spanish Republic, people who engaged in armed political struggles. In the 1940s, a psychologist coined the term "rebel without a cause" to describe Americans alienated from society in ways simultaneously both more broad (not just political but social and psychological) and more narrow (particular to an individual), people estranged from their parents, teachers, and bosses, their neighborhoods, and the conventions and expectations with which they had been raised. The modifier "without a cause" countered the strong military and political connotations of the word "rebel." Increasingly in the 1950s, however, the phrase became redundant as a new rebel figure emerged, an image of individual defiance within the very mass culture accused of producing conformity.

"Culture" has always been a notoriously slippery and yet useful term. At mid-century, the meaning of the concept underwent something of a metamorphosis in common usage. Intellectuals since the early twentieth century, led most importantly by the anthropologist Franz Boas and the sociologist Robert Park, had developed a conception of culture as everything a people produces, all its symbols and meanings, its gods and laws and hopes, as well as its clothes and songs and homes. Boas, Park, and their followers used this conception of culture to fight the white supremacist beliefs entrenched in "scientific" thought about human nature and racial hierarchies, promoting in its place a kind of relativism. Differences between people were not natural but cultural in this thinking, and no culture was inherently more valuable than another. Gradually, this definition of culture began to blur the boundaries around an older understanding of the term as what might now be called high culture—classical music, opera, and fine art—coupled with ideas about education, background, respectability, and class. After World War II, intellectuals on both the left and the right used the term "mass culture," often quite negatively, to split mass-produced varieties of expression from older popular forms. In this view, radio serials, hit songs, pulp fiction, magazines, and movies were different from other cultural forms celebrated as "folk" culture and the "higher" forms of art and learning once known simply as culture.[46]

Although definitions varied, "mass culture" suggested forms of expression created for commercial rather than for artistic purposes and for large anonymous audiences rather than discriminating individuals. While these lines of distinction would prove difficult to draw in practice, at mid-century many intellectuals quickly adopted the concept, focusing on a perceived lack of quality, on the alleged "meaninglessness" of many cultural products. Members of the New York School, an increasingly powerful group of mainly former leftists associated in the postwar period with the magazines *Partisan Review*, *Commentary*, and *Dissent*, avoided discussion of who controlled production and the unequal distribution of these other goods, the critique offered by the left during the 1930s and early 1940s. They also avoided judging these products in the traditional moral terms embraced by conservatives, which would have required excluding abstract painting, experimental fiction, and other modernist and avant-garde experimentations. The idea of mass culture enabled critics across the political spectrum to dismiss the cultural products of America's booming postwar consumption.[47]

New York School intellectuals like Lionel and Diana Trilling, Irving Howe, Mary McCarthy, Hannah Arendt, Dwight Macdonald, and Clement Greenberg drew on the ideas of earlier scholars in forming their postwar critiques of mass culture. José Ortega y Gasset, a Spanish philosopher and supporter of the Spanish Republic, published his *Revolt of the Masses* in 1930, but his ideas did not have much impact on American thinkers until after the war. "The mass," in his analysis, was not a "social class, but the kind of man to be found today in all social classes." "The mass crushes beneath it everything that is different, everything that is excellent, individual, qualified and select," he argued. "Anybody who is not like everybody, who does not think like everybody, runs the risk of being eliminated." For Ortega y Gasset, this conforming collective destroyed the very possibility of individualism. In the late 1930s and 1940s, the then leftist critics Macdonald and Greenberg began using the German term for rubbish or muck, "kitsch," to refer to cultural products embraced by large numbers of people. Theodor Adorno and Max Horkheimer, part of a group of Marxist intellectuals that fled wartime Europe for America and became known as the Frankfurt School, also denounced mass culture. In *Dialect of the Enlightenment* (1944), they argued that radio and the movies left "no room for imagination or reflection on the part of the audience . . . They react automatically . . . Capitalist production so confines them [consumers] body and soul, that they fall helpless victims to what is offered them." In Adorno and Horkheimer's analysis, mass culture numbed people to their own exploitation, propping up the political economy of capitalism and its class inequalities. In a secularizing age, it was the new opiate of the masses. James Burnham, a liberal anti-Communist rapidly moving to the right, also denounced mass culture. America, he argued, was a "semi-barbarian superstate of the periphery." "This is the generation, after all, of the triumph of the Book Clubs, columnists, and radio, the relative decrease in the number of book titles published, the Hollywoodization of a continuous series of writers, the persistent banality of opera taste and production, a dull local tradition in painting . . . and a philosophic waste."[48]

During the Depression, some future members of the New York School, then leftists, had criticized American capitalism for promoting individual freedom over equality in the realm of the economy. The masses were the many, the good, common folk, and they were being deprived to fatten the few. At mid-century, in reaction to Stalinism and the rise of the cold war, this group of writers and critics including MacDonald, Greenberg, Philip Rahv (cofounder of the influential magazine *Partisan Review*), Alfred Kazin, Lionel Trilling, and others, moved right. The New York intellectuals began criticizing the masses for their willingness to not just endure but to purchase the products of the growing entertainment industries. Mass culture, they argued, was killing in the realm of culture the very individualism American democracy needed in order to defeat the totalitarian menace of the Soviet Union. The masses, in their analysis, became the people whose bad or easily manipulated taste was ruining the culture for the few. For these thinkers, what had been a political category became an aesthetic and cultural category. The old masses had been outsiders politically and economically, people without power. The new masses were insiders culturally, people who read and watched and listened to the products of consumer capitalism. In this new metaphor of space, outsider no longer meant left and insider right. Instead, outsiders were people who lived isolated lives beyond the reach of a brutish, leveling culture. Rebels, their allies, were the artists and writers and intellectuals who actively opposed this bad culture, not people who attacked the state to change the distribution of political and economic power. During the early years of the cold war, this relatively small group of intellectuals shifted the Old Left spirit of opposition from criticism of the political economy to cultural criticism.[49]

Nowhere was this stance clearer than in the editorial statement for the 1952 *Partisan Review* symposium "Our Country and Our Culture." America, the editors argued, "must be defended against Russian totalitarianism." Political theorist Hannah Arendt's 1951 book, *The Origins of Totalitarianism*, traced the commonalities in modern forms of mass politics, Nazism and Stalinism, despite their reliance on different political ideologies. Totalitarianism, she argued, destroyed the possibility of individualism. Clearly drawing on her ideas, the editors of the *Partisan Review* series asserted that American intellectuals and writers understood this threat and therefore no longer thought of themselves as "rebels and exiles" in a political sense. "The democratic values which America either embodies or promises" were "desirable in purely human terms," whatever their "cultural consequences." Still, those consequences had proven daunting. Mass culture created a "new obstacle" for creative people: "The artist and intellectual who wants to be a part of American life is faced with a mass culture which makes him feel that he is still outside looking in." Mass culture eroded the old cultural boundaries and harmed both high and folk culture. It produced bad art and banal entertainment and deprived important work of an audience. It killed deep thought and real emotions. Committed intellectuals, many contributors to the series argued, needed to oppose cultural alienation, instead of that Old Left target, economic inequality.[50]

Other liberal scholars and writers worried about the fate of the individual in America saw the threat as related not only to mass culture but also to the growing size of entities of all kinds, from businesses and governments to suburban developments and schools, a kind of "massification" of life. For sociologist David Riesman, the problem was less the mass media—he loved the movies—but the bureaucracy growing everywhere, especially in corporations. The motivating spirit of America, he quipped, had shifted from "the invisible hand to the glad hand." The "inner-directed" American, acting according to his own internal moral compass, was disappearing, and an "other-directed man," responding to bureaucratic and social pressures, what his bosses wanted and his neighbors had, was taking his place. Riesman and his coauthors, like most mid-century intellectuals, assumed the individual was a middle-class white man. Other studies made the vulnerability of a particular vision of American masculine autonomy even more clear. In *The Man in the Gray Flannel Suit*, Sloan Wilson turned the fate of the anonymous corporate mid-level manager searching for a more meaningful life into a best-selling novel. William Whyte, another sociologist, called this kind of American "the organization man" and offered a sad survey of his plight. For Whyte, work in the corporate world and home life in the suburbs both assaulted individuality. The suburbs, he joked, were "a Russia, only with money." The middle-class white American man who acted according to what he thought others wanted him to do was almost as great a threat to individualism and American democracy as Communism. Where exactly this thinking left white middle-class women, who were supposed to live for others, remained unclear.[51]

On the right, the philosopher and novelist Ayn Rand saw threats to the survival of the individual everywhere, in the government and the economy and the culture. Her heroes and occasionally heroines, the opposite of Riesman's "other-directed" people, lived purely for themselves. Selfishness, putting the self first, she argued, was the most important virtue, the foundation of her philosophy, objectivism, which she popularized in her novels. From Howard Roark in *The Fountainhead* (1943) to John Galt in *Atlas Shrugged* (1957), Rand's businessmen heroes rebelled against what Rand saw as the anti-individualism—what she called collectivism—of contemporary American life. They rejected a world that asked people to always value the taking care of others over the freedom of the individual. They acted for themselves. Though Rand clearly believed women (including herself) could embrace objectivism, in her novels male characters most fully embody her ideals.[52]

"The new domesticated male" may have been, as *Life* announced in 1954, "a boon to the household and a boom to industry," but for many intellectuals he was a problem. He was not the opposite of totalitarian man. He was not the embodiment of the freedom that supposedly flowed from democratic capitalism. He might not even be a real American.[53]

In response to these fears, the rebel offered a model of hyper-individuality without requiring any explicit reference to politics. Dwight Macdonald described this reaction in reference to the literary marketplace: "The more literature became a branch of industry, the more the craving for the other extreme—individuality. Or rather, a somewhat coarser commodity, Personality." The biographies of writers, he lamented as part of his critique of mass culture, had become more important than their works. The literary critic Leslie Fiedler took a more historical angle on the issue in *Partisan Review*'s own symposium, contending that "the concept of the 'alienated artist' itself was as much a creation of the popular mind as of the artist." "The melancholy and rebellious artist," he argued, "has always been a collaborator in American culture." Intellectuals, writers, and artists could be inside the culture and yet still oppose it. They could be a part of America—not exiles but participants—in their role as critics of mass taste and mass thought. They could save individualism simply by producing original thought and original art, by offering an alternative to conformity and "personality."[54]

The New York intellectuals and other critics and scholars were at least partly wrong and more than a little self-serving in their diagnosis of a crisis in American culture. The mass production of entertainment was not new, although many Americans had more money to spend on entertainment and more leisure. The cultural boundaries these critics often praised were arbitrary, elitist, racist, and sexist, as scholars ever since have loudly argued. As these thinkers thought through their own place in postwar America, however, they began to change the meanings of concepts like the masses, inside and outside, and the rebel. Instead of fighting the fact that cold war Red-baiting narrowed the range of political choices, they politicized questions of aesthetics and artistic expression. Their fusion of aesthetic and political questions, their sense that every act of expression was political even as they usually ignored the everyday practice of politics, profoundly affected the thinking of people far beyond the readership of their magazines. Paradoxically, they helped create the framework within which the mass media they often criticized—in this case national magazines, newspapers, and television—covered postwar cultural developments. In their thinking, rebels became men and much less frequently women who self-consciously positioned themselves in opposition to mass culture.[55]

The growing popularity of Freudian thought and psychological theory more broadly also shaped mid-century thinking about the relationship of insiders and outsiders and the meaning of rebellion. Psychologist Robert Lindner's rebels were the alienated, disaffected people, mostly men, that he cared for in his Baltimore practice, Maryland's state prisons, and a nearby federal penitentiary. In the fifties, as use of the term "juvenile delinquent" exploded in the popular press along with a corresponding rise in white middle-class anxiety about young criminals, he argued that the cures proposed by educators, religious leaders, doctors, and even social workers only made the problem worse. These professionals simply wanted to "smooth rough-edged personalities so that they [would] not rub too harshly on their fellows." "Philosophy, recreation, and pediatrics," he lamented, were all "infused with the rot—producing the idea that the salvation of the individual, and so of society, depends upon conformity and adjustment." Young people, Linder said over and over again in his more scholarly works and in articles by and about him in popular magazines, needed more freedom. His piece for *McCall's* made this point clear in the title: "Raise Your Child to be a Rebel." "Conformity" was "not a good," he argued, "but an evil." It was not "the path to the good life." And young people were most "affected by" the loss of individuality generated by "the twentieth century's mass political movements, social and industrial giants, wars, and economic upheavals." "Mass man," he asserted, was a "psychopath." If Americans wanted to save individualism, they needed to start with the teenagers, the most vulnerable members of society. The cure for the juvenile delinquent was "positive rebellion."[56]

Though Lindner talked specifically about teenagers, adults often responded to his descriptions of growing alienation as well. "The cult of the mass has come in as the standard," a reader wrote *Time* after a piece about the psychologist's work appeared in the magazine in 1954. "Mass production, mass education, mass markets for the commercial press, for literature, for art, movies, everything." Unlike the New York City intellectuals, however, Lindner provided a workable solution. How, for example, could writers and editors and reviewers persuade people to read "better" books? What could they do that they were not already doing? Lindner, a psychologist whose practice was treating individual patients, proposed instead that people oppose the institutions and practices that constrained their self-expression, that they adopt an oppositional stance in the relationship with the world. "Man," he argued, in *McCall's*, not *Partisan Review*, was "by nature a rebel." Mass culture must be resisted, not on aesthetic and philosophical grounds but for therapeutic reasons. Individual rebellion just might begin to restore Americans' deteriorating mental health.[57]

People living in this slippery entity called mass culture absorbed a tangle of contradictory messages. Most parents, teachers, ministers, rabbis, and political leaders told them they should be happy, even as some intellectuals, therapists, writers, and professors preached resistance and rebellion. Mass culture provided attractive examples of men and women happily conforming. Nothing captured the ideal of a conventional white middle-class suburban life better than the television show *Father Knows Best*, one of several hit sitcoms in the 1950s that featured these families living in suburbia. Mass culture, however, also made the rebel real. In the episode "Brief Holiday," which aired in 1957, the mother, Margaret Anderson, played by Jane Wyatt, has become bored with her work as a housewife and takes some time off. When she sits for a portrait by a local artist, she quickly finds herself immersed in the bohemian life. Later, the artist drops off the painting at the Anderson house and her husband, Jim, is jealous. "Brief Holiday" simultaneously makes fun of this form of rebellion and reveals that even a happily married, full-time mother might identify with outsiders. What better place for people to explore their contradictory desires to be a part of the American center and yet separate from it, to fit in and to oppose, than mass culture, this space of contradictions?[58]

For all the intellectual worry about conformity, in the early postwar period rebellion seemed to be breaking out all over American culture. Widely circulated magazines like *Life* helped transform Jackson Pollock, an abstract expressionist artist, into a crossover success, known outside the rarified art world as a crazy "action painter" who used sticks to sling ribbons of house paint at giant canvases. Jazz musicians including Charlie Parker, Dizzy Gillespie, Thelonious Monk, and Miles Davis worked versions of a rebel persona onstage and invented a cool, dissonant, rhythmically complicated sound called bebop that became the soundtrack of late forties–early fifties opposition to the white middle-class center. Hugh Hefner's *Playboy* debuted in 1953 with slickly produced pages, photographs of nude women, and an overtly sexual style of masculinity. The first issue—featuring a Marilyn Monroe centerfold and an article attacking marriage—sold an unprecedented ten thousand copies within days. The television program *The Ed Sullivan Show* brought Elvis Presley's music and only occasionally censored hips into middle-class homes in late 1956 and early 1957. Jack Kerouac's autobiographical novel of rebellion, *On the Road*, launched in 1957 by a laudatory review in the *New York Times*, became a paperback best seller. That same year, newspapers and national magazines covering the effort to censor Allen Ginsberg's poem "Howl" and criticizing Beat poetry spread knowledge of avant-garde writers far beyond the limited audiences that grew up around literary magazines and small, idiosyncratic bookstores. The rebel persona, in its many guises from bohemian to black, reconciled all the contradictions. It offered a way to salvage individualism through an opposition to mass culture that also remained a very profitable part of mass culture. For white women, who sometimes identified with male rebel characters, this balancing act proved much more complicated and often, much more dangerous.[59]

Lost Girls

Holden Caulfield, the iconic lost boy of mid-century American culture, had no female peers. Models of white middle-class female alienation were hard to find, even as male rebellion became increasingly popular in literature and films. As the sociologist Wini Breines has argued, white middle-class girls growing up in the early postwar period found few compelling models or outlets for their dissatisfaction with visions of adult femininity grounded in white middle-class family life. Alienated middle-class girls existed, she has demonstrated, but they lacked characters they could identify with and use to think through their feelings and organize their rebellion. Doubly lost, left out of the popular culture of the period as well as popular accounts of its history, these young white women did not make their alienation visible until the sixties, when they went to work in the civil rights movement and the New Left and helped create the women's liberation movement.[60]

Women rebels were uncommon and rarely fared well in the work of the white male writers who dominated literary fiction in the fifties. In *Catcher in the Rye*, the character "old Phoebe," Caulfield's younger sister, exists to sharpen her brother's deep angst. Her role is not to share his alienation but to give him some connection to the world outside himself. In *Franny and Zooey*, Salinger's 1961 novel published originally in 1955 and 1957 as two separate pieces in the *New Yorker*, Franny Glass also suffers a kind of existential crisis. Yet unlike Holden, who sets out to find meaning in the city, Franny holes up in the family apartment and prays. Even her alienation plays out in a domestic setting. In his 1955 novel, *Marjorie Morningstar*, Herman Wouk created perhaps the most compelling portrait of female rebellion published in this period. Nineteen and beautiful, Marjorie Morgenstern leaves her nice middle-class Jewish home, her parents and their values, and even her Jewish name in pursuit of her dream, becoming an actress. In a sharp reversal at the very end of the novel, however, Wouk buries his female rebel in a conventional marriage and suburban life. "You couldn't write a play about her that would run a week, or a novel that would sell a thousand copies," a character comments near the end of the novel. "The only remarkable thing about Mrs. Schwartz is that she ever hoped to be remarkable, that she ever dreamed of being Marjorie Morningstar." April Wheeler, the heroine of Richard Yates's 1962 novel, *Revolutionary Road*, suffers a worse fate. Living with her husband and two children in a Connecticut suburban neighborhood in the mid-1950s, she concocts a plan to move to Paris, where she will work to support the family while her husband pursues his dream of becoming a real writer or artist of some kind. Frank Wheeler, however, does not really have any repressed creative ambitions. Escape from white middle-class suburban life is April's dream, not his. Relieved when she becomes pregnant, he insists they call off their trip. While he is at work, she tries to give herself an abortion and later dies from the loss of blood.[61]

In pulp fiction and films, white middle-class rebel girls had fun, though in the end they suffered for their pleasures or renounced their unconventional ways. They had sex with stable boys, household servants, college coeds, or gang members. They acted up and acted out. They became bad girls and tomboys, refusing the role of the good student, the obedient daughter, or the chaste girlfriend. Like their male counterparts, these girls rejected the model of the future laid out in their parents' lives. Frequently, rebel girl characters seemed created to satisfy the desires of male readers and viewers as much as female ones. Still, as the scholar Leerom Medovoi has argued, bad girls like Natalie Wood's character in the 1955 film *Rebel Without a Cause* and tomboys like Sandra Dee's character in the 1959 film *Gidget* demonstrated that middle-class white girls could be rebels too, especially if they formed friendships or relationships with rebel boys. In this sense, these characters did suggest alternatives. Alienated girls could express their oppositional feelings most easily by identifying with and romanticizing male rebellion.[62]

Many women writing about female rebellion had also tried to live it, to resist the conventional road from girlhood to mature femininity. A few of them published fiction based on their own experiences. In a letter to her mother, the future poet Sylvia Plath announced boldly, "I need to practice a certain healthy Bohemianism, to swing away from the gray-clad clock-regulated, responsible . . . economical, practical girl." In Plath's account of her young adulthood, *The Bell Jar*, the lost girl character Esther Greenwood describes her state of mind at the start of the story: "I wasn't steering anything, not even myself . . . like a numb trolley-bus . . . still and very empty, the way the

eye of the tornado must feel, moving dully along in the middle of the surrounding hullabaloo." Working at a women's magazine as an intern, she hopes
to find something that will wake her up and make her the driver of her own
life. "The last thing I wanted was infinite security and to be the place an arrow
shoots off from," she confessed. "I want change and excitement and to shoot off
in all directions myself, like the colored arrows from a Fourth of July rocket."
Over the course of the internship, Greenwood does not figure out how to be
those arrows. Instead, she attempts suicide, taking an overdose of pills and
crawling under the family house to die in an act modeled on Plath's own first
suicide attempt. If Greenwood must live a kind of waking death in middle-class
family life, she might as well die in middle-class family life. In early 1963, a
month after the publication of *The Bell Jar*, Plath stuck her head in an oven
while her two children slept in the next room. This time she succeeded.[63]

Diane Di Prima found change and excitement when she fled college and
her life as the academically successful daughter of Italian American parents to
become a poet in New York City. In her fictionalized account of her life in the
fifties, *Memoirs of a Beatnik*, Di Prima described the rebellion of a character
also named Diane Di Prima. Under pressure from her editor—Di Prima wrote
her "memoir" to earn money to support the child she was raising alone—much
of the book consists of loosely strung-together sex scenes that are wild, passionate, and often unconventional, full of odd couplings and multiple and
overlapping partners. In love with a WASP college friend who wrote like Dylan
Thomas and J. D. Salinger, Diane ran away with her to the city. She confessed
her "old longing to be a pirate, tall and slim and hard, and not a girl at all." And
she followed the rules of "Cool," the implicitly male code of bohemia, which
forbade anyone from provoking or displaying emotional vulnerability. In
return, she experienced "light and freedom, air and laughter, the outside
world." She made a life beyond the "nightmare" of monogamy with its "claus-
trophobic" and "deadening" boundaries. She lived and made love and art like
she pleased, like a man. Still, Di Prima did not publish her account of female
rebellion until 1969, too late to provide any guidance for young middle-class
white women lacking her courage.[64]

Di Prima grew up in New York City and knew where to find bohemia, in
the coffeehouses and bars of Greenwich Village and around the fountain in
Washington Square Park, before most middle-class white Americans had even
heard of the Beats. Other middle-class women went looking in these places
too. Joan Vollmer, a single mother who later married the writer William S.
Burroughs, provided the apartment in which the budding literary lives of
Burroughs, Jack Kerouac, and Allen Ginsberg intersected and sparked in 1944

and 1945. Six years later, Burroughs killed her in a drunken game of William Tell gone awry. Other lost girls also made a small mark in the historical record because they were connected with famous men. Edie Parker, Kerouac's first wife, participated in the life around Vollmer's apartment and lived there for a time. Elise Cowen dated Ginsberg in 1953, spent time with his friends, and wrote poetry. She later killed herself by jumping out a window. In New York City and elsewhere in urban America, white women sat in the audiences in jazz clubs. They performed music and poetry and mingled with the crowds in coffeehouses. They were there, helping create alternatives to "conformity" and what they understood as blind acceptance of mass culture.[65]

Joyce Johnson, a girlfriend of Beat writer Jack Kerouac, and Hettie Jones, the first wife of poet LeRoi Jones, both published retrospective accounts of their transformation from middle-class white girls into bohemians. Their memoirs provided a sense of the sparkling promise of life outside middle-class conventions, and the hard costs as well. For the young Johnson, Greenwich Village in 1957 and 1958 "seemed to promise something I'd never tasted in my life as child—something I told myself was Real Life. This was not the life my parents lived but one that was dramatic, unpredictable, possibly dangerous. Therefore *real*, infinitely more worth having." Out at bars with Kerouac's circle of male friends and fellow writers, Johnson felt she sat "in the exact center of the universe," "the only place in America that is alive," and the place "the dead culture is surely being awakened." Haunting the conversation, listening to the excited talk, "merely being there" was enough. Hettie Jones described the seductiveness of bohemian difference more bluntly: "We lived outside, as if. As if we were men? As if we were newer, freer versions of ourselves." Johnson wondered where these ideas about the greater value of the outsider life originated. "In trying to trace the derivations of this notion of experience, I come into blind alleys," she confessed. "It was simply there all of a sudden, full-fledged, like a fever I'd come down with." The romance of the outsider spread like germs, in her metaphor, carried by the air.[66]

Some middle-class white women clearly identified with male rebel characters, from the fictional Holden to the male artists, writers, and musicians who gathered in Greenwich Village. Growing up in small-town Texas, the future rock star Janis Joplin remembered wanting "something more than bowling alleys and drive-ins." There, she recalled, "you got no one to learn from because there is not a reader down the street you can sneak off and talk too. There's nobody. Nobody. I remember when I read that in *Time* magazine about Jack Kerouac," she confessed. "Otherwise I'd've never known. I said 'Wow!' and split." Mass culture, not the air, spread the romance of the outsider, and young white middle-class women as well as men felt its power.[67]

The romance of the outsider proved extremely costly for women who tried to live as rebels. Female participants in New York's late 1940s and 1950s bohemian circles paid for their freedoms in emotional pain and financial insecurity. Most difficult, women living beyond white middle-class gender conventions had little ability to shape the behavior of the men who were their lovers. Jones and Di Prima, for example, raised children alone with few resources. More troubling, with families far away and often estranged, and relationships based on "freedom" and being cool, women rebels had little in the way of a safety net. When their physical or mental health deteriorated, they had few options. Vollmer became a drug addict and neglected her children. Cowen killed herself. Parker disappeared. Self-destructiveness and suicide haunted female rebels outside the Beats' New York circle as well. Plath and fellow poet Anne Sexton both killed themselves. Joplin died of a drug overdose. Alienated women who violated the harsh and unforgiving boundaries of white middle-class womanhood not yet stretched by second-wave feminism paid dearly.[68]

Still, male rebels suffered as well. Among the Beats, Ginsberg spent time in a mental hospital. Sometime writer Herbert Hunke was a junkie. Kerouac suffered from alcoholism and eventually drank himself to death. Their friend Lucien Carr spent time in prison for murdering an older man who had stalked and propositioned him. Poet and long-term Ginsberg partner Peter Orlovsky suffered severe mental health problems. Ginsberg's 1955 poem "Howl" famously chronicles the damage suffered by both male and female outsiders trying to live through the fifties, "the best minds of my generation destroyed by madness," "the angel-headed hipsters burning for the ancient heavenly connection." Men as well as women became casualties. The successes, the icons, the models for those rebels that followed, however, were almost always male.[69]

Lost girls lived in a patriarchal world. But they also lived in a place and time in which the logic of mass culture reinforced and to some degree supported white middle-class male rebellion while working against expressions of female alienation. If mass culture threatened to swallow American individualism, as intellectuals feared, then it feminized Americans. Mass culture, at the symbolic level, was a woman. Popular male rebels provided reassurance that an always mythic but no less powerful white middle-class American individualism would survive. Male rebels made mass culture acceptable. Female outsiders, on the other hand, simply ratcheted up anxieties about the emasculating effects of "conformity," consumption, and white-collar work. At the symbolic level, mass culture made space for lost boys even as it worked to strengthen a kind of neo-traditional model of womanhood grounded in the nuclear family and the suburban home. It did not make much space for rebel girls. Alienated white middle-class women often identified with male outsiders and rebels, especially before some of them went to work to create the women's liberation movement of the late 1960s.

CHAPTER 2

Rebel Music: Minstrelsy, Rock and Roll, and Beat Writing

I don't want no other love.
Elvis Presley

If J. D. Salinger had set his coming-of-age novel *The Catcher in the Rye* half a decade later, Holden Caulfield would not have needed to wander New York City looking for an alternative to phoniness. By the mid-fifties, rebel sounds filled the air. The tinny speakers of the new televisions buzzed with the speech of segregationists angry at African Americans' demands. Streets in Little Rock, Montgomery, and elsewhere rang with shouts and barks and sirens, voices speaking through bullhorns, and the footsteps of large crowds. And everywhere middle-class kids lived, black-sounding music blared its shouted vocals and fast beats: on televised teen dance shows, at screenings of the new teen films, and on the transistor radios and portable record players blasting in suburban bedrooms. Within this defiant cacophony, ringing out in contradiction to an image of America as a place of rising conformity, middle-class white kids learned that rebellion sounded black.

In the mid-fifties, as the historian Brian Ward has argued, no place in Jim Crow America was more racially integrated than the airwaves. The year of the *Brown* decision, a song recorded by a black rhythm and blues group from the Bronx called the Chords appeared on *Billboard* magazine's white pop chart. Before "Sh-boom," other records had occasionally crossed over from the hit lists reserved for songs by black musicians. But something was different about this song's success. "Sh-boom" started a stampede. Young white fans helped rhythm and blues double its market share that year. Crossovers—songs by black musicians that found large white audiences—became increasingly common. Integration occurred in the other direction as well. A skinny white guy from Memphis recorded the blues song "That's All Right" and began performing and dressing like a black musician. Elvis Presley's young white fans loved the fact that he sounded "black." Presley remembered that when his first record came out, "you could hear folks around town saying, 'Is he, is he?' And I'm going 'Am I, am I?'" The racial mystery was part of the attraction. The white group Bill Haley and His Comets also played with racial mixing, fusing a raw rhythm and blues beat and shouted lyrics about escaping school in their recording "Rock Around the Clock." As the theme music for *Blackboard Jungle*, a popular movie about juvenile delinquency at an integrated urban high school, the song became a number one hit on the pop charts in the summer of 1955. That year, the African American singer and guitar player Chuck Berry brought this crossing full circle. Sounding like a hillbilly trying to sound like Haley, Berry turned the traditional country song "Ida Blue" into the early rock and roll hit "Maybelline."[1]

Despite the differences between these songs, in all of them musicians combined sounds, gestures, and styles white audiences usually designated as racially distinct. Previously, many white listeners imagined the black moves they watched and the black voices, black rhythms, and black riffs they listened to as circulating in distinct spaces and categories. The recording industry had institutionalized this segregation, selling secular music by black musicians as race music and, after 1948, as rhythm and blues, no matter what it sounded like. The new musical miscegenation, however, played right over this fantasy of aural and physical segregation. Rock and roll arrived less as a coherent musical genre than as a cluster of songs that mashed together elements of rhythm and blues, blues, gospel, and hillbilly music while acknowledging and even celebrating the racial mixing.

The "blackness" of rock and roll made it a perfect vehicle for white middle-class kids growing up with segregation to use in creating and expressing their felt sense of difference from their parents and their middle-class world. The music enabled a kind of fantastic cross-racial (and often cross-class) identification. Listening to songs like "Rock Around the Clock," white middle-class teenagers fell in love with the sounds and moves performing black bodies made, with the sounds and the emotions singing black bodies expressed, even when the bodies making the sounds and the moves and expressing the emotions were white. Dancing and singing along, white teenagers could make their bodies "black" too and the music their own. Rock and roll sounded and looked like rebellion.[2]

This racial crossing proved highly unstable, however, because early rock and roll simultaneously assaulted the very idea that sounds could be segregated, that they could ever actually be black or white. If a black man, Chuck Berry, could sound to some people like a white man trying to sound like a black man, what did these classifications mean? How much different, in the end, was "sounding" black from "being" black?

To understand how "sounding" and "being" could be similar and yet also different and how rebel music taught white middle-class kids to love outsiders requires some historical backtracking. It requires briefly revisiting earlier historical moments of popular music making and white love for black outsiders. It requires taking seriously the scholar Eric Lott's suggestion that the roots of rock and roll lie in the "love and theft" of blackface minstrelsy.

Minstrelsy and its descendants gave its white and black performers and fans lessons in how to act black by defining what blackness looked and sounded like onstage. And it taught them why to act black. Blackness could be anything. Blackness could be everything. African Americans might be enslaved, Jim Crowed, disfranchised, lynched, raped, abused, cheated, and discriminated against, but the minstrel show made "blackness" into a medium of transformation and transcendence so powerful that at times, within limits, it even worked for black people. In the 1950s, rock and roll and, to a lesser degree, jazz gave many white teenagers, Beats, beatniks, and other bohemians access to this magic. With the right rebel sounds and the right rebel moves, white middle-class kids and even adults could dance right over the contradiction between their desire for self-determination and their desire for deeply rooted social connection. They could project their impossible longings for autonomy and rootedness onto African Americans and in their identification with blackness reabsorb a magical mix cleansed of contradiction. And if rock and roll did not work, if they were too old or too serious or too sophisticated for it, they could take up other white fantasies of black life and black people. They could imagine a whole hipster philosophy. They could write like a bebop horn. Black sound in white ears or white mouths or white pens became a threshold, a symbolic ground simultaneously inside and outside white life, a medium whites could use to reinvent themselves. As white Negroes, they could at last have it all, at least for the moment, at least for the length of the song.

Sounding and Acting Black

Painting the face black and pretending to sing and dance and play like a slave or ex-slave would have seemed to many young white rock and roll fans absurd, not to mention old-fashioned and unsophisticated. Yet in sounding and acting black, early rock and roll played within a soundscape layered with the long history of white attraction to black expressive culture. The legacy of blackface performance remains especially powerful whenever Americans encounter people they imagine as different from themselves and cultures they under-stand as different from their own. Nineteenth-century minstrelsy established a set of aural and visual codes for exploring the relationship between loving dif-ference and wanting to be different. In important respects, the romance of the outsider is a late twentieth-century reworking and expansion of these nine-teenth-century minstrel conventions.[3]

In the late 1820s, the white entertainer Thomas Dartmouth "Daddy" Rice created a song and dance called "Jump Jim Crow" that became wildly popular in antebellum America. Rice would saunter onstage, dressed in ragged, patched, and mismatched clothes with his hat at a rakish angle. Thrusting out his bottom, lifting his knees, and swinging his lower legs to the music, he would grin widely. Then he would start to sing:

> Come, listen, all you gals and boys, I'm just from Tuckyhoe;
> I'm gwine to sing a little song, My name's Jim Crow.
>
> Wheel about, an' turn about, an' do jis so;
> Eb'ry time I wheel about, I jump Jim Crow.

As Rice told it, he based his performance on the singing and dancing of a black man in Cincinnati named Jim Cuff or Jim Crow. All kinds of audiences—middle-class and working-class, northern and southern, black and white—loved "Jump Jim Crow," and many other entertainers performed versions of the routine over the next two decades. Looking back, the *New York Tribune* reported in 1855, "Never was there such excitement in the musical or dramatic world, nothing was talked of, written of, and nothing was dreamed of, but 'Jim Crow.' The most sober citizens began to wheel about, and turn about, and jump Jim Crow."

From the moment of its origins in the early nineteenth century, blackface minstrelsy meant face paint, "Negro" dialect, and racist ridicule. African American commentators have long condemned the racist implications of blackface performance. Frederick Douglass argued before the Civil War that minstrelsy did not, as most whites believed, present an accurate picture of African American life. A century later, Ralph Ellison agreed. Blacking up white men circulated images of blacks that served the needs of the minstrel show's white fans. The "darkey act," Ellison's term for minstrelsy and all related forms of blackface performance, staged white perceptions and white fantasies of black people.[4]

Douglass and Ellison also admitted that racism alone could not account for the enormous appeal of the blackened faces, widely drawn mouths, mangled speech, and mismatched clothes on the stage. Minstrelsy was never one-way theft, never a medium in which whites simply stole from blacks. Exchange and subversion occurred in all directions. Slaves created dances like the cakewalk, for example, that copied, transformed, and made fun of the dances of their masters and mistresses. When T. D. Rice and other white entertainers first created blackface performances, they incorporated these "whiteface" elements along with other sounds and gestures they saw African Americans performing on street corners and in working-class bars. Later, blacked-up black men used the conventions of minstrelsy to make fun of whites. In this sense, although the musical recording industry in the 1920s pushed songs into categories based on assumptions about the color of the performers and potential listeners, there was simply never any pure white or black music.[5]

As the most popular form of entertainment in nineteenth-century America, minstrelsy generated musical and dramatic performance styles, outrageous costumes, and rich and famous stars. It produced beloved characters, well-known sketches, and hit songs. It explored topics like slavery, women's rights, and sexual desire, all deemed unfit for respectable discussion. And it made space for contradictory messages, emotional exchange, and indirect challenges to authority. As Constance Rourke noted in her classic 1931 book, *American Humor*, "Little Jim Crow appeared at almost the precise moment when *The Liberator* was founded." Abolitionists and anti-slavery activists like Harriet Beecher Stowe used comic and sentimental minstrel characters in their work. Minstrelsy signaled what Eric Lott has called "a profound white investment in black culture," an interest broad enough to encompass abolitionism and the possibilities of a racially mixed urban working class as well as support for slavery and white supremacy. Even Douglass admitted attending an 1849 performance of the black troupe Gavitt's Original Ethiopian Serenaders, "partly from love of music, and partly from curiosity to see persons of color exaggerating the peculiarities of their race." In the blink of an eye or the beat of a drum, minstrelsy could flip between love and hate, insult and envy, liberation and enslavement, black and white. It had more than a little in common with rock and roll.[6]

Scholars Lott and W. T. Lhamon have worked hard to restore the radical ambiguity of early blackface minstrel performances. Lhamon has emphasized the intensely heterogeneous world of the urban working class at the beginning of the nineteenth century, particularly the polyglot New York City population from Catherine Market to Five Points, in which, he has argued, blackface minstrelsy originated. Blackface performance there became a language in which different groups increasingly recognized their similar oppressions. In one minstrel character's story of "burst bondage portrayed as comedy," "various spurned peoples and their narratives came together under the blackface sign." In the bars and cellars of working-class New York, whites and blacks performed in blackface before mixed audiences and gave form and meaning to an emerging mixed-race working-class world.[7]

Lott, on the other hand, has emphasized the role of young white working-class men in the origins of minstrelsy and the complexity of their roles as both blackface performers and blackface audience members. For these men, blackface worked as an expression of resistance to new middle-class conventions of masculinity and sexuality. Acting black, they played with alternative visions of male desire and imagined African American men as naturally virile and sexually free. Blackface also worked to help white men slip the noose, symbolically at least, of a changing economy in which a shift to wage labor threatened their hopes for material independence. Free white laborers saw slaves as their opposites, as powerful symbols of economic, political, and social dependence. Impersonating them, white workers could give meaning to their own shrinking freedom and express otherwise unspeakable desires, including their nostalgia for what they imagined as southern slaves' happy-go-lucky life of country ease, their anxieties about their own worsening economic situation, and their attraction to what they understood as black culture. Blackface minstrelsy expressed love as well as hate and represented an act of cultural theft as well as political and social repudiation.[8]

Despite the differences in their accounts, both Lhamon and Lott have emphasized that blackface performance emerged from the mix of urban working-class life and enabled multiple and even contradictory interpretations and uses from the start. It was both racist and anti-racist. It was radical, presenting and celebrating cultural miscegenation, and yet it was also conservative, confirming the dominant social and political order. It was about a rural world way down south, and yet it was about the urban North. It played an essential role in defining what race meant in nineteenth-century America. Minstrelsy enabled performers to rebel and yet also to hide that rebellion right in plain sight.

If minstrelsy was always oppositional, exactly who was rebelling and just what they were rebelling against continually changed, both within the minstrel act and over the course of the century. In the early 1840s, minstrel troupes like E. P. Christy's Virginia Minstrels and Dan Emmett's Virginia Minstrels expanded the individual blackface songs and dances that Rice and others had popularized into a whole evening of theater put on by white actors pretending to be plantation slaves. A form evolved in which troupe members played standard minstrel show characters. The Interlocutor, for example, wearing what was presented as a slave's take on his master's style and dress, worked hard to tame the "charismatic insouciance" of the end men, or Tambo and Bones characters. These minstrel show characters then performed sketches and dramas—stump speeches on women's rights or courtship tales, for example—in which they in turn acted out other roles. Over time, the songs, dances, and sketches grew more stylized and, most scholars have argued, more invested in asserting white middle-class visions of order. Still, the multiple layers of playacting made it hard to be sure exactly which person or character of which race—the actor or the blackface character the actor was playing or the character in a skit that this blackface character was playing—was the brunt of the joking.[9]

The post–Civil War minstrel revival eroded many of early minstrelsy's ambiguities. Many white Americans used blackface performance to rebel against the outcome of the Civil War. Minstrelsy for them expressed the loss of the Old South, romanticized as a plantation pastoral—the happy slaves, the clear and stable roles for men and women, rich and poor. In songs like "My Old Kentucky Home" and "Carry Me Back to Old Virginny," for example, whites took on African Americans' expressions of longing for family left behind on what the historian Ira Berlin has called a Second Middle Passage, the internal migration of slaves from the east coast to the new southwest frontier. But white singers and fans used these emotions for different purposes, to express their own nostalgia for their mythical Old South. The minstrel singer's borrowing of emotions generated in a different time and place to express her feelings about her own place in the world—an emotional ventriloquism—was central to minstrelsy's appeal. This kind of affective borrowing would also become a central feature of rock and roll.[10]

Many white minstrelsy fans in the period after the Civil War believed that minstrelsy presented a true picture of African American culture. Sometimes they even seemed to forget that blacked-up white men were not actually African Americans. By the late nineteenth century, African Americans like

Bert Williams had become stars of the profitable minstrel show business, blacking up and dressing in drag and billing themselves for white audiences as well as black as the "real" Negro minstrels. Blacked-up black men highlighted the theatricality of blackface performance: The nature of the act was to act. They acted in ways characters defined as black by the conventions of minstrelsy were supposed to act and thus were black in the terms in which minstrelsy defined blackness for American popular culture. For an audience attuned to this play, blacked-up black men demonstrated the theatrical and thus illusory nature of white American understandings of race. Double blackness, black paint on black skin, paradoxically lightened these black musicians, giving them the freedom to make money playing with white fantasies of blackness in ways that would literally get them lynched off the stage. Yet for some white audiences, African American minstrels displaced even more fully the theatrical conventions of minstrelsy, making blackface performance appear as the "natural" behavior of black people. Blacked-up black men highlighted the complicated and shifting relationship between "playing" black and "being" black.[11]

African Americans, however, did not just perform in blackface. They also formed an audience for minstrelsy. From the antebellum period through the 1930s, black fans attended minstrel shows, listened to black musicians play hit minstrel and coon songs, and, when they became available, bought minstrel recordings. Through the 1930s, southern rural and working-class black audiences continued to patronize black musicians like Papa Charlie Jackson who performed both minstrel songs and the blues. Urban blacks purchased records made by white blackface singers in the period before 1920 when an emergent recording industry recorded few black musicians. Like Douglass decades earlier, later black minstrel fans enjoyed the music and the chance to see black entertainers exaggerating whites' exaggerations about African Americans. They went to see actors playing with race, with both white and African American ideas about blackness and with what those ideas about blackness suggested about whiteness. If a white person could act black onstage and make some people believe in the act, then anything was possible. Minstrelsy, for these audiences, revealed no essential quality of African American culture. It was not about transcendence, the circulation of some authentic piece of African American expressive tradition that broke the bonds of time to carry the truth. Instead, what it revealed about African American life was transformation, blackness as multiplicity and ambiguity, blackness as movement.[12]

Minstrelsy in turn deeply shaped the blues, the new musical form that African Americans invented in the U.S. South in the late nineteenth or early twentieth century. Academic and amateur folklorists and white blues fans have written most blues histories, and their accounts have placed the new music in a "black" musical tradition linked most importantly to a "pre-modern" past in antebellum America and Africa. Commercialized, mixed-up musical forms like minstrelsy, in this kind of thinking, were inauthentic and their influence corrupting. They had little role to play in the evolution of "authentic" black music like the blues. While many African American musicians were blind (playing music was one way they could earn a living), they were not deaf as well. And in the early twentieth-century South, a person would have had to be deaf not to have heard any minstrel songs. The blues emerged in a world long saturated with minstrelsy. However much they drew on African musical forms, African American musicians also consciously worked against and within minstrel conventions as they crafted this new form. Most importantly, they took up the minstrel tradition of playing with blackness.[13]

When Mamie Smith's recording of "Crazy Blues" became a huge hit in 1920, African American musicians finally broke through the segregation that had kept most of them out of recording studios. Through the early 1930s, the blues dominated the broad commercial category called race records. African American women like Ma Rainey and Bessie Smith became superstars. Singing the blues, they attracted huge audiences, sold thousands of records, and earned large incomes. Many of these women blues singers literally got their start performing minstrel material in medicine shows, vaudeville houses, and bars in the early twentieth century. While Ma Rainey sang in tent shows in small towns in the South, for example, her husband and stage partner, Pa Rainey, entertained audiences by cramming crockery in his mouth. Rainey, in turn, mentored the biggest female blues star of all, Bessie Smith. These blues women learned from minstrelsy the shape-shifting acts that would make them famous. They learned, like blackface performers, to play with what cultural critics call personas, to consciously craft characters.[14]

In the blues, musicians sang these personas into being in a strongly first person voice. The lyrics of Bessie Smith's 1923 recording "'Tain't Nobody's Bizness if I Do" reveal this process at work:

> There ain't nothing I can do, or nothing I can say
> That folks don't criticize me
> But I'm goin' to, do just as I want to anyway
> And don't care if they all despise me . . .
> If I go to church on Sunday

> Sing the shimmy down on Monday
> Ain't nobody's bizness if I do, I do.

The personal rebellion she expresses here—"If I should take a notion/ To jump into the ocean/ 'Tain't nobody's bizness if I do, do, do, do"—takes on added meaning in the 1920s as northern urban spaces like Atlantic City become increasingly segregated. But the personal freedom here is not all about leisure time. She can give away all her money and choose to accept domestic violence too, if she chooses: "I swear I won't call no copper/ If I'm beat up by my poppa/ 'Tain't nobody's bizness if I do, if I do." The blues persona Smith creates will not only live outside middle-class morality and respectability. She will live outside the law, too. Blues lyrics, in fact, do not make much of a distinction between the two. In "Beale Street Papa," also recorded in 1923, Smith's singing expresses both longing and pain over the loss of her man and yet emphasizes that her sexual expression, her existence, is her own:

> Mmmm hmmmm, I'm blue
> so how come you do me like you do?
>
> I'm cryin,' Beale Street papa, don't mess around with me
> There's plenty pettin' that I can get in Tennessee
>
> I still get my sweet cookies constantly.

Smith here sings into being a vulnerable and yet sassy character who acts on her own sexual desire.[15]

Whether sung by men or women, blues lyrics conjured a black character who was sexual and violent and anything but good, a black person free to be bad, a dark (no pun intended) sense of humor, a tragic sense of life. The minstrel, on the other hand, played the fool for the white folks, even when blacked-up black men played the fool on the white folks. The point is not that whites controlled one image (the minstrel) and blacks controlled the other (the blues). Neither form of music could be traced to a moment of "pure" white or black origins. Instead, the mediums played with different images of blackness: the black man or woman who tries to go along, at least superficially, and the black man or woman who says no, at least superficially—who wants to play her life her own way.[16]

Early blues scholars and critics emphasized the importance of personal voice in the blues. John W. Work, one of the first black blues scholars, emphasized the individualism of the form by contrasting the blues with sacred music: "The spirituals are choral and communal, the blues are solo and individual . . . The spiritual creators thought of every happening in nature as epic . . . The blues singer translated every happening into his own intimate inconvenience." Yet this personal voice was not a strictly autobiographical voice. The "I" of the song was a character, a persona that might overlap with but was not identical to the singer.[17]

The emphasis on personal performance in the blues in turn made sex the perfect subject and metaphor for its personas. Sex was a way of asserting the self in the world, of stealing some pleasure out of the grind of work and poverty. Sex too was about performance. In the blues, Ellison wrote his good friend Albert Murray, "sex means far more than poontang, but the good life, courage, cunning, the wholeness of being colored, the beauty of it . . . as well as the anguish, and the deep capacity of [a character] to stand for, to symbolize it all."[18]

Women blues singers proved sex would sell. In her 1928 recording "Hear Me Talking to You," Ma Rainey sang:

> Ramblin' man makes no change in me
> I'm gonna ramble back to my used-to-be
> Ah, you hear me talkin' to you, I don't bite my tongue
> You wants to be my man, you've got to fetch it with you when
> you come

Smith and Rainey and other female blues singers sang their rebel personas into existence in their expression of sexual and other desires. These characters they created, in turn, resisted both black men and white men and women's plans for them. In the *Chicago Defender* ad for Ma Rainey's 1928 recording "Prove It on Me Blues," Rainey is dressed like a man, surrounded by small and feminine women. The song describes her desire for sex with other women:

> Went out last night with a crowd of my friends
> They must have been women, 'cause I don't like no men
> It's true I wear a collar and a tie
> Makes a wind blow all the while
> 'Cause they say I do it, ain't nobody caught me
> They sure got to prove it on me.

Here Rainey cuts men entirely out of the loop. Not only is her sexuality her own, but she does not need men at all. Her characters are not always this strong. In "Victim of the Blues" (1928), she is heartbroken. In "Traveling Blues" (1928), her man leaves her, and she threatens to kill him. In "Sweet Rough Man," she loves (both sexually and emotionally) a man who bashes her bloody. But there is always another figure here too: Ma Rainey the singing superstar, Ma Rainey with her beautiful clothes, Ma Rainey with her powerful voice.[19]

The blues, like minstrelsy, highlight the knowingness of the performance—theatricality, illusion. Ma Rainey was a blacked-up white man or a black man performing in drag, an auntie or a whore of the minstrel stage. Ma Rainey was a poor black girl from Georgia. Ma Rainey was a respectable middle-class matron. Ma Rainey was a lesbian or a dominatrix or a masochist or a nymphomaniac, a powerful woman and a slave to love. Ma Rainey was a rich white woman. All of these images were performances. Some had roots in reality and some did not—no matter. Early blues fans, like black fans of minstrelsy and even some white fans, knew they were consuming artifice and illusion. They did not care about the real Ma Rainey. Being able to be many Ma Raineys—expressing many different individual selves—that was power. Self-expression did not mean confession. Asserting the "I" against the world did not mean exposing the inner life, some essential private self. It meant art, art in the older meaning of the term: art as skillfully making something, art as making love or fighting, art as making music. And it was significant that women, far from standing in as only the resources, both material and cultural, out of which men made their own transformations, could make this art too.[20]

Blues women performed their success, that they could change characters, that they could conjure with their sound and their words the whole journey from rags and cotton, hunger and humidity, to worldly success and freedom from the constraints of conventionality. That they had actually made the journey themselves was less important, although many of them had. Their music was not about their authenticity, about their hard origins in the South, or what scholars have called the folk expression of "the Negro" or the voice of Africa. It was about their performance of the whole exhausting journey, the turning of painful, lived history into a story of a transformation, the way they wore all the contradictions, the sexism and the sexual freedom and their own desire here standing in for all the power relations in the world. For the length of a song, the blues could chase the blues away. There was, of course, a whole category of blues songs about that too, like Bessie Smith's "Jail House Blues."[21]

The culture of segregation, named Jim Crow after the minstrel character, turned many interactions between white and black people into minstrel acts. Jim Crow was all about performance: blacks' public embodiment of their inferiority through visible rituals of deference and visible use of inferior spaces.

If whites could not ensure that every African American *was* actually inferior to every white, they could make African Americans perform inferiority everywhere. The blues played with blackness to create a different kind of Jim Crow subjectivity, a way of talking about feelings and desire in order to assert an individual self in a violent and segregated world.[22]

In the 1940s, Langston Hughes described a performance of the blues singer and guitar player Memphis Minnie. Sitting "on top of the ice box at the 230 Club in Chicago," Minnie "beats out blues on an electric guitar." Minnie, in Hughes's description, is all contradiction. She looks "like a colored lady teacher in a neat Southern school about to say 'Children, the lesson is on page 14 today, paragraph 2.'" She is tiny and thin and neat up on her chair up on the cooler. But

> her gold teeth flash . . . Her ear-rings tremble. Her left hand with
> dark red nails moves up and down the strings of the guitar's neck.
> Her right hand with the dice ring on it picks out the tune, throbs out
> the rhythm, beats out the blues.
>
> Then, through the smoke and the racket of the noisy Chicago
> bar float Louisiana bayous, muddy old swamps, Mississippi dust
> and sun, cotton fields, lonesome roads, train whistles in the night,
> mosquitoes at dawn, and the Rural Free Delivery that never brings
> the right letter . . . Big rough old Delta cities . . . border cities,
> Northern cities, Relief, W.P.A., Muscle Shoals, the jooks. "Has
> Anybody Seen My Pigmeat On The Line," "See-See Rider,"
> St. Louis, Antoine Street, Willow Run, folks on the move who
> leave and don't care.

Minnie plays "chords that come through the amplifiers like Negro heartbeats mixed with iron and steel." Transformation, momentary, fleeting, not transcendence, is on offer here. Transcendence would mean lifting the limits of human existence. Transcendence would mean otherworldliness. No, these fans know well the folly of this kind of thinking. These fans know the hard times never go away, but a change comes, change is coming, change can come.[23]

Rock and roll inherited magic and contradiction as well as sound and rhythm from minstrelsy and the blues. When white kids in the 1950s fell in love with black rebellion through rock and roll, they gave new life to old minstrel definitions of blackness as freedom from social constraints. They also drew on the blues idea that self-expression lies at the heart of both individualism and social connection.

Elvis's Hips

Like minstrelsy over a century earlier, rock and roll music set off a storm that eventually blew through most of American culture. It too worked as music and dance, and its full effects emerged most clearly when fans could see and hear the person making the music. It too raised troubling questions about the meanings of manhood and womanhood, love and sexual desire, and class relations as well as the relationship of black and white. And it too represented a profound white investment in what whites understood as black culture.[24]

Listening to rock and roll, white teenagers embraced what they thought of as black music. And, as had many white minstrel fans a century earlier, many of them missed the theatricality of the performance. They heard and understood the new music not as the assertion of an individual self against an oppressive world, but as the assertion of *the* individual self, some innate and authentic blackness. They did not hear black transformation. They heard black transcendence. Blackness, understood as synonymous with authenticity, again became a medium in which whites could express their own felt sense of difference and with which they could enact their own transformations. White artists used gestures, sounds, moves, and themes that commercially successful minstrel and blues acts coded as black to express their own feelings of alienation, betrayal, desire, and love. White rock and roll fans, in turn, like minstrelsy fans and white blues fans, kept the possibilities for release found in knowing the act was an act for their own psychic liberation.[25]

In the story of rock and roll's origins, Elvis Presley played the role of T. D. Rice. Between 1954 and 1956, Presley's rapid rise to stardom coincided with the growing popularity of the new music. Like the story of how Rice created minstrelsy, the story of the origins of Presley's musical career has become as much legend as history. Scholars disagree about many of the details. Despite layers of mythmaking, the story reveals a great deal about what early white fans heard in Presley's music and why the working-class teenager from Memphis became the first rock and roll star.[26]

According to the legend, in the early 1950s, Sam Phillips, the owner of a storefront Memphis recording studio and record company, was searching for a white man who could play the blues. White kids liked the music by the black musicians that Phillips recorded and distributed. But "the southern ones," he told an interviewer in 1959, "weren't sure whether they ought to like it or not. So I got to thinking how many records you could sell if you could find white performers who could play and sing in this same exciting way [as black performers]." Phillips, of course, had the benefit of hindsight in recounting this story, since Presley had become a huge star by then. Whatever Phillips's motivation, in July 1954, after spending hours working with Elvis and musicians Scotty Moore and Bill Black on the trio's first recording sessions, Sun Studio's owner did not feel certain at all. Then Presley spontaneously broke into a blues song. Arthur "Big Boy" Crudup had made "That's All Right (Mama)" a hit a few years earlier. The lyrics worked the same expressive territory used by a thousand blues songs before:

> Well, that's all right mama
> That's all right for you.
> That's all right mama
> Just anyway you do,
> That's all right.
> That's all right.
> That's all right now mama,
> Anyway you do.

The rest of the band jumped in, sloppy and loose. Phillips hit RECORD.[27]

The record label owner then asked his friend, the popular WHBQ deejay Dewey Phillips, known locally as "a man who just happened to be white," to feature this version of "That's All Right" on his own primetime radio slot. In the early fifties, a handful of white deejays, like Phillips in Memphis and Alan Freed first in Cleveland and later New York not only played rhythm and blues; they also began to talk and act "black" by adopting black urban slang and style, becoming what would eventually be called "white Negroes." Phillips's show, both in its playlist and its audience, exemplified the new airwaves integration, and it kept its black listeners even as it began to draw a young white audience. When Dewey played the new Sun Records song on the evening of July 8, dozens of people called the radio station. No one could quite place the singer. Dewey cued up the cut over and over and finally fetched the musician out of a movie theater and put him on the air. Pointedly, he asked him where he went to high school. His answer told the listening audience—Memphis had segregated schools—that Elvis Presley was white.[28]

The young Elvis Presley played with blackness like a blacked-up black minstrel or a blues musician. Somehow, Sam Phillips believed, Presley's own sense of inferiority at growing up poor and without future prospects fused with a raging ambition and arrogance to produce a tone, a set of gestures, even a way of inhabiting his body that mirrored the style of great black bluesmen. Yet Presley's borrowing was more conscious than Phillips thought. Presley remembered cruising Beale Street, the African American commercial district of Memphis, even before he recorded for Sun, people watching and window-shopping. As soon as he got some money, he went back to Lansky's, a mens-wear store on Beale, to buy clothes. Elvis got his style—the suits (bright colors, darker shirts against lighter jackets, pegged legs, and piping), the flashy shirts, and the two-tone shoes—from black men in Memphis. Presley also listened to rhythm and blues and gospel records, and he heard the music Memphis blacks enjoyed on radio programs aimed at black listeners. Growing up poor, he had every reason, like many African Americans, to embrace the magic of transfor-mation. He created a persona—a white minstrel performer without the face paint—that acted out the most American transformation of all, a poor boy becoming a rich man who mattered in the world.[29]

Presley, on those first Sun recordings, certainly did not sound exactly like Muddy Waters or Little Richard or even Crudup. Like blacked-up white men a century before, he did not try to produce exact covers of recordings black mu-sicians were making at the time. That was not the point. Like Rice and other white minstrel stars, Elvis played with sounds and, as importantly, dress, ges-tures, and dance moves that white audiences labeled as black.[30]

Presley also used facial expressions, movements, and makeup (he often wore mascara and eye shadow onstage) in ways that white audiences labeled as female, and he sometimes danced like a burlesque star. This willing embrace of femininity, a kind of voluntary emasculation, often circled back around to blackness in a broader southern and also national popular culture that emas-culated black men. In the same way, identifying with black men circled back around to femininity. Only a man already lacking in power and position, this kind of interpretation suggested, would embrace his own marginalization. On the other hand, Presley's femininity made his overt expressions of sexual desire less threatening to the young, screaming white girls who filled his shows. Female audience members could both love him and identify with him. He seemed to understand and like them. He seemed to get what it was like to be vulnerable, to swoon with desire, to want to let go but to have to hold back.[31]

Observers' descriptions of his performances at the time reveal how Pres-ley seduced and shocked audiences with his self-conscious playing with the categories. Biff Collie, a deejay on KNUZ in Houston, searched for the words to capture Presley's appeal. He sounded like "a Mississippi gospel singer singing black music," Collie remembered. "That's about as real as I could fig-ure." A Louisiana record executive also scrambled to define how Presley was different. He "sings hillbilly in r & b time. Can you figure that out. He wears pink pants and a black coat." A journalist described a Presley show in 1955 in

Kilgore, Texas: "He had this sneer on his face and he stood behind the mike for five minutes, I'll bet, before he made a move. Then he hit his guitar a lick, and he broke two strings." Descriptions of Presley's concerts in 1955 and 1956 often mentioned his dramatic facial expressions, loud moans and hiccups, and wild guitar playing. Experienced musicians believed he broke his strings on purpose. Others suggested he toyed with his audiences. A record company promotion manager described Presley's performance in Richmond, Virginia, around the same time: "The body language—I don't remember exactly what he sang, but there were frequent belches into the mike, and the clincher came when he took his chewing gum and tossed it into the audience." Burping, sneering, and throwing his gum—all of these acts emphasized Presley's body and set off the screaming of his young female fans.[32]

In photographs from this period, Presley's hair, clothes, and even the way he stands clearly separate him from other hillbilly musicians who share his working-class white southern background. In an October 16, 1954, photograph of Presley performing with his band on the *Louisiana Hayride*, Presley looks like an R and B musician out for a stroll down Beale Street. He wears a black shirt with a light suit and bow tie and black-and-white two-tone shoes. His bandmates Moore and Black, in Western snap shirts with contrasting yokes and dark pants, look like they are going to a hoedown. Three months later, at another *Louisiana Hayride* performance, Moore and Black have changed their style. A color photo shows them wearing black shirts and matching patterned vests in the same shade of pink as Presley's suit. On this evening, the entire band stood out in sharp contrast to the other acts on the show, which dressed and danced in a recognizably hillbilly style.[33]

On August 5, 1955, Presley played the eighth annual Jamboree at Memphis's Overton Park Shell. Webb Pierce, a honky-tonk singer and country music hit machine, was the headliner. Presley drew second billing, on a long list of hillbilly acts. Presley knew some of these musicians, and he knew this audience. Two photographs taken backstage reveal an artist visually separating himself from his fellow performers. Even in a posed, still shot, he manages to convey that he is not going to use his body like just any country crooner. He stands alone, with his legs apart, his feet pointing slightly sideways, his knees bent, and his pelvis thrust forward. His guitar hangs from a strap and rests on his left hip. His hands hang by his sides. He smiles, staring openly at the photographer, and he is almost laughing. He wears a dinner jacket with wide lapels, a light shirt with a light brocade pattern, a dark tie, pegged pants, and white bucks. The clothes accentuate his stance, although the black-and-white image does not reveal whether he is wearing his by then trademark pink. Perhaps he has toned down the colors for the hometown crowd, just as he has left off the mascara. He appears confident, ready even to conquer the world.[34]

In another image taken backstage the same night, Presley seems to have become a different person. The clothes and guitar are identical. The same concrete wall and floor fill the photograph's background. But the Presley posing here with Texas Bill Strength, a deejay, labor organizer, and musician, looks ten years younger. He appears nervous and awkward. His mouth seems stopped halfway between an "oh" of astonishment and the smile the photographer requires. Close beside him, Strength stands with his right arm around Presley and his hand on his hip. He seems at ease—he smiles broadly and stands loosely with his feet together and his knees slightly bent. Strength wears a cowboy hat, a Western snap shirt with contrasting yoke and piping on the pockets and placket, and matching pants with piping. A bandanna circles his neck. The contrast between Strength's and Presley's images in this photograph makes clear the kind of choices the young musician was making. Strength looks like a successful hillbilly performer with his hat, neck scarf, and easy confidence. Presley does not. In this particular photograph, he seems—for at least the time it takes to snap the shot—to be unsure about his decisions and his relationship to this hillbilly musician.[35]

The other white acts with which he shared the stage through the first three years of his career made it clear that Presley did not look or move or even stand like a country star. He was different. He was, he hoped and dreamed as his career grew and his second manager schemed, bigger than hillbilly music. As if to make this clear, at the end of 1955, Presley's new record label, RCA, placed a full-page ad in *Billboard* magazine. In the photograph that makes up much of the ad, Presley wears a light suit and a dark dress shirt without a tie. He holds his guitar up high, and his right arm is poised for a downward strum. He stands with his legs apart. His head tilts backward slightly, his mouth is open, and his eyes are closed. If there is a barn dance or a horse around, he does not notice. Presley looks like a man who is having sex. In the mid-century pop music universe, country music was white. Presley's audiences would have seen the difference, the blackness, in this particular historical context, of his act.[36]

The persona Presley created singing and dancing onstage around this time and the persona he crafted in interviews produced the same sort of startling contrast as a pink dinner jacket next to a cowboy costume. Talking to journalists, deejays, and fans, Presley could not have been more polite. He might have grown up poor. He might speak with a rural southern accent. But he made a great effort to demonstrate that he was respectable in the terms valued by white southerners and available even to a young man from a working-class family. He used formal manners. He acted out thankfulness, humility, generosity, and graciousness. Some fans, journalists, and even famous variety show hosts took this character as the "real" Presley. The musician, however, working in a manner indebted to minstrel and blues performers, was playing different characters. The polite, "white" Elvis made the singing and dancing character seem more wild, and for many white fans more black. The polite Elvis rarely broke character, daring respectable audiences to call his bluff. The wild performing Elvis cracked constantly, laughing at his own popping eyes and flirting tongue, grinning at his own growls and moans. The contrast between the two characters revealed that the act was an act.[37]

Viewers could see both of these Presleys at work in the star's many 1956 television performances. On January 28, he made his first appearance in this new medium, on Jimmy and Tommy Dorsey's *Stage Show*. Presley wore the kind of clothes he had been experimenting with on tour, a loud tweed jacket, a dark shirt with a light tie, and lots of mascara. And he played two songs written and performed by African American musicians, Big Joe Turner's "Shake, Rattle, and Roll" and Ray Charles's "I Got a Woman." In "Shake, Rattle, and Roll," in particular, when Presley drops back toward the band in the breaks, the camera tracks a full body shot. Presley leans back a little with his knees bent, seeming to get more force into his strumming, and his legs and hips jump forward in time to the rhythm as he takes a break from singing. Though he will appear much more relaxed in his later television appearances, here in his very first song he does the dance his critics will label obscene. Many white viewers would see the clothes, the song choices, and the dancing style as black.[38]

Four months later, in his June performance on *The Milton Berle Show*— his sixth television appearance—Presley made the sexuality of his act even more explicit. He wears dark dress pants, a two-tone light and dark shirt, no tie, and a light jacket, an urban, swanky costume full of the contrast that shows up so well on black-and-white screens. With his longish hair gelled and pushed into a high pompadour and makeup highlighting his eyes, he conveys an almost feminine vulnerability. He does not wear women's clothing any more than he wears minstrel paint, but there is a bit of drag in his look and his moves. "Hound Dog" describes a love affair gone wrong from a woman's point of view—it was a hit for Big Mama Thornton, a very large and talented, deep-voiced African American blues singer, before Presley recorded it. Like minstrel performers before him, he crosses racial and gender lines to play a black woman. Presley, however, sings the lyrics in a higher voice than Thornton's and

Elvis Presley, wearing a velvet shirt, plays with his puppy, Sweet Pea, in October 1956. *Associated Press*.

with less aggression, even as he impersonates her, adding a layer of gender ambiguity to the racial play at the center of his act. Thornton, not Presley, is the stronger woman in the personas they create through the song.[39]

In this performance, Presley does not strum his guitar as he sings, and, free from the way the instrument partially blocks and confines him, he performs a stunning dance. Though the camera cuts several times to images of screaming teenage girls, the soundtrack reveals that many in the studio audience do not seem to know how to react, and they shift between screaming and expressing outrage, shock, and sheer astonishment. In no other surviving footage from this period are Presley's moves this sexually explicit. In the song's first break, Presley spreads his legs wide and shifts his butt from side to side, shaking his whole body. Without the guitar in front of him when he sings, he seems to straddle the mike, which stands in all its phallic glory bolt upright between his legs. He slides into a kind of squat with his knees bent over his feet and his butt thrust out behind him, before he quickly shifts his weight to push his pelvis forward. The dancing continues until Presley sings and then stops, seemingly ending the song. After a weighted pause, he and the band start in again at half tempo, and he slows and exaggerates every gesture and move to fill the space between the beats. At this speed, his thrusting movements become a kind of back-and-forth and side-to-side grinding, and his trademark leg shakes become slow jerks. When he tucks in his butt and shifts his pelvis forward and backward while holding the mike, the movement he is mimicking becomes impossible to miss. His vocal tics—moans and almost-hiccups and held-out "ahhhhhhs"—add to the effect, echoing the sounds of lovemaking. The overt sexuality of his dance moves references the long history of burlesque and the drag eroticism of minstrelsy. Is he playing the man, the more traditionally aggressive actor in sexual exchange, or the woman? Is he playing black or white? One thing is certain. He is not playing the role of the respectable middle-class teenager, even though Milton Berle came out as the song ended and asked the audience to give a round of applause to "our boy."[40]

The banter after the song is almost as revealing as the performance. Berle starts by comically mimicking Presley's dance moves, which releases the tension. He then asks Presley for dating tips and makes some comments about his own desire, all coded in double entendre as patter about cars. Presley tells Berle that he does not like all the screaming young women who rip his clothes off. He wants a quiet girl. He "digs" Debra Paget, he says, breaking into black slang. "She's real gone." Berle retorts with a quip that suggests Paget is out of his league in class terms. Then Paget actually comes out onstage, Berle introduces them, and, screaming, she rushes Elvis, grabs at his clothes, and tries to kiss him. He may not be a "class" act, the scene suggests, but all the women love him.[41]

This performance of Presley's set off a storm of criticism. Ed Sullivan, host of the most popular television variety program of the period, refused for months to book the increasingly controversial musician. He later relented, but when Presley finally appeared on *The Ed Sullivan Show*, on September 9, 1956, the camera often tracked the singer from the bottom of the guitar up, and only the studio audience could always see what he was doing with his by then famous hips. Still, the surviving footage reveals that Elvis managed to do quite a lot with his lips, and anyone watching him on television who had seen him dance before could certainly guess from his facial expressions what he was doing with his hips. Over the course of the show, he performs twice and participates in the required banter, and he shifts easily between polite and wild versions of the performing Elvis.[42]

Guest host Charles Laughton stands in front of Presley's four gold records and describes them as he introduces the star. Then Presley, who recorded his performance in Hollywood while the rest of the show was taped in New York, appears wearing a high pompadour, eye makeup, and a loud checked sports coat with a diamond-patterned dress shirt open at the neck. The screaming starts. Playing his wild Elvis persona, he looks around, looks down and laughs as if he is trying to do something he cannot quite pull off, and then looks around again and makes a sound halfway between a snort and a growl. The audience laughs and squeals, and he moves his head from side to side and makes a chewing motion with his mouth. Then he looks at the camera and addresses viewers as polite Elvis: "Thank you, Mr. Laughton. Ladies and gentlemen. Wow," and he rakes his hand over his brow. "This is probably the greatest honor I've ever had in my life," he continues. "There's not much I can say except it really makes you feel good. We want to thank you from the bottom of our heart." He looks down, seemingly choked up for a second, taken in by the enormity of the moment. When he introduces the song "Don't Be Cruel," he shifts back into wild Elvis, smiles as if he is laughing at the whole setup, and starts to sing.[43]

Presley's performance is fairly subdued by his standards. At the end of the very first phrase, "You know I can be found," he makes the facial gesture—a kind of scowling pout—that sets off the screaming fans, then smiles at his own prank and keeps singing. The soundtrack includes the four Jordanaires, singing backup, but the camera does not show them until the middle of the song, and their disembodied, harmonizing voices haunt the first half of the performance. Presley shakes his head around and bounces to the rhythm, suggesting his legs and hips are shaking outside the camera's frame. He plays with his studio audience, seemingly setting his face to make one of his pouting moans but then not actually offering up what he has made them anticipate. Then he laughs. Finally he gives them what they want—pouting, full lips, an intense, eye-popping scowl, and a sound that starts off as a kind of higher-pitched moo and morphs into a lower-pitched, close-mouthed moan that suggests a kind of eroticized, adult version of "yum, yum." Before and during this move, his eyes, his mouth, and his sound do the work of his hips. After this move, a standard part of Presley's performance of "Don't Be Cruel," the audience squeals, and Presley smiles as if he is laughing at his own acting and at the response it never fails to produce. Then the camera angle shifts, and viewers can finally see the four white backup singers.[44]

Presley peppers the rest his performance of "Don't Be Cruel" with eye tics and pops and smiles, all gestures with a deep blackface history. When he finishes the chorus again—"I don't want no other love,/ Babe it's just you I'm thinking of"—the audience screams in anticipation of his eye-popping moan, but he does not give it to them. They scream more, and he laughs. The tension is left to build until the end of the song, when even more screaming and clapping provide the needed release. Presley smiles and waves his arm at the Jordanaires, including them in the circle of the applause. He says, "Thank you very much," and more screaming follows. Then he adds, "Thank you ladies," and laughs, and the audience laughs too and screams some more.[45]

Presley's performance of "Don't Be Cruel" on the Sullivan show built on his many previous television appearances that year. Whatever Presley actually did with his body and however the camera framed him, the audience expected him to act "black," to move and groan with abandon, to use his hips and his lips. The tension and screaming built when he gave them these acts and even when he did not. The camera could tame him, and when he performed a second set on the show, leading off with Little Richard's "Ready Teddy," it pulled back to show Presley's famous moves. His legs shook, his hips gyrated, his eyes popped. His dance was yet another version of the long and deeply layered history of minstrelsy, another twist of the unending spiral of whites copying blacks copying whites copying blacks.[46]

As in earlier blackface performances, Presley's identification with African Americans functioned as medium of connection as well as co-optation. Wild Elvis exploited the connection. Polite Elvis buried the transgressions of segregation in formal manners, blatantly daring anyone to be so crude as to mention anything unpleasant. Elvis the musician rode the rise of rock and roll to superstardom. As Ray Charles said:

> When you get a guy who comes up and say, like Elvis Presley, let's face it, man, you had more people goin' out and shakin' their asses and stuff like that. You know where Elvis *got* that from—he used to be down on *Beale* Street in *Memphis*. That's where he say *black*

people doin' that. Ain't no way they'd let anybody like us get on TV and do that, but *he* could 'cause he's white.

Acting black helped free his fans' emotions. Acting black felt good. Acting black worked as a very powerful form of rebellion. Acting black made Presley a superstar.[47]

Once in a while, all the layers of acting came crashing in on the young performer. Right before his fourth Dorsey show appearance, Presley and the country music duo Charlie and Ira Louvin passed the time in the dressing room playing the piano and singing hymns. Presley, as Charlie later remembered, said, "Boy, this is my favorite music." Ira lost his temper and started yelling: "Why you white nigger, if that's your favorite music, why don't you do that out yonder? Why do you do that nigger trash out there?" Presley replied, "When I'm out there, I do what they want to hear—when I'm back here, I can do what I want to do." Ira responded, in Charlie's recollection, by trying to strangle Presley. But there was no holding back the tide that Presley was riding as much as making. In the mid-1950s, rock and roll was busy creating a whole lot of white Negroes.[48]

Two Elvis Presley fans, sisters Oralee and Sharyn Davolt, covered every inch of wall space in their bedroom with pictures of the star. *Associated Press.*

Mailer and Kerouac Blow

While "white nigger" was clearly an insult, the term "white Negro," made famous by Norman Mailer, presented identification with blackness in a more positive light. Too old for Presley and rock and roll, Mailer was by taste more of a jazz fan. Yet when he mixed together romanticism, existentialism, and what he imagined about African American musicians he knew in New York City, he came as close as anyone to describing in serious terms what rebel music—both the new rock and roll and then contemporary jazz forms like bebop—did for white fans at mid-century. In his now canonical 1957 essay "The White Negro," Mailer labeled this new darky act, yet another dance in the more than century-long history of white men imitating and identifying with blackness. Blackface performance without the face paint seemed to be popping out everywhere in the 1950s, from Beat poetry readings and urban jazz clubs to radio and television programs like deejay Alan Freed's *The Moondog Rock and Roll House Party* and *The Ed Sullivan Show*. A 1953 tongue-in-cheek editorial in *Ebony* laughed at all the white Negroes: "Whites have out-eaten the Negro right down to Saturday's neck bones and Sunday's red beans and rice. They have aped his style of music so well it is sometimes impossible to tell when the blues are black or white."[49]

Mailer, however, seriously describes African Americans as if the characters created by minstrelsy and blues songs have come to life. The devil-may-care tales of sex and violence and life lived in the present become, in Mailer's analysis, not self-conscious play but essential pieces of a black worldview that might just help whites adapt to a post-Holocaust, post-Hiroshima world. "Incompatibles have come to bed, the inner life and the violent life, the orgy and the dream of love, the desire to murder and the desire to create," Mailer argues, but

> what a man feels is the impulse for his creative effort and if an alien
> but nonetheless passionate instinct about the meaning of life has
> come so unexpectedly from a virtually illiterate people, come out of
> the most intense conditions of exploitation, cruelty, violence,
> frustration, and lust, and yet has succeeded as an instinct in keeping
> this tortured people alive, then it is perhaps possible that the Negro
> holds more of the tail of the truth than the radical.

As outsiders in society, Mailer reasoned, as people who had always lived with violence and hopelessness, African Americans offered alternative visions of the meaning of life. "So no wonder that in certain cities of America, in New

York, of course, and New Orleans, in Chicago and San Francisco and Los Angeles . . . this particular part of a generation was attracted to what the Negro had to offer . . . In this wedding of black and white it was the Negro who brought the cultural dowry." In a letter he wrote a friend, he admitted that the white Negro, the "hipster," was "immature, irrational, unimportant, lumpen, etc." Still, this hipster life or "barbarism" was "preferable to totalitarianism for the radical, or at the very least, poses a real alternative."[50]

What exactly was this black cultural dowry? In Mailer's argument, blacks brought unfettered sexuality. They also brought their rebel music, jazz, "the music of orgasm, good orgasm or bad." Music then also circled back around to sex. African Americans lacked repression, which he identified as white. Practiced in the art of survival, they lived with hopelessness by focusing on the present, on the joys and pleasures that could be snatched from the music and the body. They felt and expressed intense emotions, especially sexual desire, rather than deferring gratification to plan for a future that might not come. And they understood how violence could be a kind of agency, a natural "high," one possible way in which an outsider could experience a heady sense of power. Mailer's ideas about African American life would not, with appropriate costumes and jokes added, have been out of place on the minstrel stage. Brilliant insight and deep offensiveness go hand in hand here and arise from the same source, a by then well-worn minstrel model in which a white artist used what he imagined as blackness for his own psychic purposes. Again, the trick worked by projecting contradictory desires onto African Americans and then taking them back up, rinsed of all limits, through a fantastical identification with blackness and especially fantasies of black male sexual power.[51]

In "The White Negro," Mailer actually called the polite Presley's bluff by writing explicitly about what drew many white fans to the wild Presley and to rock and roll and bebop more broadly, as well as to other forms of identification with African Americans. He described unrestrained sexuality and even violence as essential characteristics of "black" life worthy of white emulation. And he boasted that he was only saying what other people thought but would not say. Jack Kerouac's *On the Road*, on the other hand, seduced and shocked its white readers, pulling many of them into its racial romanticism.

At the end of the fifties, two runaway white boys drove across the country in love with the very motion of their journey, each other, and themselves. "What's your road, man?" Dean Moriarty asks his friend Sal Paradise. "Holyboy road, madman road, rainbow road, guppy road, any road. It's an anywhere road for anybody anyhow." Drafted in 1951 on the now infamous roll of

'Advertisements For Myself' book cover by Judy Scheftel, 1959

Norman Mailer used this photograph for publicity for his 1959 collection of essays, stories, and autobiographical writings, *Advertisements for Myself. Associated Press.*

taped-together paper, Jack Kerouac's experimental novel, rejected, edited, revised, and finally published in 1957, somehow became a best seller. Sal and Dean, stand-ins for Kerouac and his friend Neal Cassady, zoom back and forth across the country just for the thrill of the ride. "Be in love with your life every detail of it," Kerouac wrote a friend, and his characters attempted to follow this advice. *On the Road* tells the story of what might have happened to Holden Caulfield if he had grown up poorer and smoked some pot.[52]

Sal's travels begin, like Caulfield's, in a period of emotional distress. "I first met Dean not long after my wife and I split up and I had just gotten over a serious illness that I won't bother to talk about, except that it had something to do with the miserable split-up and my feeling that everything was dead." Dean, who grew up poor and hustling, shows the more middle-class Sal—he had gone to college for a while—that if he cannot feel anything else he can feel motion. As the trip begins, Sal has just met Dean. Yes, Sal admits, he wants to know Dean because he is a "writer and needed new experiences," and was bored "hanging around the campus." He knows Dean is conning him "for room and board and 'how-to-write.'" But Dean reminds him of some "long-lost brother," and "somewhere along the line I knew there'd be girls, visions, everything." "We gotta go," Dean says, "because, man, the road must eventually lead to the whole world. Ain't nowhere else it can go—right?" So Sal "shambles" down the street after Dean and Carlo Marx, the character Kerouac based on his friend Allen Ginsberg, "because the only people for me are the mad ones, the ones who are mad to live, mad to talk, mad to be saved, desirous of everything at the same time, the ones who never yawn or say a commonplace thing, but burn, burn, burn."[53]

With its rapidly multiplying meanings, the word "mad" in *On the Road*, like the word "phony" in *Catcher in the Rye*, becomes a mantra that ties together the hero's wanderings. *On the Road* overflows with mad people, mad visions, mad days, mad schemes, and mad rides. Sal feels overwhelmed by "the whole mad swirl of everything." He stands in awe of "mad drunken Americans in the mighty land." He hears Marx read his "apocalyptic, mad poetry." The "little shoulders" of a Latina woman drive Sal mad. He sees a cop become "red-faced mad." And he sets up the context of his story—1947—when "bop was going like mad all over America." Mad is emotion, a state of mind, the sign of wildness, and a mental health condition. Madness is good, bad, or pushing the edge, intense and rebellious, a symptom of existential despair, speeding confusion, or ecstatic and mystical joy. Above all, madness stands in opposition to parental and social expectations, the establishment of a career, a suburban home, and a family—adult responsibilities. Mad stands in opposition to what *Catcher* labels phoniness.[54]

Like Kerouac and Cassady before them, Sal and Dean tour the margins of mid-century white middle-class life, urban bars and rural diners, the places where African Americans, Latinos, and poor whites live, and bohemian enclaves. When they are not driving, they drink wine, smoke marijuana, listen to jazz, and try to pick up "colored" women, pleasures Dean calls "old-fashioned spade kicks." They do a great deal of what writer and critic Toni Morrison calls "playing in the dark," projecting onto African Americans their fantasies of liberation. Kerouac's letters to Cassady often display this kind of racial romanticism: "Here I am sitting in a shack, writing on a board table, as it rains, and as the radio plays colored music in this land where the colored are pushed back & scorned & 'kept in their place.' And Neal, there's a woman called Mahalia Jackson who sings real sad . . . You see how it makes me feel, don't you?" In Kerouac's travels and his fictional accounts of them, people, places, and music he imagines as black enable would-be white rebels to access their deepest emotions.[55]

In *On the Road*, Sal and Dean visit a San Francisco jazz club patronized mostly by whites, "great eager crowds of young semi-intellectuals," where they hear Slim Guillard, "a tall, thin Negro with big sad eyes," play guitar, piano, and bongo drums: "He does and says anything that comes into his head. He'll sing 'Cement Mixer, Put-ti Put-ti' and suddenly slow down the beat and brood over his bongos with fingertips barely tapping the skin." Then slowly, into the mike, Slim sings, "Great-orooni . . . fine-ovauti . . . hello-orooni . . . bourbon-orooni . . . al-orooni . . ." Later, the musician "sits down at the piano and hits two notes, two C's . . . and suddenly the big burly bass-player wakes up from a reverie and realizes Slim is playing 'C-Jam Blues.' And he slugs in his big forefinger on the string and the big booming beat begins and everybody starts rocking and Slim looks just as sad as ever, and they blow jazz for half an hour." Sal, Dean, and the white bohemians love it, and Slim, in Kerouac's words, can't stop. He "goes mad and grabs the bongos and plays tremendous rapid Cubana beats and yells crazy things in Spanish, in Arabic, in Peruvian dialect, in Egyptian, in every language he knows." Dean, Kerouac writes, "thought Slim was God."[56]

Later, Sal takes the bus to Denver, trying to conjure the wild joy and companionship he had found there with Dean and other friends two years before, looking for the answers Dean had been looking for in Slim. Wandering with envy through the city, he feels instead an overwhelming sense of alienation and yet also understands at last a potential cure:

> At lilac evening I walked with every muscle aching among the lights
> of 27th and Welton in the Denver colored section, wishing I were a
> Negro, feeling that the best the white world had offered was not
> enough ecstasy for me, not enough life, joy, kicks, darkness, music,
> not enough night. I stopped at a little shack where a man sold hot
> red chili in paper containers; I bought some and ate it, strolling in

the dark mysterious streets. I wished I were a Denver Mexican, or even a poor overworked Jap, anything but what I was so drearily, a "white man" disillusioned.

Alone, a rebel without his friends and too "white" to make a life with his Mexican lover, Terry, he is only his own narrow self, "sad, strolling in this violet dark, this unbearably sweet night, wishing I could exchange worlds with the happy, true-hearted, ecstatic Negroes of America." Kerouac's *On the Road* gave middle-class readers what Presley's performance refused to provide and what Mailer's argument offered only implicitly, the mind and soul of a white Negro.[57]

Kerouac had been writing since he dropped out of Columbia, got thrown out of the navy, and met the circle of friends that included Ginsberg, the writer William S. Burroughs, and Cassady. In an October 1948 letter to Cassady, Kerouac wrote: "Did you realize that a new literary age is beginning in America? Sinclair Lewis *et al* sum up people by their social and cultural 'positions.' This is American Lit. in general . . . especially Lewis & magazines, and leftist writing, all. But . . . we young Americans are turning to a new evaluation of the individual: his *'position' itself*, personal and psychic." Kerouac wanted to put the "broad, rugged" country in a novel, "an American-scene picaresque, 'On the Road,' dealing simply with hitch-hiking and the sorrows, hardships, adventures, sweats and labors of that (two boys going to California) . . . arriving in California where there is nothing . . . and returning again."[58]

After publishing his first novel, *The Town and the City*, in 1950, Kerouac worked to create a new style, a prose free enough to embody the emotional intensity of his experiences. "I yearn to be non-literary," he wrote in a letter to Cassady. "I have nothing to offer but the words that spring from my heart and mind in this enormous story" of two friends "rip[ping] the guts out of reality." Later, he would codify his new form in a piece, "Essentials of Spontaneous Prose," that he wrote for his friends Ginsberg and Burroughs. His work, he argued, grew out of "jazz and bop, in the sense of a, say, tenor man drawing a breath, and blowing a phrase on his saxophone, till he runs out of breath, and when he does, his sentence, his statement's been made . . . That's how I therefore separate my sentences, as breath separations of the mind," he confessed. Black music, particularly the jazz form bebop, opened up his creativity; "then there's the raciness and freedom and humor of jazz instead of all that dreary analysis." "The best writing is always the most painful personal wrung-out tossed from cradle warm protective mind—tap yourself the song of yourself, *blow!—now!*" he urged. "*Your* way is your only way—'good'—or 'bad'—always honest, ('ludicrous'), spontaneous, 'confessional' interesting, because not 'crafted.'" Beginning with *On the Road*, jazz horn playing served as both a metaphor and a model for his writing style.[59]

September 1957 was a good time to publish a white Negro novel. Acting and sounding black, musicians like Presley, Bill Haley, Carl Perkins, and Jerry Lee Lewis appeared on television and played sold-out concerts. Their hit singles broke all the records, topping at times the country, pop, and R and B charts. Teenpics, often featuring a rock and roll soundtrack, drew young people away from the television and back into theaters. Marlon Brando in *The Wild One* (1953), James Dean in *Rebel Without a Cause* (1955), and even Presley in *Love Me Tender* (1956), his film debut, created a new model of the white male hero as a blackened and feminized outsider who expresses his feelings and desires. Even ambitious, literary novelists like Mailer started acting black. Blackness, for these white artists and their white fans, was release. Blackness was freedom. Blackness was sex. Identifying with African Americans, "white Negros" could have it all, individual autonomy and collective authority, originality and history, the power of being inside and the power of standing apart.

Jack Kerouac too had the advantage of appearing to be a part of a movement. Jug of wine in hand, he had attended the now infamous event "6 Poets at 6 Gallery" on October 7, 1955, that publicly launched a new group of experimental writers, including Ginsberg. The next year, Lawrence Ferlinghetti's City Lights Books published *Howl and Other Poems*, a collection of Ginsberg's poetry. Hearing that the poet Richard Eberhart was working on an article on West Coast poetry for the *New York Times*, Ginsberg wrote to him to explain the meaning of "Howl." "The title notwithstanding," Ginsberg explained, "the poem itself is an act of sympathy, not rejection . . . I am leaping *out* of a preconceived notion of social 'values,' following my own heart's instincts . . .," he continued, "overturning any notion of propriety, moral 'value,' superficial 'maturity,' . . . and exposing my true feelings—sympathy and identification with the rejected, mystical, individual even 'mad.'" Like Mailer and Kerouac, Ginsberg found these seekers in what he imagined as the blackened margins, what he calls in "Howl" "the Negro street at dawn." Eberhart's piece "West Coast Rhythms" came out in September and helped transform a loose collection of new writers into a literary movement, the Beats, a group knit together in their rebellion. Although not primarily a poet, Kerouac became a part of this movement.[60]

Censorship, however, worked much better than literary criticism in popularizing these writers. In March 1957, U.S. Customs seized the second printing of *Howl and Other Poems* on the grounds that the work was obscene. Law enforcement officials objected to Ginsberg's explicit lines about drug use and sex, his descriptions of rebels, for example, "who let themselves be fucked in the ass by saintly motorcyclists, and screamed with joy,/ who blew and were blown by those human seraphim, the sailors." That summer, San Francisco police arrested Ferlinghetti and a City Lights employee for selling the book, and the trial took place in September. "Howl" kept the Beat writers in the news for much of the year. *Life*, for example, published a photo-filled article about the trial and the new "James Dean school of poetry."[61]

Kerouac's publisher, Viking, shrewdly marketed *On the Road* to capitalize on this publicity. "After World War I a certain group of restless searching Americans came to be called 'The Lost Generation,'" the original book jacket copy announces. "For a good many of the same reasons after World War II another group, roaming America in a wild, desperate search for identity and *purpose*, became known as 'The Beat Generation.' Jack Kerouac is the voice of this group, and this is his novel." In an interview published that October in *Saturday Review*, Kerouac said, "I guess I was the one who named us the 'Beat Generation.'" The group included not just writers, he claimed, slipping into urban black slang, but "everyone from fifteen to fifty-five who digs *everything*, man. We're not Bohemians, remember. Beat means beatitude, not beat up. You *feel* this. You feel it in a beat." Playing the role of spokesman for a generation, Kerouac tried to distinguish his peers' rebellion from the alienation of an earlier generation of writers and their friends. "The Beat Generation loves everything, man," he insisted. "We go around digging everything. Everything's a symbol. We're mystics." Kerouac emphasized the Beats' romanticism, spiritualism, and debt to African American language and music.[62]

Many early reviewers approached *On the Road* in these terms, as a portrait of young (white) American rebellion. Comparing it to Hemingway's *The Sun Also Rises*, the *New York Times* critic gushed that Kerouac's novel was "an authentic work of art," "the most brilliantly executed, the clearest and most important utterance yet made by the generation Kerouac himself named years ago as 'beat,' and whose principal avatar he is." The reviewer for the *New York Herald Tribune* did not like the novel much—he called it a "newsreel" close to "mindless incoherence"—but he too linked *On the Road* to a new generation of rebels and their predecessors: Kerouac "dreams of America in the authentic rolling rhythms of a Whitman or a Thomas Wolfe, drunk with eagerness for life." The *New York Post* called these rebels James Dean's generation, folks with soul and too-fast cars, "a curious amalgam of jazz and intellectualism, hoodlumism and tenderness, marijuana and the literary life." "Bright and creative, but committed to a willful and narcissistic ethos," the Beats were "religious without a God, insurgent without a program; hell-bent on a self-transcendence which can find release only in speed and narcotics." In the *Saturday Review*, the critic Ralph Gleason linked *On the Road* to the long history of jazz and the way musicians lived on the edge of society, in the gray area between "the underworld" and the world of respectability—homeless, in the sense of uprooted, always traveling. Some white young people, he observed, had taken up this oppositional attitude and constant movement as a way of life. The *Village Voice*, only two years old and the self-conscious voice of the new bohemians, simply praised *On the Road* as "lusty, noisily lyrical," with "pages of hilarity, of despair, of tremendous excitement about merely being alive, of horror at being alive in today's America." Kerouac "offers a belief, a rallying point for the elusive spirit of rebellion of these times, that silent scornful sit-down strike of the disaffiliated which has been the nearest thing to a real movement among the young since the end of World War II."[63]

For a few years, Kerouac proved willing to play the role of generational spokesperson. He appeared on television occasionally and talked about the Beat Generation. On *The Steve Allen Show* in November 1959, the host plays jazz piano as Kerouac uses the end of the instrument as his table. His expression and gentle tone suggest depth and thoughtfulness as he reads excerpts from *On the Road*. He ends with the end of the book. "Nobody knows what's going to happen to anybody besides the forlorn rags," and he emphasizes and drags out the sound of the words "of growing old." "I think of Dean Moriarty," he intones like a prayer. "I even think of Old Dean Moriarty, the father we never found, I think of Dean Moriarty." Then he repeats the last phrase like a jazz riff: "I think of Dean Mor-i-ar-ty," he finishes, pulling the syllables into a chopping rhythm, ending the reading like a song.[64]

Over the next few years, Kerouac gave public readings. He also recorded an album of readings with Allen on piano and another with saxophone players Al Cohn and Zoot Sims. He wrote a piece for *Esquire*, describing how in the late 1940s, he, the novelist John Clellon Holmes, and Ginsberg stayed up nights drinking coffee, "talking madly," and listening to bebop. Somehow together they came up with a vision of "a generation of crazy, illuminated hipsters suddenly rising and roaming America, serious, bumming and hitchhiking everywhere, ragged, beatific, beautiful in an ugly, graceful way." He wrote a piece for *Playboy*. Sometimes he was brilliant, and sometimes he was drunk. His letters suggest he possessed an ambiguous relationship to the role he was playing, as volatile as his moods. Other writers, particularly Ginsberg, proved more consistently effective as speakers and representatives of the Beats. When an obviously drunk Kerouac appeared on the conservative journalist William Buckley's television show, *Firing Line*, in 1968, he railed against the very types of people who had been his earliest fans. Yet across the fifties and into the sixties, increasing numbers of middle-class white kids shaped their lives around Kerouac and others' vision of self-consciously seeking the margins of society and the limits of experience.[65]

By the end of the decade, all this media attention, praise, and criticism had helped transform the Beats into their caricature, the beatniks. Ridiculed and admired, often simultaneously, beatniks appeared everywhere in late 1950s pop culture, becoming an instantly recognizable, hip-talking social type. With their goatees, longish hair, turtleneck sweaters, berets, and sometimes horn-rimmed glasses, beatnik men stood out sharply against the crisp short hair and preppy clothes of most middle-class young people. Beatnik women, too, were easy to spot. They wore long skirts, black leotards, and flat leather sandals. Their hair hung natural and long, and their faces and lips were usually bare. In particular, 1959 seemed to be the year of the beatnik. That year, *Life* magazine publicized the Beat rebellion even as it blasted the lifestyle in an article entitled "The Only Rebellion Around: But the Shabby Beats Bungle the Job in Arguing, Sulking, and Bad Poetry." The television show *The Many Loves of Dobie Gillis* premiered with a regular beatnik character, Maynard G. Krebs. A musical comedy about beatnik characters, *The Nervous Set*, opened on Broadway with a number titled "Man, We're Beat." And MGM made a sensationalized film about the phenomenon, *The Beat Generation*. A year later, the popular entertainer Bob Hope dressed up like a beatnik and played the stand-up bass on his television variety show. Even cartoons featured beatniks, from a 1960 Mr. Magoo episode called "Beatnik Magoo" to the Looney Tunes cartoons about the hip character Cool Cat.[66]

From white middle-class teenagers' love for rock and roll to white urban young people's love for jazz and the beatniks' adoption of black slang, white rebellions in the fifties often shared a common set of racial assumptions. Blackness meant primitive. It meant the absence of modern artifice. It meant free access to feelings uncontaminated by "civilized" repression. In "Howl," black streets mapped a geography of possibility, the place to find "the angel-headed hipsters burning for the ancient heavenly connection." In *On the Road*, black neighborhoods hummed "with the vibration of really joyous life that knows nothing of disappointment and 'white sorrows.'" In rock and roll, black sounds and black moves freed white feelings and white desires. Black spaces were the places where magic happened, where contradictions—free individual expression and social connection—coexisted, where fantasies came true. When these white Americans rejected the social and aesthetic and moral terms of their own worlds to make and find new communities, their journeys increasingly led them to black neighborhoods and black music. In the 1950s, whenever a white man adopted an oppositional stance, he could not seem to help borrowing from the old tradition of blackface minstrelsy.[67]

CHAPTER 3

Black as Folk: The Folk Music Revival, the Civil Rights Movement, and Bob Dylan

How does it feel?
Bob Dylan

Murray Lerner, a filmmaker and folk music fan, took his camera to the Newport Folk Festival to engage in a little conservation. Old or odd or both, increasing numbers of shape note singers, Gullah-speaking and spiritual-singing vocal groups, hillbilly string bands, and Delta blues guitarists performed on the stages and at workshops and mingled in the crowds at the three festivals in 1963, 1964, and 1965 that the documentary maker shot. Lerner believed he could help preserve these commercially marginal musical forms. The fans he filmed had larger plans. They were using the resources associated with folk music to save not just the musical genres, song repertoires, and performance styles they believed were in danger of dying. They were using the music to save the very idea of an alternative expressive culture. They were using the resources of people they imagined as marginalized, isolated, and poor to save themselves. Lerner's footage not only salvaged old music, capturing Newport's spectacular juxtaposition of young, middle-class musicians and fans and musicians the folk music community labeled "traditionalists." It also recorded the birth of the broad and homegrown American bohemia that would become the counterculture.[1]

At the beginning of the 1967 documentary *Festival* that Lerner made from the film he shot in Newport, Fritz Richmond, a member of the Boston-based

Jim Kweskin Jug Band, wears dark shades and acts stoned as Lerner interviews him. Why, he asks, would he want to tell the filmmaker about himself since he would only come across as strange? He does not need to talk for that. "When I pick up a jug and start playing it," Richmond says as he looks into the lens, "you know I am a freak, right?" Lerner's camera pans to his bandmate Mel Lyman, who wears a dark fisherman's cap and cultivates a direct and disarming eccentricity. "We're trying to take, like, our understanding or our perception of truth," Lyman says, "and put it in a form so you can hear it sensually, like with your ears, like a painter takes what he knows of the truth and puts it on canvas so the people can dig it in a sensual way. Music just happens to be an ear thing, that's all." A member of the early sixties folk group Peter, Paul, and Mary defines folk music more earnestly: "Folk music is really the personification of a human being extending his hand to another human being, without losing his dignity. The music says, 'We feel this way about it. Walk with us.'"[2]

Extending a hand became more than a metaphor in the now iconic 1963 Newport sing-along that Lerner left out of his documentary. Except for the microphones, the scene looks like a picket or a voter rally or a march. Blacks and whites stand singing with their arms linked and crossed, ready for a charge or a blow. The blacks wear dark suits, crisp white button-downs, and pleated dresses, the middle-class clothes civil rights activists use to tell the country they are citizens. Their faces are serious, earnest even, and their voices are strong.

> We shall overcome,
> We shall overcome,
> We shall overcome someday.
> Oh deep in my heart, I do believe,
> We shall overcome someday.[3]

In photographs and film footage of the Friday night finale, the stage is crowded. Peter, Paul, and Mary are there, at the height of their fame. Joan Baez is there too, the beautiful star of the folk revival, in love with the music and Bob Dylan. Pete Seeger brings the gravitas, over two decades of political and cultural work—the Old Left, the folk song movement, playing with Woody Guthrie, the Red baiting of the Weavers, and the blacklist. Well practiced in joining his politics and his music, Seeger had been playing benefit concerts for the Student Nonviolent Coordinating Committee (SNCC) since the fall of 1962. But it is SNCC's Freedom Singers, the four field workers Bernice Johnson, Cordell Reagon, Rutha Harris, and Charles Neblett, who bring the authenticity and the romance to this stage. These singers did not just sing on stages. They led hot churches full of worried people in song after song. They sang on marches and picket lines, at sit-ins and voter registration rallies, and in the paddy wagons and crowded jails in Selma and Albany and McComb. They were the conduits of an "authentic" African American rural culture that stretched back centuries. They were the "real" folk. With them on the Newport stage, the other folk-singers and the audience could evoke, at least temporarily, a simple world where black and white, the old and the new, the people left out of the present and the people alienated from it and looking to the past, can come together, where people can clasp hands and sing and conjure integration. Exactly one month later, Dylan and Baez and the Freedom Singers reenacted this powerful merging. Standing in front of the Lincoln Memorial, they lent their voices as Mahalia Jackson led one quarter of a million marchers in "We Shall Overcome."[4]

In the late fifties and early sixties, the Newport Folk Festival sat at the center of a new folk music revival that formed an important part of popular culture even as it critiqued that culture. Listening to and making their own folk music, young people learned that romanticizing "the folk" was a form of rebellion against mid-century middle-class values and what people then called mass culture. Modern America, folk music implied by providing a counterexample, was fake, plastic, slick, mass-produced, usually segregated, and new. Feelings were packaged and clear there. Passions were tidy and controlled. Folk music was the opposite of all these things. It could be gentle and pure or wild and raw, but it was always deep and real and full of feeling. It was something to be crazy about, something to love. It was the opposite of mainstream commercial music with its slick production values and racially segregated genres. It seemed like a living piece of a time before the world was mass-produced, advertised, and sold. A fan could listen to all four-plus hours of the *Folkways Anthology of American Folk Music* straight through or go to a folk festival and see musicians like Mississippi John Hurt walk out of the past of the records and onto the stage to play. She could spend days trying to master every nuance of Maybelle Carter's or Elizabeth Cotton's guitar style. Or she could sing along in Washington Square or in a neighbor's den or in a coffeehouse near her college. Mass culture asked people to make a purchase. The folk revival asked people to participate. And participating, joining with the folk, the real outsiders—and it was crucial that some of them were black—made young middle-class whites outsiders too.[5]

If early rock and roll had given many white middle-class teenagers a taste of what rebellion in the form of playing black could feel like, by the late 1950s the liberating force of the music seemed spent, buried under derivative product and an outpouring of criticism from politicians, ministers, and parents, as well as the growing force of the segregationists. Folk music filled in the gap. It gave these white middle-class teenagers a seemingly pure and noncommercial version of the last decade's teenage rock rebellion. It gave them a music they could grow up into but that still signaled their opposition to their parents' culture. It offered a rich and serious story, locating the outsider in a specific place and time, a pre-modern, pre-capitalist historical moment when people made music for the pleasure of expression rather than for cash. And it smoothed over the contradictions between self-invention and meaningful connections. Rock and roll worked like minstrelsy, displacing incompatible desires onto fantasies of blackness and then taking them back up, cleansed of contradiction, through identification with African Americans. For many white middle-class fans, folk music provided this kind of release or psychological disassociation as it broadened minstrelsy's fantasies to include rural whites as well as blacks. But folk music also offered a temporal and geographic displacement as well. Identifying with another place and time where people seemed to live connected to the land, their past, and each other enabled folk music fans to evade the incompatibility of their dreams. And identification could quickly shift into impersonation. Playing "the folk," acting like a farm lass or a member of a chain gang or a hobo, satisfied the desire for self-invention while also offering a sense of being grounded in something old and deep. Playing "the folk" enabled revivalist musicians and fans to create an alternative world filled with sounds, symbols, clothes, food, and even values that stood in opposition to the suburban middle-class prosperity in which most of them had been raised. Identification became impersonation. The folk music revival, like Lerner's documentary *Festival*, fantasized about the past to build a future.[6]

Civil rights activists, on the other hand, learned that playing the part of "the folk" provided access to white middle-class sympathy and support outside the South. No organization did this better than SNCC, which used whites' fantasies about southern blacks as the folk to raise money, educate people, and recruit new volunteers. SNCC's Freedom Singers toured college campuses and liberal churches and synagogues, playing the part of the singing black folk and teaching folk fans about the southern civil rights struggle.[7]

In the mid-1960s, it looked like shared feelings of alienation from American society might serve as the basis for a new politics. Folksinger Bob Dylan anchored one end of this dream by transforming these emotions into songs people could hear and feel and sing. And he modeled the life story, the way white middle-class kids could remake themselves as outsiders by playing the folk. For a moment, Dylan's art and life made the romance of the outsider seem capacious enough to hold back the conflicts between being black and being white, between being poor and being middle-class, between loving and using the folk.

On those stages in Newport and at the March on Washington, two streams of people came together to try to change history. For a moment there, the children of postwar plenty, the insiders, the people the whole postwar world was supposed to be for, met and joined the people they thought of as the outsiders, Americans locked out of the dream by the color of their skin. One group wanted to get out, to express their alienation from the suburbs, the Ivy League expectations, the late-model cars and other markers of status, the whole life completely laid out for them. And the other group wanted to get in, to the good jobs and the good neighborhoods and the possibility of upward mobility, to have the very security that the first group was fleeing. It was an odd coalition, shaky at best, full of irony and dependent on the romance of the outsider.

"I Shall Be Free"

In the fifties, simply listening to something called "folk music" marked a fan as rebellious. After the peak of the Red Scare, clubs, little magazines, and concerts began to draw scattered folk fans together, and a small folk music movement emerged. In 1959, this movement broke into the broader popular culture when the Kingston Trio's earnest cover of the North Carolina murder ballad "Tom Dooley" became an unlikely pop and country hit. Folk music, an ever-evolving category in the music business, remained hugely popular well into the sixties.[8]

From the standpoint of American history more broadly rather than the history of the pop charts, the folk music revival appeared as a particularly high peak in the long history of folk revivalism. In the late nineteenth century, song collectors and folklore scholars combed Appalachia in particular looking for "Anglo-Saxon" ballads, traces of the medieval old country surviving unchanged in the new. In this revival, the folk were white and the politics were generally conservative. In the early twentieth century, scholars like W.E.B. DuBois, Howard Odum, and John Lomax challenged this revivalism by studying and collecting the spirituals and "the secular songs of the Southern Negros." White southerners Odum and Lomax, however, celebrated African American music using a kind of sentimental racial primitivism that would have been at home on the minstrel stage. This kind of romanticism became a key characteristic of the rapidly professionalizing folklore field, even as folklore scholars saw their own position as promoting a kind of scientific knowledge of African American expressive culture at odds with both white racism and blackface minstrelsy's images of black life.[9]

In 1933, John Lomax filled the trunk of his Ford sedan with a then state-of-the-art 315-pound acetate disc recorder and set off with his teenage son Alan across the rural South looking for what they understood as traditional, non-commercial music. The discs they made on this trip—recordings of African American musician Huddie "Leadbelly" Ledbetter at a Louisiana prison—and the many trips that followed formed the basis of the Library of Congress's new Archive of American Folk Song. Following the Lomaxes' example, scholars and collectors increasingly preserved folk music as audio recordings rather than textual transcriptions.[10]

In the late 1930s and 1940s, another wave of revivalism peaked in what became known as the folk song revival. Folk singing then became closely linked to the Popular Front, the Communist Party's broad Depression-era effort to make allies across the American left by finding, circulating, and even inventing an alternative, indigenous radical culture. Folk songs, in this kind of thinking, provided evidence of the long history of class struggle. Communist Party cultural politics firmly linked folk singing and interest in both black and white folk music to the left. Folksingers performed at union meetings and political rallies, and the party helped popularize the songs of striking mine and mill workers like Gastonia, North Carolina's Ella Mae Wiggins (killed by the mill's armed men) and Harlan County, Kentucky's Aunt Molly Jackson, who fled the mines to live in New York City. Blues musicians like Josh White and Big Bill Broonzy wrote and recorded blues protest songs in the thirties and early forties for the Popular Front audience. When the musician and song-writer Woody Guthrie brought his Okie songs and leftist politics to New York City in 1940, the radical community embraced him. His "This Land Is Your Land," written as a Marxist response to "God Bless America," eventually became a kind of alternative national anthem.[11]

Alan Lomax played an essential role in creating the stars of this revival. He met Guthrie in 1940 when they both played a New York City benefit, a "Grapes of Wrath Evening," for a Popular Front group, the John Steinbeck Committee for Agricultural Workers. Lomax helped make Guthrie, Leadbelly, and Jackson into the biggest stars of this revival. Lomax, like Pete Seeger and other participants in this revival, worked a kind of earnest, left populism. As Lomax wrote in the preface to the 1947 collection *Folk Song U.S.A.*:

> It is our identification with the common man that has carried my
> father and myself on our ballad hunt across this continent—into
> thousands of work camps and honky-tonks, into a thousand small
> houses, into the little churches up back-country roads, and through

the still horror of a score of penitentiaries. It is this enthusiasm that laid the basis for the Archive of American Folk Song in the Library of Congress, where we added the voice of the common man to the written record of America.

In this revival, folk music became the voice of the people—their past, their politics, and the basis for their future.[12]

After the war, People's Songs, founded in a Greenwich Village basement by Seeger, Guthrie, other folk singers, scholars, and union officials, kept up the Popular Front tradition. People's Songs combined song collecting and publishing, concerts, and hootenannies (a kind of secular revival meeting for the cause) with left political organizing. They sent folksingers, for example, out on the campaign trail for Progressive Party candidate Henry Wallace. Folk songs remained broadly popular, and singers backed by orchestras performed adaptations of folk songs. In the late 1940s and early 1950s, the Weavers—Pete Seeger, Ronnie Gilbert, Lee Hays, and Fred Hellerman—worked this territory to great fame. They turned the Leadbelly song "Goodnight, Irene," for example, into a number one pop hit in the late summer and fall of 1950. At the peak of the Weavers' popularity, however, anti-Communism killed the folk song movement. An informant testifying at the House Un-American Activities Committee (HUAC) hearings in 1952 attacked the Communist Party ties of the group's members. Blacklisted and unable to book concert venues or television appearances, the Weavers stopped performing. Seeger retreated with his family to a cabin in the country north of New York City. At Yale at the time, John Cohen, future member of the revivalist string band the New Lost City Ramblers, described for a reporter the small group of art and math students, "leftwing, out group and odd scene," still interested in folk music in those bleak days: "We heard of actual fist fights, held in dormitory rooms, where students tried forcibly to prevent their roommates from going to the hoots—on the grounds that it would seriously impair their future chances, particularly for Government jobs, if it were known that they associated with people like us." The very word "folk" conjured up the Communist menace so strongly that the music industry changed the name of "hillbilly" music again, replacing its postwar labeling of "folk" with the less tainted term "country."

Record collector Harry Smith and Folkways Records founder Moe Asch could not have had worse timing when they released a six-record set of folk music in 1952. Smith, an artist, filmmaker, and, for a time, graduate student in anthropology, had begun buying "exotic" records, odd music "in relation to what was considered to be the world culture of high-class music," in 1940.

After collecting the blues, he had moved on to the hillbilly acts. In the early fifties, he tried to sell some of his records. Asch bought some, but he also suggested Smith should put out an anthology of the music he had collected.[13] In 1952, Folkways released the collection Smith assembled from his records as the *Folkways Anthology of American Folk Music*. It took a while for the multiple-record set to catch on, and Folkways never made much money from it. Asch kept almost all his releases available for years, though, and as a result, a record set that should have disappeared stayed available throughout the decade, listened to in dorm rooms and cheap apartments by a growing number of folk fans. Eventually, the songs on the *Folkways Anthology*, along with some Library of Congress field recordings, became the canon of the folk music revival.

Unlike the Library of Congress materials collected by the Lomaxes and others, however, Smith's 1952 anthology presented music recorded commercially in the 1920s and 1930s for smaller markets—country blues sold to black Deep South migrants recently settled in cities, for example, and hillbilly music sold to mountain whites living in mill towns—as folk music, as some kind of indigenous form of avant-garde art. Most importantly, Smith drew no racial distinctions:

> Before the Anthology, there had been a tendency in which records
> were lumped together into blues catalogues or hillbilly catalogues,
> and everybody was having blindfold tests to prove they could tell
> which was which. That's why there's no such indications of that sort
> (color/racial) in the albums. I wanted to see how well certain jazz
> critics did on the blindfold test. They all did horribly. It took years
> before anybody discovered that Mississippi John Hurt wasn't a
> hillbilly.

Smith's collection forced people to listen across the categories, which had always been more about marking racial boundaries for commercial purposes than about the sound of the music. The blues and other forms of black music, Smith insisted in the way he arranged the songs, were as important as the Anglo-American ballad singing tradition. All of these forms, in turn, influenced each other. On the *Folkways Anthology*, African American musicians reworked the blatant racism of the coon songs, popular late nineteenth-century minstrel hits sold as sheet music, into expressions of their own sexuality. Hillbilly artists adapted blues songs to new instrumentation and used them to express their own sense of loss. Musically, the songs were integrated. The *Folkways Anthology* aurally asserted, in a way the Library of Congress recordings accompanied by their careful scholarly notes and racially defined musical genres could not, the musical miscegenation at the heart of American folk music. As the later blues revivalist Dave Van Ronk remembered, "That set became our bible. It is how most of us first heard of Blind Willie Johnson, Mississippi John Hurt, and even Blind Lemon Jefferson. And it was not just blues people . . . It was an incredible compendium of American traditional musics, all performed in traditional styles."[14]

Like the anthology, major folk music concerts too were integrated, even if the fan base was mostly white. In 1959, Alan Lomax organized Folksong 59, a concert at Carnegie Hall that popularized the new folk music revival. The recording of the concert captures Lomax offering up his own live version of the Smith anthology: Jimmie Driftwood, a Mountainview, Arkansas, schoolteacher and ballad singer who hoped "you all can understand my southern brogue"; Earl Taylor and the Stony Mountain Boys, a bluegrass band "discovered" by Mike Seeger, a member of the New Lost City Ramblers; Memphis Slim playing, Lomax drawled as MC, "a blues you can relax on"; and Muddy Waters, a Lomax "discovery" from Mississippi and by then famous bluesman, singing, Lomax announced, " 'Hoochie Coochie Man,' a song about voodoo down in the Mississippi valley. Go ahead, Muddy." That same year, the first Newport Folk Festival, a day of folk singing held the weekend after the well-established Newport Jazz Festival, featured Robert Pete Williams, a blues musician "found" by a folklorist at Louisiana's Angola State Prison, a group of Nigerian dancers, and a gospel choir, along with the bluegrass banjo player Earl Scruggs and a very young Joan Baez. At a time when the FBI listed racially integrated gatherings as a sign of Communist influence, the racially mixed folk music scene with its miscegenated history and its live mixing of black and white performance seemed subversive to many Americans.[15]

All these pasts, the long history of folk revivalism, remained alive in the present. A racially ambiguous, bohemian, vaguely leftist and thus forbidden aura, completely at odds with white suburban middle-class plenty, made folk music popular. Tainted by its connections to Communism and the Old Left, folk music gave many young musicians and fans a way to push against the pervasive liberalism of mid-century America. Liberalism insisted that the past did not matter, that there were no limits on what the individual or the nation could accomplish, that the future would inevitably be better than the past. Folk revivalism suggested instead that the past had value, that the loss of history was something not to be celebrated but to be mourned.[16]

As folk music became popular yet again, overt radical politics were largely missing. Alan Lomax, for example, had traded in his past ties to Communism for vaguely political statements like "The recording machine can be a voice for the voiceless." The press presented folk music fans as bohemians, cultural rebels, or at least wannabe rebels, not socialists and Communists. And in New York City's Washington Square every Saturday afternoon, when they put their difference on display, their clothes were much more conspicuous than their political ideology. Young women wore black leotards, Mexican sandals, and peasant skirts, their hair unset and natural and their faces bare. Young men wore flannel shirts, overalls, raggedy jeans, and railroad caps. Many women and men brought guitars, banjos, harmonicas, and autoharps. A reporter described college students attending the 1960 Newport Folk Festival who "carried their sleeping bags and instruments down to the beach" and there, around fires built in holes scooped out of the sand to keep off the fog," played folk music until dawn. "Many of them, in some small detail of their appearance, looked ever so slightly beat," the beard at odds with the "expensively tailored Madras shorts," the "wrought iron jewelry" at odds with the crisp blouse:

> There is a connection, one begins to suspect, between the way a lot
> of students like to look and their feeling for folk music . . . This
> generation of college students is not exactly beat, but it is composed
> of young people who are desperately hungry for a small, safe taste of
> an unslick, underground world. Folk music, like a beard or sandals,
> has come to represent a slight loosening of the inhibitions, a
> tentative step in the direction of the open road, the knapsack, the
> hostel . . . Some of the trappings and tastes of a Bohemian minority
> group have been gradually assimilated and adapted by a student
> middle class.

The folk music revival helped democratize bohemian cultural rebellion. But what exactly attracted these middle-class college students to folk music?[17]

Hootenannies and festivals, concerts and cafés and singing in Washington Square Park—sharing folk music, its fans claimed, created a kind of communal warmth and elation. The music, they insisted, simply made them "feel good," "a part of something." It often started with a more commercial song like the Kingston Trio hit "Tom Dooley" or Harry Belafonte's hit "Grizzly Bear," a song originally collected in 1951 by Pete Seeger and John Lomax in a southern prison camp. Soon the new fan was buying records and making small devotional steps on a pilgrimage toward the sacrament of the *Folkways Anthology* or the very bones of the saints, what *Time* magazine called those scratchy recordings of "all the shiftless geniuses who have shouted the songs of their forebears into tape recorders for the Library of Congress." Jeff Todd Titon, a folk musician and scholar, remembered learning to play a few chords in high

Folk music fans square dance in Washington Square Park in 1959. *Associated Press.*

school, listening to popular folk musicians like Peter, Paul, and Mary, and playing Atlanta coffeehouses. By the time he entered college in 1962, he had begun to listen to musicians like Joan Baez "who tried to sing and play what they regarded as a traditional body of material." Soon he "spent hours a day practicing the finger-picking style of Etta Baker or Elizabeth Cotton." Authenticity became a folk musician's most important quality, "who was 'more ethnic' (as the saying went) than whom." Participation, on a continuum from singing along to learning to play to forming a string band like Mike Seeger's New Lost City Ramblers, was the key. Folk music made its fans part of a new community of outsiders.[18]

What this new community did was share its feelings. For Alan Lomax, emotions were central to the new folk music revival. "In order to acquire a folk singing style, you have to experience the feelings that lie behind it, and learn to express them as the folk singers do . . . Here," Lomax argued, "the city singer of folk songs is playing his full and serious role—that is, to interpret for his city audience the lives and feelings of the past or a far-off society—to link them emotionally." Without this emotional connection, folksingers merely represented the "shell of the song." Scholars claimed this "psychological and imaginative identification with the folk" was essential. Even critical press reports described this practice. A 1959 *Mademoiselle* piece laughed at a "young woman in a tweed shirt and sandals" who "sang in a wispy plaintive voice" from the steps of the Washington Square fountain: *Early in the morning, as the sun was rising,/ I heard a maid sing in the valley below./ Oh, don't deceive me. Oh, never leave me./ How could you use a poor maiden so.* "Yet in actuality—that is, on weekdays—Sally is a fashion copy writer," the reporter sneered. "Her long black pony tail is a false hair piece she discovered advertised in the shopping column of the magazine she helps to write. What's more, the depth of feeling she invested in her song had originated in a highly emotional but inconsequential tiff she had the night before with her account-executive beau." Other "fountain musicians" were also fakes. "The Scholar or Folk Bore" with the bad voice used every song as "an excuse for an explanation." "The Weeper," wailing "in a barely audible alto, cried always that true love is never true." "The Peacemonger" shouting his songs of protest, his look and tone full of indignation and belligerence, was simply "an injustice-collector," "equally happy complaining about Welsh mining conditions as about neighbors who refuse to tolerate his guitar playing after midnight." The new city folksingers, critics claimed, could not possibly be sincere. Their use of traditional songs to express their contemporary feelings was, for some commentators, a nasty kind of emotional ventriloquism, a form of minstrelsy in beards and sandals instead of paint.[19]

For many fans and performers, the shared emotions were exactly the point. Joan Baez, the revival's first big star, sang an integrated repertory of folk songs categorized as "Anglo-American" (the ballad "Black Is the Color," for example) and "Negro" (the lullaby "All My Trials"). Fans praised her for avoiding the "fake ethnic" approach. "Joan does not pretend to be a Negro or a British Maiden broken by a feudal lord," an admirer argued. "What she gives are her own feelings about these people. She's like a passionate biographer; and more than that, she makes these songs contemporary by identifying with their emotional content as herself—as Joan Baez." In that way, "her audience immediately identifies with *her*." The point was not historical truth or even knowledge. "I don't care very much where a song came from or why—or even what it says," Baez told a *Time* reporter in 1962. "All I care about is how it sounds and the feeling in it." Baez and her fans cared about the emotional truth. "The songs are so clear emotionally," Baez claimed, "that they can speak for themselves."[20]

Mike Seeger was a very different type of folk musician, for many folk purists the most serious and talented of the young white revivalists. But his fans too praised him for getting the emotional truth of the old hillbilly or country music right. "Imitation of specific individual vocal mannerisms and labored mirroring of unique instrumental techniques" was one "obvious" way of "approaching country style." Some of these revivalists, called by one critic "the imitators," even began to dress and speak like Appalachian whites. Seeger practiced this form of mimicry, taking on "the mannerisms of the southern mountaineers" and wearing old-fashioned clothes like plain white cotton "Sunday" shirts with narrow bow ties like the people whose music he was trying to master. Critic John Pankake felt that what made Mike's music great, for all Seeger's positioning as a serious musical revivalist and folk scholar, was the same quality Baez's fans found in her music: "It is the texture, mood, and depth of country music that distinguish his performances, thoroughly integrated into and reshaped by his own personality, itself colored by over a decade of close proximity with both the musical and non-musical aspects of the country experience."[21]

White bluesmen Dave Van Ronk, John Hammond Jr., and John Koerner followed similar strategies. Van Ronk, one of the first of the "new city blues" players, began performing and recording the blues songs he heard on Smith's anthology and old 78s in the late fifties: "I first came into contact with Negro traditional songs through a chance encounter with a recording of 'Stackolee' made by Furry Lewis, a southern street singer." He had never heard white people perform black music before, he recalled, except his mother when she sang old "cakewalk and ragtime songs" around the house. "So, having only such singers as Furry Lewis, King Solomon Hill, and Leadbelly for models, when I tried to sing these songs I naturally imitated what I heard." Though he did not think about it this way, he combined his own imitation of African American musicians with the example his mother gave him of the tradition of whites singing like blacks.[22]

Robert Shelton, the New York music critic who a year later would help launch Bob Dylan's career, described Van Ronk's style in 1960: "a distinctive, rough-hewn voice that alternates from a rough, representative 'gravel-pushing' sound to a purring trail of lonesome country memories; a rock-of-Gibraltar rhythmic sense on guitar, and a natural, yet often dynamic, stage presence." Van Ronk, like Presley before him, sounded "black." The difference was that Van Ronk played blues music popular in the twenties and thirties, as well as more recent versions of this music by black musicians like Leadbelly, not the rhythm and blues popular with contemporary black audiences. He also tried to make his voice sound exactly like the voices of the black blues singers he heard. Hammond Jr., the son of John Hammond, the man legendary in the music business for signing Billie Holiday and Bob Dylan, took his imitation even further. He left college, as the 1963 Newport Folk Festival Guide informed concertgoers, "to migrate to the South in search of the origins of the Delta blues," to hear and learn the music in its original context. Back in the city and up on the stage, Hammond Jr. displayed the scruffy clothes, rough voice, and country blues guitar style he had picked up on his trip.[23]

While white performers could still impersonate poor whites, this kind of imitation, white performers impersonating poor African Americans, became increasingly difficult to pull off after the mid-sixties. Critics railed against "young city-bred whites . . . who try to sing as if they had been born black and on the land fifty years ago . . . Until we have a time and color changing machine, it is impossible to recreate someone else's history." "Well-intentioned white singers in blackface" had a hard time convincing some fans and critics that they could express the emotions of poor southern blacks. After all, the early twentieth-century Society for the Preservation of Spirituals, a group of rich southern whites who dressed like antebellum planters and sang black sacred songs in dialect and in Gullah, had sounded "black" too. A music critic's mention of Hammond's 1964 album *Big City Blues* in a review of recent records put it bluntly: "I wish he hadn't." Another reviewer wrote that the album shows "his obvious infatuation for the sounds of the greatest old bluesmen. But it should be a private love affair."[24]

Defenders of white middle-class blues musicians stressed the centrality of feeling. "The blues is a general expression of feelings engendered by an event," a self-identified eighteen-year-old folk fan wrote in *Sing Out!* in early 1965 in defense of white bluesmen. "The event is not the important thing. The emotional content of the event is what is important . . . The important thing is sensitivity, not skin color." Revivalists' adaptations of folk songs were important not as historical reporting—old recordings survived to accomplish the task of providing information on poor rural life—but as emotional reporting. It was not what the lyrics said, exactly, as much as the tone and the mood a revivalist's live or recorded performance conveyed. It was the feelings. Revivalists helped build an emotional connection between the people and traditions imagined as folk and white middle-class folk fans. These connections, in turn, helped white young people build their own music-centered alternative culture.[25]

If the old definitions of authenticity did not work—and the problem existed for revivalists, whether they played music originally performed by either blacks or whites, and for traditionalists, who could no longer really claim they grew up in isolation from outside cultural influences—then one solution was to change the meaning of "authenticity." Performer and scholar Sam Hinton mused about this dilemma. Folk music, he argued, was "not so much a body of art" as it was "a process, an attribute, and a way of life." Hinton, however, had no organic access to this process. He could only be a revivalist, imitating the songs and performing styles of traditionalist musicians. Still, "unless the performer has an extraordinary sense of dialect and of musical expression, the imitation will not be a faithful one, and may easily descend to caricature. If a folksong loses its sincerity, it loses its most poignant attribute— and it ceases to be a folksong." Folk sound, in this kind of thinking, can only grow out of genuine feelings. The answer, "the one facet of folklore" that Hinton could "try to preserve intact," was "its emotional content": "My desire is to arouse in the audience emotions similar to those felt by the 'original' folk audience." This emphasis on feelings made authenticity into an internal rather than an external quality. Being alike on the inside, as people who shared emotions and the need for self-expression, replaced being alike on the outside, as people who shared a history of oppression and isolation. Emotionalism replaced materialism. Revivalist imitators served as important intermediaries in this cultural shift. Feelings, not historical connection or faithful reproduction, created the new community of outsiders. As the critic Nat Hentoff claimed, "The quest for authenticity must be pursued from within."[26]

Somehow, the emotions of the songs—the twangy heartbreak of the new mill worker who has lost his mountain home, the wailing lament of the black man, forced to travel for work, at finding "another mule in his doggone stall"— gave the new fans access to their own feelings. As one very perceptive reporter suggested, "When they sing about the burdens and sorrows of the Negro, for example, they are singing out their own state of mind as well." Traditional black music articulated not only "the Negro's longing for liberation"; the songs also expressed "any man's bid for freedom." As John Cohen argued in reply to Lomax's criticism of city folksingers, "The emotional content of folk songs is a different thing to different people—and it is hard to say that there is a simple, correct way to emotional content . . . If we from the city are attracted to folk music, it is because we appreciate the clarity of the limitations within which folk music developed. But ultimately, what we appreciate is the order that comes out of these limitations . . . If it is order for which we search, we can make and find that within ourselves. There is no truth except that which we make for ourselves." In playing folk music, "each person's individuality finally asserts itself." Unlike Lomax, many new folk fans and musicians did not see emotional connections with people of different times and places as the main point. They saw folk songs as a way to express their own feelings. "The need for their own self expression," Irwin Silber insisted in *Sing Out!*, had always been the reason people everywhere wrote and sang folk songs.[27]

The folk-loving kids of the fifties and sixties turned to fantasies about the past to find their way. It was important that in this revival folk music circulated in an aural rather than a written form. Changes in technology made this possible, from the invention of field recording equipment to the development of the LP record, the most important format in which the music circulated, and the inexpensive phonograph. Fans and performers mostly heard rather than read the music, and the songs published in *Sing Out!* and elsewhere were intended to help readers learn to play the songs. In the foreword to *The New Lost City Ramblers Song Book*, for example, Silber quoted a letter written by the transcriber soon after she signed on to work on the project: "Learning from listening is the unquestionably best way, the only way that suits this kind of music . . . If you could do it, it would be good to have a legend across each page reading: Listen to the record if you want to learn the song." The *Folkways Anthology* and the Library of Congress recordings seemed like little pieces of the real. The pop and crackle of old records, the indecipherable lyrics, the tinny high end—these quirks only made the songs sound more like messages from a lost world.[28]

Recording brought the past into the future, and when musicians like Mississippi John Hurt stepped off the *Folkways Anthology* and onto the Newport Folk Festival stage in 1963, it almost seemed like ghosts had learned to play and sing. The fact that the past seemed so literally to be in the present suggested that other things were possible, that maybe there was an alternative to the white suburban vision of the good life. Maybe there was more to feel than contentment and smug satisfaction and optimism. If there had been a different past, maybe there could be a different future.

Folkies attached their feelings to the songs and lives of people in other places and times. How else, exactly, could they describe a threat as abstract and real as nuclear annihilation? How could they express their desire for a different world when McCarthyism had pushed political alternatives on the left underground and conservatism was still understood as preserving the status quo? When, as a scholar insisted, they were part of a "people of plenty"? When politics seemed closed off and their problems, less material than psychological, even cultural, seemed impossible to put into words? "When I started singing," Baez remembered in 1962, "I felt as though we had just so long to live, and I still feel that way. It's looming over your head. The kids who sing feel they really don't have a future—so they pick up a guitar and play. It's a desperate sort of thing, and there's a whole lost bunch of them." "Studying a song," Israel "Izzy" Young, owner of the Folklore Center in Greenwich Village, told a reporter in 1960, made "a student feel allied to it. It enables a girl who grew up surrounded by the best of everything to sing with some conviction the kind of blues and spirituals that theoretically could be sung honestly only by a prisoner on a southern chain gang." As Bob Dylan remembered half a century after the revival, "Folk music was a reality of a more brilliant dimension . . . and if it called out to you, you could disappear and be sucked into it . . . It was so real, so more true to life than life itself. It was life magnified." Folk songs conjured another world. One college student fan in 1960 explained, "My great desire is to go to the places where these songs began so I can know these people and their lives . . . and learn their music firsthand. Only then can I feel content reproducing their songs with my voice, finger tips, and emotions." Knowing "the folk" suggested the possibility of transformation. An alternative to the present existed somewhere. Revivalist musicians from Hammond Jr. and Mike Seeger to Jack Elliott and Bob Dylan increasingly claimed, in their songs and their dress and their mannerisms, that they had found this better, more authentic place. Maybe fans could find it too.[29]

Folk fans, mostly white college students, usually experienced a very different kind of alienation—a sense that political and economic struggle were over and yet the world still needed saving—than the traditionalist musicians, often working-class people with rural roots, whose work they championed. But the message that self-expression —cultural rebellion—was what was possible resonated deeply with both groups. A college boy performing Leadbelly's "Rock Island Line" could feel like he was working the rail line or the prison farm.

> Maybe I'm right, maybe I'm wrong
> Lawd you gonna miss me when I'm gone.
> Oh the Rock Island Line is a mighty fine line.
> Oh the Rock Island Line is the road to ride.

Old African American lullabies and Scottish folk songs wove the same spell, making a performer or even a fan into a slave woman calming her baby while boiling the white family's clothes or into an innocent girl, in a castle tower or a plantation cabin or a mountain shack, mourning the loss of her love. Joan Baez was a medieval Scottish maid or a slave mother, not the daughter of a Mexican physicist. Ramblin' Jack Elliott, reviving old cowboy and Okie songs and channeling Woody Guthrie, was a raggedy hobo hopping the freights or a bow-legged cowboy riding the trail, not the son of a Brooklyn ophthalmologist. In the folk song revival, middle-class young people could sing themselves into almost anything. All they needed was a record to copy, an instrument, and, even if it was only their parents back home in Boise upset about their new clothes or change of career plans, an audience.[30]

Pete Seeger described the process quite clearly:

We are used to this happening in the opposite direction; a country youth goes off to college and then gets into business in the city . . . Nobody calls him abnormal . . . My guess is that there will always be young people who for one reason or another will feel that they have to violently, radically reform themselves. A personal revolution. They abandon the old like a hated mask and rebuild on new foundations.

But Seeger mixed his metaphors. Masks are superficial and decorative while foundations are structural and essential. Masks suggest the playacting of minstrelsy, the act that knows it is an act, while foundations suggest fixed materials that provide grounding and stability. Seeger here conflates a change in class status with a phenomenon more accurately described as a change in psychological status. Choosing to "violently, radically reform" oneself is not the same as moving away from a rural home in order to make more money. Romanticizing the folk—listening to and performing their music, traveling through the places where these traditions lived and might somehow still survive, and even, at the extreme, trying to live in the present in an imagined folk past—all of these acts suggest a class status, a middle-class or higher level of privilege. And this class identity, money but also an education and a sense of mattering in the world, could not be given up as easily as a taste for pop music and a preference for preppy clothes.[31]

The major difference between the traditionalists and their original fans, on the one hand, and the revivalists and their mostly white middle-class fans, on the other, was that the middle-class fans did care about the "real" Ma Rainey. Actually, they did not care much about Ma Rainey and her 1920s blues hits at all. She was too obviously urban and modern for them, too powerful and too directly sexual, too free of the bonds of family, despite the "Ma," to fit easily into any fantasy of "folk" womanhood. Revivalists were interested in country blues and early hillbilly music, in forms forgotten enough to give free reign to their fantasies, in materials they could discover and control and fix in place and time. They wanted folk music to help them find their bearings, to help them find themselves. As Dave "Snaker" Ray, a white blues musician, made clear, "I play the blues because I feel it is important to me to express myself." They needed to see folk music as old-fashioned, as pre-modern, as the music of poor, rural people different from themselves, in order to see it as a fixed alternative to the present.[32]

In taking the possibility of transformation for themselves, they took it away from the people they imagined as "the folk." Musicians had long traded in the transformative possibilities inherent in other musicians' forms, the way the emotions growing out of a particular situation could be used to express the emotions of a very different place and time. This potential for emotional ventriloquism drew Jewish singers to blackface at the turn of the twentieth century. It drew blues musicians, in an ever more circular fashion, to rework coon songs, already acts of emotional impersonation, for new expressive purposes. It drew white southerners like Presley and Carl Perkins to rework rhythm and blues songs. This kind of appropriation and exchange was exactly what made American popular music so rich. But the revival insisted that "the folk" give up on transformation and borrowing and hold steady. In order for the new folk fans to "radically reform" themselves, the folk had to be authentic, set in some essential identity. The folk had to stay the same. Jack Elliott, in Seeger's words, "reborned himself 'in Oklahoma.' He didn't just learn some new songs; but he changed his whole way of living." An Okie who came to New York and learned to play classical violin, on the other hand, would no longer be a member of the folk. The older minstrel model of performing a self, of valuing transformation, became the new, revivalist model of performing the self, of valuing authenticity. Other identities were mutable, but the folk must stay the same.

Libba Cotton was no Ma Rainey. She was revivalists Mike and Peggy Seeger's maid, and "Libba" was Peggy's childhood name for Elizabeth Cotton. The Seegers were the royal family of folk music—parents Charlie (a musicologist) and Ruth Crawford Seeger (a composer and transcriber) worked on writing down the music, as opposed to the lyrics, of songs collected by the Lomaxes, and half brother Peter was already a legend for his work with the Almanac Singers and the Weavers. According to family lore, little Peggy got lost one day in front of a department store in downtown Washington, D.C. Elizabeth Cotton, who worked in the store, found Peggy and brought her home to the Seeger house in Chevy Chase. Her "reward," as one article phrased it, was a job as a "Saturday" maid at the Seegers'. There she ironed, baked bread, and performed other household tasks, one of which was listening to the growing Seeger kids practice folk songs on banjo and guitar. One day she announced to Mike that she had played the guitar herself as a girl before giving it up for God. He gave her his instrument, and she strummed and picked a few notes and phrases left-handed and then played him some songs. "Libba," as the Seegers called her, had been quite the player as a young girl and had even written a few songs. The Seeger kids were awed. They had discovered their very own live authentic folk musician right in their home.

Cotton later began performing with Mike's New Lost City Ramblers around Washington. She even put out her own record on Folkways in 1958, *Negro Folksongs and Tunes*. Cotton earned a little money (several versions of her best-known song, "Freight Train," became hits, although there were copyright problems) and a little fame (she performed at Newport in 1964). As importantly, she gave Mike and Peggy Seeger a way to claim a kind of deep connection with the folk. Cotton had lived most of her life without playing the guitar, but what those years had been like and who she was with her own family and friends, away from the Seegers and her revival celebrity, was not part of this act. In Cotton, the Seegers had their very own folk-singing mammy.[33]

For many white middle-class fans and musicians, the folk were real precisely because they were isolated and marginal, somehow outside of time. The folk were real when they acted out the revival's romantic fantasy. Robert Shelton went south to hear the singers in mass meetings, and he compared the music of the civil rights movement there to the music of the urban folk scene then flourishing in places like New York: "The beatnik guitar-pickers of Greenwich Village are trying to say something in their music, but they don't know quite what it is that they want to say. The Negroes of the South know what they are singing about and what they want out of life. Because they know their music rings with more meaning and conviction. Because their music is not just a 'kick,' a hobby, a form of exhibitionism, or a 'gig,' it is a different story of folk music than one encounters among the pampered, groping, earnestly searching young people one meets in the Greenwich Villages of the North." Theodore Bikel, star of the Broadway musical *The Sound of Music* and a popular folksinger as well, claimed "that Negroes, by tradition and natural inclination, are incapable of conducting a gathering without punctuating and underlining what is being said with music and song." Traditionalists like Mississippi John Hurt, Skip James, Son House, Dock Boggs, and Hobart Smith were the "real" folk.[34]

The mid-century revival, however, never acknowledged its minstrel influences, the way revivalists' efforts to copy not just the songs but the vocal tones of older folk musicians they worshipped drew from the performance conventions of minstrelsy. A great deal of self-conscious acting went into making these "real" folk. In this sense, old musicians like Mississippi John Hurt and Dock Boggs, who had second careers in the revival, and younger musicians like Leadbelly, who had their main careers there, performed a role similar to that of blacked-up black men ("the only real coons around") on the turn-of-the-century minstrel stage. What the revival hailed as the "real" folk were actually musicians playing revivalists playing the folk. The folk, the musicians *Time* called "country 'authentics' " and "all but unapproachable gods," were looking for work, and they adapted their repertories and performance styles to fit the folk music revival. Music critic and folk music fan Paul Nelson argued that before 1965, the "traditional musicians" at Newport played "the unhappy role of the Masses, tolerated, present to be philosophized over, talked down to, [and] abstractly worshipped as minor saints."[35]

Fan Tom Hoskins "found" Hurt—the musician, of course, did not consider himself lost—living in the same town, Avalon, Mississippi, where he was born and had been farming since his 1920s recording career ended. In 1963, Mike Seeger found the hillbilly banjo player Boggs living in his hometown, Norton, Virginia, where he had worked in the mines after the Depression ended his musical career. Hobart Smith, another Virginian musician, remembered, "I went into this popular stuff and got to playing on that and then when I got in with Alan Lomax in 1942, he wanted me to pull back into the old folk music. And he said, 'Don't you ever leave it again.' " Around the same time, Pete Seeger sent Smith the first banjo he had owned in twenty-five years. Both these men were happy to play their old songs for new audiences. In fact, the folk revival did not just resurrect particular musicians. It also revived entire genres of music like bluegrass that seemed destined to disappear as forms of commercially viable music and gave them a second life. Under the influence of the revival, many country musicians became more traditional—Johnny Cash, for example—adding "old-timey" and hillbilly songs to please this new audience. Revivalists even managed to supply the "the gods" with some "new" old songs. Revivalist Paul Clayton, recording in the mountains around Charlottesville, Virginia, collected the song "Laid Around and Stayed Around." Someone then recorded Clayton singing it with Roger Abraham at an informal concert. The recording traveled, and someone carried it to Nashville, where Bill Monroe heard it and added it to his repertory. "Authentics" understood they were performing more than their music, as traditional musician Clayton McMichen made clear when he yelled at the crowd at a Newport Folk Festival workshop in 1964, "You don't know anything about the music. I could play the worst fiddle in the world and you'd still applaud. You just like us because we're old." Ironically, the folk music revival cut traditionalist musicians off from the possibilities of transformation that their music often celebrated.[36]

The folk music revival gave middle-class musicians and fans, however, a way to change themselves. Playing and listening to folk music, they rebelled against the culture they had been given and found their own means of self-expression. In their fantasies of the folk and in the relationships they built around the music, they found the paradoxical sense of historical and social grounding they also craved.

For young white Americans, the folk music revival's acknowledgment that black as well as white people made American folk culture suggested, however vaguely in terms of political strategy, that a precedent existed for some integrated future. Joining black and white gave revivalists a way to stress other categories, to build a rough fence between the commercialized mass culture they grew up with and some "real" folk culture carrying over from the past. Their folk music, of course, was never so pure—there simply were no songs or playing styles left untouched by commerce. But the boundary they created and worked to maintain—all the ranting against "folkum" music, or fake folk music, for example, in the pages of the *Little Sandy Review* and even in the national press—gave young people a way to escape mass culture. Even the most casual fan, listening to Harry Belafonte (dubbed Belephony by the purists) on the radio, believed she was stepping outside American life at mid-century. But more dedicated revivalists also learned that they could take a more serious step outside of American mass culture, that they could "discover," the making and the finding all mashed up together, an alternative. Maybe, the revival suggested, American mass culture was not so monolithic as the word "mass" implied.[37]

The paradox, of course, was not only that the folk music revival revived earlier commercial music as folk music, but that the revival itself was commercialized. As Joan Baez told a reporter in 1961, "The public may demand this and that, but if you don't want to give in, you don't have to. I just don't think in terms of being well known or not well known." A folk music concert promoter said in response: "If she keeps on feeling and acting this way, she'll make more and more money, no matter how genuinely uninterested she is in such irrelevancies. Her kind of audience must believe that she is entirely truthful . . . With these kids, it's a different kind of show business. To be commercial, you have to be non-commercial." The folk music revival was simultaneously a rebellion against American commercialized mass culture and a part of it.[38]

The folk gave revivalists a way to separate themselves from the pervasive middle-class character of mid-century America. In all of these versions of romanticizing the folk, people of one class (and sometimes race as well) used the cultural forms and resources of people more marginalized and isolated, poorer, than themselves. Even as folk revivals, on some level, celebrated the art and lives of poor people, then, these movements also highlighted the divisions between people. They crossed some boundaries and courted sameness in order, ultimately, to strengthen other boundaries. In the late nineteenth century, educated and wealthy whites cultivated an interest in folk ballads to separate themselves from the many Americans who preferred Tin Pan Alley hits and coon songs. The fans and musicians of the left-wing folk song revival of the Depression era positioned themselves, with their participatory sing-alongs and protest songs, against the popular mass culture of Hollywood movies and big band swing. "Success and folk music are, by rights, at opposite extremes of the American spectrum," Irwin Silber, cofounder and editor of *Sing Out!*, wrote in 1964. "Folk music, after all, is the voice and expression of generations of ordinary folks who were on familiar terms with hard work, poverty, hunger, and homemade, handmade culture. They kept their art alive outside the pale of professional show business and despite the impact of successive Establishments. Success, on the other hand, is the 'American dream,' the middle class confusion of illusion and reality." Folk revivalists, no matter their individual intentions, set themselves apart symbolically from the American middle class. And this act, in turn, made these revivals politically promiscuous. The folk could be a medium for being anti-middle class without being explicitly aristocratic. It could also be medium for invoking left ideas without using overt ideology. Playing both top and bottom against the muddled mass middle of American life, folk revivals could go either direction, toward the right or the left.[39]

But revivalists did not become the folk. Moving to the mountains or the Delta, learning to play the banjo or the guitar, wearing string ties and vests, beards or workingmen's clothes, long hair, coarse skirts, and sandals—none of these acts stripped young educated Americans of their class psychology, of their sense that they mattered in the world. Folk fans accepted few limits on their own self-invention. They believed transcendence—escape from the limits of history—was possible. Again, revivalists confused illusion and reality. Playing the top and bottom against the middle, revivalists positioned themselves as a cultural, if not material, elite. They built their coalition on the new definition of authenticity—emotions, raw, real, and shared. The folk music revival of the late fifties and sixties rehabilitated American individualism by re-imagining class status as a cultural choice.

The possibilities of transformation and transcendence, however, moved in two very different directions. For musicians who learned to play folk music in the Ozarks or the Appalachian Mountains or the Delta, the revival gave them a new audience, another way to make a living, another self, "the folk," to perform. In the twenties and thirties, the blues had given musicians and fans a view of transformation, change, a way out of poverty, a way up. The goal was not authenticity but a better life, richer in terms of dollars or experience, less isolated, more pleasurable. Each person made his own call. But the new psychological understanding of authenticity only worked if revivalists could believe they knew the folk. The folk, whether black or white, must give up transformation. They must stand still. They must be knowable, down to their emotional core. The fact that some of the folk still lived, the fact that these people were supposedly unchanged in any meaningful sense by the postwar world, meant that the revivalists too could go back, could travel to a simpler world, a place without the bomb and the cold war and the corporate life, a world of innocence. Revivalists—insiders wanting out—allied themselves with outsiders, the poor and the oppressed, the victims of racial discrimination. What the revivalists got in return for giving up their belonging was some of the innocence of people without the agency to be responsible for the present. What they got was a new morality.[40]

Black Music, the Folk, and the Civil Rights Movement

No single group of people evoked this simpler world and this new morality better than southern blacks. The folk music revival and the mass movement phase of the southern struggle for civil rights reached the peak of their influence simultaneously in the middle of the sixties. Young white middle-class Americans from outside the South often learned about the southern civil rights movement in a context framed by the revival. Folk music taught them to love the folk just as people who fit the folk image created a successful and growing political movement. Southern civil rights activists were often black. Some of them were poor. They came from places few middle-class white kids could find on a map. And they sang.

Music became a central tool of the civil rights movement in the South because activists found that singing together connected people, gave them courage, and aurally marked their claim to spaces segregation denied them. Outside the southern movement and its local contexts, however, the sounds and pictures of singing protesters helped produce and circulate an alternative image of the South as a place where African Americans preserved a distinct and "authentic" rural culture. If the South was the place that racism flourished, it was also the place, paradoxically, where "real" black folk survived. The idea of southern black people as the folk helped broaden support for the southern movement by attracting many folk music fans to the cause. The folk music revival suggested real music and real morality went together. The momentary merging of the revival and the southern civil rights struggle gave the vague coalition of the alienated—the children of plenty and the other Americans—a powerful and concrete form.[41]

No one did more to fuse the folk music revival, the civil rights movement, and the idea of southern blacks as the folk than Pete Seeger. For Seeger and other folksingers with connections to the earlier Old Left folk song movement, songs about contemporary events and politics were folk songs because "the people" had always "created songs about things happening around them—hard times, the struggles of unions, peace and war." The Freedom Songs of the civil rights movement, in this way of thinking, were authentic folk songs, songs that linked the old singing traditions to the present struggles.[42]

Sometime in the first half of 1962, the black attorney Len Holt wrote Jim Forman, executive secretary of SNCC: "We have sang the song 'We Shall Overcome' so much that it seems that by the mere force of the song[']s timbre the theme is coming true. What am I talking about? Simply this, Pete is concerned enough to give SNCC a helping hand, a helping voice, and a helping banjo . . . There is a need for a bard of the Southern protest movement, an entertainer whose life reflects the ideals they are singing for or portraying. I hope that the Pete Seeger tour will push some SNCC person in that direction." This kind of cultural program "could serve the same function for the movement as the Jubilee Singers did for Negro education."[43]

Beginning in the 1870s, the Jubilee Singers had traveled the nation and Europe, singing "authentic" Negro spirituals polished and adapted to appeal to audiences more accustomed to hearing classical music, in order to raise money for Fisk University. The Fisk students had not grown up singing these songs—they were largely part of the upwardly aspiring black middle class in the South that worked hard to distance itself from behaviors and forms of cultural expression linked to slavery. But the Jubilee Singers and other groups inspired by their success sang right over any easy distinction between interpreting a historical form of black cultural expression and playing music that appealed to rich white people by confirming their folk image of blacks. In fact, explorations of black folk culture throughout the twentieth century displayed this tension, whatever the politics of the revivalists or audiences.[44]

Seeger, like the Jubilee Singers, would be performing in a folk tradition that he had not grown up with but that he had self-consciously learned. The Jubilee Singers, however, were black. Schooled by white supremacy and the long history of minstrelsy, most whites did not need much imagination to see these middle-class college students as the literal embodiment of rural, pre-modern black folk. In 1962, however, SNCC was broke and in no position to turn away help, and Seeger was popular. "If I Had a Hammer," a song he had written, was a top hit for Peter, Paul, and Mary on the *Billboard* charts. And Seeger, who had played a benefit in Birmingham for Martin Luther King Jr. and the Montgomery Improvement Association back in 1956, had a deep interest in civil rights. As the press reported on the growing role of music in the movement, Seeger could hardly contain his excitement. Here at last was a successor to the union drives of the thirties, a movement that combined folk music and leftist politics at a grassroots level. Seeger wanted to be a part of it.[45]

That fall, the man Alan Lomax called "America's greatest folksinger" played a series of benefits for SNCC across the South. In Texas, Mississippi, Alabama, and Georgia, he performed at historically black colleges, where informal SNCC support groups tried to raise volunteers and funds. At Miles College, the student council joined SNCC in sponsoring the Pete Seeger Freedom Concert, and the Alabama Christian Movement for Human Rights endorsed the event: "Come and hear Pete Seeger as he sings about the Freedom Riders and the sit-ins." SNCC heavily promoted the Seeger concert at Morehouse College in Atlanta, writing to ministers, past supporters, and local folk music fans: "You, no doubt, are aware . . . of the tremendous power of music to convey the deepest and most fundamental convictions of people. These mass movements for social justice obviously are expressions of the most elemental concerns of the people of our time." An integrated audience turned out for the event.[46]

Still, Pete Seeger often called his concert at a mass meeting in Albany, Georgia, that October the worst performance of his life. Activists there had invited Seeger to come and share his years of experience joining his music and his politics. He remembered arriving alone at the church as Georgia State Patrol cars circled the building like buzzards, waiting for trouble. A crowd of jeering whites, some of them armed with lead pipes, stood outside the church. Seeger was scared, he recalled, as he grabbed his gear and went inside. The meeting had already started, and the air was hot, sticky, and full of song: "And before I'll be a slave/ I'll be buried in my grave/ And go home to my lord/ and be free." Bertha Gober led the next song, a commemoration of the murder of civil rights worker Herbert Lee, which she had adapted herself from a traditional hymn: "We been 'buked/ and we been scorned/ We been lied to, sure's you're born/ But we'll never,/ No we'll never turn back." As the meeting progressed, people stood up and described how they had been harassed and beaten trying to register to vote. After a while, the minister introduced Seeger.[47]

From the start, Seeger made all the wrong choices. Many African American Christians saw banjos as secular instruments, good for accompanying minstrel songs and rowdy dances, definitely not acceptable in church. But there was Seeger, at the front of the sanctuary, singing and playing "If I Had a Hammer" for all he was worth. Few joined in. Next he sang the union version of "Hold On," but his verses, his rhythm, and his key all clashed with the way his audience tried to sing along. People stirred in their seats, confused, and Seeger, worried that they were tired, launched into a long ballad: "There I was, repeating the same unrhythmic melody over and over with little or no variation . . . The story was so ancient and so unfamiliar as to have little meaning to the listeners. I sang with a deadpan expression purposefully not to detract from the words. And this only made the melody seem more boring." After muddling though more songs, Pete finally played "We Shall Overcome," and the audience at last joined in and sang along.[48]

Seeger's mistake had been to try to educate the audience on the history of left politics and folk song, on how in the days of the Old Left union organizers had adapted hymns for use in their own struggles. These people in Albany did not care. They were right in the middle of their own fight—one thousand protesters had already been arrested and jailed. More would face arrest in the days and weeks to come. How was this skinny middle-aged white radical going to teach them anything when he did not even know how to play their songs?[49]

Despite his reception in the Albany church and on historically black campuses, where most students preferred rhythm and blues to folk, Seeger was popular on historically white campuses outside the South and at folk clubs in New York, Chicago, San Francisco, and other cities. He saw all his concerts, whether they were SNCC benefits or not, as chances to educate folk music fans about the civil rights movement. "We'll tell your heroic story everywhere we possibly can," Seeger wrote Bob Moses and others in Alabama's Kilby State Prison in May 1963. "We'll sing it, we'll speak it until the whole country knows about it. You guys are working for the freedom of our whole country." Seeger might not sing the songs as well as that congregation in Albany, but he was mobile—he went on a world tour in the second half of 1963—and he was at the height of his popularity. "We Shall Overcome" and other Freedom Songs became, for people who heard Seeger perform them in concert or on records, folk songs simply because he was singing them. Seeger made the music of the civil rights movement part of the folk music revival. That, in turn, connected the civil rights movement, especially the young activists of SNCC, to a whole new group of potential supporters and volunteers, young white folk fans. But Seeger also understood the power of authenticity, of performances of folk music by "the folk" themselves. "Don't forget to make sure that the Freedom

Singers or some group will be coming to the Newport Folk Festival the last week in July," he wrote Jim Forman in 1963.[50]

The Freedom Singers had their own link to Albany. Sometime in late 1961 or early 1962, folksinger Guy Carawan had gone there and recorded an audio documentary of the movement. *Freedom in the Air*, originally sold by SNCC to raise money for the Albany Movement, was later released on Folkways Records. Like Seeger, Carawan believed the music of the movement had the power to make folk music fans into civil rights supporters. "I am convinced now after playing the Albany documentary for a number of good-sized audiences of people who are not in the South and are uninformed about what goes on there that it can really move and exhilarate them," he wrote to Forman in May 1962. Forman wrote back in November that SNCC had formed its own "group of Freedom Singers." The Seeger tour had not "raised that much money." Why not send out a group with a direct connection to the movement and the songs?[51]

SNCC's group had its genesis in Albany that fall, the same fall Seeger toured the South, when Cordell Reagon began to pull together a changing lineup of musicians to travel and perform Freedom Songs. Forman encouraged him. The Freedom Singers, SNCC's top administrator believed, could become a powerful tool for fund-raising, and SNCC desperately needed funds. Rutha Harris and Bernice Johnson (who would become Bernice Johnson Reagon in 1963) were right there in Albany. Reagon had met the talented Charles Neblett in the Cairo Movement. Carver "Chico" Neblett, his younger brother, and Bertha Gober also sometimes joined them. In October, the Freedom Singers performed a few songs in a civil rights benefit in Chicago, the Gospel Sing for Freedom, that failed to raise much money for the cause. Still, people who heard the group there praised their work. Their formal debut occurred on November 11, 1962, when they played with Pete Seeger at his benefit concert at Morehouse.[52]

Johnson, then just nineteen, met Pete Seeger in the home of the Southern Christian Leadership Conference's Andrew Young the day of the concert and talked to him about her interest in singing. By then, Johnson had been expelled from Albany State and joined SNCC's full-time staff. Seeger told Johnson about the Almanac Singers, the group he, Woody Guthrie, and others had formed in the forties to sing folk and labor songs to raise support and funds for the union movement. Inspired, Johnson envisioned the Freedom Singers touring the country performing the same function for the civil rights movement. After Pete left Atlanta, Johnson called his wife, Toshi Seeger, and asked her to set up a tour for the Freedom Singers. No one knew better than Toshi, who had been booking Pete for fifteen years, how to put folk music to work for a cause. Until the Seegers left the country on a world tour in August 1963, Toshi served as the Freedom Singers' unpaid manager, giving SNCC the benefit of her connections and fund-raising knowledge and connecting the group with sympathetic activists and journalists across the country. Toshi sold the Freedom Singers to the remaining Old Left audiences that had loved Leadbelly and Woody Guthrie in the past and the growing audiences of young folk music fans that loved Peter, Paul, and Mary and Pete Seeger.[53]

In the folk music revival, "great" meant "authentic," defined either as being a representative of the folk, a traditionalist, or as perfectly copying or representing the musical style of the folk, a revivalist. From the perspective of SNCC leaders, Johnson, Reagon, Harris, and Neblett were authentic because they had worked and suffered in Albany and other SNCC projects—they had been expelled from school, arrested, beaten, and jailed. "The primary importance of this music," the Freedom Singers' earliest press materials argued, was "not the tune or the beat, but the words and the desperation with which they are sung." For the larger folk music world, the Freedom Singers were authentic not only because of their movement activities—rare was the press release that did not mention their arrests and time in jail—but also because of their song choices and their performance styles. As music critic Robert Shelton wrote in the *New York Times*: "The unaccompanied voices, the rhythmic drive, and their sense of conviction put the Freedom Singers in the top level of American folk groups." "If folk music is an expression of the forces at work in the people," music critic Ralph Gleason wrote in the *San Francisco Chronicle*, "this group is as authentic an American folk singing group as ever walked the earth. They are real, they write their own material and above all, they can sing . . . There is a 'mystique' about SNCC."

Even SNCC staffers fell under their sway. As white staffer Dorothy Zellner remembered, the Freedom Singers "practiced in the SNCC office and when they sang, it was impossible to do any work. You just sat there transported." Most SNCC people, she recalled, were "really musical"—people sang as they worked in the national office, and singing played an essential role in the periodic national staff meetings. Still, Zellner suggested, "I don't know if the SNCC people really knew we were in the presence of one of the greatest singing groups of the century. Peter Seeger probably knew and Bob Dylan. But I don't know if we knew they were really that great . . . They were just real—no orchestral backup, no [instrumental] arrangements. They were just extremely hip."[54]

For white middle-class folk fans, the Freedom Singers were folksingers because they sang versions of old-time songs like "Pick a Bale o' Cotton" as well as protest songs like "We Shall Not Be Moved" on their album *We Shall Overcome*, sold to raise money for SNCC. They were folksingers because 1963 was the height of the folk music revival, and they sang a cappella. And they were folksingers because they were black. Their race and their politics made them traditionalists—actual representatives of folk communities—even as most of them were in fact former black college students, more like revivalists.[55]

The Freedom Singers, performing for mostly white audiences outside the South, raised a lot more money than Seeger had trying to sing for mostly black audiences inside the South. In their first tour, from February to June 1963, the group played sets at the Club 47 in Cambridge, Community Church in Boston, Judson Memorial Church in New York, a series of reform synagogues in Connecticut, and the Newark YMCA. They joined Pete Seeger onstage at his concert at Civic Auditorium in Chicago. They played benefits sponsored by young, mostly white middle-class Christian groups—the University Christian Association at Penn State, the University Christian Fellowship at the Storrs campus of the University of Connecticut, and the Christian Family Movement in Chicago. One area council of the National YMCA alone set up about ten of the 1963 college dates in states like Wisconsin, Minnesota, and Iowa, and they played concerts sponsored by other campus groups at colleges and universities including Bucknell University, West Virginia University, Swarthmore, Ohio Wesleyan, Miami University (Ohio), Iowa State, and the University of Missouri.

Future tours would concentrate on college campuses outside the South. Over the next three years, with an ever changing lineup of musicians, the Freedom Singers played everywhere from elite universities like Yale and Columbia to liberal colleges like Reed, Oberlin, and Smith and big state universities like the University of Illinois and Ohio State. "Our real purpose is to carry the story of the movement to the North," Charles Neblett told a student newspaper in 1963. "Newspapers and UPI won't give the real story and SNCC had to find another way to get it out." Descriptions of concerts and reviews of SNCC records circulated SNCC's name and reports of its activism in college newspapers, music magazines, and national publications like the *New York Times*.[56]

The Freedom Singers became an essential part of SNCC's effort, beginning in 1962, to create a northern white fund-raising network. Dinky Romilly and Betty Garmen, white SNCC Atlanta staff members charged with coordinating the new SNCC offices in Chicago, New York, and elsewhere and with creating Friends of SNCC support groups outside the South, quickly saw how the Freedom Singers might generate interest in and money for the organization among white middle-class folk fans. While some politically active students would come to meetings to hear the southern student activists SNCC sent on tour, campus Christian action groups like the Dartmouth Christian Union and Friends of SNCC groups like University SNCC in Berkeley could tap into the growing campus interest in folk music by hosting the Freedom Singers. More students turned out for concerts than speeches. In 1963, the money began to pour in, just as the Freedom Singers began to perform around the country. In 1963 alone, their solo concerts and larger benefit events at which they appeared with other performers raised about one third of SNCC's funds for the year, approximately $93,000. Presenting the Freedom Singers as genuine singing black folk created an image of SNCC as the most "authentic" civil rights organization and attracted young white liberal supporters.[57]

Press materials certainly promoted the Freedom Singers as "the folk." Under a photo of a young black man looking out a barred window and striped by its shadows, the caption reads, "The songs the Freedom Singers sing come from the country churches, the stockades, the prisons and the dusty roads of the South." "Freedom singers are the freedom movement for everyone in the movement sings the freedom songs," another promotional sheet announced. "They sing them in the field; they sing them at rallies and conferences, and they sing them when they leave the South, bringing to others the spirit of freedom. All civil rights workers, all persons who work for justice are freedom singers . . . The Freedom Singers have traveled widely across the country, raising the spirits of Americans everywhere, giving them a feeling of what it means to break the bonds of oppression." Indeed, the letters, college-paper press clippings, and even bad student poetry that groups hosting the musicians sent SNCC afterward suggested that their audiences saw and heard the Freedom Singers as missionaries coming to tell the outside world about the folk and their fight for civil rights.[58]

At SNCC benefits and concerts, the Freedom Singers described the story of the fight for equality in local movements in places like Albany and then sang Freedom Songs. Singing along became a way for audience members to share the emotions of the struggle, to hear the sounds of the jail and the mass meeting, to feel the power of the picket and the march. "Everywhere they sang," Dottie Zellner remembered, "people jumped up and wanted to go south." Not everyone who heard them, of course, could drop everything and go. But singing was a way to participate, to experience the movement and not just financially support it. The Freedom Singers, Bernice Johnson Reagon argued, made "people who were not on the scene feel the intensity of what was happening in the South." Somehow, the Freedom Singers' records never quite did it, and SNCC never made much money selling them. Only singing along in person took people there. The trip did not require white college students to quit school or work and live on a SNCC salary, a pittance the organization only sometimes even paid. It did not require them to confront their racist or worried parents and friends or to face being beaten, gassed, kicked, arrested, and even killed. Singing together enabled people to feel the music. Deep in the heart, singing was not an argument or an ideology. It was a feeling. It was the tap of the foot and the leap of faith. While some people were inspired to go south and work, all a person had to do to "feel" like part of the movement was to sing along.[59]

It did not matter that the sources and the contours of the alienation that brought people to hear the Freedom Singers concerts were different from those of the performers. Being denied a decent-paying job or the vote was not the same thing as rejecting the vision of the good life society promoted, but for a moment, in the singing, these differences did not matter. Certainly the opponents of integration had no trouble seeing what these groups had in common. Someone sent the Atlanta office a copy of a SNCC fund-raising ad that ran in the *New York Times*. Across the text in thick capital letters he had written "NIGGER LOVERS." In the corner of the ad, over the coupon with SNCC's address made for cutting out and sending in with a contribution, he had written "Beatnicks." The manager of the radio station at Bob Jones University returned SNCC's "cheap trashy record entitled 'The Freedom Singers Sing Freedom Now!'" with its "obnoxious music" and accused Mercury Records of "crusading for a few beatniks." Beatniks, folk music fans, supporters of equal rights—what was the difference?[60]

The association between folk music and the civil rights movement made support for civil rights in the South popular among many middle-class white kids—another way for them to express their rebellion against the world of their parents. *Time* explored the rising popularity of "integration songs" among folk music fans: "In a cocktail lounge in Ogunquit, Maine," *Time* reported, "a college girl shouts out 'Sing something about integration.'" The fact that folksingers supported the civil rights movement helped turn many folk fans into movement supporters too. Some of those college girls asking for integration songs would go hear the Freedom Singers. Some would send money. Some would join northern Friends of SNCC support groups. Some might even go south themselves.[61]

In July 1963, SNCC was at Newport to take advantage of the power of the folk music revival. The Freedom Singers played an early set on Friday night, before returning to the stage for the all-star sing-along. Festival audiences crowded SNCC's photo exhibit—a throwback to the presentations of FSA photographs at farm fairs across the South. And on Saturday night, after the concerts ended, Baez and SNCC organizers led more than five hundred people on a march through the town of Newport. The march ended in a rally, where the Freedom Singers sang again and Jim Forman asked the audience to join SNCC a month later at the March on Washington. The day before that event, Harry Belafonte chartered and paid for a plane to fly the Freedom Singers from California, where they were touring, back to Washington. Their last-minute inclusion on the program, along with long-scheduled folk stars like Baez and Peter, Paul, and Mary, suggested that March organizers too recognized the role the "real" folk could play in attracting white supporters to the cause.[62]

The folk music revival taught white students—and folk fans were mostly white—to love blacks, especially rural southerners, as the folk, as the real outsiders. These were the people who created the Negro spirituals and blues that whites like Baez and Dylan sang. Mississippi John Hurt and Son House were the folk in the flesh, never mind their actual histories. And so were the Freedom Singers, with their pure voices and their real politics. Folk music concerts and Freedom Singers benefits gave some whites the South as they wanted to see it, a place of good and evil, black and white, where innocence fought against hatred and violence. Listening to the music, white audience members could connect with the "authenticity" of the folk and renew their own innocence. They were not responsible for the evil down there. They were on the side of morality and right.[63]

Never mind the messy protests the Congress of Racial Equality (CORE) was busy sponsoring in suburban Boston and all over New York City, activities that occurred as SNCC held concerts in these cities. Never mind the local movement in Philadelphia. Folk music and the romance of the outsider pushed white young people from outside the South to care about the fight there. As longtime civil rights activist Virginia Durr noted in a letter to a friend in 1965, "The South and the Negro has become rather a fashionable cause as you can . . . make a big splash by spending a few weeks in the South, when the people in Harlem also need help very badly, but the South is more glamorous." While SNCC was carrying out the most radical civil rights work in that region, the organization's use of the romance of the folk and the Freedom Singers to raise funds for those programs helped some white northern liberals ignore the organizing work under way right outside those concert halls.[64]

The romance of southern blacks as the folk, as authentic outsiders, as different, a romance circulating in folk music and elsewhere, helped advance

Joan Baez and Bob Dylan perform together at the 1963 Newport Folk Festival. *Associated Press*.

the long African American freedom struggle in the early sixties. It appealed to white folksingers, folk fans, and northern college students, and it generated positive national press. Once again, music as a cultural form helped prove to some whites that African Americans had a culture. Some civil rights activists, with varying degrees of self-consciousness, decided to use this romance—they could not have stopped it if they wanted to—in their fight for equality.

Romanticizing southern blacks as outsiders just might, paradoxically, help end African Americans' status as outsiders, as people left out of American economic prosperity and American democracy. In this way of thinking, African Americans deserved equality because they were better than other Americans. But dependent as it was on the idea of black difference, of blacks as more authentic and real than other Americans, the romance of the outsider could not help generate equality on an individual, psychological level. It also had little to offer African Americans in the urban North, where people did not live in shacks and farm for whites and did not need to march and sing to get the vote, where people were not the folk. The greatest beneficiaries, in the end, were those white middle-class young people who used their attraction to blacks as the folk to transform themselves.

Bob Dylan and the Magic of Transformation

In the early 1920s, a black pianist and composer and a white arranger published a pamphlet called *How to Sing and Play the Blues like the Phonograph and Stage Artists*. It covered all the basics, "blue notes," "minor keys," "breaks," and "wailings, moanings and croonings." The music would not take too long to learn, the pamphlet insisted. Just don't forget to "play the role of the oppressed or depressed." Bob Dylan probably never read it, but when he came to New York City in 1961, he figured out on his own how to play the role by copying Woody Guthrie.[65]

Woody Guthrie's music was not widely known around 1959 when Dylan first heard the musician and songwriter playing and singing solo on a set of 78s. There had been a concert in New York City in 1956 to raise money for Guthrie's children because their dad had become too sick to play. A grand reunion for the old left-wing folk community, the Almanac Singers and the old People's Songs folks and others, the concert put the full range of Guthrie's songwriting on display and ended with a crying Pete Seeger leading the whole hall in a cheering rendition of "This Land Is Your Land." But Red baiting had discredited the once popular musician. For Dylan, listening to Guthrie was the most formative moment in his young career. He still remembered the impact of those Guthrie records half a century after he first heard them. Woody was "so poetic and tough and rhythmic. There was so much intensity, and his voice was like a stiletto . . . His mannerisms, the way everything just rolled off his tongue, it all just about knocked me down. It was like the record player itself had just picked me up and flung me across the room."[66]

In high school in Hibbing, Minnesota, in the 1950s, Robert Zimmerman had fallen in love with the romance of the outsider. He listened to Hank Williams, Elvis Presley, and rhythm and blues, watched Marlon Brando and James Dean movies, wore his hair long, and played in rock and roll bands. And as soon as he graduated, he moved "out of the wilderness" of rural Minnesota to Minneapolis, where he enrolled at the University of Minnesota in the fall of 1959.

Minneapolis had its own bohemian enclave, full of real-life rebels, right next to campus. For Zimmerman, Dinkytown was magic. At the Ten O'Clock Scholar coffeehouse, young white men like him played the blues. There, he met Dave Morton, a local musician who not only played folk standards but also wrote his own songs about civil rights to old folk melodies, and Dave Whitaker, an intellectual and political radical who read Henry Miller and the Beats. Whitaker had spent part of the late 1950s on a kind of bohemian world tour. Checking off odd characters and music scenes the way other travelers visit cathedrals and monuments, he met William S. Burroughs in Paris and Allen Ginsberg and Jack Kerouac in San Francisco and hung out with musicians in London's skiffle scene and Greenwich Village's folk scene. Whitaker introduced Zimmerman to pot and gave him a copy of Guthrie's out-of-print memoir, *Bound for Glory*.[67]

In 1960, Zimmerman learned the art of transformation. In the spring, he began playing local venues like the Purple Onion Pizza Parlor. Sometime that year he read *On the Road* and later insisted the book "changed my life like it changed everyone else's." In the summer, he copied the adventures of Jack Kerouac's semi-fictional characters Sal Paradise and Dean Moriarty and hitchhiked to Denver. He ended up playing in nearby Central City for tourists looking for the Wild West. Like other young folk musicians, he began playing Guthrie songs, but he also adopted Guthrie's left politics and his hobo style and speech: work shirts, worn jeans, few baths, and bad grammar. In October 1960, when Robbie Zimmerman got his own gig at the Ten O'Clock Scholar and the owner asked him his name for the bill, he replied, "Bob Dylan."[68]

Being a college student did not fit the Guthrie model, and in December 1960 Dylan left school. College, Dylan later explained, was "a cop-out from life, . . . from experience." Like Guthrie or Kerouac, he needed to be out on the road or at sea in the big city. In January, Dylan arrived in New York "wearing a pair of dusty dungarees, holey shoes, [and] a corduroy Huck Finn cap" and carrying "a beat-up Gibson guitar and two squeaky harmonicas." He headed straight for the Greenwich Village coffeehouses. Cafe Wha? was holding its weekly hootenanny, the folk music revival's version of those Popular Front sing-alongs, a song swap where anybody who stopped by could play. Dylan performed a few of what he called his "folky" songs. The next day, he took the bus to Greystone Hospital in New Jersey to meet Woody Guthrie.[69]

The move to New York City gave Dylan, like a thousand kids from the sticks before him, the chance to remake himself completely. Israel "Izzy" Young, the founder of the Folklore Center on MacDougal Street in the West Village, a small, second-floor hybrid music store, concert venue, and archive where many musicians and folk fans hung out, kept records in his diary in the fall of 1961 of his conversations with Dylan. Young talked about folk music and played songs for Dylan from his vast collection of 78s, sides like blues musician Big Bill Broonzy's "Somebody's Got to Go." Dylan in return talked about himself, using the opportunity to work on manufacturing a folk past. He told Izzy he was born in Duluth in 1941 and went for a while to the University of Minnesota. About the rest of his past, he lied. He had lived, he told Young and others, in Iowa, South Dakota, Colorado, Wyoming, Kansas, North Dakota, and New Mexico. At ten, he picked up guitar and piano and played in carnivals. Four or five years ago, Dylan told Young, a blind Chicago street singer named Arvella Gray had taught him the blues. While he had written "hillbilly" songs for Carl Perkins in the past, he now wrote "Talking Blues on Topical things." In Young's descriptions, Dylan was both defensive and proud of his personal style. "The less hair on my head, [the] more hair inside my head," he told Young in a line he would often repeat over the next few years. "Let my hair grow long to be wise and free to think." In Cheyenne, Dylan claimed, he learned "cowboy styles" from "real cowboys." Dylan did, however, have a source closer at hand. He told Young he had come to New York to meet Woody Guthrie, and he visited the folksinger often in his first year in New York. Picking up Guthrie's jerks and tics and odd speech, Dylan did not seem to realize he was mimicking the symptoms of Huntington's disease, a hereditary disorder then crippling the older man, a fact well known in New York folk circles.[70]

Amazingly, Dylan not only copied Guthrie's identity. He somehow absorbed Guthrie's way with identity, what Guthrie before him had learned from blues and hillbilly musicians—about playing with personas and the power of transformation. In their music, Ma Rainey and Memphis Minnie, two singers Dylan later remembered listening to and loving in the early sixties, could, at least temporarily, be anybody they chose. Performance did not always have to stop at the edge of the stage and the end of the song. Fans did not care who early blues stars really had been—they wanted to see who they were onstage, who they could become. Guthrie had not been an Okie, a Dust Bowl refugee, when he became popular playing protest songs in the early forties, just as he had not been a cowboy when he played country music on the radio in the 1930s. He became those people in his songs and in the articles he wrote for a West Coast Communist Party newspaper.[71]

When Guthrie came to New York in 1940, however, he faced a dilemma. Transformation, the play with masks and lyrics and styles that animated his music, was at odds with the political ideology and the image of the worker central to the Popular Front–era folk song revival. His music sounded "folk" to the folk music enthusiasts and leftists who first championed him in California and then in New York. The leftists, Communists mostly but also socialists and others, were concerned more about his politics than about his musical style. The fact that, beginning in the late thirties, Guthrie wore his political radicalism on his sleeve was good enough for them. In New York, he developed an easy integrationism in keeping with the Popular Front vision, playing and staying with blues musicians Leadbelly, Sonny Terry, and Brownie McGhee, African American stars of the Popular Front–inspired folk song revival. On one notable occasion, he even overturned the buffet at a banquet gig when he was told he would not be able to eat with the musicians he had just played with because they were black. But the leftists wanted him to have a working-class background, to be part of the great proletariat, to be a real live member of the folk. The scholarly folk music crowd wanted Guthrie to be one of the folk in order to see the songs Guthrie was writing as real folk music, as the past in the present, the old folk creativity surviving the flood of commercialism and offering an alternative to it. So Guthrie took the minstrel model of identity, the transformation, play, and self-invention, beyond the edge of the stage and out into the world. His best-selling 1945 memoir anchored his act, creating a romantic image of "a dusty little man wandering around the country with a guitar slung over his shoulder, making up songs that helped people to understand themselves and encouraged them to fight back." Guthrie had succeeded not only in sounding like but also in being the folk. He performed both the music and the identity.[72]

Dylan probably did not learn this magic directly in his visits with Guthrie. The young musician would have had no way to know the long history of Guthrie's life. Guthrie certainly did not give out the facts—he used them instead like phrases and melodies from old songs, as useful materials with which to build something new. Dylan must have brought some sense of how making music offered the possibility of transformation with him to New York. He had listened to early rock and roll growing up and to rhythm and blues and hillbilly music in Minneapolis. Minnesota might not have been on the main touring circuits for these acts, but Dylan must have seen some country and rock and roll musicians on television. Minstrelsy's playing with characters, its focus on transformation, still haunted these recordings and performances. Dylan also picked up the romance of rebellion floating around the youthful edges of fifties culture, from *Catcher in the Rye* (he later claimed he dreamed about playing Holden Caulfield in a movie version of Salinger's novel) to *On the Road* and the Beats. Guthrie's music, with its evocation of a folk past outside of modern time and a working-class leftist politics completely different from the middle-class mid-century present, offered Dylan a vision of an alternative life. "Woody's songs were having that big an effect on me," Dylan later recalled, "an influence on every move that I made, what I ate and how I dressed, who I wanted to know, who I didn't."[73]

Dylan was not the first young folk revivalist to channel Guthrie. Ramblin' Jack Elliott, previously Buck Elliott, had also started life with another name, Elliot Adnopoz. Elliott was older than Dylan and had actually traveled and played with Guthrie, learning his music and his style firsthand. Dylan, however, possessed a lot more talent. He had also learned, by the time he started to get noticed in New York, to play Guthrie, not just in the sense that Elliot did but also in the way that Mike Seeger played a folk song. He absorbed the texture and mood as well as the more obvious external manifestations and reproduced the hobo, Okie, traveling-man-with-his-guitar, leftist voice-of-the-people performance that was Guthrie for Dylan's own place and time. Dylan began to write songs about the events of his day and connect himself to the current left cause, that equivalent of union organizing in the thirties and forties, the civil rights movement.[74]

Just as Woody Guthrie had, Dylan solved the dilemma of the contradiction between the self-invention that made the music magical and the folk music revivalists' obsession with authenticity by inventing his own folk autobiography. While Guthrie had actually ridden in boxcars, slept in hobo camps, and met working men at union meetings all over the country, Dylan read about and listened to Guthrie describing these experiences. Dylan performed another performer—Guthrie—performing the Popular Front's vision of rural poor people as the folk. He copied a copy of a fantasy.

Young was certainly not the only person Dylan lied to in 1961 about his past. All his friends from this period remember different versions of these stories and that Dylan had told everyone he was an orphan. The journalist Robert Shelton saw through the act from the start. In his influential *New York Times* review of Dylan's performance at Gerde's Folk City in September 1961, Shelton wrote that Dylan's voice was "anything but pretty," a conscious effort "to recapture the rude beauty of a southern field hand musing in melody on his back porch. All the 'husk and bark' are left on his notes and searing intensity pervades his songs." Dylan, then, in Shelton's description, sounded like the folk—like Guthrie playing an old hillbilly tune. Yet Shelton did not believe that Dylan had any more in common with farm laborers than a love of music. "Resembling a cross between a choir boy and a beatnik," the performer, Shelton noted politely, was "vague about his antecedents and birthplace, but it matters less where he has been than where he is going." Sheldon was using an understanding of authenticity as a perfect copy, as, in the case of music, the aural fidelity of a contemporary musician to the sound of musicians now dead.[75]

But Dylan understood the folk music fans who made up his first audience better than Shelton did. More people would buy the music if they could buy the authenticity—defined not as sounding like the folk but as being of the folk—of the man. In February 1962, a little over a year after Dylan moved to New York, Columbia released his first album, *Bob Dylan*. Dylan's takes on folk songs fill the record, which includes only two of his own compositions, "Talking New York," a description of his first days in Greenwich Village, and "Song to Woody." This Guthrie tribute, the first good song Dylan wrote, fused Dylan's lyrics with the melody of Guthrie's own song "1913 Massacre," an account of the deaths of seventy-three Michigan children, trampled when armed men hired by the mining company locked all the doors at the Christmas party for the miners' kids and yelled "Fire!" Dylan's lyrics evoke the man who wrote songs about the murder of working people:

> I'm out here a thousand miles from my home,
> Walkin' a road other men have gone down.
> I'm seein' your world of people and things,
> Your paupers and peasants and princes and kings.
>
> Hey, hey, Woody Guthrie, I wrote you a song
> 'Bout a funny ol' World that's a comin' along.
> Seems sick an' it's hungry, it's tired an' it's torn,
> It looks like it's a dyin' an' it's hardly been born.

Dylan's "Talking New York" used Guthrie's talking blues style, a little-known musical form he had borrowed from blues musicians, to narrate his own arrival in New York City as the Woody of his day. The train becomes a subway as Dylan, guitar in tow, arrives at a coffeehouse: "Got up on stage to sing and play,/ Man there said, 'Come back some other day,/ You sound like a hillbilly;/ We want folk singers here.'" The song even quotes Guthrie: "Now a very great man once said/ That some people rob you with a fountain pen." Unlike his album, Dylan's performances in New York, Boston, and Chicago at the time were full of his own songs, all Guthrie inspired, that had not made it onto the record—from the farcical blast at anti-Communists, "Talkin' John Birch Paranoid Blues," to his first civil rights song, "The Death of Emmet Till."[76]

Folkies generally liked *Bob Dylan*. But Dylan's second album, *The Freewheelin' Bob Dylan*, released in May 1963, left them baffled. The editors of the *Little Sandy Review*—folkies Dylan had known in Dinkytown—wrote: "Dylan bases everything here almost 100 percent on his own personality; there is hardly any traditional material, and most of the original material is not particularly folk-derived. It is pure Bob Dylan (Bob Dylan's dream, as it were), with its foundations in nothing that isn't constantly shifting, searching, and changing." Dylan, people who heard him said either as an insult or a compliment, sounded like no one but himself. "Sopping up influences like a sponge," as Shelton had written in the *New York Times*, he combined Guthrie with Leadbelly, traditional ballads with the blues and country music, to make his own sound. It was, of course, a fine line. Folkies in the early sixties liked a musician who made a song his own and still somehow remained true to the original. In what sense, though, could Dylan be an authentic folk musician if he was not born folk and wrote his own songs?[77]

The answer, of course, could be found in the new kind of "authenticity" that Dylan's growing success helped create. Dylan was authentic because the folk traditionally wrote songs to protest their oppression and Dylan was continuing the practice. Still, he composed and recorded a lot of songs in the early sixties that were not protest songs. More important in the long run, though, Dylan was authentic because he experienced, shared, and expressed not so much the details of the daily lives of the folk but their emotions. Guthrie's life on the road with the hobos and Leadbelly's firsthand acquaintance with white southern injustice were no longer required. Dylan helped create a new kind of popular musician who fused the seeming contradictions of the folk revival's obsession with authenticity with the playacting of minstrelsy, a performer whose authenticity lay in expressing the emotions he shared with the folk. This paradoxical melding of invention and authenticity, of freedom and grounding, helped generate the seductive power of mid-sixties rock and roll.[78]

By 1963, Dylan was famous. His April performance at New York's Town Hall, his first solo show at a major venue, was the hippest ticket of the spring. In May, *The Freewheelin' Bob Dylan* came out to critical acclaim, despite its dismissal by diehard folkies. "Blowin' in the Wind," Dylan's vaguely leftist questioning of contemporary society, became a college anthem. "Masters of

War" was an angry anti-war dirge: "How much do I know/ To talk out of turn/ You might say that I'm young/ You might say I'm unlearned/ But there's one thing I know/ Though I'm younger than you/ Even Jesus would never/ Forgive what you do." "A Hard Rain's A-Gonna Fall" fused poetry and politics in a wail against the threat of nuclear apocalypse: "I saw a black branch with blood that kept drippin',/ I saw a room full of men with their hammers a-bleedin',/ I saw a white ladder all covered with water./ I saw ten thousand talkers whose tongues were all broken . . ." "Oxford Town" describes the bloody integration of the University of Mississippi. Love songs like "Girl of the North Country" and absurdist romps like "I Shall Be Free" balance the seriousness and politics well. "I Shall Be Free," in fact, has fun with all the things serious folksingers in 1963 were supposed to love. Dylan's lyrics even manage to laugh at southern segregation while suggesting the image of blackface:

> I's out there paintin' on the old woodshed
> When a can of black paint fell on my head.
> I went down to scrub and rub.
> But I had to sit in the back of the tub.

In another verse, President Kennedy calls for advice—"My friend Bob, what do we need to make the country grow"—and Dylan seems to predict here the fact that critics and fans will soon call him the spokesman for his generation. He also tells them even then that he does not have the answer. Still, the protest songs fueled Dylan's fame, a trend he continued on his January 1964 release *The Times They Are A-Changin*. He did not have to be Guthrie the hobo Okie anymore. He was Guthrie the voice of the oppressed, the post-blacklist, not particularly ideological sound of the New Left. He was Guthrie the protest singer. He was "Bob Dylan."[79]

In early July 1963, Pete Seeger took Dylan along when he and Theodore Bikel traveled to Mississippi to join the Freedom Singers at a SNCC voter registration rally outside of Greenwood. A photograph by SNCC photographer Danny Lyon shows Dylan with his guitar behind the SNCC office in Greenwood, surrounded by staff members and local activists, talking, drinking cold drinks, and just hanging out. Bernice Johnson Reagon leans close as Dylan looks at her intently, plays a chord, and sings a line now lost. Later that month, Dylan conquered the Newport Folk Festival, singing a list of his protest songs, both solo and with folkie queen Joan Baez, who became his lover and whose support that year helped make him a star. His song "Blowin' in the Wind" closed the festival.[80]

In interviews with the *National Guardian*, a radical newspaper, and the *New York Daily News*, Dylan both encouraged journalists to present him as a spokesman for the left—"the same guy who sucked up my town wants to bomb

Cuba"—and discounted the role—"there is nobody that looks like me or represents the way I feel." Dylan's ambivalence, his angst and his ambition and his playing with positions, demonstrated his debt to the minstrel model of transformation even as one of the characteristics he performed was authenticity. "You ask 'how it feels t' be an idol?'" Dylan wrote in the liner notes of *The Times They Are A-Changin*. "It'd be silly of me t' answer, wouldn't it . . . ?"[81]

By 1963, it was no secret that Dylan had manufactured his rebel past. A *Newsweek* exposé that November revealed his middle-class, midwestern, Jewish roots and his living parents. Dylan, the article insisted, hid his past because it spoiled "the image he works so hard to cultivate—with his dress, with his talk, with the deliberately atrocious grammar and pronunciation in his songs." But by then, the facts hardly mattered. His fans believed his songs expressed emotional truth. Dylan had become less a folksinger than a "religion," as even *Newsweek* admitted, to his fans. "I am my words," he told the magazine. The performance was everything. The new Dylan refused to be bound by the revivalists' image of the folk. The artifice of his early identity played in 1964 and 1965 as a kind of protest against the strictures of the folkie revival and its obsession with the past and only increased his later status as a rock and roll star. A rebel, his act suggested, had to keep moving. Opposition was a performance that could not stand still. Dylan responded to people who said he was not who he said he was by announcing he was not the person they thought he was, that "Bob Dylan." He fused the old quick change of minstrelsy with the new authenticity of emotions. He insisted that the truth was that there were many Bob Dylans.[82]

His August 1964 *Another Side of Bob Dylan* sounded like exactly this kind of rebellion. The album did not contain a single song demanding civil rights or condemning war. Instead, he pushed the dense symbolism and sexuality of his poetry even further in songs like "Chimes of Freedom," which celebrated a much more interior kind of release. "I Shall be Free No. 10"—its title is clearly a joke—laughs at critics' and fans' desires to see meaning in his songs: "Now you're probably wondering by now/ Just what this song is all about/ What's probably got you baffled more/ Is what this thing here is for./ It's nothing." Both these songs played with the message and form of the by then increasingly well known Freedom Songs. In "All I Really Want to Do," Dylan rejects his role as a model: "I ain't looking for you to feel like me,/ See like me or be like me." "It ain't me babe," Dylan insists in a song with this name, "it ain't me you're lookin' for." Life in his protest songs, he says in "My Back Pages," is "black and white . . . but I was so much older then/ I'm younger than that now." *Another Side of Bob Dylan* serves as Dylan's protest against his status as a writer and singer of protest songs, against having to have the answers. Dylan had adopted the blues model of identity.[83]

Many of Dylan's most popular protest songs had advanced a rather vague politics. Like Jack Kerouac's ellipses and Jackson Pollock's drips, the allusive symbolism and vague questions of Dylan's songs enabled listeners to fill up the ideological space themselves. It was arguably more democratic, a creative process that enlisted the listener in the process of making meaning, blurring the lines between the artist and the audience and between the art and the creative act. But the answer in the wind or the changing times could be filled with many different kinds of desires—Dylan was brilliant at being political without actually expressing a political ideology and thus being polarizing—and journalists and critics filled these spaces with the artist himself. Fans could pour themselves into the gaps. Dylan's political vagueness, a quality he shared with the early New Left, made the emotions, and not which political plan might actually solve the problem, the point.

By 1964, Dylan's short career had already evoked the whole history of postwar rebellion His early songs presented a 1960s version, channeled through Guthrie and others, of 1930s Popular Front culture and the image of the rebel as a working-class hero seeking justice for his people. An older meaning of rebellion meant some connection to organized political protest, and the folk music revival resurrected traces of this kind of politics along with the traditional ballads. Mid-1950s popular culture from James Dean movies to rhythm and blues and less popular productions like Beat writing imagined a much more psychological and individual rebellion—sex, drugs, and emotional freedom. When Dylan began writing songs that explored a whole range of feelings beyond the righteous anger and absurdist humor of his early work, he did not invent this new version of rebellion. But he brought with him from the folk scene a sense of seriousness that, fused with his poetic imagination, made the Beats' and the teen films' emotional alienation seem deep and important, even mystical. And unlike the Beats in the fifties, Dylan was increasingly, hugely popular, and covers of his songs by other musicians were often even more successful than his own versions. His new protest songs imagined alienation as an individual state of mind rather than a communal condition. Dylan romanticized cultural rebellion for the masses.[84]

Notoriously lax in the studio, Dylan treated his recordings as the record of an act, how he played a song on a particular day, not a piece's Platonic, perfect form. Dylan kept, for example, the false start as the beginning of his 1963 song "Bob Dylan's Dream." Somehow, beginning, going back, and beginning again only added to Dylan's distance from his own barely passed past, making more poignant his nostalgia for his early days in New York when he wrote songs in his friends' cheap rooms: "As easy it was to tell black from white / It was all that easy to tell wrong from right./ . . . I wish, I wish, I wish in vain,/ That we could sit simply in that room again,/ Ten thousand dollars at the drop of a hat,/ I'd give it all gladly if our lives could be like that." Like the folksingers and fans that were his first audience in the mid-sixties, Dylan went back to the beginning, using his own past as the place of origins, as a substitute for the premodern, anti-modern, anything but modern revivalist vision of the folk. The folk music revival saw all folk music, whether or not the lyrics originally expressed this nostalgia, as a lament for a "world done gone." (The earliest blues, not surprisingly for music made by people so recently enslaved, were not nostalgic, while early hillbilly songs, not surprisingly for music made by people experiencing their first industrial employment, did express this wistful longing for a romanticized past.) Dylan brilliantly got the emotions right by turning his nostalgia back on himself. In the past, before Dylan became famous, he was not responsible, just as the folk, as imagined by the revival, were not responsible. What he was looking for, like the revivalists, was a little bit of innocence. The pieces of his autobiography became, like the old melodies, song forms, and performance styles used by the new folksingers, the raw materials of his new art. He would use his own life the way a folksinger used the folk even when he was not playing folk music.[85]

At the Newport Folk Festival in July 1965, Bob Dylan walked out onstage in an orange-yellow shirt, black leather jacket, and pointy boots, strapped on an electric guitar, and sang three songs. For the folkie establishment, playing an electric guitar was a gesture equivalent to giving the audience the finger. The folkies had listened to the whiny-voiced kid from small-town Minnesota who covered his middle-class Jewish past with lies about hopping freights and playing the streets for change with old black bluesmen. They had made him a star. He belonged to them. But the times, as Dylan himself had sung, were a-changin'. At Newport, backed by a rock band, Dylan played "Maggie's Farm" and then his new ballad of psychological alienation, "Like a Rolling Stone." "How does it feel," Dylan drawled with an undercurrent of rage on the bootleg recording, "To be on your own/ Like a complete unknown/ With no direction home?" The crowd, in the myth anyway, booed him then. They are certainly yelling something on the available recording, although some who were there remember that people were shouting because the guitar was so loud in the sound mix that they could not hear Dylan's voice. As the band and Dylan finished and fled backstage, Pete Seeger stood in the wings and cried. The booing continued throughout Dylan's new tour, from Forest Hills, New York, to

London's Royal Albert Hall. Still, Dylan emerged from this transformation more popular than ever. "Like a Rolling Stone," released as a single in the summer of 1965, peaked at number two on the pop music charts in August. The folk musician had become a rock star.[86]

No matter how much folk revivalists criticized him, Dylan had succeeded in pushing their own definition of authenticity as emotional truth to its logical limit. In Dylan, transformation and transcendence merged. Becoming someone else, with all its theatricality, was a form of self-expression too. If your emotions demanded reinvention, who was to say that this change was not your own emotional truth? Who was to say that transformation was not authentic? Transformation, change, imagined now not as class mobility but as insisting that everything was possible, that the present does not have to flow out of the past, could be its own form of transcendence, a way paradoxically to escape the limits of history. Change could be the new truth. Dylan, of course, did not single-handedly transform rock and roll from the soundtrack of sock hops and parking spots into the soundtrack of the radical politics and the counterculture. No musician did more, however, with the possible exception of the Beatles, to fuse the contradictions, to meld authenticity and self-invention into a new whole, to transform rock and roll in the second half of the sixties and the early seventies into the music of rebellion.

Throughout his career, Dylan continually reworked his own image the way blues musicians reworked their songs. His life was a gesture, an act in every sense of the term. He was still at it when he published his memoir, *Chronicles*, in 2004, returning to that moment before fame hit, before he was responsible, crafting a much more subtle image of his own connections to the folk than he had years before in Izzy Young's Folklore Center. Rather than claiming his own folk past, he instead placed his artistic career in a genealogy reaching from Walt Whitman and Mark Twain to Jimmie Rodgers, Robert Johnson, Bessie Smith, and Big Bill Broonzy. Dylan helped make transcendence, self-expression sliding completely into self-invention, and the privileging of emotional rather than material truth into the sixties definition of "authenticity": I exist because I express myself. In 1966, an interviewer asked Dylan about the turn away from the politics of his protest songs like "The Ballad of Medgar Evers" and "Masters of War" in the music he had recently recorded. "Every one of them is a protest song," Dylan insisted; "all I do is protest." Four decades later, in *Chronicles*, Dylan demonstrated that he was still a master of this act.[87]

In the late fifties and early sixties, the two versions of this "I exist because I express myself" blues identity, this romance of rebellion, collided in a particularly

Bob Dylan wears jeans and a plaid shirt and holds an acoustic guitar in this photo taken in early 1965 at the height of his fame as a folksinger. *Prints and Photographs Division, Library of Congress.*

interesting moment, the mass movement phase of the civil rights movement. Transformation (I need to feel for a moment that I could be somebody else, somebody with more resources) and transcendence (I need to feel for more than a moment that I really am somebody else, somebody with different emotions and morals), the recognition of limits and the giddy sense that history did not have to apply—both played their roles in building a new politics. Perhaps it didn't matter in the end if your imagination of the folk was wrong, colored by more than a century of romance, by cakewalks, coon songs, Uncle Remus, and Appalachian jugs, Child's ballads and Alexander's Ragtime Band, summer camp singing, *Porgy and Bess*, and college song swaps. It didn't matter so much that you were playing both ends against the middle, the history of elite romanticism and poor lives against the postwar middle class's suburban vision of mass-produced plenty. It didn't matter that your politics were completely contradictory, coupling liberalism's sense of the individual's unlimited ability to make her very self with conservatism's belief in the essential otherness of the poor. It didn't matter. Folk singing required you to feel someone else's life, just for a moment, even if that life was more a product of your own imagination than any life lived in Mississippi. Performing the songs, performing the feelings, meant feeling them too. The mid-century folk music revival was flawed as both political analysis and social history, but it was a perfect exercise in empathy. And this, in the end, despite some revivalists' lack of a sense of the politics of their own appropriations, proved to be a route into politics. "While the great blues tradition of the Mississippi Delta was being kept alive at the Newport Folk Festival," Irwin Silber insisted in 1964, "the urgent freedom songs of today became the same Delta's most vital expression." By the early sixties, the music had traveled a long way back home to the South.[88]

CHAPTER 4

Rebels on the Right: Conservatives as Outsiders in Liberal America

I am already a revolutionary against the present liberal order.
William F. Buckley Jr.

William F. Buckley may have been postwar America's most important rebel. At Yale from 1946 to 1950, Buckley displayed an arch conservatism at odds with most of his fellow students, the faculty, and the administration. Far from attempting to hide, Buckley went looking for a fight. His first book, *God and Man at Yale*, published the year after he graduated, attacked the university for refusing to teach both Christianity and free market economics. Already, Buckley had begun to conceive of liberalism as "an orthodoxy," "the limits within which its [Yale's] faculty members must keep their opinions if they wish to be 'tolerated.'" Professors had to be curbed, through alumni control of appointments and course offerings.[1]

Over the next few years, Buckley polished his sense that liberals dominated mid-century American life. And he would, he insisted, in his words and his manner and his style as well as in his politics, rebel against it all. By 1955, he had founded his own journal of conservative ideas, *National Review*, and announced its attack on not only "liberal orthodoxy" but also time itself. *National Review*, the publisher's statement in the first issue asserted, "stands athwart history, yelling Stop." On Mike Wallace's television show in New York in December 1957, Buckley called himself a revolutionary:

W: Are you for majority rule in the U.S.A.?

B: Yes, unless the majority decides we should go Communist. I
would try to subvert any Communist society.

W: You mean you would turn revolutionary?

B: Yes. I am already a revolutionary against the present liberal order.
An intellectual revolutionary.

W: What would you like to overthrow?

B: Well, a revolution in the U.S.—or a counterrevolution—would
aim at overturning the revised view of society pretty well brought
in by FDR.[2]

Over the next half century, Buckley broadened his rebellion, opposing not
only liberals but also John Birch Society members and other people he called
"the irresponsible right," as well as moderate Republicans. He even rebelled
against the parochialism of the rising tide of modern conservatism he had
helped create. By the late sixties, his longer hair and libertarian tendencies
flapping in the wind, Buckley was riding his Honda 50 motorcycle all over the
East Side of Manhattan and publishing his articles in *Playboy* and *Esquire*. Five
years later, he supported the legalization of marijuana. Interviewed for a *Time*
cover story in 1967, Buckley confessed, "I feel I qualify spiritually and
philosophically as a conservative, but temperamentally I am not of the breed."
Baiting opponents and provoking outrage in his syndicated newspaper columns, at *National Review*, and on his own television show, *Firing Line*, Buckley
in the late 1960s appeared to love nothing more than a good fight. *Time* suggested that Buckley had even succeeded in making conservatism "fun."[3]

Paradoxically, only strong political conservatism could have made the rich,
witty, and white William F. Buckley an outsider in the mid-fifties American establishment. "Conservatives in this country," he argued in 1955, "are non-licensed
non-conformists; and this is dangerous business in a Liberal world." By the seventies, in part because of his own success in making conservatism politically and
intellectually respectable again, "the Buckley style," that way he had of standing
apart and implying his lack of concern about whether others approved, his body
language and his sarcastic wit, alone guaranteed his rebel stance. Buckley almost
single-handedly created the sense that conservatives were outsiders in the postwar
era. "Radical conservatives," Buckley called his fellow travelers, not preservation-
ists but Americans for change, people opposed to the liberal status quo.[4]

Joan Didion, attending the Jaycees' thirty-second annual conference of
America's Ten Outstanding Young Men in the late sixties, called conservatives
"the true underground, . . . the voice of all those who have felt themselves not

merely shocked but personally betrayed by recent history. It was supposed to be their time. It was not."[5]

Some of these young white men, often from elite universities, followed Buckley in seeing conservatives as outsiders who should be insiders in late-fifties America. Under his guidance, they founded Young Americans for Freedom (YAF) in the fall of 1960 and went to work creating a conservative student movement to combat the liberalism that then reigned on most campuses. Other white middle-class college students read Ayn Rand, whose best-selling novels, *The Fountainhead* and *Atlas Shrugged*, presented wealthy and successful capitalists as outsiders in America. Rand's novels worked to draw alienated young white readers to the right as Salinger's *Catcher in the Rye* and Kerouac's *On the Road* did to the left. Hunter S. Thompson, though he identified himself as a Democrat for much of his life, read Rand, Salinger, and Kerouac and took up a kind of libertarianism that sat at the intersection of left and right. More than any other single figure, Thompson exemplified how the romance of the outsider produced an ambiguous politics.[6]

Chronologically, conceptually, and politically, the rise of the New Right (if not its origins) followed the rise of the New Left. In the fifties, Buckley created the public role of the conservative rebel and worked to forge a new conservative majority by rebelling against liberalism and its allies. He made little progress in attracting a broad base of supporters, however, until the mid-sixties, when the growing rebellion against liberalism from the left became increasingly visible in the newspapers and on television. As the John Birch Society and other radical right groups faded and the civil rights movement threatened insular communities of southern segregationists and urban Catholic ethnics, Buckley and *National Review* conservatism became more popular. Attacking the New Left—both as it actually existed and as a figment of some American nightmare—worked much better to attract new followers than rebelling against the liberals. Eisenhower was not a Communist, as the Birchers contended, but Tom Hayden just might be. The sixties—the decade has become symbolic shorthand for the postwar transformation of American culture and politics: civil rights, feminism, the student movement, the anti-war movement, the black nationalists, and the counterculture—created the New Right.[7]

Buckley and his young followers and Hunter S. Thompson illustrate early conservative use of the romance of the outsider. This history, in turn, began to shift the very meaning of the categories "right" and "left." As people on the left talked about values, the emptiness of contemporary society, and the need for cultural self-determination, they started to sound like conservatives. As conservatives began to see themselves as outsiders opposing the liberal status quo, they began to sound surprisingly like leftists. Gestures, rhetoric, symbols, and styles converged, blurring the ideological distinctions among conservative support for a mostly unfettered free market and the idea that individual agency determines a person's fate, the liberal argument that government must act to ameliorate the structures that make some people less equal than others, and the left's demand for active redistribution of resources. White middle-class Americans increasingly defined outsiders in terms that had little to do with class status. In this way, the romance of the outsider nurtured the conditions in which middle-class Americans could become conservatives.[8]

William F. Buckley, Conservative Rebel

As early as 1952, perceptive critics and journalists saw William F. Buckley as a rebel. "He has the outward and visible signs of the campus radical," Dwight Macdonald wrote in 1952 in a review of *God and Man at Yale*, and yet "the inward and spiritual qualities of the radical's wealthy grandfather." That same year, Irving Kristol compared Buckley to that rebellious academic who would be known in the future as the intellectual founder of the New Left: "Far from being recognizably conservative, Mr. Buckley is a gay dissenter, having more in common with C. Wright Mills than any other contemporary writer one can think of." A 1961 *Esquire* piece described what Buckley shared with the most popular Beat writer: "He is becoming 'incorporated' into the public rituals of the society he attacks. In a sense, the process Buckley has undergone is similar to the experience of Jack Kerouac—first attacked by the majority voices of the society he is criticizing; then, after more books offering the same violent criticisms come forth, the rebel is treated with increasing 'tolerance,' detachment, even wry amusement and patronizing camaraderie." Kerouac, although he would become politically conservative as he slowly drank himself to death, stood out at that time as an icon of bohemian license and rebellion. "Increasingly the rebel becomes a favorite performer before audiences who wholly disagree with what he says," the *Esquire* journalist continued, "but would defend to the death his right to entertain them by saying it—and the louder he says it, the louder they applaud." Buckley's strong sense of his position as an outsider, all these critics and journalists understood, marked him as a different kind of conservative.[9]

By the late sixties and early seventies, Buckley was rebelling against much more than what he called the liberal establishment. "His enemies, laid end to end," a journalist wrote, "would reach from here to Southern Purgatory, to which they variously damn him for inciting racial hatred, dividing the

Republican Party, defaming Democracy, and betraying the John Birch Society." Accumulating opponents only made Buckley more of a rebel—and a successful writer and later television host. His enemies, as well as his admirers, became his audience—reading *National Review* and "On the Right," his syndicated newspaper column, and watching his television interview show, *Firing Line*. As Buckley's popularity grew in the second half of the sixties, *Time* announced, "The Buckley substance is forgiven for the Buckley style . . . He stands in grave danger, in fact, of being adopted by the liberal establishment he deplores." Norman Mailer wrote Buckley around 1967, "I think you are finally going to displace me as the most hated man in America. And of course the position is bearable only if one is number one." Indeed, Mailer and Buckley became good friends. They debated each other in public and traded barbs in print. Both men even ran for mayor of New York City in the sixties. Buckley told the journalist Dan Wakefield he had sent Mailer a copy of his latest book, after having written "hi" beside his rival's name in the index. "Knowing Mailer," Buckley said, "he'll immediately go the index to evaluate his own role, and that 'Hi!' will just kill him." Buckley had become that double paradox—a popular conservative and a conservative rebel. He was read, watched, and discussed because, in the words of the critic and editor Irving Howe, for the first time "the archetypal American reactionary" was not a "stumbling primitive" but a man who could "write a paragraph of lucid prose and make a clever wisecrack." By the end of the sixties, Buckley's rebel identity was playing better than his political ideas. Still, his ability to fuse the two changed the course of postwar America.[10]

The way his family and friends tell it, William F. Buckley may well have been an outsider since birth. Journalists and critics certainly described him that way, making archetypes of alleged incidents in the life of the little rebel Bill. At age six he wrote the king of England demanding that the country repay its World War I debt. Years later, at the Millbrook School, a teenage Bill broke into a faculty meeting to criticize his teachers. As a young officer just arriving on a Texas army base, Buckley wrote his commander a letter describing how the post could be better managed. He clearly saw himself as a rebel long before he arrived at Yale. "I don't deny that I have a tendency to be attracted to combatant positions," he recalled years later. At the Millbrook School, "to the extent other people were Protestant, I became sort of obnoxiously Catholic."[11]

Paradoxically, young Bill learned to rebel by following the example of his parents. All ten Buckley children learned to use pranks and verbal combat of all kinds, not to oppose their family's values but to get closer to their father. None of them ever challenged their parents' Catholicism and conservative politics. Buckley told an interviewer from *Time* in 1967, "Perhaps the reason we did not rebel is that Father was a dissenter all his life." Rebellion, in the form of a provocative and oppositional style, was the Buckley family tradition, and no one was better at it than Bill.[12]

At Yale, Buckley showed much more interest in extracurricular activities than in his studies. He had learned his Catholicism and capitalism at home, and he regarded his Yale education as a way to acquire skills—learning to communicate more persuasively his convictions—and credentials. His ambitions lay elsewhere, in the debate team and, most importantly, winning election as the chairman of the *Yale Daily News*. The liberalism of the faculty and many of the brightest students seemed to make him even more conservative. Buckley recalled years later, "My point of view was so generally disdained that it probably acquired, for that reason, a kind of stylistic pretension. It was very important for me in those days publicly to disdain the judgment of the audience . . . I have a feeling that affected my style on into the future." In his editorials as chairman of the *News*, Buckley began to work out the conservative ideas that would become *National Review* conservatism.[13]

All this youthful opposition would be of little but autobiographical interest if Buckley had not gone public with his rebellion, first by publishing *God and Man at Yale* and then by founding *National Review*. In *God and Man at Yale*, Buckley began to develop the idea of the liberal establishment that would over time enable conservatives to make their own use of the romance of the outsider. "Sonorous pretensions notwithstanding," Buckley argued, "Yale (and my guess is most other colleges and universities) *does subscribe to an orthodoxy*." And this orthodoxy did not tolerate Communists. The president of Yale had announced in a June 1949 speech that he would not "knowingly hire a Communist to the teaching faculty," in conjunction with an National Education Association resolution then circulating that had been signed by many college presidents. This policy, Buckley argued, "represented an overt departure" from Yale's explicit principles of academic freedom." Indeed, this orthodoxy banned other ideas besides Communism. "I should be interested to know," Buckley mused, "how long a person who revealed himself as a racist, who lectured about the anthropological superiority of the Aryan, would last at Yale?" Yale, he argued, "looks upon anti-Semitic, anti-negroid prejudices as false values, though of course they are value-judgments just the same."[14]

Yale and comparable institutions, Buckley suggested, could actually embrace pure freedom and "tolerate . . . racists, totalitarians, and Stalinists." Yet instead, Buckley argued for a different direction, a way to improve on the existing "wide" limits "prescribed by expediency, not by principle." Yale, he argued, should narrow the existing limits. There was no academic freedom at Yale, so why use the concept as a pretense for accepting professors' attacks on Christianity and individualism (Buckley's term for free market capitalism)? Why use the concept to enshrine liberalism as Yale's orthodoxy and make political and religious conservatives outsiders? Narrowing what was acceptable would make room for political and religious conservatives.[15]

The problem at Yale, Buckley insisted, was the gap between ideology and practice, between the pious pronouncements of the administration and the actual teaching in Yale's classrooms. This discrepancy, the most perceptive critic to tackle the book, Dwight Macdonald, pointed out, characterized most American universities. Buckley was just "rude" enough, with his brash attitude, so unlike that of most American conservatives, to dwell on it. Yale, Buckley claimed, "derives its moral and financial support from Christian individualists and then addresses itself to the task of persuading the sons of these supporters to be atheistic socialists." Alumni and students needed to fight back and overthrow the rule of the liberal elite—the administrators and the faculty. Buckley assumed the majority of Yale alumni and even most "real" Americans shared his views, and he never gave up his belief that the majority of Americans were conservatives. This idea would come to characterize the New Right. Conservatives might be outsiders because of the power of liberals, but they actually formed a majority and needed to rebel to claim their deserved authority.[16]

The Yale administration and most critics hated *God and Man at Yale*, but the book sold twelve thousand copies in its first month. The bad reviews generated more press about the bad press, and Buckley became a conservative intellectual celebrity overnight. Few reviewers seemed to have read the book carefully, and many critics displayed an appalling anti-Catholicism. The Catholic press, on the other hand, almost unanimously condemned Buckley's economic views. "He quite unwittingly succeeds in contravening Catholic moral doctrine on almost every topic he takes up," the Catholic magazine *America* argued. "Mr. Buckley's own social philosophy is almost as obnoxious to a well-instructed Catholic as the assaults on religion he rightly condemns."[17]

Only Dwight Macdonald seemed to understand that the most interesting thing about Buckley's book was not its content but its fusion of conservative politics with a youthful rebelliousness more often associated with the left:

> It was an earnest, extreme, and irreverent book, a book that, in its
> mockery of authority, its impetuous logic, its relentless hewing to
> the line of Reason, letting the sacred cows fall where they might,

followed the old familiar script: CAMPUS REBEL FLAYS
FACULTY. But the script was all balled up, for the author was
more reactionary than any of the dignitaries in their black robes,
and his book damned Yale as a hotbed of atheism and collectivism.

Macdonald described a Buckley it would take years for other critics and political observers to see—a political thinker "passionate about first principles, articulate to an almost frightening degree," who combined "opportunism and
conviction in a sometimes bewildering way" and "would obviously rather
argue than eat." "Since the New Deal there has arisen in academic and intellectual circles, where the best arguments take place, a new liberal orthodoxy,"
Macdonald wrote, ". . . while of late years a countertendency, a reaction against
liberalism, has gone far in the country as a whole. The line Buckley has taken
permits him to enjoy the pleasures both of unorthodox rebellion (within Yale)
and of conformity (outside Yale)." Buckley, for his part, responded to Peter
Viereck, one of the self-named "new conservatives," by announcing that if conservatism meant supporting the status quo, then he was not a conservative.
Accused by many, including Macdonald, of being a reactionary, Buckley
insisted that "radical" and "reactionary" were synonyms and that conservatives needed to become more radical.[18]

Over the next several years Buckley worked for the CIA in Mexico City
and then for *Mercury* magazine and wrote a book with his best friend from
Yale, an old debating partner who had become his new brother-in-law, Brent
Bozell. *McCarthy and His Enemies* attempted to criticize Joseph McCarthy
while defending the ideas that became known as McCarthyism. Indeed, Buckley and Bozell pushed McCarthyism beyond the senator's own conception of
it, far past a concern with Americans who belonged to the Communist Party
or Communist Party–organized front groups. Buckley and Bozell wanted to
police people who favored "*those policies that are not in the national interest as
we see it,*" to drive them out of government service. Again, Buckley had written
a radical book, not a conservative one—he and Bozell proposed not a defense
of the present order but its destruction. As important for Buckley's future as an
outsider as his first book, *McCarthy and His Enemies* ensured his permanent
ejection from eastern intellectual circles. Once again, Buckley savored the
pleasures of rebellion. Once again, as invitations to speak and debate and be
interviewed, on the radio and in person, poured in, Buckley also enjoyed the
pleasures of belonging, of being at home in a group of fellow outsiders, this
time not only conservative businessmen and a tiny vanguard of conservative
intellectuals but also conservative Catholics.[19]

William F. Buckley was not just a conservative in an age in which liberals dominated intellectual discussions and policy-making in America. He was also an idealist in an age in which most American intellectuals used materialist and structural analyses, of systems and groups and "mass society," to explain the world. Sociology and statistics were popular. Belief in the power of ideas was not. Nothing mattered more to Buckley than ideas. Still, he was part of an intellectual trend—the growing revolt against mass society, a particularly pejorative epithet for contemporary America. Intellectuals across the political spectrum used the term as shorthand for all that was wrong with the world. The sociologist C. Wright Mills began the attack, condemning mass society for depriving people of individual freedom and even identity as early as the 1940s. Some thinkers began, more often implicitly than explicitly, to attack liberalism itself. Reinhold Niebuhr denounced "the illusion of liberalism" directly in *Moral Man and Immoral Society*: the fallacy that "the egoism of individualism is being progressively checked by the development of rationality or the growth of religiosity inspired goodwill, and that nothing but the continuance of this process is necessary to establish social harmony." Published in 1932, the book did not become popular until the 1950s. Michael Harrington's 1962 book *The Other America* criticized liberalism too. From the New Deal to the Fair Deal to the New Frontier, Harrington argued, liberal government had failed to eliminate poverty despite multiplying government programs and bureaucracies. But for both Mills and Niebuhr, politics—the distribution of power—and not reason or the right ideas determined the fate of individuals in societies. Buckley was a rebel both because he attacked liberalism from the right and because he also believed so strongly that ideas shaped historical events.[20]

In 1955, William F. Buckley founded *National Review* as a place where he and other conservatives could work out their ideas and communicate with each other. Buckley infused his new journal with his own sense of rebellion. "I want some positively unsettling vigor, a sense of abandon, and joy, cocksureness that may, indeed, be interpreted by some as indiscretion," Buckley wrote in the early days of *National Review* to Max Eastman, then a contributor. His new magazine, he wrote a conservative publisher in 1954, would be "committed to what once was called personal journalism—the manly presentation of deeply felt convictions. It loves controversy." While most scholars then and now have described the fifties as a conservative age, conservatism in this sense has meant more a cultural mood than a political ideology. An expanding white middle class dominated American life, and its "political passivity," "avoidance of social causes," "fear of public controversy," and "preoccupation with personal gain" set the tone. Conservatism for these Americans meant life in the suburbs with like-minded people and voting for Ike. Buckley defined conservatism differently, as uncompromised support of Christianity against creeping secularism and free market economics against spreading government intervention. For Buckley and other *National Review* editors, Dwight D. Eisenhower's administration, with its acceptance of the New Deal and its willingness to negotiate with the Soviet Union, was liberal, not conservative.[21]

National Review, in fact, tried to make opposing the liberal establishment into the rallying cry for postwar conservatives. Conservatives were, in its analysis, America's real rebels. Liberals, dominating the academy, the media, and government policy-making positions, were the establishment. Somehow—*National Review* often exuded an aroma of conspiracy theory—liberals had duped the good American majority. Like many of what would in the future be called the New Right's innovations, the idea of the liberal elite had its roots in the left, specifically the Marxist pasts of two of *National Review*'s early editors, James Burnham and Willmoore Kendall, Buckley's old Yale mentor. A note attached to the bottom of Kendall's column in the first issue, an analysis of the liberal media, announced, "there is a liberal point of view on national and world affairs . . . [and] the nation's leading opinion-makers for the most part share the liberal point of view . . . We may properly speak of them as a huge *propaganda machine*." These former leftists imagined a ruling class that controlled ideas, not things, made up of the people who produced ideas, instead of the people who produced material goods.[22]

In *National Review*, Buckley tried to bring together two seemingly contradictory strands of modern conservatism—the libertarian faction, with its absolute defense of individual economic and political freedom, and the moral and religious faction, with its insistence that society promote Christian virtues. As the American majority and yet outsiders in government and the academy, conservative rebels had to come together. In the beginning, as in *McCarthy and His Enemies*, the medium of unity was anti-Communism. A politics of anti-Communism eased the contradictions between a Christian worldview that might well see intruding in the market as one way of salvaging Christian values and a laissez-faire economics that denied any intervention was ever legitimate. *National Review*'s anti-Communism brought conservative Christians, especially Catholics, into dialogue with economic libertarians. On the question of foreign policy, for example, conservatives split badly into isolationist and interventionist factions. Anti-Communism gave traditionalists a moral reason to support intervention—to stop the spread of godless and totalitarian Communism—that merged well with economic liberationists' support for anti-Communism as a way to create a global free market. In 1956, *National*

Review editor Frank Meyer wrote a series of essays that attempted to give this new definition of conservatism a philosophical grounding. Critics labeled this theory fusionism. Fusionism gave Buckley a way to define his new political conservatism, his rebellion, against the more fractured and ideologically confused conservatism of the Eisenhower era.[23]

Less explicitly than anti-Communism, Buckley's white supremacy joined different kinds of conservatives together too. Initially, Buckley and the rest of the *National Review* staff opposed school integration and African American voting rights but insisted on distinguishing their states'-rights position on constitutional issues from the blatant racism of the white Citizens' Councils and far right conservatives like Gerald L. K. Smith. In 1956, the editors argued that their "support for the Southern position rests not at all on the question of whether negro and white children should, in fact, study geography side by side, but on whether a central or local authority should make that decision." But in his own 1957 editorial "Why the South Must Prevail," Buckley sounded remarkably like the white supremacists he was trying to condemn: "The central question that emerges . . . is whether the White community in the South is entitled to take such measures as are necessary to prevail, politically and culturally, in areas in which it does not predominate numerically? The sobering answer is *Yes*—the White community is so entitled," Buckley argued, "because, for the time being, it is the advanced race . . . The question, as far as the White community is concerned, is whether the claims of civilization supersede those of universal suffrage . . . *National Review* believes that the [white] South's premises are correct." Pushed by Bozell, then an editor at the journal and supportive of the civil rights movement, Buckley then tried to retreat into a vague proposal for the disenfranchisement of uneducated voters. But it was not until 1961 that Buckley rejected the segregationists' white supremacist arguments: "No one who has contemplated a man brandishing a fiery cross and preaching hatred needs help from social science to know that the race problem has debasing effects on black and white alike." Still, federally ordered and achieved integration, Buckley insisted, was worse than the continuation of segregation for the immediate future. Change must be gradual and voluntary: "If it is true that the separation of the races is nonrational, then circumstance will in due course break down segregation."[24]

Opposing even the federal government's tepid support for the civil rights movement, however, made plain *National Review*'s rebellion against the liberal establishment. Whatever a person's position on how much the federal government was doing in the 1960s, academics and a growing number of liberal politicians came together in opposition to southern segregation. No other single issue worked as well to position conservatives as outsiders. White supremacy and opposition to government support for integration were part of the new conservatism from the start.

National Review's editors disagreed more strongly about the desirability of attacking another faction on the far right, the John Birch Society. Robert Welch, successful businessman, failed political candidate, and leader of the National Association of Manufacturers, founded the society in 1958. By 1961, the John Birch Society had at least twenty-five thousand members, including some local and state politicians and two California congressmen. Birchers fit Buckley's vision in many ways. White and extremely alienated from the federal government, they too wanted radical change. They too wanted to go back in time. Welch did not just blame Communism for America's problems—he argued that real Communists ran the country. In *The Black Book*—a text also called *The Politician* that Welch began writing in 1954 and edited and expanded throughout the second half of the fifties—he claimed that even President Eisenhower was "a dedicated conscious agent of the Communist Conspiracy." Welch had been a contributor to *National Review* in its early years, sending a thousand dollars twice, first in 1955 to help with the start-up and again in 1957 to help keep the still not profitable journal operating. He even sent Buckley a copy of *The Black Book*.[25]

While Buckley and other members of the *Review*'s staff thought Welch was "nuts," some editors cautioned against attacking other conservatives, a strategy that ran counter to the magazine's attempt to unite different conservative factions by attacking liberals. Instead, Buckley and the *Review*'s editors decided to publish articles critical of the John Birch Society written by conservatives not affiliated with the journal. In 1961, when Buckley finally decided he too had to comment on the Birchers, he wrote a less direct question-and-answer piece rather than an editorial. By 1962, Buckley was finally worried enough about the growing popularity of the group to publish a direct attack. His February 3 editorial accused Welch of harming the anti-Communist cause by "distorting reality and refusing to make the crucial moral and political distinction . . . between an *active pro-Communist*, and an *ineffectually anti-Communist liberal*." "There are bounds," Buckley concluded, "to the dictum, anyone on the right is my ally." Attacking the John Birch Society—"the irresponsible right"—made Buckley's and *National Review*'s kind of conservatism seem more responsible and moderate, even though they never entirely repudiated the segregationists.[26]

By the mid-sixties, Buckley had become a national celebrity, the most well known rebel on the right. It was time for conservatives to take on the liberals.

And in this fight, Buckley's contradictory personality and politics, his identity as a deeply religious free market absolutist who just happened to be clever, endearing, and flamboyantly entertaining in his dissent, would prove essential.[27]

As always, the man was busy. In 1961, the year he helped found YAF, he also began writing a syndicated newspaper column, "A Conservative Voice," later renamed "On the Right," which by 1964 appeared in over two hundred newspapers. Throughout the early sixties, Buckley spoke everywhere, appeared on television, and even publicly debated well-known liberals like Mailer and James Baldwin. Interviewed by *Mademoiselle* in 1961 for its early-sixties series "Disturbers of the Peace," which also included talks with Mailer, Gore Vidal, and Ayn Rand, Mailer made his free market economic views sound like part of the Beat rebellion in his support for self-expression, if not in his sense that property was more important than poetry as the means: "So I tend to feel that day by day a person's desire for freedom and desire to express himself is primarily gratified by his right to deploy his economic resources, whatever they are, as he sees fit." Economic freedom, he argued, was the freedom that made all other freedoms, even cultural rebellion, possible.[28]

In 1966, Buckley began taping *Firing Line*, on which he both served as host and debated his guests. Debuting on April 30, 1966, and quickly evolving into a showcase for Buckley's rebel style, as much a televised prizefight as a talk show, *Firing Line* mixed elite and pop culture elements—serious intellectual discussion, joking, and verbal jabbing—in a way completely unheard of in conservative intellectual circles and unique as well among television interview programs. Some fans clearly shared Buckley's beliefs, but others told reporters that they watched just to see what Buckley would say next. As a reporter for the *Wall Street Journal* wrote, "The spectacle of William F. Buckley spearing a foe . . . holds much the same fascination as the sight of a cat stalking a bird."[29]

In the first three years of *Firing Line*, Buckley convinced many liberal and left activists and scholars, as well as people representing various oppositional cultural movements, to appear, and he seemed to enjoy attacking many of them. The very first program taped, although not the first program aired, featured socialist Michael Harrington talking about America's poverty problem and commenting on Johnson's recent declaration of a "War on Poverty." Socialist Norman Thomas and New Left historian and activist Staughton Lynd argued about Vietnam. CORE directors James Farmer and Floyd McKissick and comedian and activist Dick Gregory debated civil rights. LSD proponent Timothy Leary, disc jockey Murray the K, *Playboy* founder Hugh Hefner, and poet and activist Allen Ginsberg promoted values and ways of living directly opposed to Buckley's defense of traditional Christian morality. Not surprisingly, Buckley could be harsh. He repeatedly argued that Lynd, who had gone to North Vietnam to meet with Vietnamese Communists that winter, possessed "a very dim hold of reality." "Surely, as a Marxist," Buckley commented archly, "you don't seriously believe your little vacation to Hanoi would have mid-wifed some sort of dialectical reconciliation which would otherwise not have taken place?" He could also be surprisingly engaged, as when he and Paul Goodman discussed whether public schools were necessary. And he was frequently funny. Farmer told a story about President John F. Kennedy's request that African Americans be part of the military honor guard that greeted his plane. Buckley quipped in reply, "Well, one hopes he will find more productive jobs for Negroes than simply to make them stand parade for dignitaries." Debating Allen Ginsberg on the meaning and importance of the avant-garde, he joked that Ginsberg "will wear his hair long until everybody else does; then he will cut it." In the midst of community organizer Saul Alinsky's impassioned plea for the importance of conflict in generating social change, Buckley butted in: "I, obviously, have a stake in the toleration of controversy."[30]

From 1966 to 1970, when the then hour-long show ran on commercial stations, Buckley perfected his performance as a conservative rebel. Usually wearing a gray suit, he appeared crisp and pressed in relation to his guests. Often charming and always witty, he sometimes managed the miracle of making intellectual discussion and debate into great entertainment. No television talking head did more with his eyes and eyebrows. After several seasons, his tendency to widen his eyes and raise his eyebrows when he believed his guest was offering up the intellectual equivalent of garbage was enough in itself to make his studio audience laugh. By the late sixties, his rebel style attracted viewers from across the political spectrum.

Buckley loathed the leftist politics of the sixties—Lynd's "unreality"—even as he was enchanted by the style of the counterculture. In 1964, he made an effort to listen to his young son Christopher's music collection, and four years later, in an article he wrote about rock music, he confessed that perhaps the kids were right about the Beatles: "I mean how can one prevail against them? The answer is: one cannot. And even if they are hard to listen to, there is an exuberance there that is quite unmatched anywhere in the world." In a generous mood that year, even as leftist student rebellions erupted around the world, Buckley praised the rock musical *Hair*. Interviewed by *Playboy* in 1970, the Catholic Buckley advocated giving the pill to India and legalizing both prostitution and "private homosexual acts committed between adults." He also warned against the reductive nature of rebellion, describing the pleasure of the defiant act that he knew so well: "There are, I am sure, hundreds of Americans who would like to hear a speech by Eldridge Cleaver. One reason they would like to do so is because they like the excitement . . . People like to show off their audacity," Buckley continued, "their cavalier toleration of iconoclasm—it's the same kind of thing, in a way, as shouting, 'F—— Mayor Daley' in a loud voice in the middle of a park in Chicago." Writers and activists used that rebelliousness, Buckley argued, to give "the audience the iconoclast's thrill." Influenced at least in part by his son, he explored the emerging counterculture. He rode his motorcycle, grew his hair out, and hired young editors for *National Review* who wrote favorably about Woodstock and the Rolling Stones. By 1972, he even supported the legalization of marijuana, a topic he explored on *Firing Line*. As one *National Review* editor later recalled, the most popular conservative in America loved anything new.[31]

Buckley often indirectly suggested that it was the romance of rebellion— the thrill of audacity, the pleasure of standing apart from convention and feeling unique in a crowded world—rather than reason that pulled young people toward the left. But this love for outsiders and oppositional forms among the old and young, liberals as well as conservatives, was also pushing people toward Buckley himself. Buckley drew a large audience for his public debates, his columns, and his television show, not because his readers and viewers all accepted his ideas but because he was a rebel. Many of his "fans," as well as some of his friends, were liberals. Buckley made many liberals see his brand of conservatism as a viable political choice, instead of a collective form of psychosis, even if it was not the choice they would make. While neoconservative intellectuals like Irving Kristol and Nathan Glazer helped make conservatism intellectually acceptable, William F. Buckley made it psychologically and culturally acceptable, legitimate at the level of individual identity and public performance. As his friend and yet political enemy Norman Mailer made clear, many people were able to distinguish between Buckley's political beliefs and his identity. Buckley, Mailer declared, was "a second-rate intellect incapable of entertaining two serious thoughts in a row," but he was also "wonderful company . . . You can't stay mad at a guy who's witty, spontaneous and likes good liquor." It was not, ironically, Buckley's ideas (as few people were ready to sign up for an educated franchise as were interested in alumni control of Yale's curriculum) but his rebel identity that popularized the new conservatism.[32]

In the 1960s and 1970s, Buckley was the quintessential conservative rebel, perhaps the only man in America who could claim both Robert Welch and Gore Vidal as enemies. His unabashed elitism contradicted his populist assumption that "average" Americans shared his views. His insistence on moral absolutes contradicted his unquestioned faith in free market capitalism. These inconsistencies, however, only strengthened his rebel persona, the Buckley temperament that never quite lined up with the conservative philosophy and the conservative religious faith. He understood how close the postwar idea of the rebel was, with its emphasis on absolute freedom of expression, to the conservative politics of libertarianism. As Buckley acted out his belief that in a liberal age conservatives had to be revolutionaries, he put the romance of the outsider to work for the New Right.

Young and Radical in the Sixties and Seventies

In 1961, Tom Hayden, then a student journalist, worried that young people on the right were becoming America's most important political rebels. "The new conservatives are not disinterested kids who maintain the status quo by political immobility," he observed in his 1961 piece "Who Are the Student Boat-Rockers?" "They form a bloc. They are unashamed, bold, and articulately enamored of certain doctrines: the sovereignty of individual self-interest; extremely limited self-government; a free-market economy; victory over, rather than coexistence with, the Communists . . . What is new about the new conservatives is their militant mood, their appearance on picket lines."[33]

In the early sixties, in a historical moment largely left out of standard accounts of the period, conservatism seemed as likely to spark a student revolt against liberalism as an attack from the left. A 1961 *New Yorker* cartoon laughed at the possibility. "And then we have another son," one father told another, "a radical—who's joined Barry Goldwater's conservatives." A *Time* article on campus conservatism argued that the new trend on college campuses was "involvementism," a new activism as likely to break right as left. At the same time that the southern student sit-in movement inspired liberal northern students to conduct sympathy pickets and demonstrations, other students stepped up their conservative activism. The editor of the *Michigan Daily,* the University of Michigan's student paper, claimed that "the signs point to a revival of interest in individualism and decentralization of power" on college campuses. Barry Goldwater's *The Conscience of a Conservative* was a best seller at college bookstores across America. And Nixon defeated Kennedy in 1960 mock elections at colleges like Michigan, Indiana, Northwestern, and Ohio State. *Time,* taking a cue from William F. Buckley, insisted, "The new trend is youth's rebellion against conformity, and to many the liberalism of their New Deal-bred elders is the most ironbound conformity." "You walk around campus with your Gold-water button, and you feel the thrill of treason," the president of Wisconsin's Conservative Club claimed. "My parents thought Franklin D. Roosevelt was one of the greatest heroes that ever lived," Robert Schuchman, a young Yale law student and conservative campus activist told *Time*; "I'm rebelling against that concept."[34]

In September 1960, about ninety-five delegates had answered a call to take "political action" to save "freedom" by bringing young Americans to conserva-tism. Under Buckley's patronage, they met at Great Elm, his parents' estate in Sharon, Connecticut, and founded the group they named Young Americans for Freedom. They also issued a statement of principles. "In this time of moral and political crisis," the Sharon Statement announced, "it is the responsibility of the youth of America to affirm certain eternal truths . . . That foremost among transcendent values is the individual's use of his God-given free will, whence derives his right to be free from the restrictions of arbitrary force; That liberty is indivisible, and that political freedom cannot long exist without eco-nomic freedom." The business of government, the Sharon Statement contin-ued, was to preserve order, provide a national defense, and administer justice. Moving beyond these narrow areas, the government limited the very "order and liberty" it was created to protect.[35]

Hayden had interviewed some of the Sharon delegates. Howard Phillips, student council president at Harvard, said the "main thing we're concerned with is the responsibility of the individual." University of Chicago graduate student and future editor of the conservative *New Individualist Review* John Weicher insisted that "not all of the kids who were at Sharon want to go into business, or to professional schools, nor do I think they were all very selfish, though many were. Most of them are driven by a desire to be free to see what they can do in life without interference." Robert Schuchman argued, "We do not want to be told what we must do . . . We want to be self-determined." Hayden might have been talking with future members of the New Left group he was then helping to build, Students for a Democratic Society (SDS).[36]

Like members of the early New Left, members of the early New Right shared a common background. Seventy-five of the Sharon delegates claimed college affiliations. A majority of these students attended just five schools: Yale, Harvard, University of Minnesota, University of Chicago, and Northwestern. Many were already members of young conservative organizations like Youth for Goldwater, Young Republicans, and the Intercollegiate Society for Individ-ualists, an organization founded by Frank Chodorov in 1953 to publish and dis-tribute conservative literature (including Buckley's *McCarthy and His Enemies*) on college campuses in order to "uproot the collectivist seed." Most delegates were Catholics, but some were Protestants and Jews, including early leaders Howard Phillips and Robert Schuchman. Most were men. Most were white, with ancestors from Great Britain and Northern Europe. And many, despite their attendance at elite colleges, came from lower-middle-class and upper-working-class families. About twenty older conservative leaders and staff members of conservative organizations—William Rusher, Frank Meyer, and Marvin Liebman, for example—served as delegates as well.[37]

Young conservatives envisioned an "inclusive" movement, and delegates, despite their similarities, represented all factions of conservative thought—from libertarianism and classical liberalism with its free market faith to traditional culture conservatives and religious conservatives. Debates and disagreements rippled through the conference. Future YAF leader Lee Edwards remembered that delegates argued for hours over mentioning God in a clause of the Sharon Statement and that the final vote was 44 for God and 40 against. Young conservative "individualists" or libertarians did not win all these fights, but their ideas about the power of the individual freed from government constraint shaped the conference and the organization it launched.[38]

Most important, Young Americans for Freedom embraced Buckley's vision of a radical conservatism and rebelled against the liberal establishment. Indeed, like Buckley, many members of YAF felt like outsiders on their elite college campuses and even within the Republican Party. Lee Edwards invented the term "New Right" as a way to distinguish YAF's conservative platform. The title of a history YAF published in 1969 captured members' understanding of their position, *Rebels with a Cause*. A journalist joked that YAF would make "the vest the youth symbol of the sixties."[39]

The Young Americans for Freedom were certainly ideological rebels, like Buckley's *National Review* well to the right of the Republican Party. Above all, they stressed the right to private property in their journal, *New Guard*, "the last metaphysical right" that grounds individuals in privacy, responsibility, and a place in society. But YAF, like the New Left, was committed to putting its beliefs into practice—as *New Guard* announced in its first issue, "The key word is Action!" Like *National Review* editors, early YAF leaders and advisors borrowed from the left, but this time they focused on structure and strategy. Members created a string of "front groups," organizations run by them but without any official relationship to YAF. The Student Committee for Congressional Autonomy defended the House Un-American Activities Committee, organizing a counterdemonstration of four hundred people in support of HUAC when the Eighty-seventh Congress opened January 3, 1961, against an anti-HUAC protest of two hundred. The Committee for an Effective Peace Corps urged the use of volunteers abroad to fight Communism. Other committees advocated strengthening national security and continuing the exclusion of "Red China" from the UN.[40]

Still, the majority of YAF activities, such as its Freedom Rally in March 1961, which drew over three thousand people to hear Barry Goldwater speak and turned away six thousand more, generated publicity, not protest. Many conservatives condemned political activism—the demonstrations, pickets, and especially civil disobedience that generated media coverage—for disrupting the social order. Not until the rise of the religious right and the evangelical takeover of the anti-abortion movement in the eighties would conservatives move en masse into direct action. Young conservatives also never created a separatist youth movement. YAF members remained very dependent on conservative elders like *National Review* publisher William Rusher, who became a key YAF advisor, and Marvin Liebman, another important advisor and a conservative public relations expert who gave the national YAF office space and services. They raised their budget, too, from wealthy conservative businessman. Most ironically, for a youth organization that denounced centralized power, YAF created an organizational plan that placed almost absolute control in the hands of its national office. The YAF structure did not encourage creative thinking and grassroots organizing at the local level. It did not model the society it hoped to produce.[41]

Even as conservatives in YAF and other organizations like Youth for Goldwater rebelled ideologically, however, they did not believe that there was anything wrong with the basic structure of American political life. The people in power, not "the system," were the problem. Conservatives might be outsiders, but they were "real" Americans and supported "the American way of life." Young conservatives, including the members of YAF, spent much of their time and effort throughout the sixties trying to help conservatives take over the Republican Party from the moderates so "real" Americans would have a political voice. Nor were YAF members cultural rebels in any publicly visible way. Standing up for "traditional" values—the absolute right of private property and a specifically Christian morality, for example— did not readily translate into media-ready spectacle. In the early sixties, YAF members' buttoned-down, jacket-and-tie, skirt-and-hose look matched the image that activists in the southern sit-in movement self-consciously sought to project as part of a strategy to appear as mainstream Americans. Young conservatives, then, at least until the late sixties, were mostly invisible rebels.[42]

William F. Buckley addresses the 1969 National Convention of the Young Americans for Freedom, a group he helped organize. YAF officers David Keene and Mike Thompson sit on either side of him. *Associated Press.*

Unfortunately, none of the young political rebels on the right possessed Buckley's charisma—his witty attack, his hyperarticulate talk, his impish charm, and his rebel style. They did try. "To a degree matched only by the more devout Beatle fans," a journalist wrote in 1969, "Buckley's disciples . . . imitate the gestures, facial expressions, and especially, the hair style of their hero." They also copied both his speaking style and his exact phrases. Hair parted on the side, bangs angling downward toward the right eye, little parodies of Buckley haunted conservative political circles including the YAF. They spoke in "Buckleyesque syllogisms," misused big words, and highlighted their points with "a Buckleyesque protrusion of the tongue." A young conservative described his "romance" with Buckley: "First of all I think he has tremendous style—secondly, he's a more complete man . . . He doesn't hedge—he says it, he's not afraid to say it. Lord, that's a tremendous quality in this age." During Buckley's 1965 campaign for mayor, some of them even turned a Buckley phrase—"the eschatological conceits of them Nigras," a phrase that evoked conservative opposition to the singing black Christian civil rights activists of the South—into graffiti all over New York City subway walls. In a narrow sense, their efforts had little political effect at all, and Buckley may well have lost more votes than he gained as a result of their "help." But they did begin to change the political culture by carving out a space for campus conservatives to see themselves as rebels.[43]

Still, by the mid-sixties, Hayden's earlier worries about the rise of campus conservatism seemed crazy. Young Americans rebelling against liberalism as the "political establishment" during this period were much more likely to join the New Left. Not until the Reagan era would the rebel tide turn to the conservative New Right. And a great deal of young Americans' rebellion was not explicitly political. The counterculture, usually examined as an outgrowth of the New Left, generated a kind of lifestyle libertarianism that in the long run proved politically promiscuous. Adapting the work of C. Wright Mills and other scholars, activists like the members of Students for a Democratic Society (founded the same year as YAF) built a New Left by criticizing the liberal establishment from the opposite side of the political spectrum. "The goal of man and society," SDS's Port Huron Statement announced, "should be human independence . . . Society [should] be organized to encourage independence in men." Liberalism, SDS insisted, focused too much attention on "method" and "technique" and too little attention on ideals. Most of the members of YAF would have easily agreed with these ideas. The New Left and young conservatives in the sixties even shared a sense of the source of the problem— bureaucracy, bigness, mass society, and a loss of moral values (although leftists criticized big business as well as big government). Politics, both believed, could be a tool for easing the alienation of modern life. Where the New Left and the New Right often disagreed, of course, was in proposing solutions to those problems.[44]

For a moment in the early sixties, then, the future New Left and the future New Right sounded remarkably alike. On the last night of a three-part Harvard lecture series critiquing contemporary liberalism in 1960, William F. Buckley debated a member of the Harvard faculty, and students packed Quincy House hoping for a verbal brawl. Buckley, a journalist reported, "charged the liberals with deceit and 'elitism,' [and] attacked their concern with 'normless' method—'the fleshpot of those who live in metaphysical deserts.' " Conservatism, he said in conclusion, offered "our only possibility for freedom, personality, and the survival of the West." Pops of applause rocked the hall, and then the crowd hushed, waiting for the rebuttal. Michael Maccoby, a teaching fellow in social relations, stepped up to the podium. "He was, he said, a 'radical' rather than a 'liberal' and he shared Buckley's criticism of contemporary liberalism," a reporter noted. He made some small distinctions, and then Buckley had a chance to reply: "I agree with so much that Mr. Maccoby said, it would be pettifogging to mention those of his ideas that offend me."[45]

From the start, the early New Left, SNCC and SDS, focused on values as much as on goals like better paying jobs and voting rights that could be won through the political process. Individual empowerment and creating the Beloved Community (a fragment of a better future here in the present)—these were ways of talking about morality, metaphysics, and transcendent meaning. New Leftists attacked authoritarianism, conformity, and bureaucracy—the spreading malaise of alienation. They talked about people having the freedom to decide everything for themselves. This cultural, psychological, and increasingly spiritual critique of American society linked more explicitly political activists to the spreading subculture of artists, musicians, pot and acid heads, and assorted hangers-on that scholar Theodore Roszak named the counterculture. It also linked the entire, less narrowly political end of sixties rebellion to the libertarian strand of modern conservatism.

As a political philosophy, libertarianism joined the right of self-ownership, the freedom to control the use of one's person, to free markets, the freedom to control one's property, independent of government interference. In the mid-twentieth-century United States, libertarians advocated the maximum individual liberty and the minimum state. Depending on whether they believed the power of government did more to help the rich or the poor, they divided into left and right factions. The International Workers of the World (IWW), or Wobblies, for example, campaigned for a left anarchism. In the experience of the mostly working-class members, the state used its power to support railroad and other business owners at the expense of the workers. Right libertarianism became more common by the 1950s and 1960s as liberalism with its faith in government action dominated American politics.[46]

YAF brought libertarians together with other kinds of young conservatives by emphasizing the rebelliousness of contemporary conservatism and by focusing on anti-Communism. Libertarians, in this kind of thinking, had to concede that the growth of state power in the form of military intervention in Vietnam was justified to save individual freedom from Communism. But as the war dragged on, the anti-war movement grew, and a form of radical libertarianism emerged that saw the state, including its role in defense, as the main enemy of freedom. By the end of the 1960s, libertarianism as a political philosophy sat at the intersection of the emerging New Right, the New Left, and the counterculture.

THE NEW LEFT IS REVOLTING

Young Americans for Freedom, 1221 Mass. Ave., N.W., Washington,D.C., 20005

This Young Americans for Freedom poster plays off the multiple meanings of the word "revolting" to attack the New Left. *Yankee Poster Collection, Library of Congress*.

No single figure embodied the contradictions of counterculture libertarianism better than Hunter S. Thompson, and the rich collection of letters he saved offers a rare view of the interior life of someone struggling to create an identity as a rebel in the late fifties. A founder of what came to be called the New Journalism, a reporter, novelist, and air force veteran, Thompson self-consciously crafted an enduring image as an iconoclast. His rebellion against the constraints of modern life—from the expectations and responsibilities of marriage to the limitations on individuals' rights to own and carry the weapons and drugs of their choice—was as likely in future years to break right as left. The postwar rebel's expressive individualism, as Thompson's writing and his life make clear, held the power to disrupt the old political categories.[47]

In the late fifties, young people across America, middle-class white boys especially, devoured Ayn Rand, J. D. Salinger, and Jack Kerouac. The more adventurous worked through Albert Camus's *The Rebel* and Colin Wilson's *The Outsider*, too, and anything by Jean-Paul Sartre. Reading alone, in college dorms, on merchant ships, and in shabby first apartments, they drank in a romance of psychological and cultural rebellion whose politics did not sit clearly anywhere on the spectrum of left to right. Thompson, reading this same rebel canon, was unique in that he used carbons when he typed his letters, meticulously saving his early musings on these works through all the borrowed apartments and lost jobs and poverty of his wandering early life for a future audience he was sure would someday care.[48]

In the fall of 1957, a twenty-year-old Hunter S. Thompson wrote a friend that he had just been given an honorable discharge from the U.S. Air Force: "To understand something of the philosophy I am flirting with, all you have to do is, first, consider my overall attitude—then imagine how it was affected by reading *The Outsider* and *The Fountainhead* one right after the other." He bragged to a girlfriend "just how far" he had "strayed from the popular ideologies of our time": "I can see that I shall be permanently apart from all but a small and lonely percentage of the human race, in all but the most superficial respects." Through the late fifties, Thompson pushed copies of Rand's books on acquaintances. He told the friend who had first recommended *The Fountainhead* to him, "I think it's everything you said it was and more." "Although I don't feel that it's at all necessary to tell you how I feel about the principle of individuals," he wrote, "I know that I'm going to have to spend the rest of my life expressing it one way or another." He wanted "to affirm, sincerely, for the first time in my life, my belief in man as an individual and independent entity." In another letter to a girlfriend he called himself, only half in jest, "a vicious, dangerous, radical individualist." In a news release he wrote about himself in the third person and published in the *Command Courier*, the paper he worked on at Eglin Air Force Base in Florida, Thompson called himself "an apparently uncontrollable iconoclast."[49]

Six months later, Thompson was reading Kerouac at the urging of a former girlfriend and feeling the effects of the Beat writer's confessional psychology if not his prose style. "I'm all but completely devoid of a sense of values: psychologically unable to base my actions on any firm beliefs, because I find that I have no firm beliefs," he wrote another girlfriend. "As I look back, I find that I've been taught to believe in nothing. I have no god and I find it impossible to believe in man." He confessed, "I am beginning to see what Kerouac means when he says, 'I want God to show me his face': it is not the statement but what the statement implies: 'I want to believe in something.' " Kerouac, he insisted, was "more of a 'spokesman' than most people think . . . and he speaks for more than thieves, hopheads, and whores."[50]

Eventually Thompson ended up in Greenwich Village in a cramped basement apartment with black walls he described as "something straight out of a 'low bohemia' movie" and began reading Sartre. "A man has to BE something; he has to matter," he wrote a Louisville friend in April 1958.

> As I see it then, the formula runs something like this: a man must choose a path which will let his ABILITIES function at maximum efficiency toward the gratification of his DESIRES. In doing this, he is fulfilling a need (giving himself identity by functioning in a set pattern toward a set goal)[,] he avoids frustrating his potential (choosing a path which puts no limit on his self-development), and he avoids the terror of seeing his goal wilt or lose its charm as he draws closer to it (rather than bending himself to meet the demands of that which he seeks, he has bent his goal to conform to his own abilities and desires).

"The definitive act of will which makes man an individual," Thompson argued, is making conscious choices about the patterns of life, defining and defending the individual self. No two ideas, he writes another former girlfriend a little over a week later, were "ever more incompatible than the security of conformity and the freedom of individuality." Working a string of jobs in journalism, including a stint at *Time* as a copyboy, Thompson was fired repeatedly and often broke and depressed. By March 1959, he was writing about himself, "the Hunterfigure," as a person in a Rand novel: "I am convinced, of course, that to play a role or to adjust to fraud is wrong, and I damn well intend to keep right on living the way I think I should." By that summer, he looked back at the last year and a half as a period of "near desperate evaluation, not only of self, but of all that had gone into the creation of self over the course of some twenty years." At last, missing "more than anything else" his illusions, Thompson decided to see his craft as a form of rebellion. Writing, he argued, citing William Faulkner, was a way of saying, "Kilroy was here," of imposing the individual self on reality.[51]

Thompson did not call himself a conservative. In his late-fifties letters, full of existential soul-searching, he appears apolitical and ready to damn all sides. "I may sound a little black," he joked to a friend. "Everyone who matters is a 'higher bohemian.' " He wrote his Marxist friend and old Louisville schoolmate Paul Semonin, "As for me, I have no hope for any of us: if Khrushchev and Mao don't get us from the outside, either the Arthur Schlesinger–Walter Reuther faction or the William Buckley–Gerald L. K. Smith faction will paralyze us internally." Later, his work as a journalist in Latin America brought him back into the world of politics. John F. Kennedy's assassination in 1963 completely flattened him: "This is the end of reason, the dirtiest hour in our time," Thompson wrote a friend, novelist William Kennedy. "No matter what, today is the end of an era . . . The savage nuts have shattered the great myth of American decency." How, he asked, could he communicate "the fear and loathing that is on me after today's murder?" Thompson remained involved in politics for the rest of the sixties and into the seventies. He hated Lyndon B. Johnson, saw Richard M. Nixon as his arch nemesis, volunteered his services to the Eugene McCarthy campaign, and became friends with George McGovern. Ronald Reagan, Thompson wrote Semonin in 1965 in an uncanny act of prophecy, was "the prototype of the new mythological American, a grinning whore who will probably someday be President." Thompson certainly did not vote Republican. The anarchist IWW, he wrote, "was probably the last human concept in American politics." By the mid-sixties he was attacking the liberals as "humanist conservatives" with "too much reverence for the social structure."[52]

But Thompson was no New Leftist either. He criticized the civil rights movement's nonviolent methods: "I may be sick and a bit daffy, but something in me rebels at the idea of 500 or 5000 negroes kneeling in the streets of Selma, singing 'I love State Troopers in My Heart.'" Painting signs and joining nonviolent picket lines, he wrote Semonin, was for "people who feel guilty and I don't." He did not like the Black Power movement either: "I think the idea of a Negro Nationalist party in this country is madness, because there are too many people in this country just waiting for an excuse to act like the racists they are . . . Hell," he continued, "I have a strain of it myself and the only thing that has brought me around this far is the fact that every time I've seen a black-white confrontation I've had to admit the negroes were Right. Once it turns into power politics the Negro loses his leverage on my conscience." Malcolm X, he wrote, "was a black Goldwater, and apparently just as dense." Thompson never seemed to rebel much against the racial conventions he grew up with in Louisville, Kentucky. But by the end of the mid-sixties, he was rebelling instead against the liberal–New Left, pro-civil-rights line. On the Vietnam War, too, Thompson attacked the New Leftists even as he hated the war. In 1965, he wrote Lyndon Johnson, "I am neither a pacifist nor an advocate of non-violence, but my sensibilities are grossly offended by the spectacle of a small group of old men whose mania for blood and bombing will inevitably cause thousands of young men to be killed for no good reason. As a white Anglo-Saxon Air Force veteran and shooting enthusiast," Thompson continued, "I can't be shrugged off as a politically impotent East Coast minority-group liberal beatnik draft-dodger." Pro-drugs, anti-gun-regulation, and anti-war, Thompson did not fall neatly into any political category. His most consistent political position was opposition to government intrusion into his life.[53]

On the cultural front, Thompson danced on the edge, a part of the counterculture and yet always a critic of the media's favorite rebellion of the moment. Even as he loved Kerouac, he railed against the Beat Generation, sending out queries to magazines proposing articles on the "rebellion of the ignorant" and making fun of the beatniks to a girlfriend. He even mocked his own desire to be cool and bohemian. By 1967, famous for his documentary-on-drugs-style book on life with a California motorcycle gang, *Hell's Angels*, Thompson had sold three articles on the hippies to national magazines. The hippies, he admitted, "threatened the establishment," making visible the decline of individual freedom in America. Still, these peace-and-free-love folks were not nearly, as individuals, rebellious enough. At the end of 1967, he wrote a friend, "The hippie thing is over; now they're all desperate refugees and beggars. Or serious dope freaks . . . The whole scene is glutted—bad news and losers, hostility and paranoia. Fuck it." Thompson loved pre-hippie San Francisco, "a good, wild-eyed, free-falling time" when he raced his "big-chrome-red-motorcycle" up and down the hills till the night stung his eyes. A kind of cultural and psychological anarchist and political libertarian, he fell permanently in love with his own rebellion. Opposing the popular rebels of the moment, Thompson tried to make his outsider status true by staying out ahead of the crowd. Thompson lived as if his life were the movie that would save the Western genre for another American century.[54]

Nostalgia for some lost golden age, some place where individual men, straining to make themselves from scratch, could find a home, then, linked Thompson to Buckley and future rebels on the right. The absurdity of contemporary American life became the theme of Thompson's best writing, "fear and loathing" his phrase for the death of the American Dream. Thompson's dream may have been less Christian and more frontier cowboy, but like Buckley he was a radical who wanted to remake the present in the image of the betrayed ideals of the American past. Neither Thompson nor most other countercultural rebels became ideological conservatives in the seventies. But Thompson's rebellion, his career as an "outlaw journalist," helped popularize the counterculture's anti-authoritarian, anti-institutional sentiment. And these sixties ideas, in turn, nurtured the anti-tax, anti-big-government sentiments that helped conservatives win political power in the eighties. Rebellion, the freedom to be "self-determined," the hatred of limits, was politically promiscuous indeed.Learning to Love Outsiders

PART II

Romance in Action

CHAPTER 5

New White Negroes in Action:
Students for a Democratic Society, the Economic Research and Action Project, and Freedom Summer

What a crazy country we live in. Young Negroes want to be middle-class white Americans. Young whites want to be Negroes.
   Julius Lester

There are, to be sure, only a few thousand who actively identify with the black and white poor, who reject affluence and go to the slums rather than to the suburbs for which their training and intelligence qualify them. These have a sort of mystique, a sense of oneness with all the outcasts of society, including even the junkie and the streetwalker.
   Michael Harrington

When University of Michigan student Tom Hayden met SNCC activists in 1960, he found "the models of charismatic commitment I was seeking. I wanted to live like them." Other middle-class white college students experienced similar conversions. Constancia "Dinky" Romilly drifted in confusion her first year at Sarah Lawrence. "There was nothing to work for, no struggle or activity you could sink your teeth into," she remembered. Then African

American college students in the South, joined by a few white students, began sitting in at dime store lunch counters, bus station cafés, and other segregated facilities. "That's when my life began," Romilly recalled. She packed her belongings and moved to Atlanta to work in SNCC's headquarters. Student Sharon Jeffrey, a future cofounder of SDS, found her place at the University of Michigan organizing a civil rights conference and staffing sympathy pickets in support of the sit-ins. Bob Zellner, a student at Huntingdon College in Mobile, felt "sky high" listening to King speak and meeting sit-in activists. Though he did not remember their names, he remembered that the first SNCC people he met possessed "an aura of invincibility and a charisma I had never experienced." Time and time again, young middle-class whites in the sixties described hearing about southern student activism or meeting southern student activists (mostly African Americans but also some whites) as encounters that changed their lives. Their feelings about the civil rights movement in the South sparked the process through which they began to see themselves as outsiders too.[1]

Love (what other name could describe these conversions?) is the neglected thread in the history of the origins of the New Left—middle-class whites' love for outsiders. Sometimes this love was romantic and sexual: Hayden married Casey Cason, one of the southern student activists who affected him so strongly; Romilly married SNNC executive secretary Jim Forman. Anecdotal evidence suggests that many young activists in the movement had sex with each other. More broadly, however, love means intense feelings of affection for someone, and this emotion played an essential and yet unacknowledged role in the still contested history of the sixties.[2]

A great deal of white student activism grew out of the intersection of the romance of the outsider with changing political and moral beliefs in the national and transnational context of the civil rights and liberation movements. Young activists took the tradition of cultural opposition that they had inherited from the Old Left and fused it with their new ideas about authenticity. As a result, they imagined and tried to build coalitions based in shared emotions—alienation from white middle-class suburban America and love for the rebels and the margins—rather than shared class positions and political ideology. Often, in fact, they assumed that shared emotions meant shared interests.

Opponents of the civil rights movement and the New Left more broadly realized the importance of affection in these alliances. They called white middle-class civil rights supporters and activists Communists and beatniks, yes, but just as frequently they called them "nigger lovers."

The Rise of SDS

"The cell from which I write is perhaps seven feet high and no more than ten feet long," Tom Hayden wrote his "SDS Friends" from the Albany City Jail in December 1961. He wanted "to help them see the facilities in which I'm trying to continue SDS administrative work this day (incidentally, my birthday)":

> The only light penetrates from a single bulb beyond the bars down the hall, and from the Negro quarters across the way. In a sense, I am glad for the semi-darkness because it blocks certain aspects of the cell I wouldn't enjoy gazing upon in full illumination. For instance, the stained, seatless toilet and the rusted tin cup by the water spigot at the back of the cell. For instance, the wet patches of water, excretion and spittle that cover the floor where I sleep. For instance, the brown, half-inch long bugs which I can't identify, but find more gentle than the roaches creeping upon my clothes.

"When they placed me here last night," Hayden continued, "there were five men caged with me, all of them wearing off their inebriation. The police made it clear to them that I was 'freedom riding with them niggers.'" Lucky for Hayden, the white men were not violent drunks. Some of the men talked to him all through the night. One old man constantly choked on the spittle that drained from his mouth and dried in his beard. "No nigger has life so bad as me," another cellmate claimed. "We should be fightin' for *our* equal rights." The jail was never quiet. Policemen taunted a mentally ill man in another cell who seemed to think he was a train. People shouted conversations. Hayden heard "stirring singing."[3]

He was writing on "a smuggled piece of paper with a smuggled pen," he insisted,

> not just to give you a picture of conditions, but to carry on my correspondence with you regarding the SDS meeting in Ann Arbor, Michigan, December 29–31 . . . It is imperative for people already committed to the struggle for humanism and democracy in the common life [to] come together now to ask themselves basic organizational questions: given that SDS is office space, a little money, and a somewhat amorphous program administered by a modest staff at present, what direction do we want to give it . . . Our answers cannot be abstract if we want to do more than witness to the wrongs of a fallen world.

Hayden did not explicitly answer his own question—that would violate the idea of democratic process at the center of the then almost two-year-old organization. The group would meet in Michigan and come up with a collective answer through long discussion. But his answer was there, in this letter and the reports he had been filing throughout the fall as the southern field secretary for Students for a Democratic Society. At the time, this loose coalition of about 575 campus activists shared a belief in the radical power of democracy. The members at the conference planned for that December were also becoming close friends. Hayden, in jail with the members of SNCC whom he had joined on a Freedom Ride from Atlanta to Albany, knew how he wanted the question answered. SDS should commit itself to the civil rights struggle. SDS should act.[4]

That young people their own age were risking expulsion, beatings, and jail to change the South fascinated many white students from outside the region. College students in the early sixties had grown up with the romance of the outsider, with rock and roll and rebel movies, books by Salinger and Kerouac, *Life* magazine reports on Beat writers and radical painters, and, most importantly, the folk music revival. They had learned to value self-expression and to link this kind of individualism as well as emotional authenticity with people on the margins, with artists, outcasts, and the poor, and especially with rural African Americans. The "southern student movement," as the waves of nonviolent protest that started with the Greensboro sit-ins were called, shook up white students on campuses from Berkeley to the University of Texas. In the South, white and black students moved by the courage of the Greensboro Four could simply organize their own sit-ins. But outside the region, the question of how to respond was more complicated. University of California, Berkeley students took the southern strategy of nonviolent direct action to the annual hearings of the House Un-American Activities Committee that May. Earlier that year CORE activists had helped Berkeley students organize pickets of local Woolworth's stores in support of the southern sit-ins. Using what they had learned, student activists trained volunteers in nonviolent direct action. Over two days of anti-HUAC protests at City Hall, people in coats and ties or skirts and hose formed a peaceful circle around the building, sat-in inside the rotunda, and sang "The Star-Spangled Banner" and other songs. On the second day, the police ejected peaceful demonstrators from the building and washed them down the City Hall steps with fire hoses. As news and images of the anti-HUAC demonstrations circulated, Tom Hayden remembered thinking, "Heads were being broken and . . . I never saw anything like it in my whole life. After all, the people on the stairs were like us." Berkeley students proved that students outside the South could act.[5]

In 1960 and 1961, at institutions everywhere outside the South, college students used existing campus political clubs and religious organizations or created new groups to organize sympathy pickets and other support for the civil rights movement. Christian students inspired by SNCC created the Northern Student Movement in 1961 to send white college volunteers into poor black communities in the urban North. The National Student Association (NSA), the most powerful student organization in the country in 1960 and not yet exposed as funded and controlled at the top by the CIA, invited SNCC members to its summer 1960 conference in Minneapolis. Tim Jenkins, a black SNCC member and Yale law student, became an NSA officer. By the summer of 1962, NSA was running a summer voter registration project in North Carolina. SDS was not the only student group looking at the civil rights movement and SNCC as models for national student organizing, but it was the most important.[6]

Many white middle-class students, energized by their fascination with southern black student activism, turned to politics during this time. Tom Hayden traveled south to experience the movement directly and then used the credibility he gained from his contact with the student activists there to tell its story. SDS's first president, Al Haber, brought Old Left contacts and resources into the new campus politics. Together, they and other members of SDS would use nonsouthern student interest in the civil rights movement in the South—a belief in social justice that went hand in hand with the romance of the outsider—to help forge the New Left.

From the beginning, SDS leaders displayed uncanny timing. In the fall of 1959, Haber and Sharon Jeffrey began organizing a conference on human rights in the North. Haber was president of the Michigan chapter of the student wing of the League for Industrial Democracy, or SLID, a once national Old Left student group dying out everywhere, it seemed, but Ann Arbor. Haber heard about the February 1960 Greensboro protests from NSA, which sent out notices to affiliated student governments at colleges across the country. Jeffrey and other students soon organized local sympathy pickets at Woolworth's and other chain stores in town whose southern branches practiced segregation. Haber called the Greensboro students and invited them to the conference. And Hayden, who had reluctantly joined a couple of pickets—he found protesting "uncomfortable"—wrote a fiery editorial linking the student demonstrations at Michigan to the outpouring of student protest across the country.[7]

The SDS conference, at the end of that spring of rising student activism, was a smash success. About 150 students, active on their home campuses, came together with some of the Greensboro students to hear speakers and pass a series of recommendations. SDS—earlier that spring members had dropped the unappealing name SLID—would publish a national civil rights newsletter for students, plan a national civil rights conference, take the lead in coordinating student fund-raising, and create a national network of the student civil rights groups then emerging on many campuses outside the South. For a tiny organization struggling to turn its ties to the Old Left into a new student politics, it was a bold move. The ambition and breadth of the vision on display in the three typed pages of resolutions passed by the delegates was simply stunning. SDS proposed nothing less than to make itself the national coordinating committee of all student civil rights efforts across the country. Haber sent the list off to his contacts everywhere, including participants in the Raleigh Conference, the meeting that just two weeks earlier had created SNCC to coordinate the southern protests.[8]

Throughout 1960 and 1961, SDS continued to grow by connecting with the movement down south. Its national meeting in June included a reception for Florida students jailed for participating in sit-ins. The September issue of its newsletter, *Venture*, focused on civil rights. And Haber sent letters and telegrams in support of southern activists and their work. Connecting with Tim Jenkins in the fall of 1960, for example, Haber wrote to summarize and clarify their earlier conversation and outline SDS's proposed relationship with the sit-in movement and SNCC. Again Haber pushed SDS as a national coordinator of student activism. The struggle for civil rights, he lectured Jenkins, broadened beyond "social equality" to include "questions of political power and economic organization," was "not so much a Negro problem as a problem for all liberals devoted to a democratic society." He did not have to add that thousands of southern students had participated in the sit-ins and that thousands more outside the South had demonstrated in support. What "students in the North" needed, he told Jenkins, was "greater personal knowledge of the movement": "We must be able to know what is going on, to be able to identify personalities and feel some direct involvement in the struggle."[9]

For Tom Hayden, direct involvement—experience—was everything. Not particularly tall, his face scarred with acne, his shirttails usually flapping, Hayden appeared at odds with the trimmed and pressed world that still lingered from the late fifties on American college campuses. He had not, like Jeffrey and Haber, grown up surrounded by liberal political organizing; Haber's dad was a University of Michigan economics professor active in New Deal politics, and Jeffrey's parents were both labor movement activists. In high school in a suburb of Detroit, Hayden read *Catcher in the Rye* and saw *Rebel*

Without a Cause. The year he started college, he read Kerouac's *On the Road* and fell in love with its celebration of young men exploring and embracing the wide expanse of America. Over the next three years, Hayden recalled, he spent his vacations hitchhiking "to every corner of America, sleeping in fields here, doorways there, cheap hotels everywhere, embracing a spirit of the open road without knowing where I wanted to go." In a 1972 interview, he confessed being "very influenced by the Beat Generation." He admitted that "politics was unimaginable to me. I'd never heard or seen a demonstration . . . There was no sense that there was something like a political form of protest, so whatever that was, it was mainly like trying to mimic the life of James Dean or something like that. It wasn't political." At Michigan, he read philosophy, rode motorcycles, and avoided the fraternity-sorority scene.[10]

Not yet a member of SDS in the summer of 1960, Hayden hitchhiked to the Bay Area, "already known as the Mecca of student activism" because of the HUAC protests and the oppositional politics of the campus party SLATE. He investigated the new campus activism there, traveled to Los Angeles to cover the 1960 Democratic Convention, and then caught a ride to Minneapolis to cover the NSA's annual convention. Twenty-five SNCC representatives from the South had also traveled to Minneapolis, and the conference voted on a resolution, proposed by Haber and hotly debated, endorsing the southern sit-in movement's civil disobedience. A blond graduate student and southern sit-in veteran from the University of Texas stood up to speak. Confronted with injustice, she argued, a person can do nothing, can work within the law, can revolt violently, or can act nonviolently. But

> I cannot say to a person who suffers injustice, "Wait." Perhaps you
> can. I can't. And having decided that I cannot urge caution, I must
> stand with him. If I had known that not a single lunch counter
> would open as result of my action, I could not have done differently
> than I did. If I had known violence would result, I could not have
> done differently than I did. I am thankful to the sit-ins if for no
> other reason than that they provided me with an opportunity for
> making a slogan into a reality, by making a decision into an action.
> It seems to me that this is what life is all about. While I would hope
> that the NSA congress will pass a strong sit-in resolution, I am more
> concerned that all of us, Negro and white, realize the possibility of
> becoming less inhuman humans through commitment and action.

That was it. Hayden fell in love with SNCC—with chairman Chuck McDew, a Talmud-quoting black Jew; with Bob Zellner, a white student from Alabama and SNCC field secretary; and with Sandra "Casey" Cason, the speaker who had swayed the convention. NSA voted to issue the statement of support. The SNCC people "lived on a fuller level of feeling than any people I'd ever seen," Hayden remembered, "partly because they were making history in a very personal way, and partly because by risking death they came to know the value of living each moment to the fullest."[11]

The next year, Hayden repeatedly used his position as editor of the *Michigan Daily* to return to the South. In the fall, SNCC invited sit-in activists to attend an "action-oriented" conference in Atlanta, and Hayden went. A few months later, in February 1961, he went south again. With some Ann Arbor friends, he packed up a station wagon with food and clothing for sharecroppers evicted from their land for trying to register to vote in Fayette County, Tennessee. Cason met them there. James Forman, who would become SNCC's executive secretary the following fall, was there helping the homeless and jobless sharecroppers organize "Freedom Village," a tent city by the side of a road where people were trying to survive and draw national attention to their plight. Hayden met many of the residents and was deeply moved by their struggle for "food and other physical essentials" and for "essentials of a different order—the right to vote and participate in the democratic order." It was Hayden's first trip to the rural South. "We were walking down the street" after meeting with Freedom Village members, Hayden told a reporter years later, "and we ran into a gang that was just waiting for us with belts and clubs . . . We walked the other way as quickly as possible and went into the newspaper office and called the cops. But they just joined the toughs. We got in our car and raced out of town . . . That was my first run-in with the police," he recalled. "They followed us fifty miles before we lost them." Describing his life in 1960, Hayden insisted later, "I didn't get political. Things got political."[12]

Hayden graduated in the spring of 1961, married Casey Cason at the end of that summer, and finally decided—Haber, Jeffrey, and others had been courting him since 1960—to take a job with SDS. That fall, in McComb, Mississippi, and Albany, Georgia, as he had in Tennessee, Hayden blurred the line between reporting observer and activist. He also turned his experiences into performances, speaking at Mount Holyoke, Bryn Mawr, Swarthmore, Yale, and elsewhere in the Northeast, "trying to get money and moral support for the Southern Negroes," "carpetbagging backwards." But it was Hayden's dispatches from the South, which Haber edited and mailed to his contact lists of campus leaders, student groups, and SDS members, that spread both news of the southern student movement and a sense of the actual experience of direct action there. Hayden's reports positioned SDS as the group to join for northern students who cared about the student movement in the South. If white Americans elsewhere worried that they too must act, then Hayden gave them an example of how. They could literally follow him into southern jails, but short of that, they could at least send in their dues and follow his experiences in the region.[13]

Edited by Haber, SDS's "Southern Reports" combined accounts of SNCC activism and white southern retaliation unavailable elsewhere with appeals for funds and the creation of a national support network. An October 7 newsletter described the arrests of high school students and SNCC activists in McComb, SNCC's voter registration efforts there and in surrounding counties, and the murder of local black activist Herbert Lee. SDS was working hard to bring students the news, Haber assured readers, "in the face of an almost total news blackout," and Hayden was down there. Campus activists wanted and, indeed, needed to know the truth. And the truth was that more people might be killed: "A spokesman for the Justice Department told a representative from NSA that unless it appeared there would be 'a lynching' it would be difficult for the

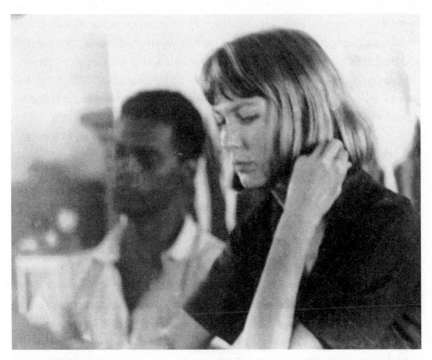

Casey Hayden traveled from SNCC's Atlanta office, where she worked, to Hattiesburg, Mississippi, in July 1964. *Randall Freedom Summer Photograph Collection, McCain Library and Archives, The University of Southern Mississippi.*

government to step in, despite the presence of FBI agents in the area." The federal government was not going to help. What the southern students needed from students outside the region was money for bails and fines and staff salaries and voter registration schools, and SDS had secured $5,000 from its parent organization, LID. The southern students also needed people to think and plan, and again SDS was on the job. Most importantly, SNCC needed people to act. There was a "revolution" under way in Mississippi: "For the southern student this is a movement for a New South, a South not only dispossessed of segregation in all its legalistic and ritualistic forms, but a South in which the entire body politic and indeed the entire society is moulded out of a different fabric . . . and the South may serve as a catalyst toward a democratic revision of the entire national outlook."[14]

At stake, then, were both the future of the South and the future of SDS. As Hayden wrote Haber in a confidential report on a September 1961 SNCC meeting in Jackson, the fight against the segregationists was transforming southern students into radicals. There was a "crazy new sentiment that this is not just a movement but a revolution, that our identity should not be with our Negro predecessors but with the new nations around the world, and that beyond lunch counter desegregation there are more serious evils which must be ripped out by any means: exploitation, socially destructive capital, evil political and legal structure, and myopic liberalism which is anti-revolutionary. *Revolution* permeated discussions like never before." He cautioned Haber, "In our future dealings, we should be aware that they have changed down there, and we should speak their revolutionary language without mocking it, for it is not lip service, nor is it the ego fulfillment of a rising Negro class, but it is in truth the fact of life in the South this minute, and unless the North or the government or nuclear war intervenes, we are going to be down here soon ourselves in jail or fighting, or writing, or being lynched in the struggle." It was, Hayden assured Haber, "a good, pure struggle, the kind that can bring hope to Africans and Asians and the rest of the hungry peoples, and it's a struggle that we have every reason to begin in a revolutionary way across the country, in every place of discrimination that exists. There is no reason for us to be hesitant anymore . . . There is no reason for us to think we can do something more important out of jail." SDS had been using the southern student movement for its own purposes, Hayden argued. "Two years ago we falsified this movement to claim it was the event with which we identified. We didn't. We saw it was something that we should extend, that we could both help in justice to ourselves and which could at the same provide a cutting edge for more reforms throughout society. Well now the Southern movement has turned itself into that revolution that we hoped for, and we didn't have much to do with it's turning at all. The southern students did . . . Now," he insisted, "they are miles ahead of us, looking back, chuckling knowingly about the sterility of liberals, tightening grimly against the potency of the racists. In the rural South, in the 'token integration' areas, in the cities, they will be shouting from the bottom of their guts for justice or else." SDS was not leading; it was following. If the organization really wanted to lead the American student movement, "we had better be there."[15]

"There" meant an actual place, of course. It meant the South, the towns and cities where the sit-ins occurred and the roads the Freedom Riders traveled. It meant Atlanta, where SNCC had its headquarters, and Jackson, where Hayden had attended a SNCC meeting and written his report. But "there" also mean an imaginative place, "the South," a place far away from the white midwestern suburb where Hayden had grown up. It meant a space outside modern America, full of authentic and yet marginal people. It meant black southerners.

It was in McComb, where the project motto was "A voteless people is a voiceless people," that Hayden became a participant in the civil rights movement, where he acted or at least was acted upon, where he put his body in the struggle. Years later, he still recalled how SNCC people had smuggled him and Paul Potter, NSA national affairs vice president and a future SDS president, into town on October 9.

> We had to stay in a motel and arrange, by clandestine means, to meet a car in a darkened section of the black ghetto in a Southern town in Mississippi. We had to be let out of a rented car, and lie on the back floor of a parked car in a parking lot. Somebody then picked it up and drove us—because it would have been too dangerous for whites and blacks to be in the same vehicle, even at night. They drove us to a house where all of the shutters were down, the windows were reinforced, and we had a meeting in the cellar with Bob [Moses] and some of the other people to talk about the voter registration campaign.

It was "devastating," Hayden remembered, to discover that we must use "clandestine means to discuss the most conventional kind of tactic, namely the registration of voters, because what we were up against was a whole organized system that was out to kill us." Crossing into the South, Hayden and Potter had become part of this "us." They too had become outsiders.[16]

In McComb, the two northern students, representing themselves as journalists, interviewed the editor of the local paper and the chief of police and spoke with local blacks. On October 11, they sat in their parked car outside the black high school and watched the students march to protest the murder of Herbert Lee and to support other students expelled for sit-in activities. The police rolled up and asked them what they were doing. "We try, but we can't protect everyone around here," the officers told them, "especially outsiders like yourselves." Told to go to the police station, Hayden and Potter drove away, with a police car trailing. After a few blocks, the police turned off. Suddenly, "the right door was ripped open by a white man, Carl Hayes, who pulled Paul into the street and beat him. He then came after me, struck me on the head and across the kidneys in the car, dragged me to the street, kicked me once, struck me again and once again, then left me alone." The plumber, as Hayes was described in the press, then ran away. Hayden "stood up from my sitting position, and noticed the students marching by us. Then the police 'escort' arrived, asking what had happened." While Hayden was talking to the police, "a fat, almost stereotypical Southern racist was screaming in a high voice that Paul and I had been fighting and fell out of the car on our heads, and now we were trying to blame a white man for having hit us." In the chaos, a person Hayden refused to identity told the "journalists" to leave the motel that night because "they are coming to take you." The police then transported Hayden and Potter to the station, where an investigator for the Mississippi Sovereignty Commission, who had arrived at the scene of the beatings just as the police pulled up, questioned the pair. Given a choice between jail and leaving town, Hayden and Potter sped north in their rental car, still wearing their bloody clothes.[17]

Years later, Hayden revealed that the man who warned them was the photographer following the march, who saw Hayes attack Hayden and Potter and took the pictures. Soon after, local whites destroyed his camera, but he had already removed the film and hidden the negatives. The next day, the Associated Press picked up the image of Hayes hitting Hayden. Newspaper readers around the country saw a skinny young white man in a suit futilely flinging his arms up to protect himself from the punch a big white man in tight jeans and a cut-off shirt had just landed on the right side of his head. In the years before the Birmingham dog and fire hose shots, this photograph circulated as an iconic image of nonviolent protest meeting segregationist brutality. A white southerner's fists and the national and local media made Hayden into a civil rights protester.[18]

Back in Atlanta, Hayden worked on *Revolution in Mississippi*, an SDS special report, published in January 1962 and read broadly by campus activists across the country. The pamphlet included authenticating documents, a preface by SNCC chair McDew, a foreword by SDS chair Haber, and a Bob Moses letter smuggled out of the Magnolia, Mississippi, jail. The title page printed *Revolution in Mississippi* over the then little known words of the song "We Shall Overcome." "How," Hayden asked at the start, "do we make the situation *real* to outsiders—those who know not the people involved, the state, the country, and most of all, the social, political, economic, cultural, religious, historic pattern we have labeled segregation? . . . This report is intended to make the facts real." Outsiders to Mississippi, Hayden predicted, would read these facts and then ally themselves with the outsiders within Mississippi, local blacks and SNCC activists. Together, they would create a new political coalition, win the revolution in Mississippi, and create a truly democratic America.[19]

Hayden's writings had their desired effect on a growing SDS. One later leader recalled that "these reports were very important to me: that's really the reason I went into SDS." From November 1961 to January 1963, membership grew from 575 to 900. More importantly, the organization was able to gain crucial national publicity. College students who did not necessarily belong learned about SDS by reading Hayden's publications or seeing the photograph of his beating in the newspaper. Haber and Jeffrey had been right to see civil rights activism as the spark that could ignite campus activism. Hayden's willingness to "put his body on the line" like his SNCC idols had given SDS's civil rights connection concrete form. For students outside the South, reading Hayden's *Revolution in Mississippi* was like singing along with the Freedom Singers, close, really close, to being there.[20]

Haber and Hayden, then, successfully used interest in the southern student movement to build SDS even as they also tried to use SDS to help the civil rights activists in the South. And it worked not just because there was great injustice in the South. There was great injustice in Detroit, right down the road from Ann Arbor, and in New York City, where Haber ran the national SDS office at the time. There was great injustice in the treatment of African Americans most places in America. It worked because popular culture had already taught many college students from outside the region how to romanticize southern blacks. It was not hard, then, for some young whites to transfer these feelings to SNCC workers. And SNCC's work was so exciting. "On a theoretical level, you can say that we believed in wanting to make history and achieve civil rights," Hayden recalled. "But there was something else: the middle-class emptiness of alienation that people talk about, and then suddenly confronting commitment. The whole emotion of defining not only yourself, but also your life by risking your life, and testing whether you're willing to die for your beliefs, was *the* powerful motive, I believe." Hayden had quoted Haber on this very point in a piece he wrote for *Mademoiselle* in August just before he went south: "Students have a mystique about action. They are thrilled by action per se," Haber told Hayden. "The passion usually associated with ideology is transferred to the actual doing of the deed." Acting, participating in the civil rights movement in the South, made whites like Hayden into outsiders too.[21]

In New York City that fall, Al Haber was busy pushing a different message. Acting now, for Haber, meant students outside the South needed to send money to support SNCC. More than a year before Seeger played his series of dates down south and the Freedom Singers became a group, Haber proposed a series of folk music concerts at colleges and high schools across the five boroughs to raise awareness about and funds for SNCC. These campus concerts would culminate in a large, citywide benefit starring "perhaps Odetta, Ola Tunji, and Harry Belafonte" and "participants from action areas of the Southern struggle." "There is no doubt," Haber wrote SNCC's Diane Nash, "that a campaign of this sort—beginning at the campus level and culminating in a mass city program could greatly contribute to the work of the committee." Later that fall and early winter, SDS's "SNCC fund raising program" held at least seven campus concerts and one citywide event for the high schools.[22]

But Haber had an even grander vision. Acting now meant not waiting to learn how to help the southern students. It meant acting here. Students outside the South needed to learn about what was happening to the region in order to imagine the ways they could act at home in this national struggle. Haber, in fact, pushed this point when he edited Hayden's reports: "We must begin not to share simply the forms of protest, but to translate the spirit of social revolution to the situations in our immediate experience that demand action." Haber called for "the complete extension of the movement to our own locales": "Support action" must "be translated into direct attack on local situations." Support activities, like Hayden's suggestion that SDS organize University of Chicago students to boycott the Illinois Central headquarters because Freedom Riders were being arrested at the railroad's station in Jackson, suggested that the fight lay elsewhere. Haber wanted SDS "to examine the character of discrimination in New York City with emphasis on housing, employment, schools, credit and political democracy." Acting now meant figuring out how to act in places like New York City. SDS would have to commit itself to the issue of civil rights everywhere.[23]

That December, Haber and Hayden decided to hold a small conference to translate their new vision of SDS as a national student movement into some more coherent organizational form. Though they thought the organization should focus on civil rights, other participants answered the call for papers by presenting other ideas including poverty, university reform, or peace. Participants could not reach a consensus but did find that they shared a rebellious style, "a kind of open Bohemianism filtered through the Beats that put a premium on honesty and naturalness." Somehow, they fused this social easiness with the passion and intellectual intensity of geeky honor students and the sense of entitlement, the belief that whatever they were doing was important, of many middle-class white kids. They shared, then, not a particular political program but a way of being in the world. At the conference, they decided to turn their disagreements into their purpose. Instead of writing a national plan for civil rights or peace work, they would codify what they believed. They would write a manifesto for the new student politics. At the bottom of the December 29–31 conference schedule were the words "January 1—the new left goes forth."[24]

What had been meant at least partly as a joke became instead a prophecy. What was lost was Haber's idea that SDS could coordinate a national student movement for civil rights, not just by romanticizing activists down south and sending money and volunteers there but also by helping generate student activism on the problem of civil rights in New York City and elsewhere in the North. The Northern Student Movement was never large enough to take up the task. Celebrating the civil rights movement in the South and raising funds for work there remained more popular on nonsouthern campuses throughout the sixties than building the movement outside the region.[25]

Unlike folk music fans, SDS leaders did not just want to feel a connection with the people imagined as living on the margins of modern America. Unlike SNCC staff members through 1963, most of whom were black college students, most SDS leaders did not just want to help local blacks engage in nonviolent direct action. Instead, the core members of SDS wanted to explain and expand the connection and articulate how an alliance of poor southern blacks and American college students could be the basis of revolutionary social change in America.

In the winter of 1962, Hayden stopped trying to be a SNCC activist and went to work instead as an intellectual. "Where," he wrote SDS members, "does one begin thinking about manifestos?" Hayden started by working on a speech, which later became a SDS pamphlet called *Student Social Action: From Liberation to Community*, in which he attempted to assimilate what he had learned in the South into a general program for student activism. Like some other early SNCC and SDS leaders, he turned to the work of two intellectuals in particular, Albert Camus and C. Wright Mills. Casey Hayden had introduced him to Camus's conception of "genuine rebellion," in Hayden's words "standing up to injustice even if life is 'absurd,' without apparent meaning." The very act of rebellion, Hayden recalled learning from Camus, "asserted a human nature worth preserving from extermination and drew the individual from solitude to solidarity." And this kind of resistance made a college student like Hayden into an outsider too. Looking for a way to weld Camus's existentialism into a practical political program, Hayden turned to Mills.[26]

Mills "became the oracle of the New Left," Hayden remembered, by "combining the rebel life-style of James Dean and the moral passion of Albert Camus with a comprehensive portrayal of the American condition." Mills gave Hayden a way of understanding America's "power elite," a much more complicated, less conspiratorial conception of the operation of power than the left's Marxist theory of the "ruling class." As importantly, Mills articulated a broader, more psychological idea of alienation and of the sources of oppression that led to political change. Mills's great subject was the inner life, the steady erosion of psychic freedom, related but not reducible to economic and political freedom. The growth of bureaucracy and the mass media and the shallow compensatory pleasures of consumerism, Mills argued, endangered the psychological independence of the American middle class. Mass society was killing not just economic independence but also individual self-expression. "The independent artist and intellectual," Mills insisted, were "among the few remaining personalities equipped to resist and to fight the stereotyping and consequent death of genuinely lively things." Individual self-expression should be the goal of left politics. Mills's analysis transformed Camus's rebellion into a political act in the restoration of American democracy and imagined middle-class Americans as a potential vanguard of political change.[27]

In "Student Social Action," Hayden fused Camus and Mills to offer a compelling vision of white middle-class college students as outsiders. The powerlessness of students on college campuses, he argued, paralleled the powerlessness of African Americans in the segregated South. Both groups were deprived of a political voice. Both groups experienced "deep alienation" from the decision-making institutions of society. College students should see southern African Americans and other oppressed groups as their allies in a new political coalition of the alienated. Together, they should work for "genuine independence": "a concern not with image or popularity, but with finding a moral meaning in life that is direct and authentic for the self." "I believe," Hayden wrote, drawing on his experiences in the South, "that independence can be a fact about ordinary people. And democracy, real participating democracy, rests on the independence of ordinary people." Following Mills, Hayden broadened his definition of independence to include psychological freedom and cultural determination, the right to self-expression, as well as economic security and political representation, the right to vote. United with "the masses of hungry, aspiring, utopian peoples intervening in history for the first time," students should act to restore "the individual personality to a creative and self-cultivating role in human affairs." "The time has come," Hayden concluded, "for a reassertion of the personal."[28]

That winter, SDS leaders had asked Hayden to write a draft of what they called an "agenda for the left" and a "manifesto of hope." "Student Social Action" was the warm-up. The plan was for Hayden to submit his work in progress to SDS members who would then form working groups at the annual conference to hammer out the final document. The manifesto that came out of this process, the Port Huron Statement, took its name from the United Auto Workers camp on the northern Michigan lakeshore where fewer than sixty SDS members and people affiliated with other organizations like SNCC met that June.[29]

Like Hayden's "Student Social Action," the Port Huron Statement radically positioned white college students as outsiders with a crucial role to play in a New Left political alliance. And it accomplished this essential revision of the Old Left's vision of a coalition grounded in economic exploitation by expanding the definition of oppression to include psychological and cultural alienation: "The goal of man and society should be human independence: a concern not with an image of popularity but with finding a meaning in life that is personally authentic, a power of mind not compulsively driven by a sense of powerlessness, nor one which unthinkingly adopts status values." Boldly, SDS's manifesto also offered a way to achieve its vision of the good life, "participatory democracy." In this "truly democratic alternative to the present," society would be organized to encourage independence and provide the means for the individual to "share in those social decisions determining the quality and the direction of his life." SDS's complicated relationship with the civil rights movement and Hayden's own romanticization of SNCC activists deeply influenced the Port Huron Statement's imagination of a new form of politics.[30]

SDS members working on the Port Huron Statement self-consciously attempted to "speak American." They understood the political capital to be gained by dramatizing the difference between democratic rhetoric and reality, by parading the fact that there were outsiders and insiders in the land of equality. Participatory democracy, in this vein, was a patriotic code word for a move toward democratic socialism. But it was also much more. As Hayden recalled about SDS, "Everything for us had to be new." Participatory democracy was a way to make the student movement into a New Left, to rebel against the Old Left as well as contemporary liberals and conservatives, for liberals, too, increasingly supported African-American civil rights, integration, and poverty programs for the urban poor. Participatory democracy was a challenge to liberal top-down, expert-heavy programs for accomplishing these goals.[31]

The concept of participatory democracy was also a way for SDS leaders to distinguish their organization from SNCC. Hayden, as edited by others at Port Huron, transformed what he understood as SNCC's "mystique of action alone" into an ideology, an understanding of the good life and how it should be achieved. Direct action became self–determination, a concept at once narrower (more individual than communal) and broader (encompassing psychological as well as material acts). Self-determination linked what many southern blacks hoped to get out of the civil rights movement—political, economic, and social equality—with what civil rights activists and people like Hayden also got out of the civil rights movement—the individual psychological freedom that came from acting under the threat of violence and even death. Activists lost their self-consciousness in the emotional intensity that accompanied the danger of organizing. "The folk," black or otherwise, supposedly lacked that self-consciousness all along. Self-determination—all the ways an individual could act to shape the world—would make everyone's life authentic, just like Hayden's heroes the SNCC field secretaries. No longer would the left simply stand for the elimination of poverty and political oppression. "The authentic life" included this old vision of utopia and so much more. With self-determination as its goal, the mostly white New Left imagined a political coalition capacious enough to include SDS members, SNCC activists, and "the folk."[32]

Feeling Real: The Economic Research and Action Project

What participatory democracy would look like in practice was anyone's guess. The Economic and Research Action Project, or ERAP, was SDS's attempt to find out. The Port Huron Statement and other SDS publications like Hayden's *Revolution in Mississippi* gave SDS a growing influence among student activists. But SDS was not known for action, or for organizing anything other than about twenty campus chapters and a lot of meetings. Jeffrey and Hayden, who had worked in the South, wanted to move beyond analysis and providing ideas and into action. As Hayden, then SDS president, wrote in the March–April 1963 *SDS Bulletin*, grassroots activists worked unseen in every community: "What we need is a way to transfer these invisible rebellions into a politics of responsible insurgence. Can the methods of SNCC be applied to the North? . . . Can we spread our *organizational power* as far as our *ideological influence*," Hayden asked, "or are we inevitably assigned to a vague educational role in a society that increasingly is built deaf to the sounds of protest?" In March, Hayden had written Walter Reuther of the United Auto Workers. In early August, the UAW gave SDS $5,000 for a project devoted to economic problems. On August 28, many SDS leaders participated in the March on Washington, where King and others spoke of an integrated mass movement to create a better America. Days later, at the 1963 National Student Association convention, Stokely Carmichael and other SNCC activists advised white students to organize in white communities. The leadership of SDS met right after the convention to discuss how their organization might respond. They had a model: SNCC's community organizing in places like McComb and Albany. They had a vision: They would organize the white as well as black poor and unemployed, in places like northern cities and the mining country around Hazard, Kentucky, where SNCC was not working. They had the funds. And they believed they could recruit college students to provide the labor. They founded ERAP to create the plan.[33]

SDS leaders disagreed about whether ERAP should focus more on action or research. Did making a plan mean conducting extensive preliminary research or deciding quickly where to create community-organizing projects that would then generate their own data for analysis? Carl Wittman, a Swarthmore student, SDS member, and the leader of a campus group that successfully allied with African Americans in nearby Chester, Pennsylvania, in a series of nonviolent mass actions in November, wrote a SDS working paper with Hayden that winter. "An Interracial Movement of the Poor?" argued that poor people across the nation were natural allies because they had common needs: "improved housing, lower rents, better schools, full employment, extension of welfare and social security assistance. These are not 'Negro issues' per se; rather, they are precisely those issues which should appeal to lower-class whites as well as Negroes." And white students as well as African Americans could organize the poor by living among them at their economic level: "*We are the people and we work with the people.* Only if conscious *cooperative* practice is our main style will our ideology take on the right details, only then will it be tested and retested." SDS needed to put participatory democracy into practice. "It is the role we play in the community, in developing a voice and a power among the poor," they argued, "that will give us a legitimate and radical place." into practice. Activists would become radicals—achieve their own "authentic" lives and express their own values—by helping the poor realize their self-determination too. Hayden, Wittman, and their allies wanted ERAP to stop studying community organizing and actually do it.[34]

In the winter and spring of 1963–64, these disagreements about the future direction of ERAP and indeed SDS erupted into open debate. Haber led a group of SDS leaders who opposed "ghetto-jumping," their term for community organizing. An even smaller group, led by New York City native Steve Max, one of the few SDS leaders who had not attended college, advocated what he called realignment. SDS should work in the South, Max argued, not because northern college students wanted to help southern blacks but because expanded voter registration in the region would break up conservative southern Democrats' hold on Congress. Working in the South was not about feelings and finding authenticity. It was a way to move the Democratic Party to the left. Hayden and his allies eventually won the debate. Haber did not give up quietly, however, and his and others' critique of using ERAP to move SDS into community organizing predicted many of the problems that would emerge as activists tried to build a new politics on the romance of the outsider.[35]

Todd Gitlin, then president of SDS, allied with Hayden in support of community organizing. In his analysis, "social change originates with the most dispossessed . . . Other classes will cluster around the dispossessed as they organize, since they are the most dynamic." This was certainly how many SDS members felt about southern civil rights activists. But for Haber, this "into the ghetto" enthusiasm ignored "our role as a *student* organization." It generated "an unfortunate anti-intellectualism in SDS," pushed "students to leave the university," and granted "a moral superiority for those who 'give their bodies' . . . 'In the world' has come to mean 'in the slum,'" an analysis Haber found "slightly sick." "Is radicalism subsisting in the slum for a year or two?" he asked. "The cult of the ghetto has diverted SDS from its primary and most difficult task of educating radicals. It says 'come and do radical things.' But when the student decides he has to make a living, SDS has given him no help in functioning as a radical in the middle class, professional world." SDS, Haber concluded, "will have people deny what they are, and hence never learn how to apply their values in what they do." At the June 1964 summer convention, a group calling itself Touch and Sex wrote a plan for action parodying the supporters of community organizing and their "feelie" politics.[36]

As these arguments raged, SDS leaders who supported community organizing were already at work creating what they envisioned as a northern counterpart to SNCC's southern projects. By June 1964, they had chosen nine cities—Baltimore, Boston, Chester, Chicago, Cleveland, Newark, Philadelphia, Trenton, and Louisville—and one rural area, Hazard, Kentucky. They had selected about one hundred participants and held a six-day training institute the week before the NSA convention. Projects had already opened in Chicago and Cleveland. In response to President Johnson's "unconditional war on poverty in America," Congress was at work on a massive anti-poverty program based on the "maximum feasible participation of the poor," an idea that like participatory democracy emphasized poor people's ability to act to help themselves. ERAP put these ideas into action. SDS would lead American college students on the newly high-profile issue of poverty. Jeffrey, who went to work in Cleveland, believed they were doing nothing less than changing the world.[37]

ERAP participants arrived in their cities with a few dollars, a scattering of local contacts, and a general idea, often wrong, about where to find the poor whites many projects most hoped to organize. They rented run-down apartments and houses, often more than one, at least initially, so male and female activists could live separately and not upset community residents. An ERAP project's first order of business was often its own community—how to make participatory democracy work in participants' living arrangements. Most often, people decided to live communally, to pool their money and divide up tasks like buying and cooking the food and repairing the houses. They held long meetings on internal organization. How could they avoid hierarchies and differences of status? How could they make all decisions democratically? Was it okay to take off one day during the summer and go to the beach? They even invented new terms like "research keeper" and "broom keeper" to try to promote a sense of the equal value of all common work. Men, many groups decided, would have to learn to cook.[38]

Quickly, groups became proud of living in poverty. Since the organizing work itself yielded few results in the first months, ERAP members' most tangible achievement was surviving in the slums. In the detailed letters they sent back to the SDS office, compiled into a national newsletter, projects competed to see who could survive on the smallest food budget, a steadily dropping number that reached less than fifty cents per person per day. Some groups passed out little cups of orange juice like communion wine. Everyone ate endless meals of peanut butter and jelly and powdered milk. Journalist Andrew Kopkind, in one of the first articles in the national media about SDS, insisted few "on the 'outside'" could "imagine the completeness of their transformation, or the depth of their commitment . . . They are part of the slums," he continued. "They get no salary; they live on a subsistence allowance . . . Most of the time they are broke . . . In the dining room of the Cleveland 'project house' last week," he wrote, hung a sign: "Panic point. Bank balance $4.09." Project participants often had to call "friends in the suburbs" for five or ten dollars in order to eat. They did not just organize the poor—they also lived the poverty. They tried to become poor people themselves.[39]

The organizing effort proved much harder than living on meager funding. Often it was difficult to find local people even interested in coming to meetings. ERAP workers fanned out through their neighborhoods daily, knocking on doors. They talked to women watching toddlers in hot apartments and men drinking on stoops and people waiting in line at unemployment and welfare benefit offices. They asked these people to participate in short surveys—what did they want to change in their neighborhoods? They collected and studied the answers and discussed the people they met. In each project area the greatest challenge proved to be finding a group to organize around some local issue in order to begin working toward the "real" goal of building "the Movement," the larger coalition for radical change. In the summer of 1964, throughout the next year, and in the summer of 1965, SDS members experimented with ERAP projects in a changing list of cities across America.[40]

Groups that had the most success, such as those in Cleveland and Newark, took on specific local issues like welfare rights, daycare and recreation facilities, and traffic lights, jokingly called GROIN, for Garbage Removal or Income Now. Poor people, they found, came to meetings to work on immediate, concrete problems and did not often share organizers' interest in participatory democracy and building a radical political movement in coalition with college students and poor people elsewhere. If life in the ghetto was "authentic" and "real," then locals wanted a little less reality. As Hayden remembered about his experience working in Newark, "We finally saw that only the organizing experience itself, going through the struggle, was enough to unify the people." ERAP activists learned to generate agitation around roaches and rats or the absence of stoplights or playgrounds. People mad about the way the city government was treating them—the welfare check denied or the slumlord protected—sometimes took the next step into political organizing. "Tragedy and protest," as Hayden wrote sometime after that first summer, were "but one and the same."[41]

In Cleveland, for example, ERAP discovered that welfare mothers were an ideal organizing target and helped reactivate a defunct community group,

Citizens United for Adequate Welfare (CUFAW). Welfare mothers, raising their children on little money in bad housing, had, in Jeffrey's words, "life skills," unlike chronically unemployed men. With the Cleveland ERAP project's help, welfare recipients won fairer treatment from the city and the payment of benefits owed and yet denied. Buoyed by these individual successes, CUFAW and ERAP project members pushed for and won a citywide free lunch program in the public schools. They planned and hosted a poor people's conference, bringing community people from other ERAP locations together with civil rights activists. Former sharecropper turned SNCC activist Fannie Lou Hamer, for example, traveled from the Mississippi Delta to speak to the conference. After the day's meetings, she led conference participants in singing as they marched through Cleveland. In 1966, Cleveland welfare mothers, politicized by SDS, became a strong organizing center in the new National Welfare Rights Organization.[42]

In Newark, where Hayden lived for four years in what would become the longest-running project, ERAP organizers created the community union approach. Newark Community Union Project (NCUP) took on whatever protests and actions community members expressed an interest in pursuing. One SDS and NCUP member described the range of activities in 1965:

> filing housing violation forms, demanding housing inspection,
> organizing rent strikes, demonstrations at a landlord's house in the
> suburbs, testifying about housing conditions before the Human
> Rights Commission; a sit-in at the Mayor's office to protest police
> and court mistreatment of a rent striker, large scale protest of police
> brutality through marches, pickets at the precinct level; testimony
> on general conditions before the Human Rights Commission, the
> Mayor, and other officials, before the War-on-Poverty agency, the
> Powell Committee investigating the War-on-Poverty; frequent visits
> "downtown," often with no notice, to ask for assistance or informa-
> tion from a wide range of officials, demanding that their offices be
> open to the public; protest of particular welfare abuses.

NCUP, in ERAP's greatest success, eventually took over the local federal anti-poverty program. Its motto, "Let the People Decide," participatory democracy's broad ideal of self-determination, became a rallying cry throughout SDS and the New Left more generally. Even SNCC watched the ERAP projects closely and increasingly adopted SDS's rhetoric after the summer of 1964. SDS members, wanting to be like Bob Moses and other black activists in SNCC, had surpassed their models.[43]

While many ERAP projects disbanded as key organizers left to go back to school or to other work, the better-run projects did not fail—they helped politicize community members who continued to work, for example, in anti-poverty programs and welfare rights organizations. But ERAP did fail to attract widespread student attention, as the sit-ins, the Freedom Rides, and the later work of SNCC had done. Community organizing in the slums did not become the next wave of the revolution. In part, the effort lacked a concrete goal, like ending the segregation of public facilities and the franchise, which could be measured and publicized. The analysis behind ERAP's arguments for community organizing was wrong. Poor people were not naturally allies. Like any other category of people, they had to learn to recognize their common concerns. A related problem was the fact that the issues organizers addressed were small locally—it was hard to see getting rid of roaches in an apartment building as part of the revolution—and overwhelming in the aggregate: How could organizers, whatever their race or resources, stop suburban flight?

But these difficulties actually increased organizers' interest in living the revolution, in modeling the utopia to come in the midst of the struggle, in changing their own lives. SNCC workers, an SDS member argued, "managed to impress ERAP with the image of an organizer who never organized, who by his simple presence was the mystical medium for the spontaneous expression of the 'people.'" "Organizing," Hayden wrote in an "Open Letter to ERAP Supporters and New Organizers," "can be a way of life . . . Students, "he urged, "should consider whether their own needs are satisfied by life in the univer-sities." As Michael Harrington argued in his *New Republic* appraisal of the "young radicals," ERAP organizers "identify precisely with the *lumpen*, the powerless, the maimed, the poor, the criminal, the junkie. And there is a mystical element in this commitment which has nothing to do with politics." Hayden did not deny that students worked to help both the poor and them-selves: "Students and poor people make each other feel real . . . If poor people are in the Movement because they have nothing to gain in the status system, students are in it because in a sense they have gained too much . . . Working in poor communities is a concrete task in which the split between job and values can be healed." The students would give the poor a sense of the possibilities of democracy and help ease their political and economic alienation. The poor in turn would teach the students the truth, "that their upbringing has been based on a framework of lies," and help them heal their cultural and psychological alienation and find their innocence. At the margins, from the people already there, students would learn to separate from existing society and live "outside" its boundaries, in opposition to its values.[44]

The idea of letting the poor decide, envisioning the role of the student volunteer more as magical catalyst rather than as dedicated organizer, dominated SDS thinking about community work by 1965. If the urban poor and people on the margins more generally possessed superior morals and values, then why should SDS members to try to lead them anywhere? SNCC's Bob Moses and Hayden, "anti-leaders," in the scholar James Miller's apt phrase, provided a model for leadership through commitment, through their very embodiment of poor rural or urban blacks' own values, without any visible exercise of official authority at all. Living and expressing poor people's estrangement from the system—acting poor—was now enough. Nothing made this clearer than the Hoboken "non-project" in which organizers simply moved into poor neighborhoods in this New Jersey city and got jobs as unskilled laborers. As one of its non-members described the effort at the 1965 SDS convention, "leaders mean organizations, organization means hierarchy, and hierarchy is undemocratic. It connotes bureaucracy and impersonality." "Getting with the people" was the key to social change. Only personal relationships changed people's values. "Alienation," he emphasized, "the quality of human life produced by the bureaucratized society," was the common problem everywhere. Young and alienated middle-class kids just needed to connect with the poor.[45]

This kind of romanticism—the idea that the outsider, either the organizer or the local poor person, was more real, more authentic than other people—hurt SDS's experiment in community organizing. There were organizational problems as well. With most of the leaders committed to community action buried deep in the day-to-day work of the projects in Chicago, Cleveland, and Newark, few people were left to push the effort nationally, coordinate ERAP efforts with the growing numbers of campus chapters, and raise much needed funding. Leaders working in the SDS national office often had other priorities or left their posts to go into community work. And ERAP's model of participatory democracy had its flaws too. A 1965 ERAP recruiting pamphlet quoted "one man in Newark" without irony: "Freedom is an endless meeting." Even the most dedicated organizers—and Hayden, who made money writing and left Newark for other political activities like his December 1965 trip to North Vietnam, was no exception—could not take the stress of living the movement all the time.[46]

But no organization could overcome the problems that grew out of the idea that organizing was a way of life that blessed its followers with authenticity and outsider status. "By going into the slum, they are doing penance for the sins of affluence," Harrington insisted. "By sharing the life of those who are so impoverished that they are uncorrupted, values are affirmed." These young radicals believed, Harrington argued, that it was "honest and moral and anti-hypocritical to be on the margin of society *whether the community organization works or not.* Indeed, there is a fear of 'success,' a suspicion that it would mean the integration of the oppressed into the corruption of the oppressors." Young radicals needed to consider, he suggested, whether this privileging of innocence and authenticity, this emphasis on the experience of organizing over the results, mattered much to the people they were trying to organize.[47]

Insiders who wanted out and outsiders who wanted in might share an alienation from modern American life, but they did not always share a vision of the good life. ERAP organizers understood their successes as small accomplishments—free school lunches, the slowing of traffic through some poor neighborhoods, the restoration of benefits to some welfare recipients, fewer rats and roaches and more working appliances in a scattering of slum apartments, more places for the kids to play, and a couple of community organizations—in a context in which the goal was the revolutionary transformation of American society. But many poor people, ERAP organizers complained, were more concerned about exactly these kinds of changes and about eliminating their poverty than they were about building a piece of a radical movement. Local people wanted into the very middle-class lives of consumption and economic security that ERAP organizers were fleeing.

What if the organizers' search for a meaningful life, the agency and expression of the poor, and the advancement of left politics were not all the same project? What if poor people discovered their agency and chose to work within "the system" and against the radicals of SDS? Or decided they did not want to be active in politics at all? Romanticism helped camouflage any potential contradictions. ERAP called its recruiting pamphlet for the summer of 1965 *a movement of many voices.* Interviews with community people who worked with ERAP projects led readers into a description of the organization, its methods and goals, and its project sites. As in a sing-along, all the voices came together to evoke a momentary sense of unity.[48]

Still, even as volunteers' romanticism made it difficult to think strategically about the projects, ERAP organizing may have been hurt even more by the fact that this romanticism was limited by the absence of any nationally popular movement celebrating the culture of the urban poor. In 1964 and 1965, there was no "ghetto revival" to circulate a romance of poor urban Americans in image and song. There were no singers reviving their authentic and charming traditions at concerts and benefits that raised funds and awareness of their plight. Most of all, there was no innocence. ERAP activists certainly presented the poor as oppressed by others and thus not to be blamed for their deprivation. The problem was that there was nothing in it for the audience, for the liberals who might be urged to give money to ERAP or to volunteer to make copies or type. There was no way for people, except the ERAP volunteers, to find their authenticity. And there was no way for people, including the volunteers, to find their innocence. Americans were exploited in cities that were the very centers of liberal power, the places where people turned out for SNCC Freedom Singers benefits. Sure, SDS activists were brash, contemptuous of older, leftist organizations and ongoing urban relief projects, and often sure with the bravado of youth that they were the smartest people— except the poor—around. But all of these faults applied to SNCC field secretaries too. It was just easier in 1964 for a white liberal to go to a concert, buy SNCC's record, or even volunteer to work for SNCC. Success, Hayden wrote from Newark, depended upon "a climate of fresh opinion in the North, a willingness to support popular movements for change here," like the willingness of people outside the South to support change there. But there was nothing like the folk music revival to generate a romantic and even sentimental view of the urban poor equivalent to the image of the folk.[49]

SDS needed Bob Dylan to do more than stop by their December 1963 New York meeting and channel Woody Guthrie: "Ah don' know what yew all are talkin' about . . . but it sounds like *yew* want somthin' to happen, and if that's what *yew* want that's what *Ah* want." They needed him to write a song about police brutality in Newark. They needed the welfare mothers in Cleveland to sing in meetings. They needed their own Freedom Singers. Without a popular romance of the outsider broad enough to encompass the urban poor, what would make people who were not poor, in Hayden's words, "transcend their pettiness to commit themselves to great purposes?" What would make them want to change?[50]

Black and White Together: The Mississippi Summer Project

With a good deal more cynicism and self-consciousness, SNCC too worked to turn white middle-class college students' attraction to outsiders into activism. SNCC benefited greatly from white romanticism in the mid-sixties. In 1963 and 1964, the organization used the folk music revival's image of southern blacks as "the folk" to spread stories of its southern projects and to raise the money and supporters it needed to spread direct action and community organizing throughout the Deep South. Favorable articles about the organization appeared in *Harper's*, the *New York Times*, and other national publications. The historian Howard Zinn called SNCC workers "the new abolitionists." Fund-raising soared. The number of paid staff grew from a little more than twenty in early 1963 to more than sixty-five in the spring of 1964. That year, the organization put this romanticism to work to recruit volunteers for its 1964 Mississippi Summer Project. Mailings and press releases called the project "a massive Peace Corps operation in Mississippi." Freedom Singers concerts, Friends of SNCC groups, and college newspapers spread the word about SNCC's ambitious plan to bring hundreds of white college students from outside the region into the state most actively and violently resisting integration. SNCC's summer project offered middle-class white volunteers a potent mix of political action, missionary work, and exotic travel.[51]

Some white volunteers, of course, were already working in the South before the summer project. In 1959, the NSA hired former member Constance Curry to direct its Southern Students Human Relations Project from an office in Atlanta. White students attended the meeting in 1960 from which SNCC emerged, and Casey Cason, Dinky Romilly, Dottie Miller, Mary King, and other white volunteers worked with SNCC as early as 1960. When the Southern Conference Educational Fund (SCEF) volunteered in 1961 to pay the salary of an activist to organize white southerners in support of civil rights, Atlanta college student Bob Zellner became SNCC's first white field secretary. Zellner quickly found this work impossible. Being a member of SNCC, he wrote in a report to the SCEF in 1962, left him "estranged from other southern white students." "How do you relate," he asked, "to the white southern moderate or liberal and at the same time relate to a group of people who are as militant and as activist" as SNCC field secretaries? Zellner ended up organizing alongside African American SNCC workers in black southern communities. In 1962, the Albany project in southwest Georgia became the first SNCC community organizing effort to actively recruit white volunteers to work with African Americans. Bill Hansen also worked in the field. Forman advocated the continuation of this new experiment in organizing. The success of white field workers there, he asserted, "opened the doors to the use of white people in other areas."[52]

SNCC activists argued a great deal about the wisdom of using whites in the movement. Staff members, who were mostly black until 1964, worried about the deep effects of bringing so many whites into a movement mainly run by African Americans. Rural southern blacks might go to the courthouse to register with a white volunteer simply because they had long ago learned that survival depended upon doing what white people asked. Too many local black people would not be able to compete with college students in terms of skills. How would locals learn to run offices, manage projects, and teach and speak and plan surrounded by talented and well-intentioned but not always sensitive young whites? The gender of volunteers also presented a problem. White women would endanger black men with their very presence.[53]

In favor of the summer project, SNCC people argued that white Americans would pay attention to Mississippi if white college students too faced racist sheriffs, Klansmen, and members of the Citizens' Councils there. If enough white kids came, the press would follow them. And if a white student got killed, the national newspapers and television news programs would investigate and report on the murder. There were possible long-term benefits as well. Giving a large group of young volunteers exposure to direct action and community organizing over the summer might transform their ideas about what they could do in their hometowns and on their campuses in the fall. The summer project was one possible answer to the question SNCC workers often asked: How could they share the experience of poor rural southern blacks with other Americans? How could they "make a fat rich country" care? The risks of using white volunteers were high, but there was no denying that the potential payoff was huge.[54]

White volunteers joined the movement out of shifting and unequal measures of commitment to social justice and an attraction to black folk. Ralph Allen, a white SNCC activist in jail in 1963 in Americus, Georgia, a small town near Albany, explained to a local white girl who had sent him a taunting letter why he joined the movement:

> It's no heaven on earth I left . . . Depends on what you mean by
> heaven. If you mean a place where everyone has so much money
> they have no sensitivity—no love, no sympathy, and no hopes
> beyond their own little narrow worlds . . . But to me the conceited,
> loud, self-centered All-American free white and twenty-one college
> boy stinks. I know. I was one. But something happened to make me
> human.

"If I didn't have my [black] friends, I would be very much alone," Allen continued. "And I don't want to eat in anyone's restaurant alone, to go to nobody's movie alone, to swim in nobody's pool alone. You dig?" Joining southern blacks in their fight turned the insider Allen into an outsider too.[55]

Danny Lyon, a white photographer who worked with SNCC from 1962 to 1964, explained his reasons for joining and staying in the movement in a letter to his parents after they sent him an underlined copy of a *New York Times* interview with Bayard Rustin. There, the long-term civil rights activist and organizer of the March on Washington argued that "many white students working with Negro students in the South could perform a more useful function if they returned home to agitate among the white people." Lyon's parents wanted him to heed this advice. He wished he could leave, he suggested in his reply. He would "rather be making money or generally enjoying myself which is the main thing I do not get to do in the South." He stayed in the movement, he insisted, because to leave would be "regarded as traitorous; or anyway a kind of retreat morally." "In many ways, I think the things I do here are good for me, to use a poor term," he pleaded. "I have responsibility, in my work here, which frankly I hate. Somehow, because of the movement and the conditions of the country, I feel forced to face that responsibility. In the particular form, it means doing some SNCC pamphlets instead of riding and photographing motorcycles . . . None of us want to be here," he continued. "Forman would like to be writing, John [Lewis] wants to go to Africa, and they all really want to leave, but can't of course. The system remains, segregation has not yet fallen."[56]

Other white SNCC workers took Rustin's critique to heart and tried to develop civil rights projects in white southern communities. White SNCC field worker Sam Shirah took up the question of white participation directly. Whites in the movement, he argued, were "crippled by guilt," and these feelings of alienation made them romanticize "blackness" as the opposite of all that was wrong in their lives. White romanticism could provide a way into "true integration," but only if white activists moved from loving blacks into accepting whites. Shirah called whites' need to come to terms with their own race "white nationalism" to suggest its similarity to black nationalism. Whites in SNCC, Shirah suggested, should recruit white students to work in white communities. In the spring of 1964, Shirah, Ed Hamlett, Constance Curry, and other white southerners working in the civil rights movement created the Southern Student Organizing Committee to recruit white students to this new kind of organizing work. Veterans of civil rights work in the South, these organizers understood how the blacks they worked with in SNCC and other organizations might like and trust them personally and yet feel that strategically, African Americans needed to organize themselves. The historic, structural weight of white supremacy was just too great, and the newer burden of some liberal whites' romanticization of rural blacks seemed, in this context, just too much to bear.[57]

When SNCC leader Bob Moses, Allard Lowenstein, a former president of the NSA, and other SNCC leaders began discussing the possibility of a summer organizing season in Mississippi, the idea of recruiting whites emerged as a divisive issue. Moses and Lowenstein had pioneered the use of white student volunteers, many from Stanford and Yale, in the small Freedom Vote experiments held in the fall of 1963, mock elections designed to prove that blacks in Mississippi wanted the franchise. White students, they found, were not only easy to recruit, they brought the national media to Mississippi and made federal officials, from FBI agents to Justice Department officials, work harder to prevent violent attacks. Based on this experience, they envisioned expanding the project the next summer. Volunteers would continue the effort to register black voters, but they would also build a set of parallel, democratic institutions: a new state Democratic Party, the Mississippi Freedom Democratic Party (MFDP), new Freedom Schools offering classes on everything from African American history to adult literacy, and community centers to house recreation and meeting facilities, libraries, and daycare centers. White volunteers, SNCC activists, and local blacks working together would bring the massive media attention and federal intervention necessary to break white segregationists' hold on the state Lowenstein called "A Foreign Country in Our Midst."[58]

At a June 10, 1964, Atlanta staff meeting called to discuss the presence of guns in the Freedom House in Greenwood, Mississippi, staff members talked again about violence and the pending arrival of white volunteers. Everyone in the room understood the dangers local blacks faced in working with SNCC. Just that January, Louis Allen, a Mississippi black planning to testify against Herbert Lee's murderer, had been shot at his home after he had asked for federal protection. Prathia Hall eloquently argued that no one could "be rational about death." SNCC should "just bring the reality of our situation to the nation. Bring our bloodshed on to the white house door. If we die here it's the whole society which has pulled the trigger." Ruby Doris responded, "We know that the summer project was conceived with the idea that there would be bloodshed, but what does it mean to say that violence will be brought to the doorstep of the white house. No one in Birmingham rose after the shootings and bombings."[59]

Talk of the summer project turned the group's attention to the question of white volunteers. Charles McLaurin wondered how SNCC could go into white communities with the idea of nonviolence. Mendy Samstein, one of at least two white staff members present, reminded the group that Ed Hamlett was "developing programs with about 25 southern whites." That project was proving very difficult to establish because, as Samstein reminded them, "when whites hit McComb they were immediately beaten." McLaurin replied, "When whites come down they rush into the Negro community.

That's why they're beaten. Whites should develop within the white, not the Negro, community."[60]

The Council of Federated Organizations (COFO) officially ran the 1964 Mississippi Summer Project, or "Freedom Summer," as a way to share resources and coordinate work with groups like CORE, also active in the state. But in its style and organization, the summer project belonged to SNCC. The mostly black veteran organizers of SNCC and other members of COFO and the local black people working with the mostly white summer volunteers put on display a version of an integrated world, a vision that overlapped substantially with white middle-class folk romanticism and SDS's coalition of the alienated. The summer project also strengthened SNCC's reputation for militant action, an image languishing as the Freedom Riders gave way to federal-government-approved voter registration efforts. SNCC was daring enough to taunt the segregationists and call on the government to make an unambiguous stand on the side of integration. "The Federal Government must take action," Moses wrote about the upcoming project in January 1964, "even if it means the imposition of federal troops or the occupation of a town or particular locality." Raising the issue of federal protection before any volunteers even arrived, Moses hoped "this is not asking too much of our country." SNCC president John Lewis, speaking at a rally in California recruiting participants and support, warned that the summer project would "saturate" Mississippi with volunteers, creating a context in which "the Federal Government will have to take over the state." Civil rights workers might provoke violence, he conceded, but "out of this conflict, this division and chaos, will come something positive." All this publicity increased the SNCC "mystique," drawing in more middle-class white supporters.[61]

For white students at elite northern and western universities and colleges, rural Mississippi seemed like a foreign land. In his reports to the NSA and speeches on campuses, Lowenstein described the state as literally an alien place where "you can't picket, you can't vote, you can't boycott effectively, can't mount mass protest of any kind, and can't reach the mass media." But the chance to leave their safe middle-class lives far behind and to make a difference working with rural poor black people attracted rather than dissuaded potential volunteers. Romanticism and a sense of social justice were often inseparable. Many volunteers left home hoping to find the real, the "authentic," black folk down south, and to become real themselves. Sally Belfrage described the not always conscious motivations that led her and other white volunteers to Mississippi: "I go where the view is a different one, my responsibility somewhat less oppressive, my guilt less evident. In the

College Students
and others
Needed

for CORE
Summer Program

This Congress of Racial Equality brochure recruited participants for the 1964 Mississippi Summer Project. *Ellin Freedom Summer Photograph Collection, McCain Library and Archives, The University of Southern Mississippi.*

backside of America," Belfrage confessed, "there is little danger of discerning a face at all, much less my own. It is a pilgrimage to a foreign country; traveling there, I can leave my guilt behind and atone for someone else's." Many potential volunteers wrote on their applications that they must act in what some called the "Civil Rights Revolution," which they understood as both a key moment in two centuries of American history and an event that was occurring in the South in particular rather than the entire country. Some candidates wanted to help people from "inadequate cultural backgrounds" and Americans who did not share their privileges. For Samuel Kipnis, a student at Reed College, the folk music revival was key. On his application, he listed his ability to play "American Folk Guitar"—he had taken "extensive lessons from Reverend Gary Davis, a Negro blind street singer from North Carolina"—as one of the skills that made him a desirable candidate. In reference to another candidate, an interviewer jotted on an application: "Has Car. Also has guitar." Paul Cowan, another white volunteer, gave Pete Seeger part of the credit for his decision to go south. Another applicant claimed he had "suffered the rebukes of James Baldwin and the laments of Peter Seeger" long enough. "The time for empathy without action is long past. I am impatient and will act now."[62]

By late spring, as a result of SNCC's and Lowenstein's efforts, about 1,200 students had formally applied to participate in the project. Between 650 and 900 nonprofessionals—people who were not the lawyers, clergymen, politicians, and folk singers that also worked in the state that summer—actually went to Mississippi. Most of these summer volunteers were the kind of people Lowenstein and Lewis helped recruit, white college students from outside the region.[63]

On the ground, at the training sessions in Oxford, Ohio, and working in Mississippi, SNCC leader Bob Moses with his quiet words, shy manner, and sharecropper style became an important focus of white volunteers' romanticism. "Don't come to Mississippi this summer to save the Mississippi Negro," Moses told one training class. "Only come if you understand, really understand, that his freedom and yours are one." The volunteers, he insisted, were working for themselves as much as for local blacks. "He is a careful thinker, expresses himself with great economy and honesty, and with every word one is amazed at the amount of caring in the man," one volunteer wrote home. "He is more or less the Jesus of the whole project, not because he asks to be, but because of everyone's reaction to him." Another described his style of leadership: "He was not in the least dynamic, but he forced you by what he said and by his manner of saying it, to want to partake of him, to come to him. He was

Pete Seeger meets with students in a Freedom School class at Mount Zion Baptist Church in Hattiesburg, Mississippi, on August 4, 1964. *Randall Freedom Summer Photograph Collection, McCain Library and Archives, The University of Southern Mississippi.*

not in any way outgoing, yet when he spoke you felt close to him." Everyone mentioned his overalls.[64]

Many volunteers adopted the modest goals Moses described during their training. "He said," one volunteer wrote home, "that the mere fact of spending the summer in Negro homes would be an important victory" and that "our connections back home will give the project more protection, and bring the Justice Dept. into Mississippi in a bigger way." "Maybe we're not going to get very many people registered this summer," a journalist and illustrator present at the training camp in Oxford recalled Moses saying to the volunteers. "Maybe, even, we're not going to get very many people into the Freedom Schools. Maybe all we're going to do is live through the summer. In Mississippi, that will be so much!" For many summer volunteers, Moses brought the romance of the activist as outsider to life.[65]

Volunteers fell in love with Fannie Lou Hamer too, present in Oxford at their training. Her story quickly circulated among the volunteers: how she had been rendered homeless and unemployed for the simple act of trying to register to vote and how, jailed for her civil rights work, she had endured a savage beating. "To watch her limp around here, encouraging the prayer sessions in which we all remember Senator Eastland and Governor Johnson and all the brutal people they sanction, is almost too much to take," one volunteer wrote. "But it's also a never-failing source of courage and determination." In Oxford and later in Mississippi, many white volunteers found the depth and strength of many southern blacks' Christian faith a source of wonder and awe.[66]

At training in Oxford, African American historian Vincent Harding gave these young white volunteers a way to think about what drew them: "Are you going as 'In' members of society to pull the 'Outs' in with you? Or are we all 'Outs'?" In going to Mississippi, summer volunteers joined what SNCC, SDS, and other New Left leaders envisioned as the coalition of outsiders that would change America. Even after the danger became painfully concrete, most white volunteers chose to remain on the side of the "Outs." Word of the murders of three activists—white CORE worker Michael Schwerner, black CORE worker James Chaney, and white summer project volunteer Andrew Goodman—in Neshoba County, Mississippi, reached many volunteers before they arrived.[67]

Just as Moses had predicted, the press followed white volunteers to Mississippi. As Julius Lester satirized the coverage, local feature stories on Freedom Summer followed a standard formula: "Blop-blop is a blue-eyed blond from Diamond Junction-on-the-Hudson, New York. She's a twenty-year-old junior at Radcliffe majoring in Oriental metaphysics and its relationship to quantum theory . . . This summer she's living with a Negro family in Fatback, Mississippi." National papers like the *New York Times* sometimes did better, but Lester's critique captured a tone present in some of their coverage as well. "Ten wide-eyed white girls" were in Ruleville, Mississippi, the *Times* reported, "to teach freedom to Mississippi Negroes." Katherine Logan, "a brunette in a blue dress, blinked in the bright sun. 'I really don't know what to expect,' she said." However much these articles exposed the brutally violent oppression at the heart of the Deep South racial order, they did not do it by promoting a vision of racial equality. They did it by telling a morality tale of America's white best and brightest giving up their summers to save poor innocent black folks. Many newspapers and magazines covered the summer project the way turn-of-the-century newspapers covered foreign mission work.[68]

Despite these articles, many white volunteers worked to fit in both with the black SNCC field workers who led their projects and with local blacks, and they made their metamorphosis, their transformation into outsiders, clear in their bodies, gestures, and speech as well as in their letters home. On dusty roads and hot porches, they fell in love with the black people they tried to organize and the community members who housed them. As staff member Charles Sherrod described SNCC's community organizing work, "There is always a 'mama,' . . . a militant woman in the community, outspoken, understanding, and willing to catch hell, having already caught her share." Summer project volunteers connected with these "mamas." "I have become so close to the family I am staying with—eleven people," one volunteer wrote her mom back home, "that Mrs. H. finally paid me a great compliment," introducing the volunteer as her "adopted daughter." "Such love oozes from this house I can't begin to explain." Another wrote home in deep admiration for the old black man who had taken them in. "He must be 75 years old, but he's tough, still working, and willing to undergo danger," and he baked "wonderful bread" too. They also greatly admired the people who tried to register to vote and came to the Freedom Schools.[69]

The relationships white volunteers formed with African Americans in Mississippi led many to compare their experiences there with their lives back home. Some admitted that the only black people they had ever really known before had been servants. Others described civil rights work in northern cities on issues like housing, trash collection in black neighborhoods, and hiring discrimination and admitted "the existence of oppressive systems in the North." One volunteer wondered "why Southern Negroes seem to be less suspicious of our intentions than would Harlem Negroes." Another felt that "this is so different from the North where there is the intense, bitter hatred which makes working in Harlem or Roxbury or Philadelphia so heartbreaking because there is this invisible wall." "Mississippi is just a start," one volunteer commented, sounding like she had read some SDS pamphlets. "This whole country needs changing so that everyone can live a life in which he is able to realize his full capacities as a human being." Volunteers wanted to be like the full-time SNCC workers who directed their projects and "stand out against the background of a lazy-dead-end society." They wanted to be like the community people who demonstrated such courage. They had found their models.[70]

In their identification with southern blacks, many summer volunteers adopted "the SNCC uniform," the jeans and overalls worn by SNCC field secretaries. Few middle-class kids in America, white or black, wore jeans then; those were mostly for "greasers" and gang members, brash working-class kids, and farmers and other agricultural workers. In many of the photos of the sit-ins and Freedom Rides, for example, only the young segregationists attacking

Jacob Blum, Mississippi Summer Project volunteer, hangs a voter registration sign in Hattiesburg, Mississippi, in the summer of 1964. *Freedom Summer Photograph Collection, McCain Library and Archives, The University of Southern Mississippi.*

the civil rights activists wear jeans. By 1963, however, middle-class black activists in SNCC had changed their dress in deference to the poor southern blacks that they were working with and trying to organize. And in the summer of 1964, some male and female white volunteers copied them. One volunteer wrote home from Greenwood, Mississippi, that "two snicks just got married . . . in a little chapel on the ground floor of the office . . . All, including the bride, wore jeans."[71]

The summer volunteers also copied SNCC veterans' speech, a ready combination of rural vernacular and urban slang, and their use of music. By the end of the summer, they were "reckoning" about possible actions and "digging" the "freedom high" and singing the songs. They had started singing in the Ohio training sessions. They sang as they taught in Freedom Schools. And they sang as they canvassed for the Mississippi Freedom Democratic Party. In a black-and-white snapshot, Heather Booth holds her guitar up high, like many folksingers, as she prepares to play for Fannie Lou Hamer. From Ruleville, Mississippi, Booth wrote her brother back home that summer about the deep fear that sometimes kept her up at night and how the words of a song could help: " 'We are not afraid. Oh Lord, deep in my heart, I do believe, We Shall Overcome Someday' and then I think I began to truly understand what the words meant. Anyone who comes down here and is not afraid I think must be crazy as well as dangerous to this project . . . But the type of fear that they mean when they, when we, sing 'we are not afraid' is the type that immobilizes," she continued. "The songs help to dissipate the fear. Some of the words in the songs do not hold real meaning on their own, others become rather monotonous—but when they are sung in unison, or sung silently by oneself, they take on new meaning beyond words or rhythm."[72]

One volunteer wrote home, "And so clothes cease to be a real concern. 'Image' ceases to be a real concern. If it ever was. In spite of the National Council of Churches' advice, we crap on the clean, antiseptic, acceptable, decent middle-class 'image.'" (The National Council of Churches had helped pay for the summer project training and sent ministers to Oxford, Ohio, and to Mississippi.) "It is that decency that we want to change, to 'overcome,'" this volunteer argued. "It is that decency which shuts these 'niggers' in their board shacks with their middle-class television antennas rising above tarpaper roofs. So crap on your middle class, on your decency, mister Churches man. Get out of your god-damned new rented car. Get out of your pressed, proper clothes. Get out of your inoffensive, shit-eating smile and crew-cut. Come join us who are sleeping on the floor . . . Come with us and walk, not ride, the dusty streets of north Gulfport." Outsiders, they learned in Mississippi, were better than other Americans. Many white volunteers, in turn, used this love for black outsiders to transform themselves.[73]

This kind of thinking, however, created another problem. If Mississippi black people, outsiders in modern America, were better than whites, then what were the volunteers in Mississippi to do? "There is some strong ambivalence which goes with this work," one volunteer wrote. "I sometimes fear that I am only helping to integrate some beautiful people into modern white society with all its depersonalization." "Let's all escape and be like the white man" seemed to many volunteers, as the summer wore on, as it had increasingly seemed to some full-time SNCC workers over the last two years, more another form of oppression than a cure.[74]

Segregationists thought of white summer volunteers as "nigger lovers" and "white niggers." Black civil rights workers, as SNCC and COFO records of debates about the white summer volunteers make clear, thought of them both as a resource and as a problem. For black activists, white volunteers' identification could be a compliment as well as a burden. Being cast in the role of the black outsider was not equality. White workers might talk about how black people fighting segregation in Mississippi, with their courage to face death, seemed so free despite the discrimination and violence they faced. But what if black SNCC activists and black locals did not feel free? What if whites' romanticism was another form of oppression? The tensions between the mostly black SNCC field secretaries and the mostly white volunteers simmered beneath the surface of summer project activities. "But we didn't have to come, did we," Belfrage wrote, trying to explain the contradictory feelings white volunteers experienced. "We could have stayed at home and gone to the beach, or earned the money we so badly needed for next semester at old Northern White. And here we are: We Came. Among all the millions who could have realized their responsibility to this revolution, we alone came . . . Don't we earn some recognition, if not praise? *I want to be your friend, you black idiot* was the contradiction everywhere evident." Being called on to make the white kids feel okay about their own racial identities was for black workers yet another burden to bear—like too little money and too much heat and the white men in the pickup truck without plates circling the Freedom House for the fourth time, something else that was always there.[75]

In October 1964, the SNCC staff met in Waveland, Mississippi, to plan for the future. By many measures, Freedom Summer was a success. Almost fifteen hundred people—college students, lawyers, doctors, ministers, and an assortment of famous folksingers—had come to the state to work for freedom. SNCC, pushed by Forman, Betty Gorman (who helped organize Friends of SNCC groups outside the South), and other Atlanta office people, had finally developed a wide fund-raising base in the North. Amidst all the articles about the summer project, SNCC ran advertisements in the *New York Times* and *Washington Post* urging people to wire politicians and send money. At the staff meeting, the number of paid workers (always in SNCC a very loose designation) increased sharply as members voted to add eighty-five new people, mostly middle-class young people, many of them white, from outside the South who had volunteered during the summer and then stayed, to the SNCC staff. SNCC was growing. SNCC was famous. SNCC was the leading edge of the southern civil rights movement. And the southern civil rights movement, in turn, was the leading edge of the New Left, the work making radical politics visible and broadly viable for the first time since the Red baiting of the early 1950s.[76]

SNCC's successes, not its failures, exposed the limits of using white romanticism. What if what some people needed to soothe their psychological and cultural alienation was not what other people needed to stop their political and economic oppression? What if black activists did not want to be non-violent saints? What if poor black southerners did not want to be other people's definition of authenticity?

It was a romance, and yet it was true. In SDS's ERAP projects and even more strongly in SNCC's Mississippi Summer Project, white middle-class young people and poor people, self-determination, rebellion, and authenticity all came together. The outsiders—people seeking political and economic self-determination— who wanted in came together with the insiders—people seeking cultural self-determination and individual self-expression—who wanted out, and for a moment it looked like white middle-class young people might turn their love for outsiders into a new left politics.

CHAPTER 6

Too Much Love: Black Power and the Search for Other Outsiders

Then I understood that I was using Black people to weep for me, to express my sorrow at my responsibility, and that of my people, for their oppression: and I was mourning because I felt they had something I didn't, a closeness, a hope, that I and my folks had lost.
     Minnie Bruce Pratt

The kids will have to decide whether they want to save their souls, or change other people's lives.
     Andrew Kopkind

In the mid-sixties, when African Americans wanted to criticize white romanticism—whites' love for people they imagined as marginal and nonwhite—they attacked the singing. Sometimes the forms of protest people chose implicitly revealed this critique. A group of young African Americans marched in a demonstration at a Philadelphia construction site in May 1963 chanting "We/ Shall/ Overcome" as they beat the palms of their hands with rolled-up newspapers. The sound of their voices turned the prayer of the popular version into a demand. Love and interracial community had nothing to do with their movement. They wanted jobs. Some leaders and artists condemned singing more directly. "Who ever heard of angry revolutionaries swinging their bare feet together with their oppressor in lily pad pools, with gospels and guitars and 'I have a dream' speeches," Malcolm X asked over a year later, taking aim at the March on Washington. Stokely Carmichael echoed this critique in 1966: "No more prayers, no more Freedom Songs, no more dreams. Let's go for power." Freedom songs, nonviolence, and integration, in this view, had become part of the problem. Whether or not they were ever effective tools for achieving equality—and African Americans disagreed on this issue—for young black radicals they had become part of a new white racism, what liberal "friends" demanded from potential African American allies.[1]

It took a musician, however, to dissect the problem of white middle-class romanticism so powerfully evoked by images of group singing. A former Fisk University student, Julius Lester helped folksinger and organizer Guy Carawan collect, transcribe, and publish Freedom Songs, wrote articles for *Sing Out!* and *Broadside*, served as a song leader in the southern movement, and composed and wrote his own music. He also worked as a SNCC staff member and was in Mississippi for the 1964 summer project. In 1966, he wrote in "The Angry Children of Malcolm X" that the eponymous children were tired of singing. The title he chose played off that of another article, widely read and discussed among folk music fans and musicians, on the influence and legacy of folksinger Pete Seeger—"Pete's Children." Blacks and whites, Lester suggested, no longer shared a common parent, a common mood, or a common sense of the goals of the struggle. "At one time black people wanted to be American, to communicate with whites, to live in the Beloved Community. Now that is irrelevant."[2]

The problem, he wrote, was the way some whites' love for blacks as authentic outsiders limited blacks' efforts to gain equality. "SNCC had been their romantic darling, a kind of teddy bear that they could cuddle," he wrote of white liberals in 1966. "The time had come, however, when blacks could no longer be the therapy for white society." White liberals had "had a cause, something that would put meaning into their lives, something that their country and society had not given them. They had it in the Negro. So they came south and they loved us when we got out heads beat, our asses kicked, and our bodies thrown in jail. They loved us as we bled, loving loving loving all the while. How noble, how courageous, how wonderful it all was."[3]

For African American activists, however, "these northern protest rallies where Freedom Songs were sung and speeches speeched and applause applauded and afterward telegrams and letters sent to the president and to Congress began to look more and more like moral exercises." White liberals "weren't really interested in solving the problem. They simply wanted to protest against it." What, he wanted to know, could love actually do? Could it stop the hurt and the want and the brutality? Lester quoted a SNCC veteran, "Man, the people are too busy getting ready to fight to bother with singing anymore." "Now it is over. The days of singing Freedom Songs and the days of combating bullets and billy clubs with Love," Lester observed, shifting his prose into the style of a song lyric: "Too much love/ Too much love/ Nothing kills a nigger like/ Too much love." Maybe sympathetic whites' own need to experience transcendence and racial unity and their vision of social justice and the needs and desires of African Americans were not in harmony. Maybe the voices did not blend. Maybe people were not even singing the same song.[4]

The New Left grew through proposing that shared feelings of opposition, rebellion, and outrage, no matter their different sources, could unite people in action. The romance of the outsider both helped generate this coalition, what supporters from the mid-sixties through the seventies called "the movement," a loose collection of organizations and causes from the civil rights movement, Black Power, and Chicano, American Indian, and Asian American rights movements to anti-war organizing, feminism, and gay liberation, and also limited it. The very fact that some people could experience outsider status as a cultural and psychological choice reaffirmed the class, gender, and racial differences that shared emotions denied.

In the second half of the sixties and into the seventies, white radicals announced that oppressed people of all kinds were allies, joined through their broad experience of alienation. The liberation of any one group of oppressed people, in this kind of thinking, aided in the liberation of all. Many middle-class whites used this idea to recognize and embrace their own position as outsiders. Moving in the opposite direction, many black radicals embraced the importance of difference through Black Power and other forms of black nationalism. In SNCC, in the Black Panther Party, and in civil rights organizing in places like Philadelphia and New York, Black Power emerged in part as a reaction to white romanticism. Pushing out white activists functioned as a psychological and cultural parallel to the strategic rejection of nonviolence and the political critique of liberalism.[5]

The role of white romanticism in both generating and limiting the movement remains largely unexamined in debates about the New Left. White romanticism was not the opposite of white supremacy but the foundation of a different kind of white privilege. If everyone was an outsider in some way, then everyone's emotions and everyone's liberation from oppression were important. This kind of thinking pushed white middle-class young people especially to imagine commonalities across race, class, and later gender divisions. Yet there were in fact differences and they did matter. Despite the love, despite the conscious intentions, some people had more freedom than others, and their freedom could limit the freedom of others. Some middle-class Americans' quest for the "real" and "authentic" limited the prospects for a new mass politics on the left by denying class and other differences in the name of shared feelings and even love.

Interest, concern, and even sympathy—too much love—had a way of making the people who were its objects less than equal citizens. As some African Americans rejected this love, many middle-class whites, especially young people with some connection to the left, could not let go of their romanticism. Some clung to their dream of one big movement—Student Power as a counterpart to Black Power; some student activists refused to give up the belief that African Americans possessed some special claim to authenticity, replacing the idea of black as folk with an image of armed, urban blacks as "real" revolutionaries. Still others reacted by searching for new outsiders to love (Chinese Communists, the Cubans, or the Vietnamese) or by claiming their own status as outsiders (radical feminism and gay liberation). African Americans' growing support for black separatism and Afro-centrism strongly shaped white middle-class romanticism, but it did not end whites' racist assertions of black authenticity.[6]

Black Power and White Romanticism

"Black Power for Black People," SNCC staffers began to declare out in the field as they tried to not only register voters but also win real political power for African Americans in the Alabama Black Belt in 1965 and 1966. "What do we want? Black Power! Black Power!" SNCC president Stokely Carmichael and young marchers chanted in June 1966 on their way across Mississippi. "We want freedom. We want power to determine the destiny of our Black Community," Huey Newton and Bobby Seale wrote in October 1966 in "What We Want, What We Believe," the ten-point program and plan that helped launch the Black Panther Party. "We believe that black people will not be free until we are able to determine our destiny." In the mid-sixties, similar calls for black self-determination rang out across the nation, from the small towns and rural crossroads of the southern Black Belt to the urban ghettos of the Rust Belt. Part strategy, part rallying cry, and part symbol, Black Power emerged as the civil rights era's flowering of the old separatist traditions of black nationalism. It drew upon the post–World War II activism of black veterans, the speeches and writings of recently assassinated Black Muslim leader Malcolm X, and the southern tradition of self-defense made visible in the work of North Carolina

NAACP leader Robert F. Williams and the Louisiana-centered Deacons of Defense. It grew out of the civil rights organizing experience in Albany, Greenwood, and Selma and in Philadelphia, Oakland, and Detroit. It responded to the racism of white conservatives and the racism of white liberals. It provided an answer to the failure of "democratic" politics to represent all American citizens and the failures of what passed as "American culture" to offer nonracist images of black Americans. It joined the struggles of African Americans to the ongoing liberation movements of people of African descent around the globe, in Algeria and South Africa, for example, and in newly independent nations like Ghana.[7]

Black Power meant African American self-determination and separatism. But black self-determination meant more than political representation. It meant cultural representation. It meant not having to play either the old Uncle or Auntie role demanded by the segregationists or the new civil rights saint required by the liberals. It meant psychological freedom. Black Power just might provide an antidote to white middle-class romanticism. And white romanticism, in turn, played an essential role in producing the media attention that fed back into and shaped this particular moment in the history of black nationalism. African American activists wanted to put black "authenticity" to work to liberate African Americans. In part, they succeeded, but African Americans' own embrace of the romance of the outsider did not escape the cultural codes of minstrelsy and worked, in turn, to generate new forms of white romanticism. SNCC's attempt to free itself from white romanticism and the Black Panther Party's emergence as the new "darling" of white radicals illustrated the limits of a New Left coalition dependent in part on the romance of the outsider.[8]

Carmichael had not been SNCC president long when the organization unexpectedly participated in a march across Mississippi in June 1966, taking up, along with other groups, the banner of James Meredith, wounded by a shotgun blast on the second day of his Memphis-to-Jackson one-man March Against Fear. Arrested in Greenwood, where he had worked as a SNCC field secretary in 1963 and 1964, Carmichael told the large crowd that gathered when he was released: "This is the twenty-seventh time I have been arrested. I ain't going to jail no more. The only way we gonna stop them white men from whuppin' us is to take over. What we gonna start sayin' now is 'Black Power' . . . The white folks in the state of Mississippi ain't nothing but a bunch of racists," Carmichael continued angrily. "What do we want?" Carmichael asked again and again. "Black Power," the crowd chanted repeatedly in return, "Black Power. Black Power." Carmichael, SNCC activists, and local blacks' call for "Black

Power" took place amidst growing black militancy in places like Oakland, where Newton and Seale founded the Black Panther Party that fall, and Atlanta, where members of the Revolutionary Action Movement were at work radicalizing some SNCC field secretaries.[9]

Newspapers and television reports suggesting that "Black Power" shocked both whites and many blacks appeared immediately and remained in the news all summer. Journalists spoke with black leaders, many of whom were quick to attack Carmichael and the phrase. Martin Luther King Jr., quoted repeatedly, criticized "Black Power" as "an unfortunate choice of words . . . that will confuse our allies, isolate the Negro community and give many prejudiced whites, who might otherwise be ashamed of their anti-Negro feeling, a ready excuse for self-justification." Roy Wilkins, executive director of the NAACP, argued that "no matter how endlessly they try to explain it, the term 'black power' means anti-white power." Much more hostile than King, he insisted "black power" meant "separatism," "wicked fanaticism," "ranging race against race," and "in the end only black death." He attacked the concept as "the father of hatred and the mother of violence." On June 11, former SNCC chairman John Lewis resigned from the organization, and later that summer, he told journalists that SNCC adopted the "Black Power" cry and the black panther symbol "to scare hell out of the white people. I agree with Dr. King that racism is implied in the slogan." Talk of Black Power alienated white supporters, he argued: "bewildered," many whites were "having second thoughts. They don't understand the talk of 'black power.' Whites who have identified with the oppressed Negroes begin now to identify with other whites who might seem threatened by the talk of black power." Hosea Williams, a staff member for King's Southern Christian Leadership Conference, accused SNCC of "racism in reverse."[10]

Editorials and newspaper columnists compared Black Power advocates to white supremacists. The *Los Angeles Times* editorial page announced, "Extremism has not been limited to white yahoos." Black "extremists," "consciously setting out to frighten whites," had halted "racial progress." The *Wall Street Journal* complained without irony that black activists "relegated" white marchers in Mississippi "to a status of second-class citizenship" and expressed "ill-feelings toward whites." SNCC's new slogan, many papers insisted, was increasing congressional opposition to the 1966 civil rights bill. Syndicated journalists Rowland Evans and Robert Novak accused SNCC of "subverting the distant dream of a bi-racial society that the movement originally fostered." Network newscasts showed footage of Carmichael speaking at a voter registration rally, a portrait described by one sympathetic television critic who criticized the coverage as "short, sharp, and demagogic."[11]

Important politicians joined the chorus. Hubert Humphrey called Black Power "apartheid." Senator Robert F. Kennedy denounced it as potentially "damaging not only to the civil rights movement but to the country." African American leaders, he argued, should not reject white help in the fight for equality. President Johnson stated forcefully, "We are not interested in black power, and we are not interested in white power. But we are interested in American democratic power with a small 'd.'"[12]

Only a few white journalists tried to explain the popularity of Black Power with African Americans and why many were angry with "white moderates" who were supposed to be their friends. The *Christian Science Monitor* criticized all the editorializing as "a panicky overreaction," and *Newsweek*, surprisingly ambivalent rather than harsh, called Carmichael "a rebel with a cause." "It is precisely the 'democratic power with a small "D" of which Mr. Johnson spoke," journalist Tom Wicker argued, "that has denied [blacks] their rights, equality, jobs and comforts for a full century . . . If the honest and needed promises of the white majority are not fulfilled with at least deliberate speed, then who is jeopardizing what?" In the *Nation*, journalist Paul Good described "the frustrating phenomenon of white power which the majority of whites were taking for granted." White Americans' power, he argued, "had a disabling influence in its ability even to recognize the powerless position in which the American Negro found himself." Maybe the new advocates of Black Power had good reasons for being angry with white liberals.[13]

Despite these exceptions, the intensity and tone of the reaction to the phrase "Black Power" made clear how much many whites' support for civil rights depended upon a particular fantasy of African Americans as outsiders. Poor rural black folks "grateful" for white northern help fit the vision, as did nonviolent activists who bowed like saints beneath the clubs of southern segregationists. Malcolm X had described these southern blacks as powerless people who "picket and boycott and beg some cracker for a job." African Americans who carried guns or ran for office did not fit this romance of the good black folk. Neither did blacks who demanded their rights rather than asked whites to grant them. For many white Americans, Black Power advocates were just too hard to love.[14]

In July and August, Carmichael traveled everywhere, taking the talent for public speaking he had developed in Delta towns like Greenwood, Mississippi, and rural crossroads like Lowndes County, Alabama, to northern cities wracked by violence. He put aside his trademark overalls and jean jacket— farmer's clothes—at times for dark suits and ties but even more frequently for the more urban attire of leather jackets, sunglasses, and slacks. Here at last, according to *Ebony*, was a black leader who "walks like Sidney Poitier, talks like Harry Belafonte and thinks like the post-Muslim Malcolm X." In July, Carmichael spoke to black militants, many of them young gang members, in a union hall in Chicago. In Cleveland in August, just after rioting there had ended, he announced bluntly, "When you talk of 'black power,' you talk of bringing this country to its knees." Black men, he argued repeatedly, should refuse to fight in imperial America's war against the colored people of Vietnam. He was always on television, frequently photographed, and repeatedly quoted in the papers. Under Carmichael's leadership, *Newsweek* argued, "SNCC speaks for a growing bloc of the disaffected when it argues that . . . a black man ought to hit back when a white man hits him, that white liberals are all right only if they know their place and stay in it." Again, without irony, journalists described whites in the kinds of terms once reserved to describe African Americans' own oppression.[15]

In his widely read, discussed, and quoted piece "What We Want" in the September 22, 1966, issue of the *New York Review of Books*, Stokely Carmichael addressed the problem of white romanticism as central to SNCC's turn to Black Power. "We cannot be expected any longer to march and have our heads broken," he said, "in order to say to whites: come on, you're nice guys. For you are not nice guys. We have found you out." Liberals were not exceptions: "They complain, 'What about me?—don't you want my help any more?'

Stokely Carmichael gives a Black Power speech at the University of California, Berkeley, in 1966. *Prints and Photographs Division, Library of Congress.*

These are people supposedly concerned about black Americans, but today they think first of themselves, of their feelings of rejection . . . Black Americans," he argued, "have been almost the only people whom everybody and his momma could jump up and call their friends. We have been tokens, symbols, objects." In the future, blacks would name their own friends and allies: "Too many young middle-class Americans, like some sort of Pepsi generation, have wanted to come alive through the black community. They've wanted to be where the action is—and the action has been in the black community." The tone and image of the nonviolent southern civil rights movement, he complained, appealed much more strongly to white liberals than it did to young blacks. African Americans did not want to hurt whites or "'take over' the country": "The white man is irrelevant to blacks, except as an oppressive force. Blacks want to be in his place, yes, but not in order to terrorize and lynch and starve him. They want to be in his place because that is where a decent life can be had."[16]

In part, white journalists reported on Carmichael's activities because he was articulate, photogenic, and provocative. But he also made good copy because he was president of SNCC. In the fall of 1966, SNCC still had an integrated staff (the remaining white staff members would be voted out of full membership in the organization that December). The organization's funding base and celebrity status, too, still depended to an important degree on white romanticism. Not surprisingly, white SNCC activists and supporters felt betrayed when Carmichael said they were irrelevant. When Carmichael and other African American activists criticized these white civil rights supporters for feeling rejected, they felt even more wounded. Writing for the *Village Voice* in late 1966, a white former SNCC activist was shockingly candid: "I'm mad. It's the kind of anger one might feel in, say, a love relationship, when after entering honestly you find that your loved one's been balling with someone else, and what's worse, enjoying it." The metaphor of intimate romance reflects the reality that for many white volunteers, involvement with SNCC produced the intense emotions—pleasure in and fear about identification and connection, tidal waves of longing and desire, the frisson of being hyperaware of the present—so often generated by sexual relationships.[17]

In the second half of 1966 and early 1967, black activists and scholars stepped up their attacks on white romanticism. Young African Americans, Julius Lester argued, had begun "to feel uneasy" with building a movement around the image of "well-dressed, well-mannered, clean Negroes . . . being beaten by white southerners:

Was this not another form of the bowing and scraping their grand-parents had had to do to get what they wanted? Were they not acting once again as the white man wanted and expected them to? And why should they have to be brutalized, physically and spiritually, for what every other American had at birth?

Black Power, they hoped, would free them from the way nonviolent direct action had taken the minstrelsy of the folk off the stage and into the streets. "It isn't my job to make black people love everybody," Stokely Carmichael told a journalist. "Whites get nervous when we don't keep talking about brotherly love. They need reassurance," he insisted. "But we're not about to divert our energies to give it to them." Historian Vincent Harding criticized white Christians, full of "hostility and fear," telling blacks "you must love—like Christ and Doctor King." Black power, they hoped, would free them from the love. African American poet June Meyer mourned that for whites, African American life remained "an imagining, a TV spectacular, the product of rank intuition, the casualty of gross misrepresentation, and grist for statistical games . . . an object, a titillation, a scare, an unknown reality and an unfamiliar voice."[18]

The journalist Andrew Kopkind perceptively argued in January 1967:

What galls SNCC people most is the way white radicals seem to have treated SNCC as a kind of psychotherapy, as a way to work out problems of alienation and boredom and personal inadequacy. A season of organizing in Mississippi, despite (or because of) the dangers and discomforts, was often more therapeutic for the white organizer than the blacks being organized. To SNCC, that was a form of unconscious racism, manipulation, and white supremacy. What is happening now is that many of those whites feel hopelessly rejected by their Negro Friends, like patients whose analyst suddenly leaves town.

By embracing separation, African Americans announced they would no longer provide the resources for white therapy. As I. F. Stone wrote, "SNCC is reacting against a new version of the white man's burden."[19]

In fact, African American psychiatrist Alvin Poussaint claimed in *Ebony* and the *New York Times Magazine*, Black Power grew out of this white problem. African American activists working in Mississippi told him that whites working in the movement there were "beatniks, leftovers, white trash, sluts, etc.," who came south "looking for excitement and adventure" and the chance to become "martyrs" and act like "big wheels." To prove they were free of prejudice, black activists told Poussaint, white workers had sex with African Americans and "indulg[ed] in all manner of unconventional behavior" that blacks believed they would never have tried at home. One young black activist said of the white summer project volunteers, "Some of them are worse than the white segregationists because they are out here feeling sorry for the 'poor colored folks' and they are doing nothing more than satisfying their own needs by being nice to the Negroes. Whites didn't do anything on my project in Greenwood in the summer of '64 but raise hell and sleep around." The experience of working with whites made black SNCC staff members in Mississippi advocate separation, Poussaint argued. Supporters of Black Power "appeared to be seeking a sense of psychological emancipation from racism through self assertion and release of aggressive angry feelings." Forty years later, Charles Hamilton, former SNCC activist and the coauthor with Carmichael of the 1967 book *Black Power*, remembered that white students wanted to work with blacks down south because they believed "the glamour and the drama were in the black community."[20]

Black SNCC activists used the growing call for black psychological and cultural autonomy as a way to frame their struggle with white romanticism. "We must launch a cultural revolution to unbrainwash an entire people," Malcolm X had demanded, a "journey to our rediscovery of ourselves." "The American Negro," James Baldwin chimed in, "can no longer, nor will he ever again be controlled by white America's image of him." It was not African Americans' fault if white liberals, in Julius Lester's words, "took this act of self-assertion by blacks as a personal insult." It was not their fault that whites felt "rejected." Even *Time* noticed the change, the fact that self-determination meant cultural as much as political power. What was new about the late sixties, the magazine argued, was "the new Negro's determination to take over his own destiny and accept no definition of blackness but his own."[21]

Some urban African Americans took to the streets to attempt to liberate their neighborhoods and make sure that no one could mistake them for singing fools. As a Watts resident put it, "Folk singing is out. Karate is in." In the uprisings in New York, Los Angeles, Newark, Chicago, and elsewhere in the summers of 1964 and 1965 and 1966 and 1967, people rebelled against both white supremacy and white romanticism. What community leader Reverend Albert Cleage said about Detroit described how many residents of these communities felt that summer: "Black people want control of black communities." Acts of violence also generated catharsis and release, the rush of adrenaline and emotion, the feeling, if just for a moment, that a person had what Carmichael called "psychological equality." Out on the streets, while the fire burned and the stuff was there for the taking, a person could feel free.[22]

Black as Militant

Seale and Newton did not start the Black Panther Party to appeal to white college kids. They designed the Panthers' ten-point program, the armed patrols to "police" the police, and the Panther uniform—black berets, black pants, and black leather jackets—to appeal to young black men in cities like Oakland. The two men quickly realized, however, that they could tap some white students' love for black outsiders. Presenting themselves as "authentic" black revolutionaries, they sold Mao Tse-tung's *Little Red Book* to white radicals on the streets of Berkeley and used the money to buy some of the organization's first guns. White radicals embraced them with all the fervor some Berkeley students had once channeled into the campus's very active Friends of SNCC chapter. After a uniformed and armed march into the California state capitol building in Sacramento in May 1967, the Black Panthers began to attract the attention of white radicals across the country. In some white left circles, militant urban blacks began to play a symbolic role similar to singing black activists—they became crucial reservoirs of authenticity.[23]

At the end of the summer of 1967, as some American cities literally still burned, white student radicals and some white liberals rushed to support African Americans' increasingly militant political demands. The National Student Association, exposed a year and half earlier in *Ramparts* magazine as the recipient of secret CIA funding, held its annual meeting that August. The mostly white delegates voted to accept the NSA black caucus's resolution endorsing the "liberation of blacks by any means necessary." Although NSA was more a vehicle for liberal than radical student activism, the organization accepted this phrase, popularly attributed to Malcolm X.[24]

Two weeks later, over Labor Day weekend in Chicago, much of the New Left—over three thousand delegates representing more than two hundred organizations—gathered for the National Conference for a New Politics (NCNP). Only about three hundred of the participants were African American, but the black caucus demanded "two tests of sincerity" from whites: the power to cast 50 percent of the votes on every resolution and the acceptance of a thirteen-point program, which included, for example, a call for the creation of "white civilizing committees" in white communities to "humanize the savage and beast-like character that runs rampant through America." The black voting plank passed two to one. Interviewed by a journalist, one white delegate said, "We are just a little tail on the end of a very powerful black panther. And I want to be on that tail—if they'll let me." A conference organizer claimed the convention "gives us entrée into the ghetto." Militant blacks would play the role, these white radicals believed, formerly held in Marxist thought by the industrial working class. They would be the agents of historical change. Still, some participants and organizers condemned many white delegates' refusal to engage in serious debate about these demands as a "travesty of radical politics at work" and "a vulgar joke." Some white radicals missed the chance to make a "new politics" by indulging in white romanticism and failing to challenge radical blacks. These white leftists' capitulation to black demands fit the long history that began when some white teenagers fell in love with black music and some SDS activists fell in love with SNCC.[25]

After Oakland police arrested Huey Newton that October for allegedly shooting and killing a police officer, white Bay Area radicals and especially Berkeley students found a way to support black militants in the Panthers' "Free Huey" campaign. Early in 1968, some of them independently formed a support organization unofficially called "Honkies for Huey." The radical and mostly white Peace and Freedom Democratic Party, founded June 23, 1967, to provide a political vehicle for opposition to the Vietnam War, became the first organization to officially and publicly ally itself with the Black Panther Party. In early 1968, an intense voter registration drive succeeded in placing the party on the ballot in California and a few other states. That summer, at the party's national convention, delegates nominated Panther Eldridge Cleaver for president. The party was strongest in California, and the state convention there also nominated Huey Newton for Congress. Peace and Freedom Party members attended "Free Huey" rallies and passed out pamphlets describing Newton as one of many African American victims of police brutality and corruption. At the opening of Newton's trial in July 1968, an orange Peace and Freedom Party truck provided sound for the rally. In the fall, the Peace and Freedom Party worked on Cleaver's presidential campaign.

Cleaver and Seale, however, openly criticized their supposed allies. As Cleaver told a Berkeley journalist to show just who was in charge of this coalition, "If the Peace and Freedom Party tried to hurt us we would have to be in a position to hurt the Peace and Freedom Party." Much like black militants at the 1967 NSA and NCNP conventions, Cleaver at least seemed to be testing just how far he could go and retain masochistic white radical support. Cleaver put the Peace and Freedom Party in an impossible position. If the party protested this verbal abuse, their actions would demonstrate they took the Black Panther Party as equals. Any complaint would also risk destroying the alliance. And Peace and Freedom Party members earned national press attention and instant radical credentials in return for their work for the Panthers, a rather large payoff given the difficulty of third-party organizing in twentieth-century America.[26]

Other organizations followed the Peace and Freedom Party into support for, if not outright alliance with, the Black Panther Party. No group fused white romanticism of black radicals and political ideology more powerfully than the SDS faction that eventually became the Weather Underground. In the spring of 1969, SDS members including Bernardine Dohrn, Bill Ayers, and Jeff Jones wrote a position paper named after a line in the 1965 Bob Dylan song "Subterranean Homesick Blues." "You Don't Need a Weatherman to Know Which Way the Wind Blows" appeared in *New Left Notes* as SDS's 1969 national convention opened in Chicago. Embracing without often specifically referencing the political analysis of Malcolm X, Robert F. Williams, and other black radical intellectuals, the Weather collective reminded the white New Left that the fight for black liberation formed an essential part of the war being waged abroad against U.S. imperialism by the Chinese, the Cubans, the Vietnamese, and other people of color. African Americans, in this form of black radical thought, were members of the third world, "part of the international revolutionary *vanguard*." This "black proletarian colony" lived scattered all over the United States.

What Weather activists understood as solidarity and identification veered toward exploitation. Once again, white activists were using African Americans' "authenticity" for their own liberation. Panther phrases, terms, and forms of analysis filled "You Don't Need a Weatherman." America was "Babylon" and "the mother country," terms used often by Newton in his speeches and writings. The call for "white mother country radicals" to work everywhere, "handing out Free Huey literature" and "bringing guys to Panther rallies," answered Newton's and Cleaver's call for white allies. And Weather quoted Newton directly, circulating the words that helped make him the newest black "darling" of the white left: "In order to be a revolutionary nationalist, you would by necessity have to be a socialist." Using the Panthers' by then famous word for the police, Weather even argued that "the fight against the pigs" would provide "the glue" to hold all the pieces together, unifying the single-issue organizations and student, black liberation, and anti-war work into "city-wide" and regionally based movements. White young people, the collective insisted, needed to look at "Mao, Che, the Panthers, and the Third World for our models." In every meaning of the term, Weather "adopted" the Panthers, approving of them and following them, yes, but also taking them up and using and incorporating them, becoming a white version of armed black men, a new form of white Negro.[27]

This kind of thinking emerged over the New Left at the end of the sixties. White radicals attacked their own "white skin privilege" and vowed "smashing the pig means smashing the pig inside ourselves." They embraced a "ghetto-equals-colony" analysis. They bought and read and discussed collections of speeches and writings by Malcolm X and Stokely Carmichael, Eldridge Cleaver's *Soul on Ice*, George Jackson's *Soledad Brother*, and H. Rap Brown's *Die, Nigger, Die*. They agreed with Brown, former militant SNCC president turned Black Panther, that "violence is necessary. It is as American as cherry pie." They wore buttons and gave money and assembled to free Huey Newton and Angela Davis and the Panther 21. If black radicals did not want white activists to work in black communities, white radicals would make sure they knew they had allies. Up Against the Wall Motherfuckers, a New York City–based anarchist group, took its name from an Amiri Baraka poem. The White Panther Party's model was obvious. Weather Underground members promised to destroy "our own honkiness." White radicals worked, in yet another of the many ironies of the long history of racism in America, to make their own separate movement equal in its militancy and its radicalism to the movement for black liberation.[28]

Was fighting to free Huey Newton organizing in the white community? It was if radicals persuaded other whites to support black liberation. Was fighting the pigs organizing in the white community? It was if the police attacked white students, white radicals, and hippies, as had happened at the 1968 Democratic Convention and elsewhere. Was the takeover of Columbia University organizing in the white community? It was if activists defined the university as a white "imperialist institution" invading "the black colony." The lines were not always easy to draw, and there were many ways to organize in white America. Still, in its founding position paper and in later communications, as some members of this collective helped dissolve SDS and went underground, Weather struggled most with the second piece of SNCC's warning, the charge that whites not use black activism as a form of therapy, as a means to white self-liberation.

Weather's political analysis insisted that black radicals formed the bridge that joined the movement in the United States to the global struggle, to Cuba and Fidel and Che and Vietnam and the National Liberation Front. African American militants connected home and abroad *materially*, as members of the third world even though they lived in the first. They connected home and abroad *ideologically*, as victims of U.S. imperialism like black and brown people everywhere. And they connected home and abroad *symbolically*, as the example of militancy that once again spurred white students on to greater activism. As the ultimate outsiders, African American militants marked an outside on the inside, a "real" home within the compromised homeland, a space of alienation at the heart of the empire. They marked a space of American innocence.[29]

A palpable desire to win black radical approval mixed with Weather's political analysis and sharp denunciation of white supremacy and imperialism. White radicals not supporting complete black self-determination, they argued repeatedly, were not really fighting American imperialism, no matter how much they spoke out in support of the Vietnamese or other third world revolutionaries. With far greater perception than many white radicals, the collective understood the white racism at work in both asking blacks to wait for a white movement to join them and allowing blacks alone to make the revolution that would free everyone. This insight left them with little space in which to plot their own actions: building "a white movement which will support the blacks in moving as fast as they have to and are able to and still itself keep up with that black movement enough that white revolutionaries share the cost." The awkwardness of the words here matched the difficulty of the task. Still, Weather members insisted on becoming the white allies of black liberation at a time when many black militants—the Panthers were of course the exception—did not want white help. But their disregard for the demands of black nationalists like Stokely Carmichael, Rap Brown, Maulana Karenga, and Amiri Baraka suggested that Weather, too, had trouble with black self-determination. Equating the police harassment of anti-war demonstrators, "youth with long hair," and other white, middle-class rebels with the long-established, brutally systematic police oppression of poor blacks brought Weather close to indulging in the racism they rightly denounced in other white radicals.[30]

Underground in the early seventies, Weather cast themselves as militant blacks' most reliable white friends. Every day, they reminded white Americans, police officers and prison officials murdered African Americans just as U.S. soldiers murdered the Vietnamese. Panther Fred Hampton and prison activist George Jackson were exceptional only because some whites knew their names. "Black and third world people were going up against Amerikan imperialism alone," and militant whites had to help them. In "New Morning—Changing Weather," issued December 6, 1970, they criticized themselves for believing "only bombings or picking up the gun" was "authentically revolutionary." A month later, the New York Panther 21, arrested in April 1969 and charged with conspiracy to kill police officers and destroy buildings, published an open letter asking Weather to continue the armed struggle. Despite sharp self-criticism of its own "military error," Weather turned away from this analysis and resumed bombing targets. Weather publications cheered Panther Angela Davis's and H. Rap Brown's escapes into the underground, and they called on white radicals "to build a new world on the ruins of honky Amerika." Some people had to prove that "even the white youth of Babylon" would use violence to destroy U.S. imperialism. When they wrote, "What we do or don't do makes a difference," it sounded more like a plea than a fact.[31]

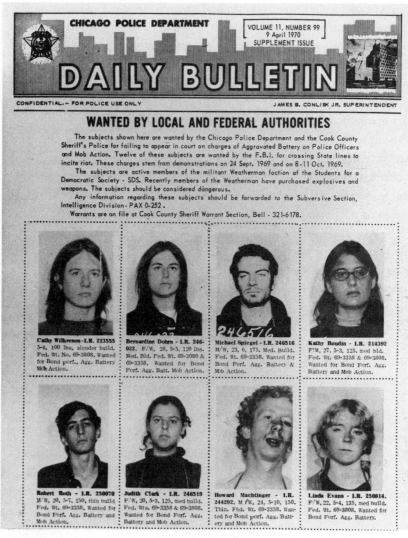

This 1970 Chicago Police Department wanted poster shows eight members of the Weather faction of Students for a Democratic Society. *Associated Press.*

Issuing warnings ahead of time and "communiqués"—they took the term from Latin American revolutionaries—afterward, Weather used literal explosions to write their condemnation of racism and imperialism on the buildings that housed government and related corporate power. On June 9, 1970, they bombed the New York City Police headquarters for its occupation of black neighborhoods. On February 28, 1971, they bombed the U.S. Capitol in retaliation for the invasion of Laos. On August 30, 1971, they bombed the

Department of Corrections in San Francisco and the Office of California Prisons in Sacramento in response to the murder of George Jackson. On September 17, 1971, they bombed the New York State Department of Corrections for the killing of prisoners, many of them black, at Attica. On May 19, 1972, they bombed the Pentagon in retaliation for the bombing of Hanoi. In at least fifteen bombings claimed by Weather Underground, the group acted eight times in response to violence against African Americans and at least four times in response to violence in Southeast Asia. They carried their commitment to attacking racism and imperialism as far as they could without attacking people. Yet they had little contact with black radicals. Even the undergrounds were segregated, with Davis and Brown moving in different circles. In the context of the early seventies, the Weather Underground wrote and acted as if they wanted black radicals to know that some white Americans, too, could be real revolutionaries. They wrote and acted as if they were perpetually auditioning for the role of militant blacks' favorite whites.[32]

Despite their political differences, other white radical organizations in the late 1960s and the 1970s, including the White Panther Party and the Symbionese Liberation Army, shared Weather's desire for the approval of black radicals and especially the Black Panthers. Like Weather, they adopted various versions of what scholar Laura Browder has called "revolutionary blackface."[33]

White Panther Party leader John Sinclair had a deep, decade-long interest in black culture. In college as the sixties began, he fell in love with beatnik poetry, the hard bop jazz of John Coltrane, and the marijuana that was an essential part of the jazz scene. He ended up in Detroit for graduate school, helped found the Detroit Artists' Workshop, and slowly came to radical politics through his own problems with Michigan cops. Busted repeatedly for possession of pot, Sinclair believed he understood what the Panthers meant when they talked about "the pigs." Released after serving a six-month sentence, he and former members of the Artists' Workshop created Trans-Love Energies (TLE) to unite student and other urban activists with the counterculture.[34]

In 1968, MC-5, a rock group connected with TLE, played at the Yippies' "Festival of Life" during the Democratic National Convention in Chicago. Sinclair, the band's manager, was there to see the musicians plug into a hot dog stand and play on the grass because the Yippies had failed to get a permit and set up a stage. He was there, too, to help the group throw equipment into a van as the police, provoked by Abbie Hoffman, closed in on the park. He arrived back in Ann Arbor, where TLE had moved to escape police harassment, convinced that law enforcement officials everywhere overreacted to gatherings of anti-war and Black Power activists and hippies. Sinclair also believed he had the experience and the skill, unlike the Yippies, to organize alienated white young people into a national movement. Fellow TLE member Pun Plamondon had spent the summer in jail on a marijuana charge, reading works by Newton and Cleaver and anything else he could find on the Black Panther Party. TLE, he suggested to Sinclair, should form a support group for the Black Panther Party. On November 1, 1968, Plamondon and Sinclair founded the White Panther Party.[35]

Quoting Newton, Cleaver, Latino land activist Reies Tijerina, and Mao, they set the White Panthers up as black militants' white counterparts, as blackface white militants. After reprinting the Black Panthers' program, the White Panthers offered their own ten-point plan. Most famously, they called for "total assault on the culture by any means necessary, including rock and roll, dope, and fucking in the streets." Again copying the Black Panthers, Sinclair and Plamondon chose for themselves the titles "Minister of Information" and "Minister of Defense." "We take as our heroes, those that we have been told to hate and to fear; Eldridge Cleaver, Rap Brown, Fidel," Plamondon wrote at the end of the document. "Black Panthers are our Brother[s], we join them in the liberation of the planet."[36]

The White Panthers described their members as former pot smokers and peace-loving hippies, forced by police harassment to fight back, just like the Panthers. Sinclair, influenced by black radical thought, saw the counterculture as a kind of oppressed "youth colony," existing in solidarity with other "colonies," from Newark and Detroit to Vietnam, oppressed by U.S. imperialism. Like African American cultural nationalists, Sinclair argued, the youth colony sought self-determination through creating an alternative culture: "We have to realize that the long-haired dope-smoking rock and roll street-fucking culture is a whole thing, a revolutionary international cultural moment." Plamondon, on the other hand, stuck close to his continuing romanticization of the Black Panthers: "Get a gun brother, learn how to use it. You'll need it, pretty soon. You're a White Panther, act like one."[37]

On one level, the White Panthers seemed like an extension of Sinclair's long obsession with jazz and black urban life, a Yippie-influenced form of performance art and an exaggerated, self-conscious playing with the old white Negro role. It was hard, in this sense, to take the White Panther Party seriously. It was also hard, at least for J. Edgar Hoover's FBI and Michigan's police, not to take the White Panther Party seriously. Whatever the intentions of the members (and the evidence suggests different members possessed different intentions), the White Panthers's white Negroism embodied all too well some whites' fears that white radicals would unite with militant blacks. Plamondon, especially, seemed over time to forget that their acts were an act. Underground in flight from charges related to the September 1968 bombing of a CIA building in Ann Arbor, he stockpiled arms and visited Cleaver in Algeria. The FBI reacted to the White Panthers' white Negroism by attempting to destroy the organization. Hoover placed Plamondon on the FBI's Ten Most Wanted list and labeled the White Panthers one of the most dangerous radical groups in America.[38]

Sinclair's belief that the counterculture could be a revolutionary political culture came true, though not as spectacularly for Sinclair's freaks and hippies as it did for Christian evangelicals in the 1970s and 1980s. Still, whether or not the White Panthers were ever much more than a kind of Black Panther Party fan club and a provocation aimed at the police, they did expose the limits of white romanticism. Plamondon's identification with the Panthers circled all the way back around into caricature. Mimicking the Black Panthers' own complicated uses of white Americans' fears and fantasies about armed black men, he played a white man's version of a black man's version of white fantasies about armed black men. The long history of American racism made it impossible, though, for this play to be a comedy. However much love motivated Plamondon's performance, it ended up looking more like another form of white privilege.[39]

The Symbionese Liberation Army (SLA) followed this kind of identification even further. Members (almost all white dropouts from the middle class) took up Swahili names and what they imagined as black urban forms of speech and body language in an effort to spark black revolution. In 1974, six SLA members died in a shootout and fire that erupted when law enforcement officials stormed their safe house in Los Angeles. This kind of play could be dangerous: Weather Underground members would later end up in prison, convicted of helping black radicals, members of a group called the Black Liberation Army, kill two police officers and a guard in a Brink's truck robbery gone wrong in 1981. White identification with black radicals began as a way to bury contradictory desires for self-invention and historical connection in the symbolic power of blackness. It ended in something real, all right, if not exactly the "real" white radicals were looking for. From one perspective, white SLA members achieved their desire. They may not have ever been able to actually become the black radicals they played. But in trying to live like black radicals, some of them certainly died like black radicals, in a spray of police bullets.[40]

Weather and other white radical groups created a self-consciously radical version of the old white "love," the belief that blacks were the ultimate outsiders. They thought that black radicals were "real" revolutionaries, and they wanted to be "real" too. Despite the difference between the political ideology of SDS in 1963 or 1964 and Weather in 1969 or 1970, this kind of thinking was entirely consistent with SDS's earlier identification with SNCC. "Being real" always carried with it, however consciously or unconsciously, the problem of white romanticism. When African Americans served as resources or objects for making white people "real," they could not be subjects. As objects, they could not be equals.

Everyone Is a Nigger

Most white radicals took their identification with African American activists in different directions than Weather, the White Panthers, and the SLA, sustained by their continuing faith in one big movement. After the Mississippi Summer Project ended and the ERAP projects gradually fell apart, some SDS members and other college students joined Old Left survivors, pacifists, and the old nuclear freeze activists in building a movement to oppose the Vietnam War. African American former civil rights activists like Robert Moses and James Bevel played important roles in this work, and SNCC remained a powerful model. These white radicals tried to organize around other left issues the way young African American activists organized around civil rights.

In late 1964, Congress nearly unanimously passed the Gulf of Tonkin Resolution, giving Lyndon Johnson tremendous power to pursue the Vietnam War and spurring older peace activists into action. Johnson's subsequent decision in March 1965 to send combat troops to South Vietnam and to bomb North Vietnam inspired some of these activists, beginning at the University of Michigan, to hold informational meetings they named "teach-ins" where they were joined by middle-class young people already politicized by the growing student movement. SDS called for a March on Washington against the war, and on April 17 at least twenty thousand people showed up in what was then the largest anti-war demonstration in American history. In August, anti-war activists formed the National Coordinating Committee to End the War in Vietnam—the name evoked the Student Nonviolent Coordinating Committee—to try to bring some organization to the scattered and diverse movement and to begin planning for direct action. That fall, Berkeley's anti-war organization, the Vietnam Day Committee, tried to block trains full of future soldiers traveling to the Oakland induction center, and activists held the first mass draft card burnings in New York.[41]

In January 1966, SNCC issued a position paper condemning the war and encouraging draft resistance, and later that year, mostly white anti-war activists began to build an anti-draft movement. In April 1967, the Spring Mobilization Committee, or the Mobe, another umbrella group, organized simultaneous protests in New York and San Francisco and drew an unprecedented 250,000 participants. Vietnam Summer began two months later, and though it received much less press attention than San Francisco's Summer of Love, several thousand volunteers canvassed door-to-door educating citizens about the war. In October, more than 100,000 people marched on the Pentagon, as the newly named "hippies" joined radical white students and older peace activists and added some drama—they tried to levitate the Pentagon—to the usual march and protest ritual. As increasingly radicalized SNCC activists had traveled to Africa, SDS celebrities like Hayden met with members of the National Liberation Front (NLF) of Vietnam in Czechoslovakia. The test, Hayden announced, sounding the same themes he had used in his earlier reporting from the South, was "whether we as Americans can identify enough with the suffering and ordeal of the Vietnamese people to feel what they feel . . . We are all Viet Cong." That November, Hayden met with the NLF in Phnom Penh, Cambodia, and proved their "decency" by bringing home three American POWs. In SDS and elsewhere, student activists modeled their anti-war work on civil rights organizing.[42]

SDS struggled once again, after the glorious beginning of the ERAP projects, to live up to its image of SNCC and CORE. Having rejected both a single focus on college student organizing and the leadership of the anti-war movement, nationally SDS remained confused about what to do with its exploding membership. At the end of 1966, delegates to the SDS national council meeting in Berkeley debated whether the national organization should get involved in draft resistance work. Again, SNCC served as a model. One plan, based on the Freedom Votes, proposed issuing potential draftees with a "freedom draft card" printed with a declaration: "I want to work for democracy. I do not want to fight in Vietnam . . . I want to build, not burn. The work done by many young Americans in Alabama and Mississippi is a prime example of what I want to do."[43]

SDS national secretary Gregory Calvert made this continuing identification with black activists clear in his January 1967 report. Neither "traditional political organization" nor "ideological clarity" was important for SDS, he wrote. "What counts is that SDS be where the action is. What counts is that SDS be involved in the creation of a cutting-edge freedom struggle." SDS, in other words, needed to be like SNCC and CORE and other radical black organizations.[44]

Calvert acknowledged how much SDS still valued SNCC's approval:

We have to admit that—like it or not—we live in urban industrial capitalist America and not in the rural South. We owe SNCC a deep debt of gratitude for having slapped us brutally in the face with the slogan of black power, a slogan which said to white radicals, "Go home and organize in white America, which is your reality."

Calvert's choice of metaphors positioned black separation as a violent attack on the very body of white radicalism. Again, the language suggested an intimate relationship gone bad, rather than a disagreement over strategy. White radicals, he made clear, did not have to give up their love for black outsiders. They just needed to work on the relationship, making their identification with black radicals less literal. Instead of copying radical black activists' particular actions—going to work in black communities in the rural South or the urban North—SDS members should look at black activists more broadly, as a model for militancy. Black radicals worked for their own liberation, their own freedom. Being a white radical meant doing the same thing, working for the liberation and freedom of the white radical. In contrast, Calvert argued, "the liberal" always fought other people's battles, translating her "conscience into action for others." She worked from a sense of distance, a measure of the space between herself, the subject, and poor African Americans, the object of her activism. "The gap," however, was "not between oneself, what one [was], and the underprivileged." Instead, the crucial motivation for radical activism was "the gap between 'what one could be' and the existing conditions for self-realization." "The radical" worked from a different sense of distance, a measure that collapsed the distinction between subject and object, between the activist and the focus of the activism. In Calvert's interpretation, radical African Americans, in embracing Black Power, made themselves both the subjects and the objects of their activism. Historically, reformers had worked to remake the existing world into "what could be," their visions of utopia. Calvert instead told white activists to make possible their vision of their best self. Radical or "revolutionary consciousness" emerged in "the perception of *oneself* as unfree, as oppressed," "the discovery of oneself as *one of the oppressed*." In this way, Calvert's model mirrored Beats' and folk fans' use of their love for outsiders to discover and make their own difference. Activism began with the activist looking inside rather than outside, at the self rather than at the world. All "authentic" activists were outsiders.[45]

Calvert's speech clearly articulated ideas long percolating in the New Left and offered a logical extension of Hayden's earlier argument. Black and white radicals shared both "gut-level alienation from America-the-Obscene-and-the-Dehumanized" and "the burden of oppression," Calvert insisted, even if they needed to work separately, in their own communities. This shared alienation, an internal and subjective perception rather than the common class status the Old Left had understood as an external and objective "fact," united blacks and whites working for change. External conditions certainly shaped that inner perception, but the key was how a person saw her own identity. The self became the subject and the object, the actor and the thing acted for. This shift aligned New Left political analysis with the broader shifts in the culture, particularly the powerful idea that authenticity, the "real," existed as an internal, rather than external, quality.[46]

Collapsing the distinction between subject and object certainly seemed more democratic. "Liberal" activism positioned the activist above the people acted for, the subject above the object. Whatever the source of the activists' privilege—race or class position, religious beliefs, country of origin, or some combination of these—activism reasserted the superiority of the person acting, even when a person worked to change the very conditions that granted this status. Black activists avoided the problem of this paradox by working to free themselves, by being the subject and the object, both the person acting and the person acted for. White romanticism, however, made this solution more difficult for the white New Left. What problems did white middle-class children of plenty have?

Many white radicals could not make this shift. They reacted to Black Power and black separatism simply by drafting other outsiders to play the role—Appalachian miners and their families, Cuban and Vietnamese revolutionaries, Latino migrant farmers, and even the white working class. They moved to eastern Kentucky to make documentaries and picket mining companies. They followed Cesar Chavez and worked for the United Farm Workers organizing strikes in California and Texas. They traveled to Cuba to help with the sugarcane harvest, or met with resistance fighters of the National Liberation Front in Budapest or Havana or even Hanoi. And they moved to Detroit or Newark or Oakland, got a job in a factory, tried to blend into the working class, and got back to the Old Left task of organizing unions. Environmentalists dropped living people altogether—they liked their fantasy Indians—and romanticized nature instead as a place uncorrupted and innocent, harmonious and pure. Ecology evolved as the study of perfectly balanced "ecosystems," "natural" alternative communities, self-regulating communes of plants and animals, water and earth. If black militants did not want their help, some white radicals went to work elsewhere, for other causes, against other injustices, and they took their romanticism with them.[47]

Still, some white radicals did go to work liberating themselves. Looking inside, making and naming the self, was often part of this process. If they were white and draft age and no longer protected by deferments, they organized draft resistance, became conscientious objectors, and fled to Canada. If they were women, they combined participatory democracy and their under-standing of Maoism and invented consciousness-raising. They built radical feminist women's organizations, discovered women's history, and created womyn's culture. If they were black women, they became black feminists or womanists because white women's feminism left them out and black nation-alist men all too often wanted to build an alternative black world with women's hands and backs and wombs. If they were gay and lesbian, they built organiza-tions like the Lavender Menace and created their own gay liberation move-ment. If they were Native American, they worked for Red Power or built the Native American Movement. If they were Latinos, they joined the Brown Berets and the Young Lords and La Raza. If they were Asian Americans, they joined the Red Guard or Wei Min She. Like black activists before them, all these people made themselves both the subject and the object of their activism. They looked, as Calvert had suggested, at the gap between what they could be and what society allowed them to be and went to work to erase it. This kind of work, the rich proliferation of many separatisms, flourished well into the seventies and early eighties.[48]

Some white Americans worked to liberate themselves by romanticizing the project of cultural separatism rather than black radicals. The hippies in San Francisco's Haight-Ashbury, New York City's East Village, Atlanta's Little Five Points, and elsewhere, the white kids building rural communes in California, Vermont, Colorado, and Tennessee—these mostly middle-class young people did not just copy earlier bohemians, the Beats and, even more recently, Ken Kesey's LSD missionaries and hippie avant-garde, the Merry Pranksters. Afri-can Americans' brash cultural nationalism, well covered if often caricatured in the national media, shaped them as well. Like some radical African Ameri-cans, they too took new names—Sunshine and Wavy Gravy instead of Afeni and Malik—and wore new clothes, created their own art, and invented their own cuisine and their own spiritual practices. They too lived self-consciously against the world, whatever they called it, the system, the machine, the main-stream. The very way of life of white middle-class America—adulthood spent chained to a career or a house, a marriage, a car, and the kids—oppressed them, killing their spirits, killing their inner lives, killing their pleasure. Free-dom meant not working. It meant having lots of sex. It meant taking drugs. But just like white middle-class folk music fans before them, they remade their own privilege by asserting their innocence. Taking up cultural separatism, the mostly white participants in what in 1968 the scholar Theodore Roszak named "the counter culture" recast themselves as outsiders. They did not make themselves the political allies of poor urban or rural blacks.[49]

Some African Americans expressed their frustration with the hippies that moved into black and poor urban neighborhoods for the cheap rents. "The hippies really bug us," one black New Yorker told a reporter. "Because we know they can come down here and play their games for a while and then escape. And we can't, man." "After the hippies go back to their middle-class homes," another African American told a reporter, "we'll still be here." "Hippies have a romantic attachment to the Negro as an Outsider," a professor wrote in the *Nation* in 1967, "but they view him as part of the hated Establishment as soon as he becomes an accepted member of the social order." "How can a Negro drop out?" a New York hippie asked a reporter. "He's there, at bedrock, all the time." For the hippies, all too often African Americans served as sources of authenticity, objects and not subjects, conveyers of coolness and realness and rebellion.[50]

Unlike much of the New Left, hippies did not use blackness to solve the contradictions between the desires for unfettered self-invention and yet for deep connection that conveyed authenticity. Journalist Tom Wolfe, a sensitive observer of the early counterculture, noticed this shift under way as early as the mid-sixties in San Francisco:

> The whole old-style hip life—jazz, coffee houses, civil rights, invite a spade for dinner, Vietnam—it was all dying, I found out, even among the students at Berkeley, across the bay from San Francisco, which had been the heart of the "student-rebellion" and so forth. It had even gotten to the point that Negroes were no longer in the hip scene, not even as totem figures. It was unbelievable. *Spades*, the very soul figures of Hip, of jazz, of the hip vocabulary itself, man and like and dig and baby and scarf and split and later so fine, of civil rights and graduating from Reed College and living on North Beach, down Mason, and balling spade cats—all that good elaborate petting and patting and pouring soul all over the spades—all over, finished, incredibly.

Instead, they dissolved the contradictions in drug trips, dancing, and spiritual practices borrowed liberally from what they knew of Eastern and American Indian religions. They lost themselves in their own bodies and inside their own minds. They experienced ecstasy, holiness, and the dissolving of boundaries. They saw visions.[51]

The counterculture was broad enough to include the Pranksters, who helped invent it with their rebellion against the black-clad, too serious beatniks, and red-diaper babies with Beat pasts like poet and anti-war activist Allen Ginsberg. It made room for dropouts from New Left organizing like Paul Potter and from the academy like Timothy Leary. A former professor turned LSD advocate, Leary told everyone to "turn on, tune in, drop out." "If all the Negroes and left-wing college students in the world," he warned in a 1966 *Playboy* interview, "had Cadillacs and full control of society, they would still be involved in an anthill social system unless they opened themselves up first."[52]

Rock and roll came back, more whitened than ever, as rock. Like some fantastical love child of the Newport Fort Festival and the ERAP projects, rock festivals like Woodstock and Altamont, for better or worse, gave the counterculture nation concrete form. The journalist John Landau wrote in the rock magazine *Rolling Stone*, founded that year, "Rock was not only viewed as a form of entertainment." It was much more, "an essential component of a 'new culture,' along with drugs and radical politics." Other bands across the country and even the Beatles took up the West Coast groups' fusion of lyrical subjects pioneered by Dylan: vaguely political rhetoric, barely disguised drug references, apocalyptic imagery, and calls for liberation. For many fans, political and cultural revolt, at the level of language and feeling, were one. Rock was the new revolution, and its demonstrations, its direct actions, were the ever larger concerts and festivals popping up like mushrooms in hippie-rich areas along the coasts. Two 1969 events—Woodstock and Altamont—came to symbolize the best and the worst of these new paradoxically countercultural institutions.[53]

Promoters of Woodstock, which was advertised as "three days of peace and music," chose this name for their August 1969 music festival to evoke the countercultural charisma of Dylan, who had a home in Woodstock, New York, even though the event was actually held on a farm over an hour away. Expecting one hundred thousand fans come to hear the music of Joan Baez, Jefferson Airplane, the Grateful Dead, and others, promoters were overwhelmed when half a million people showed up, most of them without paying. Abbie Hoffman and other political activists had persuaded the organizers to include what became "Movement City," a place for political groups like SDS to set up booths and both print and distribute literature. But what exactly was there for these groups to do at Woodstock beyond the old campus literature table model of passing out leaflets? As desperate food and water shortages and inadequate bathroom and medical facilities threatened to shut down the festival, the expensive printing press, missing key parts, sat abandoned in the rain.[54]

The journalist Tom Smucker, a member of the SDS offshoot Movement for a Democratic Society, came to the festival to try to reconcile his own commitments to both "Rock and Roll and the Movement." "They both developed at the same time," he argued, "and both, in some ways, dealt with the same problems—Race, Sex, Repression, Class." How could a fan and a political radical reconcile the fact that rock was both a part of the capitalist system the New Left by then openly opposed and yet also central to the counterculture's great cultural rebellion? At planning meetings, "politicos" suggested various approaches, ways "to relate politically to a Rock Event." Ideas ranged from "Point out to people that what they were doing isn't real. Bread and Circus, Co-optation, The Plastic Straightjacket, that it is happening under capitalism and therefore phony" to "Point out to people that Rock and Roll is good, that it is 'Ours,' but it's run by capitalist corporations and thus mistreated, stolen from 'US' . . . That, of all things, the Promoters are trying to make money off this." At Woodstock, however, Smucker found that the New Left groups were essentially irrelevant. After a bad night of rain Friday, Smucker recalled, "we awoke to hear the U.S. Committee to Aid the National Liberation Front announcing over their loudspeaker, 'Get Your Dry Che Guevara T-Shirts: Only Two Dollars.' That's called Radical Politics." It was the hippies, members of New Mexico's Hog Farm commune, Smucker had to admit, who did the real organizing—feeding people mountains of free vegetarian food and helping users come down from bad trips. Building the (temporary) alternative community, not getting people to read damp pamphlets, was for Smucker and many fans the political accomplishment of the festival.[55]

At Woodstock, people felt what journalist Andrew Kopkind called "the intense communitarian closeness of a militant struggle," without having to go south or to the cities and face the cops, without becoming urban guerrillas, without trying to take over Columbia University or build People's Park. "No one in this century," he wrote, "had ever seen a 'society' so free of repression. Everyone swam naked in the lake, balling was easier than getting breakfast, and the 'pigs' just smiled and passed out the oats." Most people at Woodstock had not participated in the great political struggles of the decade. For them, "Woodstock must always be their model of how good we will all feel after the revolution."[56]

Four months later, Altamont, of course, gave all this rock and roll community-building a bad name. The Rolling Stones decided to give San Francisco a present, a free concert that December. There, instead of peace, love, and understanding, four people died. One, a black man named Meredith Hunter, was stabbed to death by members of the Hell's Angels motorcycle gang, hired by the Stones, in a stupid gesture of romantic rebellion, to provide security at the concert. The Angels were for many on the left the white working-class equivalent of the Black Panthers, the literal embodiment of the outsider now armed to fight back, and part of their countercultural celebrity lay in the fact that they were not black. Up around the stage, the Angels beat others too. Three more men died less dramatically. One fell in a ditch and, too stoned or drunk to come out, drowned. Two others sitting by a campfire were run over by a car. Rock was still a rebellion—parents and policemen certainly hated it—but it no longer seemed like a new, post–Black Power path to the Beloved Community. The rock revolution, the magical liberation, was over.[57]

By the end of the sixties, the burned-out remnants of both radical political groups and the urban counterculture began to collect in pockets of the country. These people were still searching for meaning, but they had given up on politics on the one hand and quick routes to a new consciousness on the other. Some communes, like the Ananda Co-Operative in the foothills of the Sierras, grew up around spiritual leaders, in this case an American yogi named Kriyanda, and ran meditation centers as well as organic farms. Over the hills from Oakland, the members of Vocations for Social Change lived together in two brown shingle houses in the woods and ran a clearinghouse for information about groups, projects, and jobs. In 1968, Allen Ginsberg's nonprofit Committee on Poetry bought a farm near Cherry Valley, New York, and Ginsberg took his own nontraditional domestic arrangements—there were always lots of people staying with Ginsberg and Peter Orlovsky and a pot of soup that could be stretched for dinner—to the country, creating a commune-like retreat for himself and other poets. Other alternative communities grew up around the growing interest in environmentalism and living lightly on the earth and a romanticization of Native Americans.[58]

Some communes originated not so much to try out new spiritual practices and domestic arrangements but out of a conscious desire to step away from radical political organizing and lead a slower, simpler life. Raymond Mungo, a former peace activist, described a year in the life of a commune in Vermont in his book *Total Loss Farm*. "The farm in Vermont had fooled us, just as we hoped it would when we moved there in early '68," he admitted. "It had tricked even battle-scarred former youth militants into seeing the world as bright clusters of Day-Glo orange and red forest." But Mungo also remembered the whole sequence of events that led many radical activists to retreat to the country:

When we lived in Boston, Chicago, San Francisco, Washington . . .
we dreamed of a New Age born of violent insurrection. We danced

on the graves of war dead in Vietnam, every corpse was ammunition for Our Side; we set up a countergovernment down there in Washington, had marches, rallies and meetings; tried to fight fire with fire. Then Johnson resigned, yes, and the universities began to fall, the best and the oldest ones first, and by God every 13-year-old in the suburbs was smoking dope and our numbers multiplying into the millions. But I woke up in the spring of 1968 and said, "This is not what I had in mind," because the movement had become my enemy; the movement was not flowers and doves and spontaneity, but another vicious system, the seed of a heartless bureaucracy, a minority Party vying for power rather than peace. It was then that we put away the schedule for the revolution, gathered together our dear ones and all our resources, and set off to Vermont in search of the New Age.

Dawn, a woman drifting in the early seventies between communes and then living at one outside Taos, New Mexico, recalled the series of steps through which she too had dropped out. After attending the University of Illinois for a while, she left to work on the McCarthy campaign. "I had just started to get into SDS and that kind of thing when I went to the Chicago Convention and was arrested at a sit-in. After the Convention I was convinced that there was no way to work for change within the system . . . At first I wanted to make a new beginning, as an artist, but that meant that I'd still have to participate in the competitiveness of that society," she recalled. "So it all came down to the realization that it wasn't possible to live in that society and not feel alienated." The communes were SNCC field sites and SDS ERAP projects abstracted from their surrounding communities, shorn of any attempt to organize politically.[59]

Most communes did not last long—organic farming, earning a living from the land, many members found out quickly, was extremely hard, and impossible unless everyone contributed his or her labor. The field, the vegetable patch, was as difficult a place to work, in different ways, as the field, the Delta town or Newark neighborhood or campus, had been in an earlier life. Members adopted a voluntary primitivism—making their own clothes, eating a simple, mostly homegrown and vegetarian diet, scavenging for building supplies, and even collecting food stamps and welfare—that was difficult to sustain. The communes that survived often had outside sources of funding—they ran businesses or attracted members with money—or they were organized around religious leaders or practices. Belief, faith even, gave form to the search for meaning that animated these communal experiments, structuring individuals' explorations in ways that promoted the survival of the group. Without some kind of spiritual or religious cohesiveness, it was too easy for members' individual inner trips to work against the need of the commune. If one person's "thing" or "bag" or "yoga" was to meditate all day and other people needed to have lots of sex or explore the woods, who would weed the lettuce patch and cook the rice and beans?[60]

Other folks with weekends or weekly hour-long time slots and not whole lives to dedicate went to places like the Esalen Institute in Big Sur, south of San Francisco, or to retreats and group sessions to try Gestalt or EST, primal scream therapy or the human potential movement, yoga or the meditation practices and teachings of particular spiritual leaders. Esalen, an "experiment in living," was a model for the new therapeutic and spiritual retreats that became a weekend in the counterculture camps, the part-time way to expand your consciousness. At Esalen, Richard Perls, one of Paul Goodman's collaborators in the invention of Gestalt therapy, preached "the Now Trip," a strange fusion of encounter sessions, skinny-dipping, folk and rock music, Tai Chi exercises, and drugs designed to free people from "the Rut" and get them to live in the present and pay attention to their senses. Perls popularized the mantra "Do your own thing." At Esalen, a little romping in nature, a little nakedness, a little true communication, and a little sex, and people would find the way to inner growth and inner peace. The author Henry Miller had lived in Big Sur, and his works, especially *Tropic of Capricorn*, finally openly available after years of censorship for their sexual explicitness, became a kind of sacred map for these trips: "There is only one great adventure and that is inward toward the self, and for that, time nor space nor even deeds matter." The inner journey became the most important route to rebel legitimacy. By 1967, even the Beatles had a yogi.[61]

Black Power and black separatism did not succeed in preventing "blackness" from playing its old historical role in American culture as the ultimate marker of outsider status. The "nigger" analogy, popping up all over the place in the late 1960s and 1970s, made this clear. SDS reprinted as a pamphlet Jerry Farber's March 3, 1967, article from the *Los Angeles Free Press*, "The Student as Nigger: How to Be Slaves." Students from kindergarten to graduate school, Farber argued, were an "academic Lowndes County." They had "no voice." In October 1967, the *Village Voice* named hippies "the new niggers." East Village freaks, the New York weekly argued, faced "opposition from every corner, muggings and rape and even murder." Naomi Weisstein's article "Kinder, Küche, and Kirche as Scientific Law: Psychology Constructs the Female," originally published in the *Boston Free Press* in 1969, was reprinted in *Psychology*

Today in October 1969 as "Woman as Nigger." That same year, Yoko Ono used the phrase "woman is the nigger of the world" in an interview with a British women's magazine. Three years later, she and John Lennon made it the title of a song about women's oppression and sang it on Dick Cavett's television show.[62]

There was, in this phrasemaking, a genuine attempt to imagine and create alliances across racial and other boundaries. Lennon turned to California congressman Ron Dellums, chairman of the Black Caucus, to support his and Ono's use of the word as radio stations refused to play the single. On the Cavett show, Lennon read a statement of support from Dellums:

> If you define niggers as someone whose lifestyle is defined by others, whose opportunities are defined by others, whose role in society is defined by others, then good news!—you don't have to be black to be a nigger in this society. Most of the people in America are niggers.

On one level, Dellums's statement made political sense. A coalition of the oppressed and the alienated—the people without self-determination—could form a new majority. On another level, this kind of thinking failed to take into account the long history of white romanticism of African Americans. How could a group of people symbolize reality and yet be real? How could they confer authenticity on others and yet be people themselves?

The romance of the outsider—some white middle-class college students' identification with southern black civil rights activists—helped make the white New Left. The romance of the outsider—some white New Left activists' identification with urban black militants—also helped radicalize the New Left. In the end, however, the romance of the outsider helped destroy the New Left, or at least white activists' dream of becoming a part of a broad and effective multi-racial and multi-issue progressive political alliance. African Americans could not be resources in some white people's quest for transcendence and yet also be equal allies in a collective fight for political transformation. In the white New Left, the intersection of two ideas about reality—that the real and authentic existed inside the self and that blackness marked the richest sites of realism and authenticity—produced a whole new level of minstrelsy.

SDS member Bill Ayers was working for the ERAP project in Cleveland when Stokely Carmichael spoke at a church there in 1966 a few weeks after he began using the phrase "Black Power" in Mississippi. Black people had to take their freedom, Carmichael argued. They could not wait for other people to give it to them. Black people had to define their own standards of morality, wisdom, and beauty. They could not let others define these key values for them. White people should go organize their own people. "I thought Stokely made perfect sense," Ayers remembered. "But by that time I thought I was Black."[63]

No matter how much a white middle-class radical made common cause with the oppressed, at the deepest level her assertion of self supported the status quo. It supported a world where white middle-class people possessed the privilege of self-invention. It supported the age-old American fantasy that the limits of history did not have to apply, that a person could make herself anything. It supported the very structures of class and racial privilege radical politics was supposed to oppose. The postwar history of white middle-class Americans' love for outsiders haunted and limited New Left attempts to build a new political coalition on the basis of alienation.

In the last two decades, scholars, former activists, and public intellectuals have continued to search for the "real" politics of the period. The arguments vary. "Real" politics are interracial, nonviolent, and anti-separatist. "Real" politics focus on class and economic issues. "Real" politics shun the expressive, the theatrical, and the performative. "Real" politics are not "cultural." In a culture, however, in which "real" has long been a synonym for "authentic" and conveys not just efficacy but emotional resonance and inner truth, this kind of criticism is useless. In America, the romance of the outsider always racializes the concept of the real. And looking for "the real," no matter what the professed political beliefs of the seeker, perpetuates the politics of inequality.

CHAPTER 7

The Making of Christian Countercultures: God's Outsiders from the Jesus People to Jerry Falwell and the Moral Majority

Fundamentalists have been left out of everyone else's liberation.
Martin Marty

From southern California to Atlanta, as the sixties turned into the seventies, an odd poster began to appear among the advertisements for rock shows and housing notices plastered on kiosks, community bulletin boards, and commune walls: "Wanted, Jesus Christ. Alias: The Messiah, The Son of God, King of Kings, Lord of Lords, Prince of Peace." Under a large, all-caps lead, the text listed his crimes: "Notorious leader of underground liberation movement; wanted for the following charges: Practicing medicine, winemaking, and food distribution without a license; Interfering with businessmen in the temple; Associating with known criminals, radicals, subversives, prostitutes, street people; claiming to have the authority to make people into God's children." It also noted his appearance and his habits: "Typical hippie type—long hair, beard, robe, sandals. Hangs out in slum areas, few rich friends, often sneaks into the desert." Wanted posters had become markers of rebel status on the left as militant activists from Eldridge Cleaver and Angela Davis to Bernardine Dohrn and Bill Ayers escaped criminal charges by fleeing underground. Like the wanted flyers for these Black Panther Party and Weather members, this poster ended with a warning: "This man is extremely dangerous . . . He changes men and claims to set them free." "Wanted, Jesus Christ" called hippies to follow the ultimate rebel.[1]

In the early seventies as growing numbers of countercultural white kids took up evangelical Christianity, reporters began to see a pattern. They named the scattering of Christian cults, communal houses, new nondenominational churches, beachside baptisms, and Christian rock concerts the Jesus People movement or the Jesus movement. *Time* called this new outpouring of faith "the May-December marriage of conservative religion and the rebellious counterculture." A cover portrait of a psychedelic Jesus wore the glowing words "Jesus Revolution" like a typed halo. All the media attention, in turn, helped spread awareness of this hippie evangelicalism to young people far from its California epicenter, much as the press had helped to popularize the Beats a generation before. The Jesus People movement formed a kind of counter counterculture. It gave postwar conservatives something they had needed—their own broad and recognizable youth culture.[2]

By the middle of the decade, this path into conservative Christianity met and in some ways merged with an upwelling of faith in less countercultural enclaves. Evangelical Christianity began to spread from more working-class and rural areas into white middle-class suburbs. Fundamentalist ministers like Lynchburg, Virginia, pastor and televangelist Jerry Falwell led many conservative Christians from self-imposed exile into political power and cultural visibility. By the end of the decade, conservatives gained a more lasting oppositional culture in a growing network of evangelical social, cultural, and political institutions that gave form and voice to an oppressed "majority," what Falwell called "godly Americans." Evangelicals announced that they were the outsiders who would save the nation.

Certainly, rebels on the right defined the margins and the center of American society differently than civil rights, anti-war, and Black Power activists, and feminists, but they proved by the late seventies and eighties as adept at romanticizing their own outsider position as these earlier rebels. Conservative white Christians' desire for personal transformation and their alienation from late twentieth-century American culture also mimicked the yearnings and emotions of the hippies and back-to-the-land folks. They too institutionalized their sense of difference by building their own self-consciously separate communities, in this case secondary schools and colleges, religious institutions of all kinds, organizations for providing social services, and media empires. As Guy Rodgers, an early Christian Coalition leader, argued, "One of the best ways to understand people in the grassroots of the pro-family movement [a mid-seventies name for conservative Christian organizing] is to understand their perception of being outsiders, either because they chose to be out of the process or because they wanted to be involved but always met resistance."[3]

Paradoxically, the New Left and the related hippie counterculture made possible both the New Right's political style and its focus on cultural issues. Many civil rights and New Left activists had tried to use alienation from contemporary society as the organizing principle of a new political coalition, a community of outsiders. Marginality and separateness, they argued, could be a route back into politics. On the left, this strategy worked most effectively in the southern civil rights movement and in the anti-war movement. On the right, this strategy worked so well that conservatives used the vision of a coalition of outsiders to put aside their differences and take over the Republican Party. Conservative Christians, culturally, morally, and politically alienated from what they defined as contemporary life and rooted in their own self-conscious enclaves or Christian countercultures, played an essential role in this process.

The romance of the outsider gave white evangelical and fundamentalist Christians a story, a way to see themselves as outsiders and yet still engage in politics. Jesus, some believers decided, was a rebel, a self-conscious outsider in a region ruled by Rome. By the end of the seventies, what Buckley had grasped in the fifties became widely understood—conservatives stood not for conservation but for change. As Howard Phillips, executive director of the Conservative Caucus and a former YAF member, told fundamentalist minister Jerry Falwell at the 1979 meeting that created the Moral Majority, conservatives needed to be revolutionaries, in temperament if not moral philosophy. Belief, in this kind of thinking, required expression. It required action, from voting and partisan activism to nonviolent direct action. And these acts in turn shaped the nature of belief. The greatest irony of postwar American history may be the fact that conservative white Christians became better at loving outsiders and seeing themselves as outsiders than white hippies and middle-class members of the New Left.[4]

Hippie Christians

At the end of the sixties, a new kind of Christian began to use the clothes and slang and lifestyle of the counterculture to spread the message: "Turn on to Christ." Jesus was a "freak," these "street Christians" and "Jesus freaks" claimed, the ultimate outsider, a martyr for peace and love and human understanding rejected by the world because he told people to change their lives. As hippies, these new Christians believed, they had already rejected contemporary America and were actively searching for a new way of living. Maybe Jesus could tell them what to put in place of the world they had left behind. Maybe he could understand their alienation. A rich nineteen-year-old explained why she joined the Jesus group the Children of God: "I'd been searching, for an answer, something to give meaning to my life. I tried drugs, Zen, a dozen other things, but none of it worked. Then I met the Children of God, and I just gave up everything and joined them." Another woman in a religious commune in Oregon insisted, "What makes all of us in this new generation different is our God thirst."[5]

Many cool-talking, hip-dressing proselytizers came to Christ out of the hippie counterculture, giving up their LSD and grass and even sex for God. The founders of the first Christian coffeehouse, Ted Wise, a former sailmaker and recovered drug addict, and his wife, Elizabeth, started the first countercultural Christian ministry in 1967 on the streets of San Francisco. Churches as institutions could not give people salvation, they preached—all believers needed was Christ. The Wises literally worked on the streets. They met and converted Lonnie Frisbee, for example, a San Francisco art student who would become a charismatic Jesus People minister, as he wandered the Haight one day tripping and talking about UFOs and God. Jesus People like the Wises, even when they quietly took money from established churches, saw their new interest in Christ as a continuation of their countercultural lives.[6]

Others, like Jack Sparks, a former Campus Crusade for Christ worker and college professor who became the founder of Berkeley's Christian World Liberation Front (CWLF), self-consciously adopted New Left and hippie forms of expression as a way to convert young people. On the one hand, this practice followed the work of missionaries abroad who learned local languages and adopted native symbols and styles—trimming their robes with kente cloth, for example—to try to fit their foreign faith into the everyday lives of their intended converts. In this sense, Sparks and others like him learned to talk and dress like hippies to show young people that Christianity could be a part of an alternative lifestyle. As Sparks wrote, "It's easier to rap to a person at a language level he's hip to." But the practice of "passing" at work here, of "playing hippie," also provided a bizarre twist on whites' well-established practice of establishing some kind of connection to cultural "authenticity" by playing black. In place of face paint and black dialect, some white evangelicals grew their hair out and wore jeans and learned to say "peace" and "revolution" and "right on" in order to convince hippies that Christianity was cool.[7]

Both these paths into the Jesus People movement relied on the hippies' resurrection of symbols and forms rooted in the long Western history of romanticism and bohemian culture. That history in part traced the secularization of religious ideas and experiences like transcendence, the sacred and the divine, and conversion. The Jesus People brought interest in magic and mysticism, ritual and states of inner consciousness, out of hippie culture and back into the broad currents of religious life where they had originated.

The hippies did not invent the idea of lifestyle as a form of cultural expression, but they spread the practice much more broadly than nineteenth-century pioneers like Thoreau and twentieth-century predecessors like New York's 1920s bohemians and mid-century Beats. Clothing was key, an always visible marker of estrangement, and Jesus People readily adapted the hippie attention to dress to their new faith. Converts often kept their cutoff jeans, sandals, and beads and simply added crosses and wrote "Jesus Is Lord" on their tie-dye T-shirts. Christ gave them another reason not to cut their hair or beards—the first Christians, they assumed, had been men and women with long, natural locks. Some Jesus People even adopted "Christ couture," a peasant-style, Mexican-made combo of flowing tunics and pants or skirts. Countercultural groups like California beach kids and surfers flocked to ocean-side baptisms in places like Corona del Mar wearing their usual bikinis and shorts.[8]

Jesus People talked and lived like hippies too. Arthur Blessitt lured the freaks into his His Place headquarters on the Sunset Strip with the line "Why don't we drop a little Matthew, Mark, Luke, and John." At his "toilet services," druggies gave their hearts to Jesus and flushed their stashes down the bowl without ever having to hear the words of the King James Bible. And Blessitt and other would-be leaders narrated their autobiographies as tales of rejection by the "mainstream" and persecution by the "straight" church and even the police. Sparks wrote a "hip" version of the New Testament, *Letters to Street Christians*: "Don't get hooked on the ego-tripping world system . . . Dig it! This whole plastic bag is exactly what Jesus liberated us from." While Sparks and the CWLF used the revolutionary rhetoric of the politically active end of the counterculture, other Jesus People spoke a more flower-power vernacular. The *Hollywood Free Paper* offered Christ as the answer to "the nitty-gritty fragmentation we experience on the inside":

Well, we're not rapping about positive thinking or playing religious games. Nope. That's just as phony as the drug trip. We're rapping about a Person—Jesus Christ. And if you can dig Him (that means to depend on Him to put your head together) then you're in for some heavy surprises!! He'll turn you on to a spiritual high for the rest of your life.

The Rev. Arthur Blessitt, left, and Jessie Wise, center, carried this 105-pound cross from California to New York City to raise awareness about the Jesus People and the need for the nation to return to God. In New York City on July 8, 1970, they talked with young people in a park. *Associated Press*.

In newspapers and national magazines, these new Christians talked about getting "right" with God and finding "the higher high." In documentary films from the early seventies, Jesus freaks hugged and sang and swayed and played guitars, debating the deepest questions of life in slang and smiling beatifically as if being saved were the natural equivalent of getting stoned.[9]

Like other hippies and radical political activists of the late sixties, Jesus People believed in the power of gestures, chants, and signs. In place of Allen Ginsberg and other hippies' "Hare Krishna" and "Ommmmm," Jesus People chanted "Jesus Saves" and "One Way" (to heaven). They greeted strangers and friends alike and answered all questions with the refrain "Jesus Loves You." And they transformed leftist phrases like "All Power to the People" to "All Power Through Jesus" and "Ho Ho Ho Chi Minh, Jesus Christ Is Gonna Win." There was even a Jesus People cheer, a "Give me a *J*" chant that ended with "What will keep you up longer than speed? Jesus! What does America need? Jesus!" Most new believers adopted the movement's sign, an obvious modification of Black Power's raised fist and of the anti-war movement's peace sign, an upraised fist with the forefinger pointed toward heaven for the "One Way," Jesus Christ, to salvation.[10]

Jesus People also followed the hippies in creating their own alternative forms of media. The underground newspaper and the rock song were the counterculture's most important forms of cultural expression, and the Jesus People used both to spread their message of Christ. Jesus People everywhere published free "underground" newspapers, from the largest *Hollywood Free Paper* with a peak circulation of about half a million to the relatively intellectual *Ichthus*, "the paper of the East Coast Jesus People," to the Jesus People's Army's *Goad*. The CWLF copied the politically activist end of the counterculture and published not only the underground newspaper *Right On!* but also pamphlets, tracts, and leaflets. In one example, they copied the style and size as well as the format—a thirteen-point manifesto—of a radical Berkeley Liberation Front tract, matching the BLF's picture of Chairman Mao, the leaves of a pot plant, and the quote "Let a hundred flowers bloom" with a portrait of Christ and the quote "You will know the truth and the truth will set you free." The BLF's "We will turn the schools into training grounds for liberation" became the CWLF's "He will turn the schools into training grounds for the liberation of the inner self." "We will make Telegraph Avenue and the South Campus a strategic free territory for revolution" turned into "He will free all who come to Him from bondage to the crippled self, the maimed world, and the scheming devil." At a 1971 peace march in Berkeley, the CWLF set up a free Kool-Aid stand and passed out Christian tracts and a special edition of *Right On!* The CWLF even published a Christian underground comic book. Jesus People newspapers and other literature both proselytized and helped spread their producers' particular vision of Christian community within the broader counterculture.[11]

After the Wises opened the Living Room in the Haight, Christian coffeehouses began to emerge on the fringes of countercultural neighborhoods elsewhere and on the edges of college campuses as other new Christians set about what they called the work of the Spirit. These Christian versions of the places kids had been hanging out and playing folk music since the fifties provided a venue for the new Christian music, most often a religious version of the then popular folk-rock and emerging singer-songwriter sounds. By the early seventies, most major cities and college towns had at least one Christian coffee shop or nightclub, supported either by a more established church as a kind of mission to the counterculture—Hollywood Presbyterian's Salt Company, for example—or by an individual or a small group of believers (sometimes with covert "straight" church funding) as a place for winning converts, like Solomon's Porch Coffee House in Baltimore. In some places these spots functioned as a new kind of church, and in others they helped draw new Christians to the services of more organized groups. Christian musicians played at these spaces and at larger, often outdoor Jesus festivals and concerts.[12]

Larry Norman, the first real Christian music star, began singing his own Jesus songs at the Salt Company but later parted with the Presbyterian-supported venue over his criticism of "straight" churches. Norman songs like "Right Here in America" became Jesus People anthems, the Christian version of Dylan's protest songs.

> I am addressing this song to the church,
> 'Cause I've been to your churches and sat in your pews,
> And heard sermons on just how much money you'll need for the year,
> And I've heard you make reference to Mexicans, Chinamen, Niggers and Jews;
> And I gather you wish we would all disappear;
> And you call yourselves Christians when really you're not,
> And you're living your life as you please.

Other Jesus musicians retained ties to churches full of Jesus People. The popular Christian band Love Song, for example, played for Chuck Smith's Calvary Chapel in Santa Ana, the church where Lonnie Frisbee helped draw thousands

Members of the Children of God sing and pray before eating lunch at their headquarters building in Los Angeles in 1971. *Associated Press.*

of freaks to beachside baptisms and weekly services. In the counterculture more broadly, music worked as a symbol of the alternative community, a medium of individual self-expression, and a means of creating the connections through which new collectivities could be made. The Jesus People used their music in the same way. Bands and songs represented the particular Jesus People groups that nurtured the musicians. Listening to the music became a way for believers to physically experience feelings of connection as sound waves hit bodies simultaneously. Music, for the Jesus People—playing or singing or dancing along—became a form of worship, a way of opening up to the Spirit.[13]

Jesus People also took the idea that "community" itself could become a form of expression, a kind of symbolic statement about belief and individual identity as well as a group of people helping each other to live, from the counterculture. Many Jesus People, especially leaders and recent converts, lived in communal Christian houses—Calvary Chapel's Mansion Messiah, Ted and Elizabeth Wise's House of Acts, CWLF's Agape House, and the Shiloh Houses across the country, for example—though some groups shunned the word "commune" because it suggested an easy sexuality. In these homes, Jesus People lived apart from non-Christians, abstaining from sex and drugs, praying, reading and often memorizing the Bible for hours a day, and working together to find salvation. A journalist laughed at the odd rural-revival-meets-summer-camp feel in his 1971 description of San Francisco's Harvest House: "All the towels in the bathroom were pegged and labeled Mary, Johnny, Sue . . . and for some reason that simple Sunday School picture of Jesus-in-the-Garden-of-Gethsemane was iconed over the toothbrush rack, probably to remind early morning brushers of their oft-bannered slogan: *after Jesus, everything else is toothpaste.*" But many of the residents were earnest and serious about building alternative Christian communities. Couples a few years older than the new converts lived in most group houses, providing spiritual guidance and structure.[14]

In these Christian communes, chosen and intentional community—a family of the like-minded—became its own kind of performance art and religious ritual, a liturgy of everyday life. They were trying to solve in their own way a central question of postwar American culture, in J. D. Salinger's character Holden Caulfield's words—how can a person separate the phony from the true? How can she know what to believe in? Like many hippies and New Left activists, alternative Christians wanted to create a transparent relationship between their symbolic and material worlds. They wanted to make how they lived exactly equal to what they believed.

The parents of young converts often saw their children's conversions as yet another form of countercultural experimentation. "I guess we should have known that this might happen," said one mother interviewed for a 1971 *Life* magazine piece on the "groovy Christians" of Rye, New York. "These kids have already bugged us with every kind of classic adolescent rebellion. We'd been through long hair, peace marches, macrobiotic diets, meditation . . . Drugs, too, of course." Another mother confessed, "Sometimes I almost wish they *would* go back to something simple like smoking a little grass." What the parents called rebellion, their kids described as the cure—the feeding of their hunger for something real to believe in, their discovery at last of the absolute truth. These "ex-flesh freaks," as some called themselves, had been "hip and bright and avant-garde," had been "showered all their lives with all the material 'advantages' their parents could afford." "I've just graduated from Yale and come back from hitch-hiking around Europe, doing what I'd supposedly always wanted to do, but not feeling particularly happy about it," one of the new converts told a reporter. "I was getting ready to go to California to see what kind of flesh trip I could get into," another replied. "None of that stuff ever worked," a third argued. "I tried it all and I quit each thing whenever I heard of something else that might be a little more groovy, but it never was." "There is no difference between seeing how fast you can run a mile or how much acid you can take," another Rye convert insisted. Parents, converts, and the national media all described the Jesus People movement as another form of oppositional youth culture.[15]

Within the counterculture itself, however, the Jesus People rebelled by choosing an indigenous form of Christianity over more seemingly exotic ways of opposing white middle-class conformity and the alleged meaninglessness of mid-century American life. Beginning in the fifties, writers like Salinger, Kerouac, and Ginsberg began experimenting with Zen traditions, yoga, meditation, and chanting, their Americanized adaptations of Eastern religious practices and mystical traditions. In the late fifties and sixties, Salinger, Ginsberg, and the poet Gary Synder helped make these practices popular in the student bohemias that ringed many campuses. By the end of the sixties, cults, alternative spiritualities, new forms of analysis, and odd hybrids of religious and therapeutic practices popped up everywhere, like the psychedelic mushrooms some of their practitioners ate. Scientology, Abilitism, light radiation, psychocybernetics, astral projection, the use of alpha-wave headsets, Gestalt therapy, EST, Arica, and the Foundation were all homegrown amalgamations of mystical practices, therapy, psychological theory, and new technologies that promised to ease repression and free the individual self. Other groups adapted religious practices like Native American peyote-eating and sweat lodge rituals and Eastern Sufism, yoga, and transcendental meditation to answer white middle-class Americans' questions about life's meaning. Interest in extraterrestrials and UFOs exploded. If this world had no answers, intelligent beings elsewhere might provide wisdom or, alternately, so threaten earth that human beings might finally recognize their commonalities. Thousands of Americans rejected their former lives to follow yogis and gurus and wise men of all kinds. Yogi Bhajan, Guru Maharaj Ji, Meher Baba, Swami Satchidananda, Maharishi Mahesh Yogi, and Baba Ram Dass—the names alone expressed their followers' desire to flee mid-century American life. Across all these old and new faiths, countercultural seekers shared a common rejection of scientific and bureaucratic rationality, a longing for ecstatic and visionary experiences, and a sense that emotional intensity signified truth. There had to be more to life than what they had learned in mainline churches, colleges, and public high schools. Jesus People shared this sense of alienation and yet rebelled too against all these new spiritual rebels, instead reaching back within the Christian tradition for visions of a primitive church that they believed connected directly with the supernatural and the divine.[16]

In turn, this search for the "early church," Christianity's first few centuries, and the "simple gospel"—the divine word alone is enough—set the Jesus People against the majority of American Protestants. These alternative Christians were not just rebels in the countercultural sense—they were theological rebels as well. Rejecting the forms of Christianity practiced in mainline denominations, the Jesus People embraced more conservative forms of Christianity. These forms, in turn, had grown out of some early twentieth-century Christians' resistance to the growing dominance of liberal theology. Liberal Protestantism, according to the scholar Stephen Prothero, was a "theological movement" that originated in the nineteenth century and "adapted to the challenges of modernity by stressing the goodness of humanity, the inevitability of progress, the necessity of good works, and the immanence of God in nature, culture, and the human heart." Fundamentalism, which took its name from a published series of doctrines called "the fundamentals of the faith," emphasized instead the difference between the true Christianity of Jesus and the false Christianity of the established churches. In adapting to modern life, liberal Protestants, fundamentalists argued, had lost the supernatural Jesus. They were not really Christians at all.[17]

Fundamentalists believed, most importantly, that the Bible was literally true and that the individual found salvation only in a personal relationship to Jesus Christ. The role of the church, then, was to support this path to eternal life, to save souls. Beginning with the Scopes Trial in 1925, fundamentalists began retreating from the broader culture, seeking in separatism from modern

America a way to preserve their strict standards of behavior and Bible-based rejection of modern intellectual ideas like Darwinism. By the 1940s, fundamentalists measured their faithfulness by their distance from American popular culture—no dancing, alcohol, secular music, or drugs—and liberal Christian churches. Other conservative Christians, led by ministers like the revival leader Billy Graham, rejected what they perceived as fundamentalists' militant separatism, anti-intellectualism, and anti-modernism. They resurrected the old term "evangelical" to describe their own emotional, Bible-based, and conversion-oriented faith and differentiate themselves from fundamentalism. Evangelicals, then, were conservative Christians, but they were not necessarily fundamentalists. The Jesus People, in their fusion of fundamentalist theology and countercultural style, were hippie evangelicals.[18]

Most Jesus People followed some version of fundamentalist theology. Sitting cross-legged on the tables of coffeehouses, on the grass in parks, and on the floors of the cobbled-together meeting places of the new nondenominational churches, these alternative Christians studied dog-eared Bibles, streaked their pages with yellow highlighter, and looked for the Lord. They listened to their leaders, almost always white men like Chuck Smith and Lonnie Frisbee or Steve Heefner, a former disc jockey who led kids from Rye, New York, into the "The Way" ministry in the early seventies. In sessions of study, prayer, and singing, these "ministers," rarely formally trained, taught a simplified version of the fundamentals. The Bible was the inspired and wholly inerrant word of God, literally true and complete in itself, transparent and needing no interpretive tradition or outside texts or religious leaders to tell followers what it meant. Christ was literally born of the Virgin Mary, died to atone for humanity's sins, and rose from the dead to live again. His return to earth would create the Kingdom of God. A personal relationship with this Savior, not good works or church attendance, rituals, or creeds, was the only way to salvation: "Jesus Saves." As *Time* reported, "If any one mark clearly identities them, it is their total belief in an awesome, supernatural Jesus Christ, not just a marvelous man who lived two thousand years ago, but a living God who is both Savior and Judge, the Ruler of their destinies."[19]

Like most evangelicals, almost all Jesus People believed in the apocalypse, in the literal return of Christ and the end of the world, as prophesied in the book of Revelation. There was no need for the social gospel—a rich Protestant tradition of serving the poor as a way to express religious faith—or for an interest in politics. Only conversion mattered—how many more individuals had been brought to Christ? The end of the world was at hand. Why worry about the war in Vietnam or poverty? "Jesus," as some of these new Christians were fond of saying, "might be back before breakfast." Many Jesus People believed they were the last generation of young people who would ever live, the "terminal generation." As Chuck Smith of Calvary Chapel preached, "The last days are upon us and the Spirit of God is being poured out upon us . . . It won't be long until we see the Second Coming of the Lord." And the end of the world was not just coming fast—everything had already been predicted and explained. Whether they could cite the name or not, many new converts followed a particular type of fundamentalist theology called pre-millennial dispensationalism. In this vision of the end of the world, a series of powerful signs prophesied in the Bible would signal that the end times were at hand. Then Christ would come to take true Christians directly to heaven. Larry Norman's "I Wish We'd All Been Ready," a song that appeared on both of his first two Christian albums, *Upon This Rock* (Capitol, 1970) and *Street Level* (One Way, 1970), spread this pre-millennial belief in the Rapture. "The Son has come and you've been left behind," Norman sang quietly over a swelling soft-rock arrangement of strings and horns in one version of the song, opening with what becomes the chorus. "A man and wife asleep in bed,/ She hears a noise and turns her head./ He's gone/ I wish we'd all been ready . . . / There's no time to change your mind." If they walked with Christ, many new Christians believed, they would not even have to die.[20]

But the most important popularizer of pre-millennial thinking in this period was Hal Lindsey. Lindsey, like Jack Sparks, had worked for Campus Crusade for Christ but left the group to preach to the hippies living around UCLA in the late sixties. His JC Light and Power Company became an important Jesus People ministry in L.A. In 1970, Lindsey published *The Late Great Planet Earth*, a slang-filled, easy-to-read guide to the coming apocalypse. Lindsey relied on nineteenth-century theologian John Darby's pre-millennial dispensationalism, a Bible-based framework for understanding all of human history that stresses Christ's return before the Great Tribulation, the period of the antichrist's rule. But Lindsey pushed Darby's chronologies into the present, linking biblical prophecies to global events since the end of World War II. Citing chapter and verse like a Jesus People preacher leading a Bible study, he set out one by one the signs of the end times—the invention of nuclear weapons, the restoration of Israel, the cold war, and the rise of Communist China. As the book became the single best-selling nonfiction book of the seventies, Lindsey helped create a popular flowering of apocalyptic thinking among the Jesus People and other Christians. He also, paradoxically, helped lay the groundwork for fundamentalists' return to politics in the eighties. If the end times were here, if life on earth was indeed almost over—then perhaps believers needed to pay attention to contemporary events so they could read the signs and be ready for the Rapture.[21]

Most Jesus People, like most evangelicals, looked to the "early church," the imagined beginnings of Christianity, as a model for their own ministries. The first Christians, they believed, had discovered the truth without the aid of rituals or creeds, sacred buildings, or hierarchies of religious authorities. Again, the Jesus People flourished at yet another unlikely convergence of the counterculture and fundamentalism, a common seam of anti-institutional and anti-authoritarian ideas and practices and faith in transparent meaning.

Among both hippies and fundamentalists, this primitivism generated anti-feminism. Fundamentalists had retreated from the broader American culture in the 1920s in part because they believed the early feminist movement threatened the family's traditional gender hierarchies. Some members of the counterculture, in turn, rebelled against the surge of second-wave feminism at the end of the sixties. In both cases, primitivism reversed the gains that women had made in the larger world. In hippie communes, women had children with men they did not marry and lacked the legal protections—the ability to charge a wayward spouse with abandonment or to sue for alimony, for example—that marriage had at least provided. Child support, too, was difficult to collect from men who did not have standard employment. And women on communes still cooked and cleaned, usually without modern appliances and for forty instead of four. Jesus People often replicated these countercultural forms of gender inequality in their own group living. While leadership might be informal in the counterculture and among the Jesus People, leaders were almost always white men, possessing an often large and unchecked personal power like the ministers of notoriously independent fundamentalist and nondenominational churches. Women members, in turn, of both fundamentalist churches and Jesus People groups, often adopted forms of clothing imagined as traditional and authentically feminine and pure. Hippie Christians' long and flowing skirts, peasant blouses, and braids updated the simple, modest dresses and uncut hair of some fundamentalist women. In both cases, faith pushed members to make their difference from the larger world—their true femininity—visible on their very bodies.[22]

Fundamentalist and countercultural primitivism came together as the back-to-the-early-church movement fused with the back-to-the-land movement. Some Jesus People even formed rural Christian communes, like the Farm, started by a Jesus People group from California that later moved to Tennessee. Others, like the cultish Children of God, at times tried to live like Jesus's first followers, traveling the roads in broken-down faded yellow buses looking for something to eat and souls to save.[23]

Members of the Children of God, wearing "Christ" clothes, march down a road in Miami chanting, "No sex, no violence, and don't kill animals," in 1978. *Associated Press*.

Still, in one essential way, the primitivism of many Jesus People led them to break with fundamentalist theology. Infused with a countercultural interest in intense experience and the transformation of inner consciousness, many Jesus People fused their fundamentalist theology with Pentecostal practice, an intense, emotional, embodied form of worship that most fundamentalists disdained. Pentecostals, or charismatic Christians, as they were often also called in the sixties and seventies as belief in the gifts of the Spirit spread among Catholics and even mainline Protestants, were part of the broader evangelical category. They believed in the second blessing, a manifestation of the Holy Spirit in the saved that followed the first blessing of conversion. True believers experienced the "charismata," or gifts of the Spirit, during worship, most commonly speaking in tongues—often called the third blessing—healing the sick, and casting out devils or exorcism. They shouted and clapped and sang and cried together, "slain in the Spirit." For fundamentalists, these miracles, or manifestations of the Holy Spirit, flourished only in the early church, in the time of the disciples. For Pentecostals, the gifts of the Spirit still flowed, providing proof that the converted were truly saved.[24]

Pentecostalism has roots in the Second Great Awakening but emerged as a distinct strain of American Protestantism at the beginning of the twentieth century. From the start, the practice of "Spirit Baptism," or receiving and displaying the gifts of the Spirit, integrated both white and black forms of Christian worship and attracted white and black believers. Pentecostalism flourished at the margins of American society, among the rural poor and the urban working class. At mid-century, increasing numbers of white middle-class Americans—among them Catholics and mainline Protestants—began to import Pentecostal practices, especially the physical experience of the Holy Spirit and its manifestation as glossolalia, or speaking in tongues, into Bible studies, prayer breakfasts, and the worship services of new nondenominational churches. This spiritual move to the margins became known as neo-Pentecostalism (among mainline Protestants) and the Charismatic Renewal (among Catholics). Assembly of God minister David Wilkerson provided a key link here. His work ministering to drug addicts and street people in New York City and his 1963 best seller, *The Cross and the Switchblade*, which described his conversion of a teen gang member, helped spread awareness of the gifts of the Spirit beyond the traditional Pentecostal churches. By the mid-sixties, these new charismatic Christians had begun to come together across theological and denominational differences and did not always share most Pentecostals' embrace of fundamentalist theology.[25]

Many Jesus People practiced glossolalia as a part of their worship services. Singing old hymns like "Amazing Grace" or new Jesus songs and swaying, often with eyes closed and hands upraised, people began to feel the Spirit. Someone might start to moan or cry—the Holy Spirit might be invisible, but its presence always marked a person's body as well as her soul. Then a strange babble chant would cut through the collective hum. Charismatic worship is as difficult to capture in words as a drug trip, though an intrepid *Life* reporter tried. At the Sunday night meetings of The Way East in Rye, Steve Heefner would always ask someone to stand and speak. Then "a divinely inspired message that sounds, to an unsaved ear, like: 'Alokar shamalsh frolaniuk asapolikaj shantih'" rises to the rafters. "The prompt translation, by the same speaker, is usually along the lines of 'Be bold, my children, in spreading the Word. Thus saith the Lord.'" In other groups, a second person might interpret the sacred speech. But the words themselves were not, for worshippers, separate from the context, the fully embodied, felt experience of the faith. The Holy Spirit, these worshippers insisted, still entered into true believers, literally touching them with the words and power and presence of Jesus.[26]

Hippie Christians who spoke in tongues and called for spiritual revolution while waiting for the Rapture, the mostly white Jesus People rebelled by welding their countercultural style and interest in experience to fundamentalist theology and Pentecostal practice. They did not rebel by trying to recruit African American young people out of the urban surge of black nationalism or the established black churches or by reaching out to the urban and rural white working class. In this sense, the Jesus People were completely conventional, acting within the racial and class divisions that organized American religious life in this period.

As the counterculture faded away in the mid-seventies, the Jesus People movement as a visible, alternative strand of Christianity dissolved as well. Many converts lapsed back into their old hippie ways, while others remained active Christians, joining growing institutions like Calvary Chapel or Vineyard Christian Fellowship or other mega-churches then springing up all over late-seventies suburbia. Some former Jesus People even slipped back into Catholic parishes and mainline congregations. Still, despite their small numbers—three hundred thousand in the most generous estimate—and the movement's life span of less than a decade, these alternative Christians transformed the practice of Christianity in America, and not just by bringing guitars and casual clothes into Christian fellowship. In the Jesus People movement, young white middle-class Americans' interest in outsiders, personal experience, and the transformation of the inner self, the culmination of a long line of secularizing rebellions stretching back to European Romanticism, came together with an evangelical Christian version, evolving since the Reformation, of the same ideal. Countercultural Christians tapped into the deeply Protestant origins of the romance of the outsider and the emphasis on individual, inner transformation.[27]

The Jesus People stood in the great big plastic present and rejected modern America, not, like the fundamentalists, in some partly mythic, ancient past of close-knit, prosperous, and pious small towns. They had lived in the world they were now rejecting. And they could not, despite their intentions, entirely leave it. The fundamentalists, on the other hand, had rejected the spiritual and cultural trajectory of modernizing America half a century ago. For most Americans, their name still evoked anti-Darwinism and their ultimately futile attempt to stop the "monkey" science. Fundamentalists seemed then to many Americans to be white people living on the wrong side of history, and the success of the civil rights movement—many fundamentalists supported segregation—only made this fact even more clear. But the Jesus People embraced fundamentalist theology while keeping their countercultural forms of expression. They did not seem like backward, rural people stepping out of the past but like modern young people, raised in the postwar culture of abundance and privileged enough to play with the future. What could be more rebellious than taking up the old-time religion? The new Christians took fundamentalist theology, infused it with Pentecostalism's intensity and focus on experiencing the Holy Spirit, and attracted middle-class suburban kids raised in agnostic and liberal Protestant, Catholic, and even Jewish homes, young people who might have looked for salvation in a summer of Mississippi organizing or at a Freedom Singers concert only a few years earlier. They put Christianity back in the rebel and the rebel back in Jesus. For a time, the Jesus People made conservative Christianity cool. The counterculture may have grown out of the New Left, but it also helped nurture the New Right. Members of mega-churches at the end of the twentieth century, theologically conservative and determined to have a personal relationship with Christ and yet socially casual—wearing jeans to guitar-filled services and calling their ministers Jerry and Mike—and understanding their faith as an inward journey were just Jesus People without the long hair.[28]

Jerry Falwell and Fundamentalists as the Oppressed Majority

By 1976, the Jesus People movement was over. Jimmy Carter, a devout Southern Baptist Sunday school teacher and former Georgia governor, was running for president. When he casually told a reporter he was born again, two worlds collided once more, not this time the counterculture and evangelical Christianity but instead evangelical Christianity and the white middle-class suburban world where people attended mainline churches and did not talk about their faith at parties. Interest in the Jesus People had made a kind of conservative or "Bible-believing" Christianity into a mainstream media obsession for the first time since the Scopes Trial. But the Jesus People's hippie style made it easy for reporters looking for good copy to avoid any serious investigation into their faith. When the Democratic candidate for president announced he was a "born-again" Christian, someone had to provide an explanation for the many people not familiar with the phrase. The media tried. *Newsweek* led with a cover article called "Born Again." Gallup had polled Americans of voting age about their religious beliefs, *Newsweek* reported, and calculated that fifty million Americans—one half of all Protestants, one third of all Americans—"say that they have been 'born again.'" Almost half of all Protestants believed in biblical inerrancy, the idea that the text should "be taken literally, word for word." "A general turning inward to seek refuge from everyday pressures" and the "search for nonmaterial values in light of the fading American dream," Gallup suggested, were generating a national religious revival. The year 1976 just might be, *Newsweek* declared, the "year of the evangelical."[29]

By the mid-seventies, the meaning of evangelical Christianity had become broad enough to include fundamentalists, Pentecostals, and other Christians who put the Bible and a personal relationship with the supernatural Jesus at the center of their faith. These conservative Christians, however, were not necessarily Christian conservatives. They had mostly, in the separatist tradition of fundamentalism, stayed out of politics and away from public support for issues of social reform, however some of them might vote in the privacy of the polling booth. In their own version of the romance, outsiders, people who chose Jesus over the world, were more moral than insiders. "Men of God," Jerry Falwell preached in the late seventies, were "not interested in being the Jaycees' outstanding young man of the year in their hometown." They were "not interested in winning popularity polls." They were interested, Falwell argued, "in pleasing God, honoring Christ, and winning their cities at any price for the Lord." Citizenship, for conservative Christians, lay in heaven. Especially for fundamentalists, separateness from American intellectual and politic life and especially from popular culture had long been a measure of godliness. Distance from the modern world meant closeness to God.[30]

Like the African American Christians who had initiated the bus boycott in Alabama and the sit-in movement across the South, mostly white evangelicals began in the year of the nation's Bicentennial to describe themselves as the outsiders who would save the nation. As Falwell preached in a sermon called "The Establishment," which he gave in several versions in the late seventies:

> We are in need of a spiritual revolution that will re-establish the establishment. The hippies and the yippies have had their day . . . This is the day of the fundamentalist. We need to re-establish our homes . . . We need to re-establish our churches . . . We need to re-establish this nation. We have been second-class citizens too long.

The liberals and the left—Falwell and other conservatives did not make any distinction—had had their political and cultural revolutions. They had made America a "cesspool." "I say that as Christians," Falwell argued, "we need to take a long, long look at the moral issues that affect the future of our nation. If God's people don't stand up on these issues, who will? Who should?" Christians, he began arguing in 1978, need to "come to action." Other outsiders— anti-war activists, abortion supporters, homosexuals, and feminists —were taking over the nation. It was time for the marginalized Christian majority to take their morality back into the world.[31]

William F. Buckley had crafted the image of the conservative as a rebel, a self-conscious outsider, working against the liberal establishment. His followers in YAF copied his style and saw their conservatism as a rebellion against their generation's embrace of the sixties social movements, liberal and left ideas, and the counterculture. The Jesus People normalized the idea that Jesus and his followers were outsiders, not in the old sense that fundamentalists were anti-modern, living outside time, but in the new sense that Christians were creating another counterculture. Jerry Falwell, in turn, founded the Moral Majority in 1979 and became one of the most widely known rebels on the right of the postwar era. He helped evangelicals and especially fundamentalists develop a narrative about their reentry into politics that both justified the abandonment of their old separatism and maintained their sense of difference in a fallen world. In Falwell's journey from separatist and conservative Christian to Christian conservative, older Protestant ideas about individual transformation and difference based on the interior self met the secular romance of the outsider.

In the seventies, Jerry Falwell often preached that, unlike some fundamentalist congregations, "his church welcomed all the long-haired kids in Lynchburg." "Let's get them saved first and shaved later," he often said. But Christian men looked like men. They had short hair. For Falwell and other fundamentalists, the Jesus People were not yet real Christians. "Bible-believing Christians"—a phrase fundamentalists frequently used to distinguish their Christianity from more liberal forms—needed to reach out to these "hippies" and everyone else in America who had not been saved and pull them in.[32]

No one would ever have confused Jerry Falwell, a man who regularly appeared in a three-piece suit, with one of the Jesus People. On January 20, 1952, though, he too had gone through the experience of becoming a new Christian, conversion. Cooking a big southern breakfast, his mother woke him up that day as she did every Sunday, with the smell of bacon and the sound of Charles Fuller's *Old Fashioned Revival Hour* turned up so loud that it echoed out of the kitchen and up the stairs. The odor of frying pork was hard to ignore, and the young Falwell loved the piano playing on the radio broadcast. So he pulled himself out of bed, went downstairs, and sat down at the kitchen table. He listened to Fuller preach as he finished his breakfast, he remembered later, to please his mother. But somehow he lost the words, overwhelmed by his emotions: a lump in his throat, a desire to cry, and a sense of great excitement, "like you feel before a storm strikes or that moment in the hospital just before your first child is born." "Are you born again?" Fuller finally asked his radio audience. Falwell did not, he later insisted, know then that what he felt was the Holy Spirit. "God was calling me, but I didn't recognize his voice."[33]

Being born again is not just a moment of radical transformation—it is also a story, and fundamentalist preachers like Falwell practice telling it daily, in more formal sermons and in the casual witnessing that infuses many fundamentalists' everyday speech. Fundamentalist sermons, in fact, are as cultural forms a lot like blues songs. Based in live performances and oral traditions, they are hard to pin down. Words do not stay fixed, and rhythms change. Phrases float, too, between texts, and similar anecdotes, jokes, and arguments pop up in different sermons just as similar lyrics and melodies appear in different songs. Both cultural forms developed in historical contexts in which their original makers had little economic and political power and focused instead on individual, interior change. As forms, both fundamentalist sermons and blues songs suggest the possibilities of individual transformation, in their words and in the way their makers are always modifying their forms.[34]

By the time Jerry Falwell described the day he got saved in his 1987 autobiography, *Strength for the Journey*, the minister and founder of Thomas Road Baptist Church, Liberty University, and the Moral Majority had polished the performance until it sparkled like the diamond ring he often wore. He knew what had actually happened to him that day, and he also knew the language and events that structured the experience of becoming born again. Filling the telling particularities into a frame helped Falwell, as it did other evangelicals, to confirm both the intercession of the divine, an experience shared with other believers, and the individuality of the event that made clear his own personal transformation. If writers like Mailer and Kerouac reached through individual transformation for transcendence by turning their lives into art, believers like Falwell, people already transformed, sought transcendence by turning their lives into Bible stories. Accounts of becoming born again were by their nature stories of outsiders, of an individual's ending her separation from God and beginning instead a separation from the secular world.[35]

By Falwell's account, he spent much of that fateful day in a daze. He joined his friends—"the Wall Gang"—at a café in Lynchburg where they gathered almost daily to drink Cokes, eat hamburgers, and listen to songs like the Weavers' "Good Night, Irene" on the jukebox:

> I remember sitting alone on a stool. . . . The room was filled with noisy kids. But in and through the commotion, His Voice was speaking to me. I couldn't hear the words, but I knew something strange and wonderful was about to happen. I didn't know it then, but it was God's world breaking into my world. Why it happens when it happens is still a mystery to me.

After eating, Falwell and his gang ambled across Campbell Avenue as they always did to hang out by the wall. In the middle of a conversation, his own voice speaking shocked him out of his daze: "Does anybody know a church in Lynchburg that preaches what Dr. Fuller preaches on the radio?" Soon after, he and two friends set out for the Park Avenue Baptist Church, despite the fact that they were not "dressed for church." The crowd was singing "The windows of heaven are open and the blessings are flowing tonight" when they arrived, and the usher gave him a hymnal—*Gospel Songs from the Old Fashioned Revival Hour.* "There are no coincidences when God is at work," Falwell insisted as he told his story. An old man sitting in a nearby pew offered to go down to the altar at the end of the service with him. Together there, they knelt down and the old man said, "The wages of sin is death, but the gift of God is eternal life through Jesus Christ." Then the man—Falwell later learned he was a deacon—repeated his words again. That night in a little "cement-block building" Falwell got down on his knees with the deacon, asked Jesus to forgive his sins, and "accepted the mystery of God's salvation." "Isn't that easy?" the old man asked. "Isn't that wonderful? 'For whosoever shall call upon the name of the Lord shall be saved.'"[36]

In his autobiography, Falwell moves directly from his own story to the Bible and to the moment of conversion in all "true" Christians' lives, the moment when each person has to decide whether to stay in the security and sin of the old life or to step away, outside of that life, take up Christ, and begin anew. He cites and paraphrases the relevant Bible verses, John 3:3–6:

> Jesus answered and said unto him, Verily, verily, I say unto thee, except a man be born again, he cannot see the kingdom of God. Nicodemus saith unto him, how can a man be born when he is old? Can he enter the second time into his mother's womb, and be born? Jesus answered, Verily, verily, I say unto thee, except a man be born of water and *of* the Spirit, he cannot enter into the kingdom of God. That which is born of the flesh is flesh; and that which is born of the Spirit is spirit.

"That," Falwell insists in his conversion story, is the moment of individual transformation, "the beginning of the Christian's new life. Everything else follows that act." He wishes that he had not waited until he was eighteen, and that he had listened to his mother and others who tried to save him earlier. But he has found the path at last. "'Well, Jerry,' the pastor said, putting his arm around my shoulder, 'this is the end of your old life and the beginning of your new.' . . . From that moment everything changed for me."[37]

Being born again is the sign and the event, the symbol and the story, that forms the heart of evangelical Christianity. Conversion—the asking for forgiveness and the acceptance of Christ that brings eternal salvation—is the historical moment when a believer's relationship with Christ begins. But it is also a ritualized story, a genre—the conversion narrative—that marks a passage, the believer's separation from the secular world. The transformation imagined is so radical that the world rejected includes even the convert's previous life. "Salvation is not progressive, it is not eventual, it is instantaneous," Falwell preached in 1978. "If you are a born-again Christian, you can remember a time and a place where the miracle happen[ed]." Believers' stories of becoming born again always describe the moment of receiving God as surrender, as a letting go of the world and giving in to the Spirit. As Falwell described the process, "If any may be in Christ, that moment he is a new creation, a new creature, old things are passed away and behold all things are become new." The conversion narrative works to give the agency to God in this moment of individual transformation. Believers see this act of radical transformation as the work of the Spirit. Becoming born again, stopping one life and starting another, is a divinely assisted rebellion against the very self. The believer, filled with God, becomes an outsider in her former life.[38]

Still, beyond the supernatural explanations, becoming born again, with its focus on personal, interior transformation, has a great deal in common with broader cultural trends in the second half of the twentieth century. Conversion, in this sense, is yet another way of rebelling against some definition of the center and of using the expression of this transformation as a way to create an alternative, adversarial community. An individual is not a self-determining person in a political or economic sense, not a person who can vote or a worker without a boss. In the Jesus People movement, the outsider as a model of identity literally passes from the counterculture to the Jesus culture and flourishes there, joining with and reinforcing a powerful Protestant tradition of focusing on the individual's inner life. But cultural change is not usually this explicit and easy to trace. The broad 1970s evangelical explosion, too, grows out of the coming together of a secular obsession with individual self-transformation and the deeply Protestant vision of individual, Jesus-generated, interior change. Both these trends, in turn, deepen and strengthen each other.

Preachers like Falwell always made their own conversion stories part of their ministries. But in 1976, an amazingly diverse group of Americans began to spread the stories of their conversions beyond their churches and Bible study groups. Jimmy Carter, running for president at the time, told the national press that he had felt despondent in 1967 after losing his first campaign for the Georgia governorship and "realized that my own relationship with God and Christ was a very superficial one." Mission work with poor Americans and talking with his evangelical sister led to his becoming "born again": "a very close, intimate, personal relationship with God, through Christ, that has give me a great deal of peace, equanimity, the ability to accept difficulties without unnecessarily being disturbed, and also an inclination on a continuing basis to ask God's guidance in my life." "The most important thing in my life," Carter told many audiences on the campaign trail that year, "is Jesus Christ." The former Nixon aide and Watergate felon Charles Colson described his own transformation in his best-selling 1976 memoir, *Born Again*. A friend suggested they pray together, and Colson numbly assented. "Something began to flow into me—a kind of energy. Then came a wave of emotion which nearly brought tears." Later, he sat alone in his car. "With my face cupped in my hands, my head leaning forward against the wheel, I forgot about machismo, about pretenses, about fears of being weak. And as I did, I began to experience a wonderful feeling of being released. Then came the strange sensation that water was not only running down my cheeks, but surging through my whole body as well, cleansing and cooling as it went . . . Something inside me was urging me to surrender . . .," Colson continued. "For the first time in my life I was not alone at all."[39]

Carolyn Torbert found God after a jealous woman shot her. The former stripper Candy Bar, left paralyzed and confined to a wheelchair, had little choice but to go where her mother pushed her. Inside the tent at a revival, the Holy Spirit simply took her. "I felt so clear and pure as though I were worth something. I'd found what I had been searching for all those years." Christ, she realized, loved her profoundly, and she would change her life. Torbert decided not to press charges against her attacker: "My life is fulfilled sitting here in this wheelchair." Eldridge Cleaver, the best-selling author of the decidedly secular 1968 memoir *Soul on Ice* and a former Black Panther, also became born again that year, while waiting for his trial on charges of assault. In *Soul on Ice*, he committed blasphemy, calling his San Quentin teacher "Christ" and arguing that "the language and symbols of religion were nothing but weapons of war." But by 1976, he had experienced, literally, a change of heart:

> I was looking up at the moon and I saw the man in the moon and it was my face . . . Then I saw the face was not mine but some of my old heroes. There was Fidel Castro, then there was Mao Tse-tung . . . While I watched, the face turned to Jesus Christ, and I was very much surprised . . . I don't know when I had last cried, but I began to cry and I didn't stop . . . It was like I could not stop crying unless I said the prayer and the Psalm and surrendered something . . . All I had to do was surrender and go to jail.

The moment of surrender and the interior transformation that leads to the creation of a new and different life—the "born again" story shaped the evangelical view of how change occurs in the world.[40]

Before Jerry Falwell went through another radical moment of transformation in the late seventies, most fundamentalists were taking their new selves and rapidly departing for a separate world—independent Baptist churches, unaccredited Bible colleges, far-flung missionary outposts, church-run camps, and, beginning particularly in the sixties in response to racial integration, church-run schools. Since the 1920s, fundamentalists had lived in a largely self-imposed exile, isolated from the major currents of American public life. An earlier movement to bring conservative Christians back into the world had created a series of institutions—Youth for Christ, the National Association of Evangelicals, Fuller Seminary, the revivals of Billy Graham, and the magazine *Christianity Today*—in the 1940s and 1950s and revived the term "evangelical" to replace the tainted label "fundamentalist." In the early fifties, these conservative Christians even began to question racial segregation. Graham refused to segregate his crusades after 1953, and in 1954 the Southern Baptist Convention and the National Association of Evangelicals both endorsed the *Brown* decision. But many conservative Christians, especially in the South, maintained their militant separatism. Many, like Falwell until the early eighties, even rejected the term "evangelical."[41]

Falwell told the story of the origins and birth of his Thomas Road Baptist Church in Lynchburg almost as often as he told the story of his own rebirth in Jesus Christ. After his conversion in 1952, Falwell left home and his engineering studies at Lynchburg College to attend Baptist Bible College, an unaccredited religious school in Springfield, Illinois. By the summer of 1956, he was back in Lynchburg, founding a new church with thirty-five people from his former church, including his future wife, Macel Pate. That fall, he began a daily morning radio program on local Lynchburg AM station WBRG 1050. In November 1956, he began taping a sermon in a television studio for broadcast too. Before his new church even celebrated its first birthday, Falwell had added on to the old Donald Duck soft drink bottling plant that served as its home, doubling the size of the sanctuary space and greatly increasing the number of members. In 1964, the young minister preached at the opening of Thomas Road Baptist Church's new one-thousand-seat sanctuary, and new members soon filled all the services there too. In the sixties, he began broadcasting Sunday services as *The Old-Time Gospel Hour* directly from the church. He repeatedly preached a kind of action-oriented faith: "I do not believe God is in anything that is static or stagnant. If God is a part of something, it is on the move." In less than ten years, Falwell built a powerful ministry.[42]

Still, few people outside Lynchburg and the small world of fundamentalist Baptist colleges knew about Falwell until he preached and then widely distributed his 1965 sermon "Ministers and Marches." "Does the 'CHURCH' have any command from God," he asked, "to involve itself in marches, demonstrations, or any other actions, such as many ministers and church leaders are so doing today?" Falwell's answer was not really shocking. Fundamentalism had defined itself in the early twentieth century against the social gospel, a movement among liberal Protestants to take their beliefs out into the streets and actively work not just to save souls but to create the structural, political changes—like the abolition of child labor—necessary to relieve human suffering.

"As far as the relationship of the church to the world," Falwell argued, "it can be expressed as simply as the three words which Paul gave Timothy— 'preach the Word.' We have a message of redeeming grace through a crucified and risen Lord. This message is designed to go right to the heart of man and there meet his deep spiritual need . . . Nowhere are we commissioned to reform the externals," Falwell continued. "We are not told to wage wars against bootleggers, liquor stores, gamblers, murderers, prostitutes, racketeers, prejudiced persons or institutions, or any other existing evil as such." "Our ministry is not reformation but transformation," Falwell often insisted, repeating the old attack of the fundamentalists on social reform work. "The gospel does not clean up the outside but rather regenerate the inside." His congregation, he preached, was full of former sinners. "What changed them?" he asked. "Did we go to Richmond and try to get laws passed which would send these persons to jail? No! . . . When Christ came in, sin went out." Christians "have very few ties on this earth. We pay our taxes, cast our votes as a responsibility of citizenship, obey the laws of the land, and other things demanded of us by the society in which we live. But at the same time, we are cognizant that our only purpose on this earth is to know Christ and to make him known." While Falwell directly questioned "the sincerity and non-violent intentions" of Martin Luther King Jr., because of his "left-wing associations," he was also lashing out here at mainline Protestant ministers in the National Council of Churches and their broad support for the civil rights movement. "Preachers are not called to be politicians but to be soul winners."[43]

Christians, Falwell argued, should worry about fixing the churches, "rather than trying to clean up state and national governments." Activist ministers, he suggested, were motivated by political expedience to support "this so-called freedom movement." Otherwise, they would be just as concerned about discrimination against "negroes" in the North and "American Indians." If church leaders believed Christians should work for social reforms, "then I am forced to ask why the church is not as concerned about the alcoholism problem in America. There are almost as many alcoholics as there are negroes." "Love cannot be legislated," Falwell ended his sermon. "It is found in a Person—and his name is Jesus Christ."[44]

Because an earlier sermon that survives—the 1958 "Segregation or Integration, Which?"—uses Noah's curse on Ham from Genesis to argue that the Bible supports segregation, a common fundamentalist interpretation, some scholars have seen Falwell's position on political activism as the result of his white supremacy. The evidence (and Falwell and his associates spent a great deal of time spinning it in early eighties when the Lynchburg pastor led the Moral Majority and became a nationally recognized religious leader) suggests that Falwell shared the racist beliefs of many white southerners. Falwell had segregationist governors George Wallace and Lester Maddox as guests on the *Old-Time Gospel Hour* in the 1960s and went to visit both of them in their statehouses. When CORE activists conducted a kneel-in at Thomas Road Baptist Church in 1964, ushers threw them out, a fact Falwell did not deny in his

1987 autobiography. Thomas Road's congregation accepted its first black member in 1968, according to Falwell, as a result of a bus ministry created to reach out to minority neighborhoods. The minister's defense of those bus ministries in the late 1970s, however, was not exactly an endorsement of equality: "There are churches that actually hate a bus ministry because of the dirty, barefooted urchins who are brought in on the buses." "We are trying to make everybody equal," he preached, but "God did not create us all equal. We are very unequal. God loves us equally, but every one of us is created unequal."[45]

Falwell founded his Lynchburg Christian Academy in 1967, the year Lynchburg public schools were finally integrated, although he denied any connection between the two events. The Lynchburg Ministerial Association, a local ministers' group, met that April to condemn the use of the word "Christian" for a school that planned to exclude people who were not white. Falwell was clearly a white supremacist. He told a journalist for the *Los Angeles Times* that it was "probably 1963–1964 that I totally repudiated segregation. It was a carryover from my heritage. I would say that 99 percent of all [white Southerners] . . . were segregationists, and once we became Christians, many of us were still in that cultural society—an all-white church and pastors who preached it as the Gospel. I don't think they were guilty of racism." In his 1987 autobiography, Falwell claimed an African American shoeshine man named Lewis ministered to him every Saturday morning in 1963 as he cleaned Falwell's shoes. Lewis's probing question—"when am I going to be able to join that church of yours over on Thomas Road?"—made the young minister question segregation. Whatever was in Falwell's heart in the sixties, he supported the southern culture of segregation that economically and socially oppressed and politically disfranchised African Americans in the region. But he also shared the majority of southern fundamentalists' belief in a militant separation from the world. "Ministers and Marches" simply joined the two beliefs. White southern fundamentalists believed in separation—the segregation of whites and blacks and the segregation of true believers and the rest of humanity.[46]

Some time around 1976, Falwell changed his mind about "reforming the externals" and began to argue that fundamentalists' separation, their outsider status, was exactly why they had to act to save the country. Fundamentalists should take their born-again selves back into the world. "This idea of 'religion and politics don't mix,'" he preached in a 1976 sermon, "America Back to God," "was invented by the devil to keep Christians from running their own country." "I have heard for so long politics and religion don't mix," he argued in another sermon that year, "Conditions Corrupting America." "Now if they mean by that that Jerry Falwell shouldn't run for Congress, I agree with that. I have no time. I really don't. But if they mean that saved men, that if saved persons, ought to stay out of politics, I don't mean that for a minute. That's exactly what we have done too long. We've handed the reins over to the ungodly." Other conservative Christians began speaking out in favor of political action as well. A lobbyist for the political action group Christian Voice warned conservative Christians, "The ministers have been admonishing their people to stay out of politics because it's dirty. They're finally waking up to the fact that it's dirty because Christians haven't been involved." But Falwell's second "conversion" shook up the insular world of southern fundamentalists more than the actions of any other leader or group. Falwell was a southern minister in a kind of Christianity that granted these male leaders tremendous power and the founder of his own booming church; he claimed seventeen thousand members in the late seventies. He had, in effect, created a world in Lynchburg—church, secondary school, college, media empire (television, radio, and publishing), and counseling center—where Christians could spend much of their lives. Falwell used all this power to push fundamentalists into rebelling against their former separatism. Conservative Christians needed to express themselves in the larger culture. By the end of the seventies, many fundamentalists had accepted Falwell's and other religious leaders' calls to political action. The oppressed majority, tentatively at first and then more strongly, began speaking out on issues like school prayer, opposition to gay rights, and control over textbook selection in the public schools.[47]

In the story Falwell wrote years later, abortion was the abomination that drove him out of the pulpit and prayer room and into politics. Scholars and activists have questioned his account. In their arguments, they note the 1962 and 1963 Supreme Court decisions outlawing school-sponsored prayer and Bible reading in the public schools, which upset and angered fundamentalists and indeed most conservative Christians. No longer would these groups be able to shape public schools, even in districts where they were the majority, in ways that supported their beliefs. The success of the civil rights movement in integrating southern school systems in the second half of the sixties and the early seventies extended their outrage and fueled the movement to build private academies like Lynchburg Christian Academy. But by the late seventies, these schools too seemed threatened. In 1970, 1975, and 1978, the IRS issued ever more stringent rulings denying racially segregated private schools, including religious schools, tax-exempt status. The 1978 IRS ruling required schools to have "significant" numbers of enrolled minority students, a figure set at 20 percent or more of the minority school-age population in the area served by the school. Angry conservative Christians reacted by sending more than 120,000 letters to the IRS and about 40,000 more messages to Congress. They feared they would not be able to maintain the separate Christian schools that they believed nurtured and protected their children's faith. Paul Weyrich, a leading conservative strategist and one of the architects of the New Right's rise to power in the eighties, has argued that "what galvanized the [Protestant] Christian community was not abortion, school prayer or the ERA. I am a living witness to that I was trying to get those people interested in those issues and I utterly failed. What changed their mind was Jimmy Carter's intervention against the Christian schools." Although IRS efforts to withhold tax exemptions from segregated Christian schools began under Nixon, it was the 1978 ruling that generated mass protest. Other issues upset conservative Christians, in Weyrich's view, but they believed they could protect their own morality by simply not participating: avoiding abortions, creating their own schools, and maintaining traditional gender relations in their own families and institutions. "Suddenly, it dawned on them that they were not going to be able to be left alone to teach their children as they pleased. It was at that moment that conservatives made the linkage between their opposition to government interference and the interests of the evangelical movement." Conservative Christians' interest in protecting their separate world from the federal government made them potential allies for political conservatives working to forge a broad anti-government coalition.[48]

The IRS's nearly decade-long push to drop the tax-exempt status of segregated Christian schools scared fundamentalists because it occurred within a world they saw as deeply changed. The old threats—Prohibition-era popular culture, illegal drinking, the teaching of evolution, and the spread of liberal Protestantism—of earlier in the century looked pretty small by the seventies. In the fifties and early sixties, in Billy Graham's successful crusades, in the pages of *Christianity Today*, and in their sense that Eisenhower was a man of faith, some evangelicals began to feel that the country was turning back to God. In 1954, for example, Eisenhower signed the bill inserting "under God" into the Pledge of Allegiance. "From this day forward," he proclaimed, "the millions of our schoolchildren will daily proclaim . . . the dedication of our Nation and our people to the Almighty." But the social movements of the sixties and the changes in American popular culture—rock music, the broad embrace of the counterculture, and the sexual revolution—reversed the gains some Christians believed they had made since World War II. The success of sixties political movements, however incomplete, formed the context within which fundamentalists understood the threat of federal intervention in their schools.[49]

Southern fundamentalists like Falwell saw the civil rights movement in the region as the first blow. In the South and elsewhere, many white fundamentalists believed as adamantly in the separation of white and black as they did in the separation of their own communities from the contaminated world. The stampede of white southern Christians into the new private schools, called by their critics "seg academies," occurred as much or more because the 1954 *Brown* decision had finally reached the rural deep South as because the Supreme Court had compounded that earlier error by banning prayer in the public schools. Many fundamentalists at the time fused the two issues. The government, they said, pushed God out of the schools and put African Americans in. With limited resources, a great deal of volunteer work, and church support, conservative Christians had responded by building an alternative network of educational institutions. In the seventies, the tax issue filled them with anger because it would make it even more difficult for white Christians to fund their own school system. The form of federal government intervention that pushed many fundamentalists into politics in the seventies was forced integration.[50]

More than a decade after "Ministers and Marches," Jerry Falwell was still preaching against the civil rights movement in a sermon called "America's Lawlessness." "Our churches need to teach their people to be soul winners and not social reformers," Falwell still claimed. "The best way to overcome racial hatred, prejudice, and lawlessness in a man is to win him to Christ. When he becomes a Christian, Christ, who is love, comes to dwell in his heart. He then finds himself not only loving God, but loving all men . . . Love cannot be legislated," the minister argued as if that were the point of the civil rights movement. "Nobody can make someone love someone else against his will." The "social gospel," Falwell asserted, and fundamentalists would have understood the term to refer to contemporary social movements, began with the false assumption that people were "basically good." In fact, though, "reformation can never be the answer. It must be transformation. Jesus said, 'ye must be born again.'" Still, Falwell insisted, "I don't blame the Blacks"—he was finally dropping his old term "negro"—"for our terrible plight today." They were being used "by wicked men with wicked motives," "communists." "Communist party officials and members," the minister even alleged, "were the instigating factors" in the recent race riots in Cleveland.[51]

But in the late 1970s, Falwell never directly condemned the civil rights fight against segregation in the South, at least in the sermons that survive. He did, however, broadly condemn the New Left. "Women's lib," he preached in 1975, was "antichrist and unscriptural." Claiming the sexes were equal was like claiming people were equal to Jesus. Abortion supporters, Falwell argued in 1978 in the first sermon he devoted to the issue, were part of "the same crowd that is promoting ERA, women's liberation movement, gay liberation, the same people that are pushing towards a unisexual society, that knows no dos and don'ts and has no code of ethics." The supporters of "children's rights," he argued in a sermon televised on his *Old-Time Gospel Hour* in 1979 on which Phyllis Schlafly was a guest, were the same people again, "the anti-family people, those who promote the Equal Rights Amendment . . . the same ones [that were] in the vanguard of the pro–abortion rights efforts and are still there and they were in the anti–Viet Nam War marches and the anti–nuclear power people and you know what they're saying. We want to preserve human life." Then he attacked the New Left with its own weapon. "Gross hypocrisy," he accused. These people promoted "the murder of a million babies a year" while claiming, "We're for the protection of life." The broader cultural obsession with action finally reached the fundamentalists. "We've got to become activist witnesses, activist Christians, activist citizens."[52]

Conservative Christians angry about what they saw as potential government intervention in their schools lived in a world they saw as profoundly shaped by the New Left social movements they condemned. Elmer Towns, who moved to Lynchburg in 1971 to help Falwell build Lynchburg Baptist College into Liberty University, remembered that many fundamentalists felt under attack in the seventies: "We really had a fortress mentality: 'Let's hang on. We are losing ground every day to society, to the world, to bureaucracy, to the federal government.'" Ed Dobson, a close Falwell aide in the seventies, has argued, "I don't think people understand that the average fundamentalist felt alienated from the mainstream of American culture." As the scholar Martin Marty argued, "Fundamentalists have felt left out of everyone else's liberation." Falwell too preached in the late seventies on fundamentalists' sense of themselves as outsiders: "Did you know that the largest single minority bloc in the United States that has never been capitalized on by anybody is the fundamentalist movement?" Racial integration, the anti-war movement with its support for the North Vietnamese Communists, gay rights, feminism, and the ERA—all violated the boundaries of the fundamentalist vision of the world and their godly separatism. The fact that the protest letters that evangelicals wrote to the IRS and Congress made President Carter reverse the IRS's position, however, gave them a taste of what their political power might be. Distance had been created to promote godliness. Maybe distance would have to be violated to save it. As a direct mail letter from the Christian Voice Moral Government Fund put it in the early eighties, good people could not let "militant gays, ultra liberals, atheists, [and] porno

On May 6, 1980, the Rev. Jerry Falwell leads one of his series of "I Love America" rallies in Springfield, Illinois, with some help from Phyllis Schlafly. *Associated Press*.

pushers, pressure Congress into passing Satan's agenda instead of God's." Falwell argued, "If all the fundamentalists knew who to vote for and did it together, we could elect anybody . . . We could turn this nation upside down for God."[53]

Jerry Falwell was not the first conservative Christian to join his religious focus on the autonomy of patriarchal families and churches with a conservative political ideology that condemned (rhetorically, at least) government intervention in society and the economy. But because he was a southern fundamentalist with a large church and a popular television and radio ministry as well, his decision that social reform and not just individual religious transformation was the business of the church carried a great deal of force. As Falwell preached defensively in 1980, "I'm accused of being controversial and political. I'm not political. Moral issues that become political issues I still fight. It isn't my fault that they've made these moral issues political." In an interview in the mid-nineties, however, Falwell claimed he faced the issue directly. "When I got into politics personally, it was morally necessary for me to say out loud that 'I have misled you on the issue. I never thought the government would go so far afield, I never thought the politicians would become so untrustworthy, I never thought the courts would go nuts to the left, and I misjudged the quality of government we have. Our lack of involvement is probably one of the reasons why the country's in the mess it is in. We have defaulted by failing to show up for the fight.'" In Falwell's memory, it did not take long. Most of his congregation followed him right into politics.[54]

Falwell's surviving writings from the seventies and early eighties position abortion as only one among many moral threats. Sermons from 1975 and 1976 like "The Biblical Answer to Women's Lib," "America Must Come Back to God," and "Conditions Corrupting Politics" do not even mention abortion. In the 1979 sermon "Home: Ten Major Threats," abortion was number eight. Threat number one was divorce, followed by employed mothers and "the ERA delusion." Falwell did not actually preach a sermon on abortion until 1978, five years after *Roe v. Wade*. In "Abortion-on-Demand: Is It Murder," different versions of which were given at the Thomas Road evening service and at the morning service televised as *The Old-Time Gospel Hour* in February and April, Falwell answered the question yes but did not ask his congregation to enter politics as a way to stop "the killing of innocents." As late as 1980, the celebratory, photograph-filled book *Jerry Falwell: Man of Vision* presented abortion as "perhaps . . . the most distasteful legalized sin," one of the many causes of the "moral decay" killing America. Homosexuality was the first threat Falwell described in this book—he had supported Anita Bryant's campaign against gay rights in Miami in the late seventies and hosted her as a guest on *The Old-Time Gospel Hour* in February 1980. Next, the preacher denounced the soaring divorce rate, the fault, he argued, of the feminists and the ERA. In the 1980 version of his "America Back to God" sermon, abortion again followed homosexuality as the major threat to American morality.[55]

But Falwell eventually settled on abortion as the evil that set his personal transformation and the resulting radical reorganization of fundamentalism in motion, and many conservative Christians today narrate their own politicization in the same way. For the New Right, abortion worked like the civil rights movement did for the New Left. In the histories and memoirs—the born again into politics stories—abortion is often the engine of the moral outrage that generates a new activism, even if only in the histories and memoirs and not at the time. Falwell used his second conversion tale—almost identical accounts appear in his 1986 book *If I Should Die Before I Wake* and in his 1987 autobiography, *Strength for the Journey*—both to explain the gap between the 1973 Supreme Court decision *Roe v. Wade* and his founding of the Moral Majority in January 1979 and to narrate his second radical break with his past. This second conversion is, fittingly, in his telling, the work of a child. And the means are not political calculations or ambitions but the evangelical model of social change, the individual interior transformation, the change of heart.[56]

In his account, on January 23, 1973, Jerry Falwell glanced over his newspaper, the *Lynchburg News*, while eating a big southern breakfast with his family. Almost buried under the banner headline "Lyndon Johnson Dies" and related articles on the front page, he read "Supreme Court Legalizes Abortion." "In one terrible act they struck down all the state laws against abortion and legalized infanticide across the land," Falwell realized as his bacon turned cold. "I could not believe that seven justices on the nation's highest court could have so little regard for the value of human life." But immediately, the eighties present from which the ecumenical and politically active Falwell is writing seeps into this tale: "Already, leaders of the Catholic church had spoken courageously in opposition to the Court's decision; but the voices of my Protestant and Christian brothers and sisters, especially the voices of the evangelical and fundamentalist leaders, remained silent." In 1973, Falwell would have cared little what Catholics said about anything. He was not even interested in evangelicals—a term he still rejected then. Only fundamentalists mattered. At that time he understood his job as one of creating new believers by helping the Holy Spirit save souls.

Falwell's second conversion tale gets slippery then, and moments of epiphany and inner transformation become hard to locate on a timeline. Despite the fact that the conventions of the born-again genre work to make it read true, the date of *Roe v. Wade* is not actually the birth date of this new third Jerry Falwell, true Christian and political activist. The form of the born-again story is there, but the materials refuse to stay neatly in the structure. Falwell, for example, remembers that he had read the evangelical theologian Francis

Schaeffer. Schaeffer believed that abortion was both the sign of people's loss of respect for the sanctity of life and its cause. Legalized abortion, he and C. Everett Koop argued in their popular book and film *Whatever Happened to the Human Race?*, would lead to legalized euthanasia and infanticide. Yet Schaeffer and Koop did not publish this book and produce this film until 1977.

Clearly, Schaeffer's thinking influenced Falwell. The theologian's 1976 book and film *How Should We Then Live?* promised Christians that everything in the world was theirs, as the earliest Christians believed: "All truth is God's truth." He exhorted his readers, "Do not think Christianity is a small thing. Do not sell it short. Christianity is intellectually viable . . . The Bible is there and it covers the whole spectrum of life. God has given us a beautiful thing . . . Do not sell it short." Schaeffer taught that nothing needed to be separate for Christians. God wanted them to take their faith and their values out into the intellectual and cultural and political life of the world.[57]

In the second half of the seventies, Schaeffer called on all evangelicals to take up politics. Falwell, he urged, should build on the popularity of his *Old-Time Gospel Hour*, which was by then being broadcast on television stations nationwide. Falwell had an audience much larger than his Lynchburg church and college. If he spoke, fundamentalists across the country would listen.[58]

Falwell's own account of his conversion leaves out these details. He describes the SEC's 1973 investigation into his bond sales to fund Liberty Baptist College and *Old-Time Gospel Hour*. By early 1974, he remembers, he could turn his attention back to abortion. Like any good fundamentalist preacher upset about morality, he preached "regularly against abortion," "hoping that words would be enough." In fact, Falwell did not preach a sermon on abortion until 1978. But in his conversion-to-politics story, historical time falls away. Falwell begins to doubt that "preaching would be enough": "To stop the legalization of death by abortion, opponents of the *Roe v. Wade* decision were protesting in the streets. For the first time in my life I felt God was leading me to join them." In fact, anti-abortion activists did not take their politics into the street until Operation Rescue led the New York City protests in 1988.[59]

In every good born-again story, the person to be converted examines his doubts. How could Falwell turn against what his teachers had taught him and a half century of fundamentalist tradition? How could he act against even his own widely publicized position against ministers' involvement in political activism? "I sincerely believed that a Christian's best contribution to social change was his or her faithfulness to our primary goals: studying the word, preaching the Gospel, winning souls, building churches and Christian schools, and praying for the eventual healing of the nation." Falwell worried that he did not know anything about politics and that he did not have the time—with all of his commitments—to learn. Still, lack of expertise had not stopped him from founding a school, a college, and a radio, television, and publishing company.[60]

In Falwell's conversion story, what ultimately pushed him into politics, though, was the voice of a child, his child. The scene is the perfect image of the American family, father and mother and children sitting "in a little circle around the fireplace, reading the Bible and praying." Falwell was describing in detail "the meaning of abortion and its effects on the unborn and their mothers." He spoke of his fear that America would not survive "the judgment of God because of this 'national sin.'" His nine-year-old daughter, Jeannie, grew angry. His seven-year-old son, Jonathan, cried. Then Jonathan "got up off the floor, walked over to the fireplace, knelt before me, and placed his hands on my knees. For one moment he looked directly into my eyes without speaking." Then Jonathan, Falwell's own son, spoke the words that "helped change our lives forever": "Daddy, why don't you do something about it?" In his second conversion tale, Falwell again cuts directly to the words of Jesus: "A little child shall lead them."[61]

Falwell's new sense that Christians needed to act—most likely reached about 1978—was pushed back in his own account into the year or two after *Roe.* But it did not matter in the end that Falwell's chronology was way off. For believers, his second conversion story conveyed a spiritual truth. When God acts, a person is born again and history ceases to matter. And the sharper the break with the past and the more radical the rebellion appears, the more the conversion story offers proof of God's power.

Falwell had already learned during his 1976 series of "I Love America" rallies, staged in state capitals across the nation, that he could bring his television audience out into the streets. That campaign had used the nation's Bicentennial to stage fundamentalist revival meetings across the nation. And best of all, local media—television and newspapers—gave Falwell's rallies a great deal of coverage. Who would not want to see them? Young women wearing long red taffeta dresses, Farrah Fawcett hair, and perfect makeup danced and sang with clean-shaven, short-haired men in three-piece white suits, dark blue shirts, and red-striped ties. Uniformed kids from Christian academies, not a black face in sight, watched and prayed. Falwell preached. It was more interesting than the day's traffic accidents and robberies or yet another story about public school children painting their trash cans red, white, and blue. Too late for Nixon and even Falwell's friend Gerald Ford, Falwell's rallies turned out the "silent majority." Whether Falwell consciously adopted the strategy or not, it was a conservative Christian version of the protest march. Falwell had to purchase the television and radio time on which he broadcast Thomas Road Baptist Church's services. In the late seventies, he figured out how to get all the exposure for free.

Falwell's series of rallies raised his profile outside fundamentalist circles. His and other religious broadcasters' success in getting their viewers to write and pressure the IRS into backing down from its 1978 decision to tax segregated Christian schools gave him a sense of his power. Other conservative Christian ministers and broadcasters, too, were beginning to talk about politics. Charles Stanley, the pastor at First Baptist Church in Atlanta, distributed thousands of videotapes of his sermon "Stand Up, America" urging Christians to become political activists. James Robison was fighting to get his nationally syndicated television program back on the Dallas ABC affiliate after the station pulled the show because of the minister's condemnation of gays. "Everybody else is coming out of the closet," Robison preached. "Let's come out from under the pew, stand up, and take this country back." Conservative strategist Paul Weyrich and others came to Lynchburg in May 1979 to court Falwell at the local Holiday Inn. Out of their meetings emerged a new organization, the Moral Majority, "pro-life, pro-family, pro-moral, and pro-American," that would make Falwell famous.[62]

Moral Majority's strategy, Falwell often joked to the press, was "get 'em saved, baptized, and registered." Twenty-five million Christians attended church at least twice a week, the Moral Majority estimated, and yet had not previously voted. "It's amazing what we've learned from feminists and the other side. Civil Rights people had the kind of backbone to stand up for their freedom, and Christians better have that kind of backbone too." In the early eighties, Falwell often compared the Christian Right to the civil rights movement: "Well, some ask, 'Don't you think it's imposing your morality on someone else to make it *legal for little children to be born and illegal to kill them*? Or to pass a human life amendment some day? We're imposing our *immorality* against the civil rights of the unborn who cannot speak for themselves!"[63]

In the end, the story (sometimes true, sometimes not) mattered as much as the particular histories of what actually caused individuals' own transformations. And the story, by the late 1980s, was that abortion, not integration, pushed Bible-believing Christians back into politics. Opposing abortion, trying to protect the weakest and most marginal of Americans, fetuses literally and legally on the border between life and non-life, made many conservative Christians into different kinds of outsiders. Southern fundamentalists were no longer Confederate-flag-waving supporters of segregation, people still, even a half century after Scopes, on the wrong side of history. And Catholic ethnics were no longer African-American-hating busing opponents. The fight against abortion gave all kinds of conservative Christians a way to see themselves on the right side of history, as civil rights supporters. It also validated their feelings, whatever their numbers, that they were outsiders too. Conservative Christians had discovered the most oppressed Americans of all, "people" with fewer rights than African Americans—"the unborn." "There is no more helpless form of life in the world," Falwell preached in 1978, "than an unborn child." And they brought their Bible-believing sense that everything was important and laden with symbolic meaning, that nothing in God's world was a coincidence, into politics. There, conservative Christians' emphasis on interior transformation and an individual, emotional relationship with Jesus linked up with the secular vision of the outsider as a real individual, worshipping self-expression and inner experience.[64]

The two conservative Christian oppositional cultures that emerged in the 1970s made profound use of the romance of the outsider. Most of the white young people who joined the Jesus People were refugees from the people of plenty, kids who had grown up in prosperous new suburbs and whose parents were educated and securely middle-class or upper-middle-class. Jesus freaks, like hippies and beatniks, formed in an anti-middle class. They romanticized outsiders because these figures seemed to model forms of behavior and ways of living that stood in stark opposition to white middle-class norms. Outsiders modeled freedom and offered a route to get there, identification. Rebellion might damage the class and race privileges of individual white middle-class men, and middle-class white women were particularly vulnerable to the additional loss of their gender privileges. Yet at the larger, collective level, the romance of the outsider worked to strengthen the white middle class symbolically in an era when its central myth—the individual's control over his or her fate—proved increasingly untenable in material terms. Jesus freaks violated the polite rules of mainline Protestant religious life at mid-century, but their rebellion worked at a deeper level to strengthen belief in the efficacy of the individual will and the truth of the inner self.[65]

For Falwell's fundamentalists, on the other hand, adopting the romance of the outsider worked to integrate them into the modern white middle class. It helped them expand their belief in the value of inner transformation and individual will, a key attribute of white middle-class subjectivity, beyond matters of religious faith. Most fundamentalists at the start of the seventies came from working-class or lower-middle-class families in the rural South, Midwest, and

West. As the Sun Belt economy boomed from California to the Deep South, many found their incomes rising. Their growing sense that their outsider status worked as an asset helped them to act in the larger world. However much fundamentalists valued their separation from modern America, however, in their faith in the value of individual inner transformation, inner truth, and the moral power of outsiders, they were much like other white middle-class Americans.

CHAPTER 8

Rescue: Christian Outsiders in Action in the Anti-Abortion Movement

Every major political change in our society has been
preceded by social upheaval. The pro-life movement
has failed to learn the lessons of history, which show
how the labor movement, the civil rights movement,
Vietnam protest, and gay liberation all occurred because
a group of people created social tension.
      Randall Terry

The romance of the outsider helped white conservative Christians navigate the post-civil-rights-movement world. It enabled them to hold on to a sense of difference and yet recast it as a strength. It gave them a way to navigate the contradictions between their feelings of alienation from and yet entitlement to the resources of modern America. And it provided a way to reconcile their growing political agency with their unshakable belief that they were oppressed. Jerry Falwell and other leaders of the emerging Religious Right led fundamentalists back into politics, in rebellion against both their own subculture's separatism and the larger American culture's secularism. But some conservative Christians went further, insisting that voting, running for office, and lobbying elected officials could never be enough in a fallen world. Like some New Leftists in the 1960s and early 1970s, they needed to bring the transformation of their inner life out into the world. They needed to act. In the 1980s, Randall Terry, the founder of the anti-abortion group Operation Rescue, pushed conservative Christians to take up direct action and make their politics as real as their faith.

Conservative Christians were not the first people of faith to take up civil disobedience in the postwar era. Many Catholics, Quakers, and mainline Protestants used nonviolent direct action in the civil rights and peace movements. "There are places and times when law so abuses the inherent rights of people that the only way to make grievances known, and begin to create a more just situation, is to violate the law," the Quaker civil rights and peace activists Martin Oppenheimer and George Lakey wrote in their 1965 book *A Manual for Direct Action*. "Every individual must decide for himself just when such a point is reached in society. We do not presume to make that decision for others, nor do we presume to choose tactics of direct action for others. The final choice is yours."[1]

For many conservative Christians, especially fundamentalists, voting and speaking publicly about politics were radical steps. Randall Terry wanted evangelicals to embrace even more radical political work. "For so many years, those in the pro-life movement have been saying that abortion is murder and then writing a letter or carrying a sign once a year at a march. If you were about to be murdered," he argued, "I'm sure you would want me to do more than write your congressman!" In what became the motto of Operation Rescue, which he founded in 1986, Terry urged, "If you think abortion is murder, act like it!" True Christians could not be satisfied with campaigning and voting. They needed to rededicate themselves to living as moral outsiders and work directly to stop the "baby-killing." "My main issue mission has never been to convert people to being pro-life," Terry wrote his supporters in 1990. "My mission has been to convert Christians into activists."[2]

When Falwell and other ministers urged fundamentalists to take up politics at the end of the seventies, they meant using white-male-led organizations like the Moral Majority to force the Republican Party to enact a conservative Christian agenda. Other conservative Christians had begun in the sixties and seventies to use more of a community-organizing model, political action as building networks of like-minded people (not necessarily Christian but sharing a moral agenda) at the local level. In the seventies and early eighties, this kind of organizing emerged on the right around rising property taxes in Orange County, California, gay rights in Miami, Florida, the textbook choices of local schools in Kanawha County, West Virginia, and the state-by-state battles to defeat the Equal Rights Amendment. White women, from well-known figures like Anita Bryant to housewives turned activists like Alice Moore, played prominent roles. In southern California, upstate New York, St. Louis, and Chicago, anti-abortion activists used these same community-organizing methods to create local anti-abortion movements. This kind of activism worked on the premise that if America came back to God, conservative Christians would no longer be outsiders and could resume their deserved position at the center of the nation.[3]

Nonviolent direct action, in contrast, moved away from interest group politics and community organizing and instead offered a model that small, committed groups of activists could use to call attention to their cause. Direct action worked through mobilizing enough bodies to create a spectacle, as opposed to other political strategies that focused on mobilizing enough voters to swing an election or win a referendum or determine a party platform. Often, this spectacle involved civil disobedience, activists deliberately and publicly breaking laws that they considered unjust. By disregarding the law, activists announced their break with a corrupt status quo. Direct action often momentarily brought into being the better world that activists imagined—the sit-in, for example, that integrated the lunch counter or halted the work of an abortion clinic for an hour. In this way, direct action worked simultaneously as a symbolic and a material form of intervention. It blurred the line between drama and action. The nonviolence of the protesters highlighted the violence of the social order. Activists performed the contrast and thus created a tension between what could be and what was. They acted out their outsider status by refusing to live in the existing world. They gave their interior sense of difference material form. For these reasons, many young middle-class whites took their activism into direct action protests in the second half of the sixties.[4]

This type of political action had a long liberal and left history in the twentieth century. The NAACP's 1917 Silent Protest Parade in response to an East St. Louis riot was an important precedent. Ten thousand African Americans marched down Fifth Avenue to mark the massacre, their startling silence pierced in a slow rhythm by the muffled beats of a drum. Politics as spectacle depended upon more urban environments where people could witness the performance with their own eyes or on well-developed, free, and widely distributed forms of media that could spread news of protest activities. As the media expanded internationally in the postwar period, more activists turned to direct action. Peace activists acutely aware of their minority status in the aftermath of World War II used direct action to oppose the emerging cold war. Liberation struggles, most famously in India, developed and spread direct action strategies throughout the decolonizing world. Back in America, the southern civil rights movement used nonviolent direct action to dismantle southern segregation. What was new about the period after the civil rights movement was the use of direct action by activists on the right.[5]

Randall Terry's Operation Rescue was not the first group of conservative activists to adopt the strategies, including direct action, widely associated at the time with the civil rights and anti-war movements. In 1974, anti-busing activists in Boston seemed to have taken SNCC activists as models as they marched on Washington, wore militant buttons on their clothes and backpacks, picketed schools, and quoted Martin Luther King on civil disobedience. In the George Wallace campaigns of 1968 and 1972, conservatives cast themselves as outsiders within the liberal, integrationist establishment. Conservative women fighting ERA and working to take over the 1977 National Women's Conference described American families as an oppressed group, under attack from the federal government. Catholic peace activists, in turn, brought a New Left style into the fight against abortion. When evangelicals began to organize against abortion, however, they could lay claim to the moral authority of a long tradition of Protestant religious dissent on political questions, from abolitionism to civil rights, as their own. Building on the growth of evangelicalism in the seventies, they fused secular and Christian ideas about outsiders' greater moral authority and access to the truth and proclaimed themselves the new civil rights movement. For evangelicals, direct action techniques possessed a strategic usefulness. But they also asserted a powerful appeal for conservative Christians who felt a great desire to make their inner psychic transformation—their conversion—visible in the material world.[6]

No other single organizer proved as skilled as Randall Terry at using conservative Christians' deep yearning to see themselves as outsiders, as a moral remnant surrounded by sinners, to push them into New Left–style direct action. Terry told evangelicals not to get too comfortable in their new embrace of the larger world. "We are in *jeopardy*," he argued repeatedly in speeches and direct mail solicitations for Operation Rescue in the late 1980s and in his 1990 book *Accessory to Murder*, because conservative Christians had failed to stop abortion: "God is handing us over to be oppressed . . . More and more, Christians and Christian principles are being mocked, scorned, and attacked in magazines, newspapers, television shows, movies, classrooms, the American Medical Association, and the American Bar Association. This barrage of anti-Christian bigotry will take its toll—on us—in the form of severe persecution." True believers needed to put it all at risk—their careers, their community standing, and even their personal freedom—to stop the "murdering" of "the unborn" and other immoral acts. Abortion was not just a sin. It was also a powerful sign of Christians' oppression in the modern world. Randall Terry made Operation Rescue into the most important conservative direct action movement in American history by reminding Christians that no matter how they voted or the faith of their politicians, God's people remained outsiders.[7]

Randall Terry carries a human fetus while leading an Operation Rescue protest at Northeast Women's Center in Philadelphia on July 6, 1988. *Associated Press*.

Anti-Abortion Activism from Left to Right

After the Supreme Court's 1973 decision in *Roe v. Wade*, a small group of anti-abortion activists began to create a direct action wing of the anti-abortion movement by consciously adopting some of the strategic methods and symbolism of the civil rights movement in particular and the New Left more generally. It was not completely clear, in the first half of the seventies, that anti-abortion activism would become so identified with the right. Scholars writing in the 1972 book *Abortion and Social Justice* argued that abortion was "nothing less than a question of *civil rights*: Does the unborn child have a civil right to life?" The book opened with an epigram from Gandhi: "It seems to me as clear as daylight that abortion would be a crime." Some Catholics and many Quakers saw the fight against legal abortion as related to their anti-war and anti-death-penalty activism and a part of their broad support for life.[8]

Direct action protest against *Roe* did not begin immediately. At the 1974 regional conference of the National Youth Pro-Life Coalition (NYPLC), young Catholics Burke Balch, Tom Mooney, and Chris Mooney heard a speech by Charles Fager. A former peace activist, Fager had just published a book on the 1965 Selma civil rights march, and he spoke that night about what anti-abortion activists could learn from the nonviolent direct action of the civil rights movement. In accepting suffering—allowing policemen, for example, to beat them on Selma's Edmund Pettus Bridge—civil rights activists made visible the violence of segregation. Fager told anti-abortion activists to enter clinics peacefully and sit-in. Their peaceful actions—let the "violence be visited on me, not the unborn"—and their arrests would make the horror of abortion visible in America, just as civil rights sit-ins and marches had made white people see the brutality of southern segregation. Fager's speech inspired the three to try nonviolent direct action in the fight against abortion.[9]

By early 1975, Tom Mooney, a former anti-war activist, had become president of NYPLC. He and his wife, Chris, decided to organize an abortion protest the next summer. Unsure of exactly how to proceed, they asked Balch to research civil disobedience. At the Library of Congress among the piles of Quaker pamphlets on pacifism and protest, Balch found Martin Oppenheimer and George Lakey's A Manual for Direct Action. Billed as "a product of the civil rights direct action movement," the book was nothing less that a practical, do-it-yourself guide to nonviolent social change. Dedicated to James Chaney, Andrew Goodman, and Michael Schwerner, A Manual for Direct Action provided detailed, pragmatic instructions on how to organize an effective picket line or consumer boycott, how to behave at a sit-in, and how to talk to reporters. Balch distributed copies of the manual to other NYPLC leaders, and soon Chris Mooney was guiding a small group of young anti-abortion activists in the Washington area in training and role-playing sessions modeled, through the guidebook, on the SNCC-led Mississippi Summer Project training weekends eleven years earlier. Oppenheimer and Lakey described three kinds of direct action: "demonstrations," which were "primarily expressions of a point of view"; "non-cooperation," or actions in which "campaigners withdrew their usual degree of cooperation with the opponent"; and "direct nonviolent intervention." This final method required "physical confrontations rather than withdrawal of cooperation or demonstrating," Oppenheimer and Lakey taught. "It carries the conflict into the opponent's camp and often changes the status quo abruptly." Balch and the Mooneys decided to stage a sit-in.[10]

On the morning of August 2, 1975, the three organizers led a small group of abortion opponents in the first acts of civil disobedience at an abortion clinic. Several men began picketing outside Sigma Reproductive Health Services in Rockville, Maryland, as at least six women entered the clinic and began to sit-in. The group had decided that only the women would actually enter the abortion clinic. "You had to get across something that would break the stereotype of misogynistic males trying to control women," Balch remembered later, aware of the power of organized feminism then and most feminists' support for abortion rights. As the women inside sang and prayed, the men outside gave out literature and spoke to women entering the clinic. Eventually, police arrested the six women inside the clinic for trespassing. Still following their New Left script, their comrades named the women "the Sigma Six," after the Chicago Eight, and tried to get the press interested in their trial. The press, for the most part, ignored them. On July 4, 1976, they staged a second sit-in at another Washington, D.C.–area abortion clinic to mark the Bicentennial. Again, they failed to gain much media attention.[11]

In the internal movement history that anti-abortion activists often tell, John O'Keefe, another leftist Catholic who followed peace activism into the anti-abortion work, gets the credit for founding the pro-life sit-in movement. O'Keefe met Balch and thus had access to what the original small group had learned from staging the two sit-ins and from studying *A Manual for Direct Action*. From Washington, D.C., O'Keefe's New Left–sounding Pro-Life Non-Violent Action Project worked to create a region-wide series of sit-ins in the Northeast, a kind of anti-abortion version of the southern student sit-in movement of the early sixties. Singing civil rights songs like "We Shall Overcome" and carrying picket signs with quotes from Martin Luther King Jr., O'Keefe and his small band of activists sat-in at clinics in the Washington area and in New England. The civil rights movement not only provided a strategic model for using direct action protest. It also provided a model for using direct action to cultivate and use moral righteousness. O'Keefe believed evoking the civil rights movement would build support for a new radical social movement.[12]

In 1978, O'Keefe wrote the recruiting pamphlet *A Peaceful Presence* to spread news about this latest round of civil rights organizing: "With Reverend Martin Luther King Jr., we must come to believe that unearned suffering is somehow redemptive. A change of heart will not occur without suffering, and we have to ask ourselves whether we are willing to suffer ourselves or only ask others to suffer . . . It is not enough to change people's minds; we are engaged in a struggle to change people's hearts." Using late-sixties, New Left–sounding language, O'Keefe argued that sit-ins would demonstrate protesters' "*solidarity with the child.*" He envisioned a new version of the civil rights movement's Beloved Community, a living example of how the whole world could be after the fight: "Any movement that sets out to change society has to provide a picture of a world that is an ideal, that is convincing, so you can compare what is going on with what ought to be, and so you can be prepared to struggle for it." And this ideal world in the moment was the group of protesters sitting in at a clinic and prayerfully, peacefully stopping abortion, putting their bodies on the line to aid the most oppressed, voiceless, and innocent Americans. He thought that other activists on the left, prodded by their alienation from a militarized America that had proved its dedication to death in Vietnam, would follow him into peaceful direct action protest against abortion now that that war had ended. He thought that people on the left who identified with marginalized and oppressed people globally would see the plight of unborn babies as part of their fight. He was wrong. Few people on the left became publicly involved in anti-abortion activism. However, many conservative Americans eventually adopted "the unborn" as the oppressed group they were fighting to save.[13]

In the late 1970s and early 1980s, copies of *A Peaceful Presence* and *A Manual for Direct Action* circulated among the small numbers of mostly Catholic, action-oriented anti-abortion activists in rebellion against the larger Catholic-led "passive" pro-life movement working to overturn *Roe*. Joseph Scheidler, one of these Catholic activists, founded the Chicago-based Pro-Life Action League in 1980. Unlike O'Keefe, he did not come into anti-abortion work from the peace movement. Drawing on his experiences protesting at abortion clinics and his work in journalism and public relations, he essentially revised and expanded *A Manual for Direct Action*, publishing it as *Closed: 90 Ways to Stop Abortion*, in 1985. *Closed* eventually replaced tattered copies of the Quaker book and other accumulated notes on civil rights and anti-war protests as the conservatives' direct action guidebook. In adapting sit-in techniques to the particularities of the fight against abortion, Scheidler advocated a more militant style of activism in the form of clinic "invasions" that pushed right up against the edge of nonviolence. Around the same time, Joan Andrews, another dedicated Catholic activist, led a small group of activists that conducted a few sit-ins and provided housing and other help to pregnant women. Andrews had grown up in Nashville, and her own experience of anti-Catholic discrimination there inspired her to participate in local sit-ins protesting racial segregation. In 1986, Andrews was sentenced to five years in prison in Florida for entering an abortion clinic and attempting to destroy equipment used to perform abortions. Andrews's refusal to cooperate with prison authorities in any way eventually landed her in solitary confinement in a maximum-security prison. After a year, many evangelical Christian radio stations took up her cause, making Andrews the first martyr of the anti-abortion movement and spreading news of her activism through the evangelical counterculture. Before hearing Andrews's story, many evangelical Christians did not understand the meaning of direct action.[14]

In the mid-1980s, activists trying to inspire people to participate in the anti-abortion fight were working in a historical moment transformed by the rising power of the New Right and the election of Ronald Reagan. O'Keefe had reached out to potential supporters by appealing to the political and cultural alienation of young middle-class whites drawn to the civil rights and peace movements, the same kinds of kids who would have headed to Mississippi for a summer of organizing or marched on the Pentagon. Yet most participants in the New Left, especially women, failed to see abortion as another fight for the oppressed. They adopted a feminist perspective focused not on the oppression of the fetus but on women. In this kind of thinking, the legal practice of abortion empowered women, giving them control over their bodies. Catholic activists who kept up the fight in the early eighties tried a different approach. They worked to tap a deep commitment to protecting all life that united some believers despite their different relationships to recent social movements. This appeal did not work well for evangelical Christians, who were already feeling alienated from what they understood as a country and culture in decline as a result of sixties activism. They saw aborted babies as a symbol of all that Americans had lost. In the fight against abortion, they found an oppressed and marginalized group they could claim. Catholic peace activists' moral outrage over abortion had somewhat different sources than the moral outrage of Protestant evangelicals. But both fused a Christian sense of believers as outsiders in an evil world with the more secular romance of the outsider, rooted in popular culture and intellectual life, that outsiders were better—more real, more authentic, and more individual—than other Americans. Anti-abortion activism gave some conservative Christians a way to both reject the secular world and yet connect with it through a shared identification with outsiders and rebels.[15]

In the late eighties, when anti-abortion activists finally succeeded in building a mass movement using direct action strategies, some participants still used New Left ideas to justify their activism. When the Catholic magazine *America* interviewed two Catholic seminary students, Martin L. Chase and James F. Vandenberg, about their role in protests at abortion clinics in New York City in the spring of 1988, Chase sounded like O'Keefe channeling an anti-abortion version of Freedom Summer participant Mario Savio's call for students to join the Free Speech movement. "The basic idea was putting our bodies in between the abortionist and the unborn child," Chase said. "That's the sort of protest that I'm familiar with from the 1960s and 1970s. I thought it worked then, and I think it works now." Many participants, however, embraced sixties-style direct action without ever having been supporters of these earlier movements and with no prior experience in civil disobedience. Some were young people who had not been old enough to participate in civil rights and peace activism.

Others had actively opposed or ignored those movements. Late arrivals to the anti-abortion fight, many white evangelicals in the South had spent the seventies on the defensive as a result of their opposition to the civil rights movement and exhausted from the huge effort of establishing Christian schools to circumvent integration. Across the country, conservative Christians had also been busy creating their own counter counterculture—a network of independent Christian schools, colleges, and churches, a growing number of organizations like Falwell's Moral Majority, and a diffuse web of Christian bookstores, radio and television programs and stations, presses, and music companies. Intrigued by the stories about Joan Andrews they had heard on the radio and lifted on a wave of growing conservative Christian activism on a range of issues from opposing gay rights to supporting prayer in schools, many evangelicals were hungry to enact their faith and their sense of themselves as outsiders in the world. Randall Terry's Operation Rescue gave them a way.[16]

Randal Terry, Radical Christian Rebel

Fittingly, before he founded the organization that brought evangelicals into direct action protest, Randall Terry wanted to be a rock and roll star. Too young to participate in the social movements that had shaped the lives of his mother and his aunts, he left home as a teenager in 1976 to play his music and find what was left of the counterculture. He seemed to find some of it—there were tales of pot smoking and maybe more drugs. Somewhere in Texas he also encountered that other counterculture. He met some evangelical Christians. Back in upstate New York after a traumatic event never fully explained, Terry lived at home and worked at an ice cream parlor. A customer shared his faith with the young worker. Sometime in September 1976, Randall Terry experienced a conversion and became a born-again Christian. "I was radically converted," Terry remembered later. "Up until that time, I was part of the rock 'n' roll culture, involved in drugs and immorality." He caught up with the local remnants of the Jesus People movement and in 1978 enrolled in nearby Elim Bible Institute. The charismatic movement, which spread Pentecostal practices like speaking in tongues and an openly emotional, prayer- and music-filled worship style to other evangelicals and even mainline Protestants and Catholics, had swept through the small religious school. Charismatic Christians fused a new secular emphasis on the truth value of the experiential and on emotion and feeling with an older Protestant faith in the centrality of the individual's experience of God. Terry, a competent musician and counterculture dropout, fit right in. He always portrayed himself as "a young rebel." "I was born out of time almost . . . I was in some aspects, I imagine, a holdout," he remembered later, displaying a revisionist historical analysis even as he revealed a great deal about his sense of himself as an outsider. "The sixties for many was an era of searching. People wanting to know the answers, wanting to know the truth. In the seventies, people just wanted to get high. But I wanted to know the answers." The head of the only abortion clinic in Binghamton, New York, the site of Terry's first anti-abortion activism and a repeated target of Operation Rescue protests, described Terry as an outsider as well, though in a less flattering way: "Even though we always thought he was a nut, he has that martyred, rabid quality that attracts people. His movement needed some kind of a figure like that, someone who's willing to go beyond the pale."[17]

The way Terry told it, a bumper sticker he saw in 1977 first made him think about the evil of abortion: "Abortion, Pick on Someone Your Own Size." Six years later he had a vision. God wanted him to implement "a three-point plan" to stop abortion: block clinics, counsel young women trying to enter clinics, and provide homes for single women who were pregnant. In some versions of his tale, he says he began to think more about the problem after seeing the film *Whatever Happened to the Human Race?*, based on the book by C. Everett Koop and Francis Schaeffer, while he was a student at Elim Bible College. After Terry watched a particularly violent scene of an aborted baby near the end of the film, he recalled, "I literally sat there and sobbed. I remember praying, 'God, please use me to fight this hideous crime.' The Bible says, 'Rescue the fatherless from the hand of the wicked.' It's my Christian duty to fight abortion."[18]

Koop was a pioneering pediatric surgeon who would become surgeon general in the Reagan administration. Schaeffer, a theologian, cultivated a kind of sage-like persona at his spiritual retreat in Switzerland by dressing in bohemian clothes, growing his hair long, and wearing a goatee. *Newsweek* named him "the guru of the fundamentalists." Garry Wills called him "the evangelicals' C. S. Lewis." Schaeffer had been urging Christians for years to use widespread civil disobedience to challenge the legitimacy of both the godless culture—what he called "secular humanism"—and the state. For Terry, Schaeffer's work "legitimize[d] the idea that there is a higher law, that God's law is above man's law, to be revered and obeyed before man's law. That had a profound impact on me." By 1979, when Schaeffer and Koop traveled across the United States promoting their book and movie, Schaeffer had settled on abortion as the issue Christians should use to create a direct action movement. The Christian's "duty," he argued in his 1981 book, *A Christian Manifesto* (his answer to *The Communist Manifesto* and *The Humanist Manifesto*), was "to disobey the state." Looking back at the emergence of mass protest in the anti-abortion movement, Terry argued: "Jerry Falwell provided the political cover, Francis Schaeffer provided the theological cover; but it was Operation Rescue that brought the two together in the street." Stopping abortions combined "civil disobedience" and "biblical obedience."[19]

In reality, Randall Terry's wife, Cindy, led the couple into anti-abortion work. Cindy and Randall met at Elim and married in 1981. After Cindy had trouble getting pregnant, she began picketing Southern Tier Women's Services in Binghamton in the winter of 1984, haunting the parking lot with armfuls of anti-abortion literature. She came every day and stayed the eight hours that the clinic was open, yelling at women as they got out of their cars, "Don't kill your baby. I'll take it. I can't have a baby." After a few months, Randall began coming too. In the summer of 1985, aided by members of their church, they invaded the clinic. Inside, they tore out the phone lines, broke up the furniture, and blocked the door. They put Krazy Glue in the clinic's locks. Other days they followed workers home and called late at night to threaten them. A member of their tiny band of activists made bomb threats. By then, Randall Terry had taken over this small group that would grow into the beginnings of Operation Rescue. It was not an equal partnership between Randall and Cindy Terry. He never seemed to worry, as had earlier protesters, that anti-abortion activism might look like men controlling women. Like the independent churches and Bible colleges that dominated the world of conservative Christianity, the organization was from the start male-dominated and hierarchical. As the founder, Terry had almost absolute power.[20]

In 1986, Randall Terry recalled, God slowly revealed for him how to use nonviolent direct action to shut down clinics. "It was like the dawn." Joseph Scheidler remembered it differently. He had been calling for sit-ins against abortion clinics for years, and his Pro-Life Action League had pioneered the kind of clinic invasion Terry and his followers were conducting in the summer of 1986. Terry invited him to speak in Binghamton in early 1986, soon after Scheidler published *Closed*. He told Terry of his dream to use nonviolent direct action to shut down clinics across the country. Mass arrests, he explained to Terry, would generate national media coverage, just as they had for the civil rights movement. A week after Scheidler left, Terry and his group blocked the entrance to Southern Tier. By the fall, Terry had named his growing group Operation Rescue.[21]

Unlike Scheidler, Terry and Operation Rescue built anti-abortion protest into a mass movement. Terry quickly learned to use direct action tactics effectively, but he also learned to talk about them effectively. Clinic sit-ins or rescues, he repeatedly told the press in the late eighties, were "designed to save lives by preventing abortionists from entering their death chamber, and to dramatize for the American people the horrors." Nonviolent mass protest prevented the "murder" of the "unborn" but also, through mass arrests, jail terms, and trials, dramatized abortion as a problem. "When pro-lifers are jailed, it forces the community to reconsider child-killing," Terry argued. "It gives credibility to our rhetoric."[22]

In the spring of 1988, Terry led Operation Rescue in its first mass protests, a series of sit-ins at abortion clinics in New York City. That summer, Operation Rescue implemented an even more ambitious plan, a series of mass protests at abortion clinics timed to coincide with the 1988 Democratic Convention in Atlanta. Terry and Operation Rescue tried out the tactical and strategic lessons they had learned from earlier activists who had studied or participated in the civil rights and peace movements. Protesters marched and picketed and passed out leaflets. They conducted sit-ins. Scattered use of this form of direct action to shut down clinics since 1975, however, had made clinics change their operating procedures and increase security. Since it was virtually impossible to get inside clinics, protesters sat-in outside, blocking entrance doors with their bodies, linking arms and sitting, lying, and even crawling on the ground. This change in protest strategy generated a wider panorama of dramatic conflict perfect for television, as well as a much greater number of arrests, and an at times brutal response from the police. Mayor Andrew Young, a veteran of the 1960 sit-in movement and Southern Christian Leadership Conference leader (he was on the balcony of the Lorraine Motel standing beside King when he died), authorized police officers to use "pain compliance techniques" to stop the demonstrators; 1,235 people were arrested outside several clinics with these methods. National media coverage followed.

That summer Terry and other anti-abortion protestors also learned to deploy the symbolic value of the civil rights movement. In Atlanta, birthplace of Martin Luther King, site of the headquarters of both the SCLC and SNCC, and a location of major civil rights organizing from the 1940s to the 1970s, the spectacle of new mass protests readily evoked comparisons to the civil rights movement. Operation Rescue leaders used the analogy often when speaking to the press. "When we first came here it was not our intention to make Atlanta a battleground," an Operation Rescue spokesperson told the Los Angeles Times that summer. "But for whatever reason, we believe the Lord has decided to turn this into something that could be another Selma, Alabama." Terry began to claim King as "one of his mentors," and he started "reading little things here and there . . . like a book of [King's] sayings." "Every major political change in our society has been preceded by social upheaval," Terry told reporters, a way of thinking about social change he had learned from King. "The pro-life movement has failed to learn the lessons of history, which show how the labor movement, the civil rights movement, Vietnam protest, and gay liberation all occurred because a group of people created social tension." He also watched *Eyes on the Prize*, the celebrated PBS multi-episode documentary series about the civil rights movement that featured extensive coverage of the sit-in movement of the early sixties and the Christian faith that inspired many participants. For Terry, the civil rights movement proved that a Christian-led, direct action movement of courageous people willing to risk arrest could succeed in helping the oppressed, changing the laws, and saving the country.[23]

In his book *Operation Rescue*, published that fall, Randall Terry described how his organization used nonviolent direct action to do God's work and laid out his vision for the future. The Bible, he argued, sanctions sit-ins at abortion clinics and other activist tactics that actually stop abortions. "Rescue those who are unjustly sentenced to death," he quoted Proverbs 24:11 as rendered in the *Living Bible*, a translation of the sacred text into everyday speech. "Don't stand back and let them die." Leading evangelical and fundamentalist ministers added their endorsements of the direct action anti-abortion movement led by Terry. Jerry Falwell wrote in one foreword: "I believe non-violent civil disobedience is the wave of the future for the pro-life movement in this country." James Kennedy, head minister of Coral Ridge Presbyterian in Fort Lauderdale, Florida, sounded like a SNCC field worker as he praised Operation Rescue members for putting their bodies on the line and filling the jails. And televangelist Pat Robertson, too, wrote yet another foreword: "Randall Terry has begun the same dramatic nonviolent protest against the slaughter of innocent babies in our nation that brought racial justice and equality in the 1960s."[24]

Sometime in late 1988, Terry condensed the arguments of his book and his frequent statements to the press into an article. "Operation Rescue: The Civil Rights Movement of the Nineties" appeared in early 1989 in the Heritage Foundation's *Policy Review*. "Today we celebrate as a national holiday the birthday of a man who helped change unjust laws through civil disobedience," he argued. "I am convinced that the American people will begin to take the pro-life movement seriously when they see good, decent citizens peacefully sitting around abortion mills, risking arrest and prosecution as Martin Luther King Jr. did." Terry played the role of King in this vision of anti-abortion organizing. He became the outsider who would lead the nation to justice.[25]

In response to anti-abortion activists' increasing use of the civil rights analogy, many prominent liberal activists expressed their outrage and revulsion. Civil rights leaders, urged on by Planned Parenthood, protested officially in 1988. Julian Bond led a group of ten civil rights leaders, including Atlanta mayor Andrew Young and Jesse Jackson, in denouncing Operation Rescue, comparing the group "to the segregationists who fought desperately to block black Americans from access to their rights." Throughout the late eighties and nineties, pro-choice activists and their supporters countered anti-abortion activists' use of the civil rights analogy by flipping the terms. Terry and his followers, they insisted, were today's Bull Connors, murderers of the Mississippi Three, policemen with fire hoses, billy clubs, and biting dogs. In 1988 and 1989, Kate Michelman, executive director of NARAL, the National Abortion Rights Action League, made this charge repeatedly. Anti-abortion activists used direct action techniques to limit other peoples' rights rather than expand them. Women were oppressed, and legal access to abortion gave them rights. Anti-abortion activists, unlike Martin Luther King and his followers, were not nonviolent. Pro-choice leaders and supporters refused to give anti-abortion activists any rhetorical claim to the moral authority of the civil rights movement.[26]

Historically, however, the most influential political movement of the period did share some commonalities with the upstart anti-abortion effort. Anti-abortion activists did work to limit the rights of women to terminate pregnancies, but civil rights activists worked to limit the rights of whites to practice discrimination. When liberals countered that ending racial discrimination empowered African Americans, anti-abortion activists claimed that ending abortions empowered "the unborn." For some, these claims may have been simply rhetorical, but for conservative Christians who believed life began at conception, they were facts. Some civil rights activists did not practice nonviolence, and others, like SNCC leader Stokely Carmichael, changed their positions over time, rejecting the nonviolent techniques they had once supported. The fact that some SNCC leaders rejected nonviolence in the late sixties did not erase the earlier history of the organization. Randall Terry's growing support for violence, first in private and then, by the mid-nineties, in public as he worked with other conservative radicals to forge an alliance between the militia movement and the activist anti-abortion movement, did not erase his earlier advocacy of nonviolence or its appeal to masses of conservative Christians. As importantly, the anti-abortion movement worked symbolically for conservative Christians much as "white love" for blacks in the civil rights movement worked for many middle-class liberal whites. It gave them a group of outsiders—"the unborn" as they imagined them—with which to identify. Romanticizing fetuses as the embodiment of human innocence gave them a way to disavow their power and see themselves as outsiders.[27]

Not everyone, however, agreed with Terry's call for conservative Christians to take up direct action. Some powerful evangelical ministers like Charles Stanley, pastor of the First Baptist Church in Atlanta, opposed Operation Rescue's use of civil disobedience. Like Falwell, in the later seventies Stanley also called conservative Christians into politics. But he drew the line at direct action. In a pamphlet entitled *A Biblical Perspective on Civil Disobedience*, Stanley and the staff and deacons of his church affirmed that abortion was morally wrong but advocated only "lawful means of protesting." In response, Operation Rescue leaders backed off from their civil disobedience argument and told the press and congregations that rescue provided a means of "saving the lives of babies scheduled to be murdered." Some fundamentalists, they admitted, were put off by the leftist-sounding call to break the law.[28]

Part of the problem was that Terry was an evangelical Christian but he was not a fundamentalist. He never completely severed his ties with the counterculture he experienced in the mid-seventies. With his wild and longish hair, his awkwardness in a suit, and his love of rock music, he never really fit in with fundamentalists like Falwell. When his first church, Bushnell Basin Community Church, a suburban Rochester, New York, charismatic congregation, spun off its youth ministry as a satellite, The Ark, that met in an old barn, Terry went with them. The Ark became a Jesus People church. Many fundamentalists, despite a strategically savvy public show of unity, distrusted the mysticism and emotional expressiveness of Pentecostals and other charismatic Christians. Charismatic worship was full, too, of nontraditional music. As head of Operation Rescue, Terry continued to write and play Christian rock. Lists of resources on sale for "educating the Christian activist" included his video, "When the Battle Raged," footage of the Holocaust, aborted babies, and actual rescues set to a song written by Terry, and cassettes of other anti-abortion and Christian songs he had written and performed.[29]

Theological arguments too divided Terry and many fundamentalists. Fundamentalist ministers denounced the *Living Bible* that Terry often quoted when speaking to the press. Terry's call to action implicitly challenged the dispensationalism essential to fundamentalist thinking. God had divided history into periods, dispensations, and preordained what would happen in each. Christians could not change the course of history—they could only affect how many people would be saved and how many would be damned. These remnants of an older Calvinist Protestantism did not fuse easily with secular or evangelical faith in the moral authority of individual acts of rebellion. Operation Rescue's calls for action suggested that Christian rebels could intervene in history. Later Operation Rescue materials described this process as making "theology into biography": "We are propelled to speak up for those who cannot speak for themselves . . . this is how the Word of God becomes flesh and theology becomes biography. This gives God an excuse to do mighty acts and bring real healing to our land." The future, Operation Rescue told potential anti-abortion activists, was not set. Christians had a duty to act.[30]

If belief in the ability to change the world came easily to many white middle-class Americans in this period, actually making change proved difficult. In the fall of 1989, Randall Terry experienced the cost of casting himself as a martyr to the cause, as the "King" of the activist pro-life movement. Convicted in September of illegally blocking the entrance to an abortion clinic during the Operation Rescue protests in Atlanta the previous year, Terry rejected his sentence of two years' probation, two years' banishment from the Atlanta metropolitan area, and a thousand dollar fine. The judge gave him a six-month prison sentence instead. Terry had lots of time to think as he sat in his cell in the Fulton County jail. The setting helped. King had spent time in this very jail.[31]

On October 10, Terry wrote from his cell what he envisioned as his version of King's famous "Letter from a Birmingham Jail." Like King, he dismissed the complaint that activists were "outside agitators." Like King, he insisted that nonviolent direct action was necessary to force people to confront immorality and injustice. And like King, he worried about the way moderation slides so easily into acquiescence; he embraced the word "extremist." "I am deeply troubled by what I see happening to the rescue movement nationwide," Terry confessed. "In city after city . . . the number of rescuer missions per week is dropping." The problem, he argued, was not extremists but moderates. Terry called abortion opponents to the struggle, to participation in clinic picketing, "sidewalk counseling," and sit-ins or rescues. As King had written a quarter of a century before, "Nonviolent direct action seeks to create . . . a crisis and establish such creative tension so that a community that has constantly refused to negotiate is forced to confront the issue." Terry pledged Operation Rescue to creating that tension. The time to act, he insisted, citing the example of his own courage in serving his sentence, was now.[32]

That winter, Terry left the Atlanta jail before his six-month sentence was up, allegedly freed by an anonymous donor's payment of his fine. Some experienced sit-in veterans understood Terry's agreement to be released as a moral failing, and he lost some of the moral authority he had gained leading people

Randall Terry speaks to the press after he receives a twenty-four-month suspended sentence and $1,000 fine in Atlanta on October 6, 1989, for his anti-abortion protests during the 1988 Democratic National Convention in Atlanta. He refuses to pay the fine and says he will serve the time. *Associated Press*.

who opposed abortion into action. He also had to fight to retain control of the original Operation Rescue. Behind the scenes, court injunctions and fines threatened to bankrupt different versions of the organization and its splinter groups as well as Terry and other leaders. In 1990, however, at the height of its power, the Moral Majority endorsed Operation Rescue's efforts with a highly publicized $10,000 check. Falwell urged Christians to engage in widespread protest: "This is a departure from anything I've ever preached," Falwell told the *New York Times*. "The only way is nonviolent civil disobedience."[33]

By the start of the 1990s, Randall Terry's public advocacy of nonviolent abortion clinic sit-ins had turned anti-abortion activism into a New Right mass protest movement. Like William F. Buckley two decades earlier, Terry provocatively fused oppositional style and conservative beliefs. The evangelical model of social change—one heart at a time—made sense to a man who had grown up on the cusp of the counterculture. And Terry intuitively understood that people of his generation retained a deep desire to act, as the generation before them had, to change the world. He pushed evangelicals into direct action protest, where they made the fight against abortion the center of an increasingly politically powerful Religious Right. For a time, he forged a highly unlikely coalition of outsiders, what the *Wall Street Journal* called the "anti-establishment"—"ex-hippies, pacifists, Reagan Democrats, Attila-the-Hun Republicans, far-right Catholics, leftish Catholics, evangelicals, fundamentalists, Protestants of no-name-brand denominations who pray in tongues and converse with Jesus"—into a powerful political force. In 1990, it seemed like this new alliance of the alienated just might win.[34]

Outsiders for Life

As the pro-choice movement fought back and the courts issued injunctions blocking anti-abortion protests, nonviolence remained essential to sustaining a mass movement against abortion and establishing the moral legitimacy of the cause. Nonviolence drew thousands of conservative Christians, many first-time participants, to the two largest mass protests against abortion, the 1991 Wichita "Summer of Mercy" and the 1992 Buffalo "Spring of Life." A flyer for the "Spring of Life Rescue" in Buffalo in April 1992 contained a list of rules and a place for participants to sign to indicate they would behave as instructed. "I understand," the pledge begins, "the critical importance that this mission be unified, peaceful and free of any actions or words that would appear violent or hateful to any witnesses of the event." Organizers tried to get participants to think about the audience, the people who would see the event in the news. "Marshals," like SNCC field secretaries, provided instructions at the protest site. Materials described in detail what would happen at protests so participants would not be caught by surprise. "A rescue," one flyer claimed, was like having a church service on the "doorsteps of hell . . . Our intervention for the little babies is an act of worship . . . Be peaceful and nonviolent at all times in both word and deed." A "Rescuers Check List" distributed by Operation Rescue California in the mid-nineties explicitly described every detail of the process—from prayer beforehand to jail afterward. "Bring a ziplock bag of trail mix" and some sunscreen, organizers suggested. Avoid underwire bras because they are banned in jails. The single, typed sheet cautioned participants to remember the training provided at pre-demonstration rallies: "If threatened, avoid even the appearance of aggression," organizers warned. "Remember the principles of solidarity."[35]

Training materials also stressed the actual mechanics of civil disobedience. "Do not talk to, touch, or call out to the police, pro-abort opposition, clinic personnel, mothers, passersby or anyone else." To block clinic doors, "walk, crawl or scooch, as directed by marshals. Never run. Always scooch to fill funnels or gaps." Rescue training materials urged participants to "remain passive during arrest . . . Do not resist the officers, but do not assist them either." By "going limp," Operation Rescue insisted, activists would "buy more time for babies scheduled to die" because it would take longer for the police to drag them away. They also mimicked the passive response of the fetus to the assaults of the abortionist. Like civil rights activists after the first sit-ins, anti-abortion activists trained and practiced and reviewed instructions. Nonviolent direct action was difficult.[36]

Instructional materials stressed that participants needed to be prepared for arrest. "Think of your jail time as the 'second part' of the rescue." Jail gave Christians "an opportunity to truly trust in God." Incarceration became a time for worship and prayer. "Being in jail for your faith," a flyer claimed, "can be a wonderful experience." Filling up the jails would tax local government resources and keep abortion in the news. Participants could use their time behind bars to think and to write letters—as Terry had in Atlanta in 1989, or Bob Jewitt in the Harris County Jail in Houston in 1992, or Keith Tucci in Melbourne, Florida, in 1993—that urged activists to continue sitting-in in the face of persecution.[37]

By the early nineties, the nonviolent direct action wing of the anti-abortion movement invoked the civil rights movement and other sixties-era social movements in almost every action they planned and executed, every publication they produced, and every media story they circulated, whether they consciously appealed to these earlier direct action campaigns or not. Traces of the sixties continued to haunt much Operation Rescue rhetoric as other leaders replaced Terry. A call to work in the Buffalo "Spring of Life" stressed that the project formed part of the long "battle for the oppressed." Abortion, another pamphlet argued, was "a violation of the rights of unborn boys and girls"—it attacked the powerless. A journalist who went under-cover in New York City to a planning meeting for clinic protests in the summer of 1992 described speakers talking about "civil rights for the unborn." "If I must go to jail for being a Christian, then I will," announced Keith Tucci, the leader of Operation Rescue National in 1992. "I will let the court know, however, that I will not be silent, for the oppression of the few leads to the oppression of the many." Operation Rescue materials frequently used as an epigraph a poem by Chris Cowgill that began "We stand for those who have no voice." "If every Christian put their lives on the line in front of abortion mills for just one day," Operation Rescue leaders argued, "we could shut down the abortion business in a matter of hours." The activ-ists should "interpose themselves between a defenseless child and the killer bent on destruction." "We as Americans," a pamphlet called *What Does One Abortion Cost?* reminded readers, "have a proud tradition for standing up for the rights of individuals." Operation Rescue materials continued to sound vaguely leftist, denouncing the "multimillion dollar abortion industry that sells abortions in the same ways that the corner drug-store sells aspirin." The people who change society, a call to participate in the 1993 summer project, "Cities of Refuge," proclaimed, are always small in number. "The pro-abortion secular media would like to portray people who risk arrest to save preborn children as fringe fanatic activists." The truth was that they were Christians, "a remnant," following "the biblical command to execute justice and defend the innocent." Operation Rescue existed to "put action behind our words."[38]

For people old enough to remember and the many, like Terry, who had seen *Eyes on the Prize*, the visual images—newspaper coverage, television footage, and the photos in Operation Rescue's own publications—continued to look like sixties-era civil rights protests. Crowds of sign-carrying people with determined faces, surrounded by police, in the commercial districts of towns and cities looked like they were reenacting earlier demonstrations. Pictures of protesters with bashed and bandaged heads visually quoted the photographs taken by SNCC workers a quarter of a century earlier. People filling police ve-hicles, jails, and courtrooms also evoked the imagery of earlier movements.[39]

On one level the civil rights movement analogy worked. It gave conserva-tives a chance to work for and imaginatively connect with their own marginal-ized and oppressed group. Identifying with the fetus—the ultimate example of powerlessness—mostly white middle-class protesters reconciled their own contradictions much as other middle-class whites had identifying with blacks. Their deep sense of themselves as outsiders coexisted with their growing polit-ical and economic power. Their profound faith in the individual united with God coexisted with their devotion to autocratic leaders and racial and gender hierarchies. With the unborn, they did not have to think about trade-offs or limits. They did not have to think about the nature of democracy in a nation of equal citizens. They did not have to feel responsible. Identifying with the unborn, they shared their innocence. The irony, of course, was that the civil rights analogy did all this work for anti-abortion protesters regardless of whether they supported civil rights activists or segregationists at the time or understood the results of the freedom movement as positive or negative.[40]

At the level of conscious adaption of civil rights methods, however, grass-roots protesters sometimes did not understand the connection. Potential recruits in Buffalo in 1992, for example, were bewildered and even offended by training sessions filled with film footage of King's speeches. Activists in the late 1970s had coined the term "rescue," in fact, to avoid the left-sounding term "sit-in." In the courts, Terry denied rescue was civil disobedience. The neces-sity defense—that Terry had to break the law for the greater good, saving a baby—demanded it.[41]

For anti-abortion activists who embraced the call to direct action, though, thinking of rescue as solely an intervention rather than also as symbolic action had a major liability. If rescues were actually about saving lives, then what effort could ever be considered enough? A pamphlet for Operation Rescue: Boston made this clear. "A rescue" was "not a demonstration." "Firemen do not 'protest arson' at the site of a burning building. They rescue people and property. Likewise, pro-life rescuers block abortuary entrances to *rescue* chil-dren*." Operation Rescue's "If you think abortion is murder, act like it"—like the Black Panther Party's "Off the pigs" and the Weather Underground's "Bring the war home"—ultimately pushed some proponents of direct action into vio-lence. In 1992, the police dug up a book in the backyard of an arrested activist. A group of anti-abortion extremists who had formed an underground group they called the Army of God supposedly distributed the anonymously authored text. *When Life Hurts, We Can Help* combined a detailed philosophical and theological justification for violent attacks on clinics with an explicit, step-by-step guide for producing explosive chemicals, building bombs, and carrying out other acts of sabotage, a version of *Closed* for the activist ready to use violence. From its first line, it described the abortion fight in religious terms: "This is a manual for those who have come to understand that a battle against abortion is a battle not against flesh and blood," the text begins, "but against the devil and all the evil he can muster among flesh and blood to fight at his side." America was "a nation ruled by a godless civil authority that is dominated by humanism, moral nihilism, and new-age perversion of the high standards upon which a Godly society must be founded if it is to endure," "a nation under the power of Evil—Satan." What, the manual asked, except a lack of knowledge would stop an activist this alienated from using violence? Where did an activist stop if protest ceased being even partly symbolic and she no longer believed in calling out the conscience of a broader public? Anti-abortion activist Michael Griffin provided one answer when he shot and killed Dr. David Gunn at a Pensacola, Florida, abortion clinic.

Direct action as a strategy of protest worked by fusing the symbolic and the material—an intervention that stopped some targeted activity momentarily and thus dramatized for others the beliefs of the protesters. When protesters no longer had faith that there was anyone out there for their drama to speak to, direct action lost this tension. It ceased to be both symbol and act, to both live inside the existing world as a thing and to make an alternative to that world. When activists lost hold of the symbolic meaning of their acts, only the material act of intervention had value. At that moment, the outsider had nothing to lose.[42]

In response to the murder of Gunn, Congress passed the Freedom of Access to Clinic Entrances Act, which President Bill Clinton signed into law in May 1994. FACE brought federal penalties against anyone using "force, threat of force or physical obstruction" to "intimidate or interfere" with a person "obtaining or providing reproductive health services" and against any person damaging facilities that provide these services. The new law made participation in the sit-ins that pro-choice activists called "clinic blockades" a federal crime.[43]

The same month FACE became law, Randall Terry and Matthew Trewhella, founder and leader of the Milwaukee-based anti-abortion organization Missionaries to the Preborn, attended a conference publicly billed as the Wisconsin state meeting of the United Taxpayers Party. Anti-hate-group activists described the convention instead as a major effort by anti-abortion and militia leaders to combine their missions. Terry told participants, "Our goal is a Christian nation ... We are called by God to conquer this country. We don't want equal time. We don't want pluralism." Trewhella called Christians to "do the loving thing" and buy their kids "an SKS rifle and 500 rounds of ammunition" for Christmas. Then he held up his toddler and asked him to show the crowd his trigger finger. When the little boy held up his right index finger, the crowd laughed and applauded. In the militia movement, the postwar romance of the outsider fused with an older celebration of vigilante "justice" and "moral" outlaws.[44]

Fellow participants and journalists disagree about the extent to which leading activists actually privately encouraged or helped facilitate acts of violence against clinics and providers as they publicly promoted nonviolent direct action. In a January 1995 letter from Allenwood Federal Prison, Terry tried to refute the charge that "taking non-violent action to save children from death inevitably leads to the use of lethal force." The violence, he argued, occurred because Americans refused to stop their attacks against "unborn" children. "Just as segregation and the accompanying violence possess the seeds for further violence, likewise it appears that the Law of sowing and reaping is being visited upon the abortion industry." FACE "turns peaceful pro-life activists into federal felons." Was it "logical to leap from non-violent life-saving activities to lethal force?" Terry asked. "Has God authorized one person to be policeman, judge, jury and executioner?" He made no mention of his speech in Wisconsin the year before, and denied that he had ever asked his followers to pray for the death of abortion providers or had any responsibility for the actions of James Charles Kopp, a former Operation Rescue member and close Terry associate who murdered abortion provider Barnett Slepian in Buffalo on October 23, 1998.[45]

The increasing numbers of murders and attempted murders—from two in 1993 to twelve in 1994, one each for 1995, 1996, and 1997, and three in 1998—made it difficult to recruit more than a small hardcore group of itinerant rescuers who lived on the road, traveling from protest to protest. The fact that federal fines shut down organizations as the courts seized assets and bank accounts and forced leaders to spend their energy staying a step ahead of the law did not help recruitment efforts either. The shocking murders of abortion providers pushed the press to publicize other acts of violence—clinic bombings, fires, and other acts of sabotage—more broadly as well. Not just pro-choice advocates but many conservative Christians too had trouble believing the direct action movement was nonviolent.[46]

In 1997, anti-abortion activist Neal Horsley created a Web site he named the Nuremberg Files. In the late nineties, activists talked less about civil rights and increasingly compared legalized abortion to slavery in America or to the Holocaust in Europe. The site asked visitors to "visualize abortionists on trial" for "their crimes against humanity" and listed the names, addresses, and even phone numbers of over two hundred abortion providers. Interviewed for a documentary on the Army of God, Horsley described how he had become an anti-abortion activist and narrated his own journey from the sixties to the nineties. As a young man, he claimed, he believed that the Vietnam War was wrong. "What will stop this war," he decided, "is if everybody in this country that presently supports it looks around and sees themselves surrounded by freaks and counterculture outlaws. And what made outlaws in those days . . . all you had to do was reach out and pick up a marijuana cigarette and you smoke[d] it. If you inhaled, [you were an] an outlaw. And all of a sudden you begin to manifest behavior characteristics of outlaws." Breaking the law made people into outsiders. "The reason I started selling marijuana was I intended to strew it all over the United States of America so that I could participate in creating the counterculture. It was my strategic input into the process. It was something I could do, and I did it, and they put me in prison for it." Once people became part of the counterculture, he argued, they understood the immoral acts that propped up the center. They could see. "What I am doing today in defense of the unborn children is that same kind of willingness to get down and understand how the system works," Horsley insisted. "And recognize that the only way we can really stop legalized abortion is if we the people can find a state that's willing to secede and then the threat of that secession movement will wake the majority up and make the majority ask themselves are they willing to see the United States of America destroyed in order to perpetuate legalized abortion."[47]

Horsley represented the growing alliance of anti-abortion extremists and the militia movement, a new right-wing coalition of the alienated, promoted at the 1994 Wisconsin meeting. However far from full equality African Americans were in America, most Americans saw the early, southern phase of the civil rights movement as such a great success that even conservatives tried to claim its legacy. This consensus, in turn, made the supporters of white supremacist arguments and members of white supremacist groups like the Klan, people who had supported the oppressive system that civil rights activists were fighting in the sixties, look like the new outsiders. Horsley's use of the secession argument revealed his ties to white supremacist, states'-rights thinking and demonstrated how the anti-abortion cause united Americans whose alienation from contemporary society seeped from a variety of sources. Ironically, the romance of the outsider that had done so much to pull young middle-class whites into support for the civil rights movement in the 1960s worked to rehabilitate right-wing extremists and white supremacists in the 1990s.[48]

Terry lied about his own actions, but he was right when he argued that direct action did not inevitably lead protesters to act violently. Some Catholic activists like Joan Andrews, for example, have participated in regular, nonviolent protests against abortion clinics for years without becoming murderers. Civil disobedience certainly depends on violence to work—acts of protest make visible the violence of the law as well as of the institutions charged with upholding it. Violent acts of protest, on the other hand, can never make this distinction. They cannot dramatize the difference between a particular vision of morality and particular vision of legality. It was not the logic of civil disobedience but the logic of the outsider romance that pushed anti-abortion activists, especially men, into acts of violence.

An oppositional stance only possesses meaning in relation to the beliefs and acts it stands against. Outsiders and rebels are not so much identities as relationships. In the second half of the twentieth century, however, the romance of the outsider has encouraged a view of the world that celebrates individual will, disavows collective white middle-class power, and imagines relatedness at a symbolic rather than a material level. In this kind of thinking, a symbolic, imaginary relationship with a fetus can become so important that it necessitates murder.

Conclusion: The Cost of Rebellion

Through the end of the twentieth century, the romance of the outsider remained a compelling tool of white middle-class self-invention, especially for men. Alienated young middle-class whites continued to fall in love with fantasies of black difference and black culture. For white young people of privilege, hip-hop in the 1980s and early 1990s worked much as rock and roll had in the 1950s. Other alienated middle-class whites followed the path of the Jesus People in rejecting secular popular culture and liberalized religious practices and turning to conservative faiths. Some became Christian evangelicals, but others converted to Orthodox Judaism or fundamentalist forms of Islam. By the beginning of the twenty-first century, these acts of opposition had grown so common that people who performed them barely registered as outsiders at all. White youth who loved black music and white adults who became more religious than their parents ceased to surprise or shock other Americans. What had been forms of rebellion turned into new norms.

A relationship rather than a fixed set of characteristics, the outsider was never an easy persona to live. By the end of the twentieth century, the popularity of outsiders and rebels among white middle-class Americans made finding the edge, the boundary where outside began and inside ceased, increasingly difficult. Christopher McCandless and Timothy Treadwell both went looking for that line, that far-out and always moving place where a white middle-class man could still be an outsider. Both men pushed the rebel romance as far as the fantasy could go, to its logical extreme. In death, they became famous for their rebellion, their lives as outsiders the subjects of books and films and fan Web sites. Like the fictional Holden Caulfield long before them, they ran away from society and ended up as compelling symbols of what they had been avoiding and yet also somehow seeking. At the individual level, McCandless's and Treadwell's stories reveal the dangers inherent in the refusal to recognize the contradictions between the desire for individual autonomy and for grounding and connection.

In August 1992, Christopher McCandless died alone in a 1940s Fairbanks city bus on the edge of Denali National Park. No one who knew his real name had heard from him in over two years. McCandless wanted it that way. He had destroyed his identification and told people who met him that his name was just "Alex." And yet he also wanted to be known. The rigid rules of anonymity and self-reliance he had developed in his years of tramping did not stop him from keeping a record of his adventures. Among the few things he carried into the Alaskan wilderness were a camera, film, and *Walden*. Like Thoreau, McCandless anticipated an audience for his solitary experiment in self-reliance.[1]

Sometime that spring, on a piece of plywood covering a broken window, McCandless scrawled a description of how and why he had come to live in the bus where his body would later be found: "Two years he walks the earth. No phone, no pool, no pets, no cigarettes. Ultimate freedom. An extremist. An aesthetic voyager whose home is the road." There, in Alaska, he was living "the final and greatest adventure," "the climatic battle to kill the false being within and victoriously conclude the spiritual pilgrimage." "No longer to be poisoned by the civilization he flees," he "walks alone upon the land to become lost in the wild." The possessions his siblings later recovered from Alaskan authorities included the documents in which he recorded his experiences: five rolls of exposed film containing many self-portraits and a diary of 113 short entries written across the last two pages of a book on the region's edible plants.

Before hitching to Alaska, McCandless left with a friend and former employer, Wayne Westerberg, a journal filled with descriptions and photographs of his earlier adventures in South Dakota. In it, for example, he described what happened after his car broke down in the Arizona desert in July 1990. He took photos as he buried most of his belongings and burned all his money. And he described his feelings of exhilaration and freedom. That fall, he sent a postcard to Westerberg praising his wandering life and complaining about the money he had earned working for his friend: "My days were more exciting when I was penniless and had to forage for my next meal. I've decided that I'm going to live this life for some time to come. The freedom and simple beauty of it are too good to pass up." Journal entries describe how that winter, McCandless paddled a used aluminum canoe down the Colorado River all the way to the Gulf of California, living on five pounds of rice and whatever he could catch.

By the time McCandless left home in 1990, the simple act of seeking salvation outside human society no longer registered as very oppositional. It too had become a new norm. McCandless used more radical actions, like burning his money and refusing to carry adequate supplies, to challenge himself and secure his rebel status. Postcards and journals revealed McCandless carefully and consciously cultivating a rebel persona. They provided the context that enabled journalists, filmmakers, and the fans who posted bus pilgrimage videos online to fit the smart and resilient young man who starved to death within a few miles of a well-stocked ranger station into the long history of the rebel romance.

The same summer McCandless died in Alaska, another alienated white man spent the first of what would become thirteen consecutive summers living with the wildlife in Katmai National Park in the southwestern part of the state. Timothy Treadwell, too, traveled to what he imagined as the edge to heal and reinvent himself. While McCandless refused to plan for the basic necessities of human survival, Treadwell rejected the boundary between humans and wild animals. Both men crafted rebel personas by ignoring the basic rules of wilderness survival.[2]

Treadwell did not share McCandless's rigid code of anonymity. He paid for his "expeditions," as he called his adventures, with the money from his 1997 memoir, *Among the Grizzlies*, and public appearances. Like McCandless, he changed his name—he was born Timothy Dexter—and did not seem to need much contact with people. He spent the majority of his time in Alaska alone with the bears. He also recorded his experiences and his carefully constructed rebel persona in journals and, for his last five years, on a digital video camera. He too anticipated an audience for the story of a life lived beyond human society.[3]

His transformation began, in his telling, on his first trip to Alaska, when he had a life-changing encounter with a bear. In one version, he fell into a river and got caught in some rapids, and a bear, also trapped, showed him the path to shore. In another version, a nearby bear unexpectedly charged him from the brush. They locked eyes. "The encounter was like looking into a mirror," Treadwell remembered. "I gazed into the face of a kindred soul, a being that was potentially lethal, but in reality was just as frightened as I was." Whatever actually happened, for Treadwell it was a kind of conversion experience. In one of his last few summers, he filmed himself describing this transformation. He had been a "big drinker," but his encounter with the bears set him on a different path: "I promised the bears. If I would look after them, would they please help me be a better person. They've become so inspirational, and the foxes too." The bears saved him, he claimed, by giving him a life.

Treadwell carried his empathy for the bears to the extreme. He refused to use electric bear fences around his camp or carry pepper spray because he believed these precautions were not "fair to the bears." He practiced bear moves and sounds and ate raw fresh fish like a bear. Some of the people he encountered in the park claim he acted like a bear, snorting and growling at them. Closely following the bears through two habitats he called "Big Green" and the "Grizzly Maze," Treadwell filmed himself singing to them, dancing for them, and even petting some of them. He gave the giant predators the kind of names kids would give their teddy bears: Cupcake, Booble, and Ms. Goodbear. He even choked up over a pile of "poop" still warm from the body of Wendy, the mother of his favorite bear, Downey. "Everything about them is perfect," he tells his camera, as he cups his hands lovingly around the steaming pile of excrement. In response to a friend who repeatedly warned him about his reckless behavior, he replied, "God forbid, if a bear takes me, let him go." Leaving for the bush every year, he always grinned as he told another friend, "If I don't come back, this is what I love doing."[4]

Alternately goofy, childlike, and vain, Treadwell in his videos speaks in a singsong, little-boy voice and shifts between reportage and confession. Sometimes he appears melodramatic and sentimental. He cries on camera, seemingly overcome by what he calls his "love" for these animals. "Downey is seven years old, and I've known her since she was a spring pup, like she was my own sister," he says, narrating as he shoots footage of a bear walking around in the grass behind him. "And we've been here together." He looks at the bear and continues, "You are the most beautiful thing." Then he turns back to face the camera and says, crying, "And I will care for her. I will live for her. I will die for her." In another shot, he pets one of the foxes that he encourages to share his campsite. "I love you. I love you so much," he says. "Thank you for being my friend." Then he turns his face away from his camera, overcome with emotion. Treadwell claimed to know "the language of the bear." He repeatedly said, "I am one of them." In his rants against the National Park Service, he chants, "Animals rule." In Treadwell's footage, the bears keep their side of the bargain, though he never actually has to protect them since he never meets any poachers, at least when he has his camera. He in turn is reborn: "I am so wild, so free, so like a child with these animals."

Over his summers in Alaska, Treadwell came to identify with bears so completely that he transformed the grizzlies into fantastical hybrid creatures, made up mostly out of his projections and wildly anthropomorphic interpretations of their behavior. He understood his bears' thoughts and behavior, which he explained frequently in his film footage. He could live with them, he argued, because he alone loved them enough to understand them and to become them. In his last letter to ecologist Marnie Gaede, he wrote, "I have to mutually mutate into a wild animal to handle the life I live out here." The grizzlies played these fantasy bear roles. Connecting with these bear fictions, Treadwell could play his dream roles too. He could forget he was human.

The bears did not forget. As Treadwell and Amie Huguenard, a girlfriend who had spent parts of the last three summers with him and the bears, were breaking down their camp—the pilot was scheduled to pick them up midday— an older male bear attacked Treadwell just outside the tent. Amazingly, either Treadwell or Huguenard somehow turned on the already capped and packed video camera. It recorded audio for six minutes as the bear mauled and killed them both. Helicopter pilot Sam Egli, hired to help clean up the pillaged camp-site and transport the bodies and gear, still had trouble describing the scene long after the event. Park rangers had to kill the bear to get into the camp. In its stomach, they found human remains: "We hauled four garbage bags of people out of that bear." Treadwell, in his view, "was acting like he was working with people wearing bear costumes out there, instead of wild animals."

Like McCandless, Treadwell made the choice to try to live on the margins. He carried the romance of the outsider as far as it would go.

At these extremes, the romance of the outsider fails to work as a way of life. While psychological issues—depression, personality disorders, and addic-tions—clearly play a role in fueling the oppositional behaviors of individuals, rebellion has a social and cultural dimension as well. McCandless and Treadwell did not invent the personas in which they acted out their alienation. They did not invent the lens through which journalists and filmmakers inter-preted their lives. And they did not invent the context in which many readers and viewers continue to be fascinated by their stories.

The romance of the outsider fails here too, at the level of collective fantasy. It fails, paradoxically, because for some people it works only too well. The lure of the outsider romance is that it enables white middle-class Americans to experience at the imaginary level the social and historical connections that contemporary life erodes at the material level. Fantasies about the "authen-ticity" of blacks—whether a white middle-class American identifies with civil rights workers, folk singers, or hip-hop stars—derail the hard task of working with actual African Americans to build equality. Fantasies about the corrup-tion of money and the morality of the poor deflect attention from the hard work of creating a system of economic justice. Fantasies about the purity and morality of religious codes and practices at odds with the modern world and particularly with more equitable gender relations block serious discussion of the issues facing contemporary families.[5]

The romance of the outsider works because it denies at the imaginary level the contradictions between the human fantasy of absolute individual autonomy and the human need for grounding in historical and contemporary social connections. It works because it enables Americans with political and economic power to disavow that power. The time has come to make a new romance.

Notes

Introduction

1. Laslo Benedek, *The Wild One* (Columbia Pictures, 1953); Jack Kerouac, *On the Road* (1957; New York: Penguin, 2002), 179; Norman Mailer, "The White Negro," (1957), in *Advertisement for Myself* (New York: Berkeley Publishing, 1966), 311–31, quote, 314; Tom Hayden, *Reunion: A Memoir* (New York: Random House, 1988), 40.
2. The John Cohen quote is in Tom Davenport and Barry Dornfeld, *Remembering the High Lonesome* (2003). The film and a transcript of the film are at http://www.folkstreams.net. Robert Shelton, *The Face of Folk Music* (New York: Citadel Press, 1968), 41. Larry Cohn's 1965 quote about Son House is in Lawrence Cohn, *Nothing but the Blues: The Music and the Musicians* (New York: Abbeville Press, 1993), 350. The Janis Joplin quote is in David Dalton, *Piece of My Heart: A Portrait of Janis Joplin* (New York: Da Capo, 1991), 38.
3. There is a large philosophical and theoretical literature on the meaning of authenticity, including Lionel Trilling, *Sincerity and Authenticity* (Cambridge, Mass.: Harvard University Press, 1972); Charles Taylor, *The Ethics of Authenticity* (Cambridge, Mass.: Harvard University Press, 1991); and Anthony Appiah, *The Ethics of Identity* (Princeton, N.J.: Princeton University Press, 2005). American historians, for the most part, have failed to historicize the term and think critically about its rapidly changing meanings in the postwar period. For an otherwise excellent history focused on the development of the New Left at the University of Texas at Austin, see Doug Rossinow, *The Politics of Authenticity: Liberalism, Christianity, and the New Left in America* (New York: Columbia University Press, 1998). For an intriguing and helpful sociological investigation, see David Grazian, *Blue Chicago: The Search for Authenticity in Urban Blues Clubs* (Chicago: University of Chicago Press, 2003). Even business writers have taken up the topic: James Gilmore and Joseph Pine, *Authenticity: What Consumers Really Want* (Cambridge, Mass.: Harvard Business School Press, 2007). For a critique of the idea of community, see Miranda Joseph, *Against the Romance of Community* (Minneapolis: University of Minnesota Press, 2002).

4. Isaiah Berlin, *The Roots of Romanticism* (Princeton, N.J.: Princeton University Press, 1999); Eric Lott, *Love and Theft: Blackface Minstrelsy and the American Working Class* (New York: Oxford University Press, 1993); W. T. Lhamon Jr., *Raising Cain: Blackface Performance from Jim Crow to Hip Hop* (Cambridge, Mass.: Harvard University Press, 1998).

5. Jack D. Flam and Miriam Deutch, eds., *Primitivism and Twentieth-Century Art: A Documentary History* (Berkeley: University of California Press, 2003); Jerrold Seigel, *Bohemian Paris: Culture, Politics, and the Boundaries of Bourgeois Life, 1830–1930* (New York: Viking, 1986); Erika Bsumek, *Indian-Made: Navajo Culture in the Marketplace, 1868–1940* (Lawrence: University Press of Kansas, 2008); David E. Whisnant, *All That Is Native and Fine: The Politics of Culture in an American Region* (Chapel Hill: University of North Carolina Press, 1983); Michael Denning, *The Cultural Front: The Laboring of Culture in the Twentieth Century* (New York: Verso, 1988).

6. Wini Breines, *Community and Organization in the New Left, 1962–1968: The Great Refusal* (New York: Praeger, 1982); Breines, *Young, White, and Miserable: Growing Up Female in the Fifties* (Chicago: University of Chicago Press, 1992); George Lipsitz, *Time Passages: Collective Memory and American Popular Culture* (Minneapolis: University of Minnesota Press, 1990); Hayden, *Reunion*; Constance Curry et al., *Deep in Our Hearts: Nine White Women in the Civil Rights Movement* (Athens: University of Georgia Press, 2000); Bill Ayers, *Fugitive Days: A Memoir* (Boston: Beacon, 2001).

7. Leerom Medovoi, *Rebels: Youth and the Cold War Origins of Identity* (Durham, N.C.: Duke University Press, 2005); Thomas Frank, *The Conquest of Cool: Business Culture, Counterculture, and the Rise of Hip Consumerism* (Chicago: University of Chicago Press, 1997); Sean McCann and Michael Szalay, "Paul Potter and the Cultural Turn," 209–20, and "Do You Believe in Magic? Literary Thinking After the New Left," 435–68, which appeared in *Yale Journal of Criticism* 18:2 (Fall 2005), a special issue on "Countercultural Capital," edited by McCann and Szalay.

Chapter 1: Lost Children of Plenty

1. "Never Before, So Much for So Few: The Luckiest Generation," *Life*, January 4, 1954, 27. On the history of the idea of adolescence, see David Bakan, "Adolescence in America: From Idea to Social Fact," *Daedalus* 100:4 (Fall 1971): 979–95; Jon Savage, *Teenage: The Creation of Youth Culture* (New York: Viking, 2007); and G. Stanley Hall, *Adolescence* (New York: Appleton, 1904). Throughout this chapter, I have drawn on James Gilbert, *A Cycle of Outrage: America's Reaction to the Juvenile Delinquent in the 1950s* (New York: Oxford University Press, 1988).

J. D. Salinger, *The Catcher in the Rye* (New York: Bantam, 1951), 52. See also *Franny and Zooey* (Boston: Little, Brown, 1961), *Raise High the Roofbeam, Carpenters, and Seymour, an Introduction* (Boston: Little, Brown, 1963), and *Nine Stories* (New York: New American Library, 1954). I drew on the following collections of material on Salinger and his work in writing this chapter:

Henry Anatole Grunwald, *Salinger: A Critical and Personal Portrait* (New York: Giant Cardinal, 1963); William Belcher and James W. Lee, *J. D. Salinger and the Critics* (Belmont, Calif.: Wadsworth Publishing, 1962); Marvin Laser and Norman Fruman, eds., *Studies in J. D. Salinger* (New York: Odyssey Press, 1963); Malcolm M. Marsden, *if you really want to know: A* Catcher *Casebook* (Chicago: Scott, Foresman, 1963); Harold Bloom, ed., *J. D. Salinger's The Catcher in the Rye* (Philadelphia: Chelsea House, 2000); Bloom, ed., *Modern Critical Views on J. D. Salinger* (New York: Chelsea House, 1987); Bloom, ed., *Holden Caulfield* (New York: Chelsea House, 1990); Jack Salzman, *New Essays on The Catcher in the Rye* (New York: Cambridge University Press, 1991); Peter Lang, ed., *The Catcher in the Rye: New Essays* (New York: Peter Lang, 2002); Eberhard Alsen, *A Reader's Guide to J. D. Salinger* (Westport, Conn.: Greenwood Press, 2002); Joel Salzberg, *Critical Essays on Salinger's* The Catcher in the Rye (Boston: G. K. Hall, 1990); Ian Hamilton, *In Search of J. D. Salinger* (New York: Random House, 1988); Joyce Maynard, *At Home in the World* (New York: Picador, 1998); and Stephen Whitfield, "Cherished and Cursed: Toward a Social History of *The Catcher in the Rye*," *New England Quarterly* 70:4 (December 1997): 567–600.

2. Salinger, *Catcher*, 1.

3. Salinger, *Catcher*, 213, 214.

4. *Catcher* has been frequently compared to Mark Twain's *The Adventures of Huckleberry Finn* (1884). For the first comparison, see Harvey Breit, "Reader's Choice," *Atlantic Monthly*, August 1951, 82. See also Alfred Kazin, "J. D. Salinger: 'Everybody's Favorite,'" *Atlantic Monthly*, August 1961, 27–31.

5. On paperback sales figures, see Robert Gutwillig, "Everybody's Caught 'The Catcher in the Rye,'" *New York Times Book Review*, January 15, 1961, 38. The novel has now sold more than 65 million copies worldwide.

6. Gilbert, *Cycle of Outrage*.

7. Grace Hechinger and Fred Hechinger, "In the Time It Takes You to Read These Lines the American Teenager Will Have Spent $2,378.22," *Esquire*, July 1965, 65, 68, 113. On teenagers, especially girls, and their emergence as a separate marketing niche, see Susan Douglas, *Where the Girls Are: Growing Up Female with the Mass Media* (New York: Times Books, 1995).

8. Gilbert, *Cycle of Outrage*; Leerom Medovoi, *Rebels: Youth and the Cold War Origins of Identity* (Durham, N.C.: Duke University Press, 2005); Timothy Melley, *Empire of Conspiracy: The Culture of Paranoia in Postwar America* (Ithaca, N.Y.: Cornell University Press, 1999).

9. On *Catcher* and the cold war, see Alan Nadel, *Containment Culture: American Narratives, Postmodernism, and the Atomic Age* (Durham, N.C.: Duke University Press, 1995), 71–89; and Medovoi, *Rebels*, 53–90.

10. C. Wright Mills, New York City, to Francis and Charles Mills [his parents], December 18, 1946; Mills, Chicago, to William Muller, undated (1949), in C. Wright Mills, *Letters and Autobiographical Writings*, ed. Kathryn Mills with Pamela Mills (Berkeley: University of California Press, 2000), 101, 136; and Mills, *White Collar* (New York: Oxford University Press, 1951), 327.

11. Salinger, *Catcher*, 172. Holden's problem here prefigures Paul Goodman, *Growing Up Absurd* (1960). Literary critics disagree about the degree to which Salinger shares Holden's romantic alienation, whether he too romanticizes rebellion or instead shows the reader that it is a false stance, an inability to see the people in other than one-dimensional terms. See the collections of criticism cited above.

12. Salinger, *Catcher*, 9, 13, 17, 26, 59, 77, 84.

13. Salinger, *Catcher*, 52, 16.

14. Salinger, *Catcher*, 61, 61, 154.

15. Salinger, *Catcher*, 174, 180, 189, 191–92, 194–95.

16. Salinger, *Catcher*, 99, 18, 141, 62, 63, 9.

17. Salinger, *Catcher*, 8.

18. Salinger, *Catcher*, 3, 43, 46, 103, 92, 93, 76, 73.

19. Salinger, *Catcher*, 170.

20. Salinger, *Catcher*, 173. Critics disagree about whether this romanticism is Holden's alone or also Salinger's, whether there is distance between the narrator and the author. For my purposes, it does not matter whether the romanticism is Holden's alone, and Salinger is critiquing it, or whether Salinger shares Holden's romanticism. Many readers have certainly confused Holden and Salinger's feelings. My point is that many readers have shared or adopted Holden's romanticism, that they see themselves in him.

21. Salinger, *Catcher*, 1, 60, 81–82, 153–54, quote, 198.

22. Salinger, *Catcher*, 104.

23. Salinger, *Catcher*, 162–63. Salinger does name a movie: *The Doctor*, about a physician turned mercy killer that Phoebe sees at the Lister Foundation. But in the novel, the film is a noncommercial documentary, used to set up a contrast with Holden's own desire to catch the children, to save them from the abyss, from adulthood, from even the adults. The Lister Foundation may refer to the Lister Institute in the UK, which is a medical research charity founded in 1891. I cannot find any reference to a film fitting Salinger's description called *The Doctor*.

24. Clement Greenberg, "Avant-Garde and Kitsch" (1939), in *Art and Culture* (Boston: Beacon Press, 1961), 3–21; Dwight Macdonald, "Masscult and Midcult" (1960), in *Against the American Grain* (New York: Vintage, 1962), 3–79; Theodor Adorno and Max Horkheimer, *Dialectic of Enlightenment*, trans. John Cumming (1947; New York: Verso, 1997); Adorno, "Culture Industry Reconsidered," trans. Anson G. Rabinbach, *New German Critique* 6 (1975): 12–19.

25. Salinger, *Catcher*, quotes, 21, 103–4, 154–55.

26. Salinger, *Catcher*, quotes, 29, 2; see also 104, 116.

27. Bernard S. Oldsey, "The Movies in the Rye," *College English* 23 (December 1961): 209–15. Mervyn LeRoy's *Random Harvest* (Metro-Goldwyn-Mayer, 1942) was nominated for seven Oscars in 1943, including Best Picture and Best Director.

28. Salinger, *Catcher*, 139–41.

29. Salinger, *Catcher*, 205.

30. Salinger, *Catcher*, 206–7, 160, 104. Salinger would not sell the movie rights to *Catcher*, and thus Holden's life literally did not become a film.

31. Sources on Romanticism include Isaiah Berlin, "The Romantics and Their Roots," *Times Literary Supplement*, February 19, 1999; Berlin, *The Roots of Romanticism* (Princeton, N.J.: Princeton University Press, 1999); Stephen Gill, *William Wordsworth: A Life* (New York: Oxford University Press, 1989); Kenneth R. Johnston, *The Hidden Wordsworth: Poet, Lover, Rebel, Spy* (New York: Norton, 1999); Richard Holmes, *Coleridge: Early Visions, 1771–1804* (New York: Pantheon, 1989); Holmes, *Coleridge: Darker Reflections, 1804–1834* (New York: Pantheon, 2000); and Andrew Motion, *Keats* (London: Faber and Faber, 2003). Johann Wolfgang von Goethe, *The Sorrows of Young Werther* (1774) was a powerful early text in the history of Romanticism. On the importance of German writers in this literary history, see Frederick C. Beiser, *The Romantic Imperative: The Concept of Early German Romanticism* (Cambridge, Mass.: Harvard University Press, 2003); and Oskar F. Walzel, *German Romanticism* (New York: F. Ungar, 1965).

32. William Wordsworth and Samuel Taylor Coleridge, Advertisement for the first edition of *Lyrical Ballads* (1798), in *Longman Anthology of British Literature: The Romantics and Their Contemporaries*, ed. David Damrosch, Peter J. Manning, and Susan J. Wolfson (New York: Longman, 1999), 332; Andrew Jackson George, ed., *The Complete Poetical Works of William Wordsworth* (Boston: Houghton Mifflin, 1904), 791.

33. William Wordsworth, *The Prelude*, in George, *Complete Poetical Works of William Wordsworth*, 137; John Keats, letter to Benjamin Bailey, November 22, 1817, in *The Letters of John Keats*, ed. H. Buxton Forman (London: Reeves and Turner, 1895), 51–55, quote, 52.

34. Salinger, *Catcher*, 154.

35. Jerrold Seigel, *Bohemian Paris: Culture, Politics, and the Boundaries of Bourgeois Life, 1830–1930* (New York: Viking, 1986), Murger quote, 3–4. On American bohemians, see Albert Parry, *Garrets and Pretenders: A History of Bohemianism in America* (1933; rev. ed., New York: Dover, 1960); Emily Hahn, *Romantic Rebels: An Informal History of Bohemianism in America* (Boston: Houghton Mifflin, 1967); Rick Beard and Leslie Cohen Berlowitz, *Greenwich Village: Culture and Counterculture* (New Brunswick, N.J.: Rutgers University Press for the Museum of the City of New York, 1993); Christine Stansell, *American Moderns: Bohemian New York and the Creation of a New Century* (New York: Metropolitan Books, 2000); and Ann Douglas, *Terrible Honesty: Mongrel Manhattan in the Twenties* (New York: Farrar, Straus, and Giroux, 1995).

36. Salinger, *Catcher*, 136, 142, 143.

37. Salinger, *Catcher*, 189.

38. On Marx's view of alienation, see Daniel Bell, "The 'Rediscovery' of Alienation," *Journal of Philosophy* 56:24 (November 19, 1959): 933–52; and Istvan Meszaros, *Marx's Theory of Alienation* (London: Merlin, 1970). Salinger, *Catcher*, 108. My point here is not that Holden's view is a correct assessment of class difference but that it is his view. Salinger weaves this idea through much of his fiction, and it is increasingly on display across mid-century American culture. On the Beats, see

John Tytell, *Naked Angels: The Lives and Literature of the Beat Generation* (New York: McGraw-Hill, 1976), and chapter 2.

39. Albert Camus, *The Rebel* (New York: Knopf, 1954), quote, 19. See also Jean-Paul Sartre, *Existentialism and Human Emotions* (1946; New York: Philosophical Library, 1957); *Existentialism* (New York: Philosophical Library, 1947); and Sartre, *Being and Nothingness: An Essay on Phenomenological Ontology* (New York: Philosophical Library, 1956). On the impact of existentialism on postwar America, see Ann Fulton, *Existentialism in America, 1945–1963* (Evanston, Ill.: Northwestern University Press, 1999); and George Cotkin, *Existential America* (Baltimore: Johns Hopkins University Press, 2003).

40. Salinger, *Catcher*, 170.

41. James Stern, "Aw, the World's a Crumby Place," *New York Times Book Review*, July 15, 1951, 5; T. Morris Longstreth, "Review of *The Catcher in the Rye*," *Christian Science Monitor*, July 19, 1951, 7; Ernest Jones, "A Case History of Us All," *Nation*, September 1, 1951, 176. Other reviews that stress young people's possible identification with Holden include Paul Engle, "Honest Tale of Distraught Adolescent," *Chicago Sunday Times Magazine of Books*, July 15, 1951, 3; and Virgilia Peterson, "Three Days in the Bewildering World of an Adolescent," *New York Herald Tribune Book Review*, July 15, 1951, 3.

42. Clifton Fadiman, writing for the Book-of-the-Month Club July report, as quoted in Laser and Fruman, *Studies in J. D. Salinger*, 72; Nash K. Burger, "A Book of the Times," *New York Times*, July 16, 1951, 32; Gutwillig, "Everybody's Caught *The Catcher*," 39; Granville Hicks, "The Search for Wisdom," in Grunwald, *Salinger: A Critical and Personal Portrait*, 191–94, quote, 192; Alfred Kazin, "Everybody's Favorite." Other positive reviews appeared in *Time*, *Newsweek*, and the *Saturday Review*.

43. Marsden, *A Catcher Casebook*; Kip Kotzen and Thomas Beller, *With Love and Squalor: Fourteen Writers Respond to the Work of J. D. Salinger* (New York: Broadway Books, 2001); Chris Kubica and Will Hochman, *Letters to J. D. Salinger* (Madison: University of Wisconsin Press, 2002); "Letters to J. D. Salinger," http://www.jdsalinger.com, accessed March 29, 2010.

44. Salinger, *Catcher*, 67, 156. The novel's frame also makes the audience—the readers—into Holden's analysts, suggesting the ways self-expression as art and self-expression as therapy become intertwined in the postwar era.

45. On the impact of the cold war on American culture, see Paul Boyer, *By the Bomb's Early Light: American Thought and Culture at the Dawn of the Atomic Age* (New York: Pantheon Books, 1985); Tom Engelhardt, *The End of Victory Culture: Cold War America and the Disillusioning of a Generation* (New York: Basic Books, 1994); Joel Foreman, ed., *The Other Fifties: Interrogating Midcentury American Icons* (Urbana: University of Illinois Press, 1997); Elaine Tyler May, *Homeward Bound: American Families in the Cold War Era* (New York: Basic Books, 1988); Medovoi, *Rebels*; and Stephen J. Whitfield, *The Culture of the Cold War* (Baltimore: Johns Hopkins University Press, 1991). On the social problem literature that explores arguments about mass culture's destruction of individualism, see Wilfred McClay, *The Masterless: Self and Society in Modern America* (Chapel Hill: University of North Carolina Press, 1994), 226–75.

46. Dwight Macdonald, "A Theory of Popular Culture," *Politics*, February 1944, 20–23; Macdonald, "A Theory of Mass Culture" (1953), in *Mass Culture*, ed. Bernard Rosenberg and David Manning White (Glencoe, Ill.: Free Press, 1957), 59–80; Macdonald, "Masscult and Midcult"; Greenberg, "Avant-Garde and Kitsch." See also Andrew Jamison and Ron Eyerman, *Seeds of the Sixties* (Berkeley: University of California Press, 1994), 30–63.

47. John Fiske, *Understanding Popular Culture* (New York: Routledge, 1991), 168.

48. José Ortega y Gasset, *The Revolt of the Masses* (1930; New York: New American Library, 1950), 79; Macdonald, "Theory of Popular Culture," Greenberg, "Avant-Garde and Kitsch"; Adorno and Horkheimer, *Dialectic*, esp. "The Culture Industry as Mass Deception," 120–67, quote, 133; James Burnham, a contributor to "Our Country and Our Culture," special issue of *Partisan Review* 19 (May–June 1952): 284–326, quote, 290.

49. Alan Wald, *The New York Intellectuals: The Rise and Decline of the Anti-Stalinist Left from the 1930 to the 1960s* (Chapel Hill: University of North Carolina Press, 1987); Neil Jumonville, *Critical Crossings: The New York Intellectuals in Postwar America* (Berkeley: University of California Press, 1991).

50. "Our Country and Our Culture: A Symposium," special issue of *Partisan Review* 19 (May–June 1952): 284–326, quote, 284.

51. David Riesman, Nathan Glazer, and Rebel Denney, *The Lonely Crowd: A Case Study in the Changing American Character* (New Haven, Conn.: Yale University Press, 1950), 126, 3–30; "David Riesman: Social Scientist," *Time*, September 27, 1954; Sloan Wilson, *The Man in the Gray Flannel Suit* (New York: Simon and Schuster, 1955); William Whyte, *The Organization Man* (1956; Philadelphia: University of Pennsylvania Press, 2002), 280; Timothy Melley, *Empire of Conspiracy: The Culture of Paranoia in Postwar America* (Ithaca, N.Y.: Cornell University Press, 1999). Melley calls cold-war-era anxiety "agency panic."

52. Ayn Rand published *The Fountainhead* in 1944, but it began to sell well after the war. *Atlas Shrugged* was published in 1957. On Rand, see Robert Mayhew, *Essays on Ayn Rand's* The Fountainhead (Lanham, Md.: Lexington Books, 2007); Mimi Riesel Gladstein, *The New Ayn Rand Companion* (Westport, Conn.: Greenwood Press, 1999); and Jennifer Burns, *Goddess of the Market: Ayn Rand and the American Right* (New York: Oxford University Press, 2009).

53. "The New American Domesticated Male: A Boon to the Household and a Boom to Industry," *Life*, January 4, 154, 42–43; Barbara Ehrenrich, *The Hearts of Men: American Dreams and the Flight from Commitment* (New York: Anchor, 1983).

54. Macdonald, "Masscult and Midcult," 21; Leslie Fiedler, a contributor to "Our Country and Our Culture," quote, 297. For an analysis of these developments that stresses the ideological function of the rebel figure in the cold war contest to win the loyalty of third world nations, see Medovoi, *Rebels*.

55. Wald, *New York Intellectuals*; Jumonville, *Critical Crossings*. For a study of a segment of early twentieth-century mass culture, see Kathy Peiss, *Cheap Amusements: Working Women and Leisure in Turn-of-the-Century New York* (Philadelphia: Temple University Press, 1986).

56. Robert Lindner, *Rebel Without a Cause: The Hypno-Analysis of a Criminal Psychopath* (New York: Grune and Stratton, 1944); Lindner with James Fuller,

Rebel Without a Cause: A Play in Three Acts (Chicago: Dramatic Publishing, 1958); "Raise Your Child to be a Rebel," McCall's, February 1956, 102, 104; "Rebels or Psychopaths?" Time, December 6, 1954; "Letters," Time, December 13, 1954.

57. "Rebels or Psychopaths;" "Letters;" and "Raise Your Child to be a Rebel." See also Kathleen Doyle, "A Bill of Rights for Teenagers," Parents' Magazine, April 1948, 20, 82–86.

58. Lynn Spigel, Make Room for TV: Television and the Family Ideal in Postwar America (Chicago: University of Chicago Press, 1992); Susan Douglas, Where the Girls Are: Growing Up Female with the Mass Media (New York: Random House, 1995). "Brief Holiday" appeared in season 3 and first aired on January 16, 1957.

59. "Jackson Pollock: Is He the Greatest Living Painter in the United States?" Life, August 8, 1949. On the "cool" image of bebop musicians, see Lewis MacAdams, The Birth of Cool: Beat, Bebop, and the American Avant-Garde (New York: Free Press, 2001); on Playboy, see Ehrenreich, Hearts of Men.

60. Wini Breines, Young, White, and Miserable: Growing Up Female in the Fifties (Chicago: University of Chicago Press, 1992); Breines, "The 'Other' Fifties: Beats and Bad Girls," in Not June Cleaver: Women and Gender in Postwar America, 1945–1960, ed. Joanne Meyerowitz, 382–408 (Philadelphia: Temple University Press, 1994); Breines, "Postwar White Girls' Dark Others," in Foreman, The Other Fifties, 53–82; May, Homeward Bound.

61. J. D. Salinger, Franny and Zooey (Boston: Little, Brown, 1961); Herman Wouk, Marjorie Morningstar (New York: Doubleday, 1955); Richard Yates, Revolutionary Road (New York: Boston: Little, Brown, 1961).

62. Medovoi, Rebels, 265–316; Rachel Devlin, "Female Juvenile Deliquency and the Problem of Sexual Authority in America, 1945–1965," Yale Journal of Law and the Humanties (Winter 1997): 147–82; Breines, "Postwar White Girls' Dark Others."

63. Sylvia Plath, Letters Home: Correspondence, 1950–1963, ed. Aurelia Schober Plath (New York: Harper and Row, 1975), 144; Plath, The Bell Jar (1963; New York: Harper Perennial, 2000), 3, 87; Anne Stevenson, Bitter Flame: A Life of Sylvia Plath (New York: Mariner Books, 1998).

64. Diane Di Prima, Memoirs of a Beatnik (1969; rpt. New York: Penguin, 1998), 24, 72, 108. Not until she published her actual memoir over thirty years later did she describe the emotional pain, the betrayals, and the failed couplings of this period in her life. See Di Prima, My Life as a Woman (New York: Penguin, 2002); Brenda Knight, Women of the Beat Generation: The Writers, Artists, and Muses at the Heart of a Revolution (Berkeley: Conari Press, 1996); Ronna C. Johnson and Nancy M. Grace, eds., Girls Who Wore Black: Women Writing the Beat Genera- tion (New Brunswick, N.J.: Rutgers University Press, 2002); and Johnson and Grace, Breaking the Rule of Cool: Interviewing and Reading Women Beat Writers (Jackson: University Press of Mississippi, 2004).

65. Joyce Johnson, Minor Characters: A Young Woman's Coming of Age in the Beat Orbit of Jack Kerouac (New York: Houghton Mifflin, 1983); Knight, Women and the Beat Generation.

66. Johnson, Minor Characters, 29–30, 261–62; Hettie Jones, How I Became Hettie Jones (New York: Dutton, 1990), 81.

67. Breines, *Young, White, and Miserable*; Knight, *Women and the Beat Generation*; Kubica and Hochman, *Letters to J. D. Salinger*; "Letters to J. D. Salinger," http://www.jdsalinger.com; Janice Radway, *Reading the Romance: Women, Patriarchy, and Popular Culture* (Chapel Hill: University of North Carolina Press, 1984); David Dalton, *Piece of My Heart: The Life, Times, and Legend of Janis Joplin* (New York: St. Martin's Press, 1985), 147, 162.

68. Knight, *Women and the Beat Generation*; Grace and Johnson, *Breaking the Rule of Cool*; Stevenson, *Bitter Flame*; Diane Wood Middlebrook, *Anne Sexton: A Biography* (New York: Vintage, 1992).

69. Ginsberg, "Howl" (1955–56), online at http://www.poetryfoundation.org/archive/poem.html?id=179381, accessed June 28, 2010. See also Ginsberg, *Collected Poems of Allen Ginsberg* (New York: Harper, 2007); Tytell, *Naked Angels*; and Ann Charters, *The Beats: Literary Bohemians in Postwar America* (New York: Gale, 1983).

Chapter 2: Rebel Music

1. Brian Ward, *Just My Soul Responding: Rhythm and Blues, Black Consciousness, and Race Relations* (Berkeley: University of California Press, 1998), 1–20; Peter Guralnick, *Last Train to Memphis: The Rise of Elvis Presley* (New York: Little, Brown, 1994); Bruce Pegg, *Brown-Eyed Handsome Man: The Life and Hard Times of Chuck Berry* (New York: Routledge, 2002); Leerom Medovoi, *Rebels: Youth and the Cold War Origins of Identity* (Durham, N.C.: Duke University Press, 2005).

2. George Lipsitz, "Against the Wind: Dialogic Aspects of Rock and Roll," in *Time Passages: Collective Memory and American Popular Culture* (Minneapolis: University of Minnesota Press, 1990), 99–132; Ward, *Just My Soul*; Meovoi, *Rebels*.

3. I take the phrase "acting black" from Eric Lott, *Love and Theft: Blackface Minstrelsy and the American Working Class* (New York: Oxford University Press, 1993), 29: "Acting black: a whole social world of irony, violence, negotiations, and learning is contained in that phrase." Other minstrelsy sources include Ralph Ellison, "Change the Yoke and Slip the Joke" (1958), in *Shadow and Act* (New York: Random House, 1964), 45–59; Robert Toll, *Blacking Up: The Minstrel Show and Nineteenth-Century America* (New York: Oxford University Press, 1974); Hans Nathan, *Dan Emmett and the Rise of Early Negro Minstrelsy* (Norman: University of Oklahoma Press, 1962); Alexander Saxton, *The Rise and Fall of the White Republic: Class Politics and Mass Culture in Nineteenth-Century America* (New York: Verso, 1990); David Roediger, *The Wages of Whiteness: Race and the Making of the American Working Class* (New York: Verso, 1991); and W. T. Lhamon, *Raising Cain: Blackface Performance from Jim Crow to Hip Hop* (Cambridge, Mass.: Harvard University Press, 1998).

4. Ann Douglas, *Terrible Honesty: Mongrel Manhattan in the 1920s* (New York: Farrar, Straus, and Giroux, 1995); Ellison, "Change the Joke;" Toll, *Blacking Up*.

5. Lhamon, *Raising Cain*; Robert Cantwell, *Bluegrass Breakdown: The Making of the Old Southern Sound* (Urbana: University of Illinois Press, 1984); Malone, *Country*

Music U.S.A. (Austin: University of Texas Press, 1968); *Singing Cowboys and Musical Mountaineers: Southern Culture and the Roots of Country Music* (Athens: University of Georgia Press, 1993); Karl Hagstrom Miller, *Segregating Sound: Inventing Folk and Pop Music in the Age of Jim Crow* (Durham, N.C.: Duke University Press, 2010).

6. Constance Rourke, *American Humor: A Study of the National Character* (1931; New York: New York Review of Books, 2004), 85; Lott, *Love and Theft*, 18; Frederick Douglass writing in *North Star* (June 29, 1849), online at http://utc.iath.virginia.edu/minstrel/miar03at.html.

7. Lhamon, *Raising Cain*, 160.

8. Lott, *Love and Theft*; Roediger, *Wages of Whiteness*; Saxton, *Rise and Fall*.

9. Lhamon, *Raising Cain*, 144; Annemarie Bean, James V. Hatch, and Brooks McNamara, eds., *Inside the Minstrel Mask: Readings in Nineteenth-Century Blackface Minstrelsy* (Hanover, N.H.: Wesleyan University Press, 1996).

10. On the plantation pastoral, see Grace Elizabeth Hale, *Making Whiteness: The Culture of Segregation in the South, 1890–1940* (New York: Vintage, 1999). On the Second Middle Passage, see Ira Berlin, *Generations of Captivity: A History of African American Slaves* (Cambridge, Mass.: Harvard University Press, 2003).

11. Tim Brooks, *Lost Sounds: Blacks and the Birth of the Recording Industry, 1890–1919* (Urbana: University of Illinois Press, 2004); *Lost Sounds: Blacks and the Birth of the Recording Industry, 1891–1922*, notes by Tim Brooks and David Giovannoni (Archeophone Records, 2005); Camille F. Forbes, *Introducing Bert Williams: Burnt Cork, Broadway, and the Story of America's First Black Star* (New York: Basic Civitas, 2008); Douglas, *Terrible Honesty*.

12. Brooks, *Lost Sounds*; Lhamon, *Raising Cain*; Miller, *Segregating Sound*; Lott, *Love and Theft*; Hale, *Making Whiteness*; Roediger, *Wages of Whiteness*; Michael Rogin, *Blackface/White Noise: Jewish Immigrants in the Hollywood Melting Pot* (Berkeley: University of California Press, 1996). On Papa Charlie Jackson, see Samuel Barclay Charters, *The Country Blues* (1959; New York: Da Capo, 1975), 49–51; and R.M.W. Dixon and J. Godrich, *Recording the Blues* (New York: Stein and Day, 1970), 34, 78. We need more research on black fans of minstrelsy.

   On the history of the blues, I have relied heavily on W. C. Handy, *Father of the Blues* (1941; New York: Da Capo, 1969); Handy, ed., *Blues: An Anthology* (1926; rev. ed., New York: Da Capo, 1990); Ralph Ellison, *Going to the Territory* (New York: Vintage, 1986); Albert Murray, *Stomping the Blues* (1976; New York: Vintage, 1982); Lawrence Levine, *Black Culture and Black Consciousness: Afro-American Folk Thought from Slavery to Freedom* (New York: Oxford University Press, 1977); Amiri Baraka (LeRoi Jones), *Blues People: The Negro Experience in White America and the Music That Developed from It* (New York: William Morrow, 1963); Samuel Barclay Charters, *The Roots of the Blues: An African Search* (New York: M. Boyars, 1981); Charters, *Country Blues*; Jeff Todd Tilton, *Early Downhome Blues: A Musical and Cultural Analysis* (1977, Chapel Hill: University of North Carolina Press, 1994); Charles Kiel,

Urban Blues (Chicago: University of Chicago Press, 1966); Alan Lomax,
The Land Where the Blues Began (New York: Delta, 1993); Paul Oliver,
Blues Fell Down This Morning: Meaning in the Blues (New York: Cambridge
University Press, 1960); Oliver, *The Story of the Blues* (Boston: Northeastern
University Press, 1998); William Ferris, *Blues from the Delta* (New York:
Da Capo, 1978); Robert Palmer, *Deep Blues: A Musical and Cultural History
of the Mississippi Delta* (New York: Penguin, 1981); Angela Y. Davis, *Blues
Legacies and Black Feminism: Gertrude "Ma" Rainey, Bessie Smith, and Billie
Holiday* (New York: Pantheon, 1998); Daphne Duval Harrison, *Black Pearls:
Blues Queens of the 1920s* (New Brunswick, N.J.: Rutgers University Press,
1988); Hazel Carby, "'It Just Be's Dat Way Sometimes': The Sexual Politics
of Women's Blues," *Radical America* 20 (June–July, 1986): 9–22; Gene
Santoro, *Highway 61 Revisited: The Tangled Roots of American Jazz, Blues,
Folk, Rock, and Country Music* (New York: Oxford University Press, 2004).
Davis, *Blues Legacies*, 42, 91, 135, argues that the image of the self that blues
musicians make in their music anticipates the new conceptions of the self of
the 1960s. My argument here is that blues songs help create these new ideas of
the self.

13. Elijah Wald, *Escaping the Delta: Robert Johnson and the Invention of the Blues*
(New York: HarperCollins, 2004); Marybeth Hamilton, *In Search of the Blues*
(New York: Basic, 2008).

14. Davis, *Blues Legacies*; Carby, "'It Just Be's Dat Way Sometime'"; Sandra R. Lieb,
Mother of the Blues: A Study of Ma Rainey (Amherst: University of Massachusetts
Press, 1981); Harrison, *Black Pearls*; Dexter Stewart Baxter, *Ma Rainey and the
Classic Blues Singers* (New York: Stein and Day, 1970); Chris Albertson, *Bessie*
(New York: Stein and Day, 1972); Samuel B. Charters and Leonard Kunstadt, *Jazz:
A History of the New York Scene* (1962; New York: Da Capo, 1981); Douglas,
Terrible Honesty. On white singers' performances of blues songs, like those by
W. C. Handy, see Miller, *Segregating Sound*.

15. Bessie Smith, *Bessie Smith: The Complete Recordings*, vols. 1–5 (Columbia,
1991–96). The lyrics of "'Tain't Nobody's Bizness if I Do" and "Beale Street Papa"
are published in Davis, *Blues Legacies*, 342–43 and 264. On the segregation of
Atlantic City, see Bryant Simon's excellent *Boardwalk of Dreams: Atlantic City
and the Fate of Urban America* (New York: Oxford University Press, 2004).

16. Ellison, "Change the Joke"; Hamilton, *In Search of the Blues*.

17. John W. Work, ed., *American Negro Songs* (New York: Howell, Soskin, 1940), 28.
It is important to remember that how blues musicians and blues fans during the
music's commercial heyday heard the music (these people were mostly black)
and how blues scholars from the early twentieth century through the present
hear the music (these people were and are mostly white) often diverge. Most
writing about the blues is more accurately described as a history of whites'
romanticization of black people.

18. Ralph Ellison and Albert Murray, *Trading Twelves: The Selected Letters of Ralph
Ellison and Albert Murray* (New York: Modern Library, 2000), 29; Davis, *Blues
Legacies*.

19. For the songs, see Ma Rainey, *The Complete Ma Rainey Collection, 1923–1928* (King Jazz, 1994). For a transcription of the lyrics, see Davis, *Blues Legacies and Black Feminism*: "Hear Me Talking to You," 221–22; "Prove It on Me Blues," 238; "Victim of the Blues," 252; "Travelin' Blues," 252, "Sweet Rough Man," 247–48. Advertisement for Ma Rainey's "Prove It on Me Blues," *Chicago Defender*, September 22, 1928, reproduced in Lieb, *Mother of the Blues*, 127.

20. William Barlow, *Looking Up at Down: The Emergence of Blues Culture* (Philadelphia: Temple University Press, 1989); Douglas, *Terrible Honesty*, 387–433.

21. For biographies of female blues musicians of the 1920s, see Harrison, *Black Pearls*.

22. Hale, *Making Whiteness*; Ellison and Murray, *Trading Twelves*; Albert Murray, "The Blues Idiom and the Mainstream," 54–69, in *The Omni-Americans: Some Alternatives to the Folklore of White Supremacy* (1970; New York: Da Capo, 1990); Walter Benjamin, "The Work of Art in the Age of Mechanical Reproduction," in *Illuminations*, ed. Hannah Arendt (New York: Schocken Books, 1968), 217–52; Miles Orvell, *The Real Thing: Imitation and Authenticity in American Culture* (Chapel Hill: University of North Carolina Press, 1989).

23. Langston Hughes, "Happy New Year! With Memphis Minnie," *Chicago Defender*, January 9, 1943, in *Write Me a Few of Your Lines: A Blues Reader*, ed. Steven C. Tracey (Amherst: University of Massachusetts Press, 1999), 321–22; Paul Garon and Beth Garon, *Woman with Guitar: Memphis Minnie's Blues* (New York: Da Capo, 1992); Memphis Minnie, *Bumble Bee: The Essential Recordings of Memphis Minnie* (Indigo, 1994).

24. Rock music sources consulted include Gillian Gaar, *She's a Rebel: The History of Women in Rock and Roll*, 2nd ed. (New York: Seal Press, 2002); Nelson George, *The Death of Rhythm and Blues* (New York: Plume, 1988); George Gillett, *The Sound of the City: The Rise of Rock and Roll* (New York: Da Capo, 1995); Gerri Hirshey, *We Gotta Get Out of This Place: The True, Tough Story of Women in Rock* (New York: Grove, 2001); Lipsitz, "Against the Wind"; Greil Marcus, *Mystery Train: Images of American in Rock 'n' Roll Music* (New York: Simon and Schuster, 1999); John Street, *Rebel Rock: The Politics of Popular Music* (New York: Blackwell, 1986); David Szatmary, *A Time to Rock: A Social History of Rock 'n' Roll* (Upper Saddle River, N.J.: Prentice-Hall, 1996). In an almost direct inversion of "respectable" opinion at the time, the standard story of the rise of rock and roll emphasizes the liberatory, anti-racist effects of its racially mixed sound and performance styles. In the work of many scholars, rock and roll became instead an effect of and even a force for progressive social change. More recently, an alternative account has arisen that sees this liberation as a lie. See Lawrence Grossberg, *We Gotta Get Out of This Place: Popular Conservatism and Post-modern Culture* (New York: Routledge, 1992); Grossberg, *Dancing in Spite of Myself: Essays on Popular Culture* (Durham, N.C.: Duke University Press, 1997); Thomas Frank, *The Conquest of Cool: Business Culture, Counterculture, and the Rise of Hip Consumerism* (Chicago: University of Chicago Press, 1997); and Sean McCann and Michael Szalay, "Paul Potter and the Cultural Turn," 209–20, and "Do You Believe in Magic? Literary Thinking After the New Left," 435–68, both

in *Yale Journal of Criticism* 18:2 (Fall 2005), a special issue on "Countercultural Capital," edited by McCann and Szalay. The best recent accounts of rock music's origins argue that the music is a part of postwar capitalism that enabled both accommodation and resistance. See Medovoi, *Rebels*. Medovoi offers a neo-Marxist account, in which white middle-class teenagers use working-class rebellion against postwar capitalism to express a sense of their own alienation and difference. See Miller, *Segregating Sound*, for the smart argument that rock is a transgression of the early twentieth-century idea that music has to be racially embodied rather than racially performed.

25. On authenticity, see Orvell, *Real Thing*; and David Grazian, *Blue Chicago: The Search for Authenticity in Urban Blues Clubs* (Chicago: University of Chicago Press, 2003).

26. Guralnick, *Last Train to Memphis*; Marcus, *Mystery Train*; Charles L. Ponce de Leon, *Fortunate Son: The Life of Elvis Presley* (New York: Hill and Wang, 2006); Dave Marsh, *Elvis* (New York: Thunder Mouth Press, 1992); Erika Doss, *Elvis Culture: Fans, Faith, and Image* (Lawrence: University Press of Kansas, 1999).

27. Guralnick, *Last Train to Memphis*, quote, 96.

28. Guralnick, *Last Train to Memphis*, 5–6, 95–135.

29. Guralnick, *Last Train to Memphis*; Marcus, *Mystery Train*. Today, Presley fans and scholars are still debating the degree to which Presley sounds "black" on his cover of Crudup's tune. Part of the problem is that there is no clear consensus on what sounding black means, because black and black-sounding are such shifting and contested terms. In fact, it is impossible with any analytic precision to describe "black" music (or "white music" either) as a historical category. See Miller, *Segregating Sound*.

30. *Elvis Presley: The Ed Sullivan Shows: The Performances* (Image Entertainment, 2006); *Elvis #1 Hit Performances* (RCS, 2007); *Elvis #1 Hit Performances & More, Vol. 2*, video (RCA, 2008); Alan Raymond and Susan Raymond, *Elvis '56: In the Beginning*, documentary film (Lightyear Video, 2000); 1950s photographs at http://www.elvispresleymusic.com.au/pictures, accessed October 27, 2009.

31. On Elvis and his female fans, see the photos in "A Howling Hillbilly Success," *Life*, April 30, 1956, 64; and "Elvis—A Different Kind of Idol," *Life*, August 27, 1956, 101–9.

32. Guralnick, *Last Train to Memphis*, 152, 182, 182, 191.

33. Photographs, October 16, 1954, and January 22, 1955, at http://www.elvispresleymusic.com.au/pictures, accessed October 27, 2009.

34. Photographs, August 5, 1955, at http://www.elvispresleymusic.com.au/pictures/1955_august.html, accessed October 27, 2009.

35. Photographs, August 5, 1955, at http://www.elvispresleymusic.com.au/pictures/1955_august.html, accessed October 27, 2009.

36. Presley advertisement in *Billboard*, December 3, 1955. The same photograph appears on the cover of the album *Elvis Presley* (RCA Victor, 1956).

37. *Presley: Ed Sullivan Shows*; *Elvis #1 Hit Performances*; *Elvis #1 Hit Performances & More, Vol. 2*; 1950s photographs at http://www.elvispresleymusic.com.au/pictures.

38. *Elvis #1 Hit Performances*; *Elvis #1 Hit Performances & More, Vol. 2*; Raymond and Raymond, *Elvis '56*.

39. *Elvis #1 Hit Performances*; *Elvis #1 Hit Performances & More, Vol. 2*. I want to thank Bonnie Gordon, a University of Virginia musicologist, for pointing out key differences between Presley's and Thornton's performances.

40. *Elvis #1 Hit Performances*; *Elvis #1 Hit Performances & More, Vol. 2*; Raymond and Raymond, *Elvis '56*.

41. *Elvis #1 Hit Performances*; *Elvis #1 Hit Performances & More, Vol. 2*; Raymond and Raymond, *Elvis '56*.

42. In addition to the videos already cited, see Guralnick, *Last Train to Memphis*, 327–50.

43. *Presley: Ed Sullivan Shows*.

44. *Presley: Ed Sullivan Shows*.

45. *Presley: Ed Sullivan Shows*.

46. *Presley: Ed Sullivan Shows*.

47. Steve Chapple and Reebee Garofalo, *Rock 'n' Roll Is Here to Pay: The History and Politics of the Music Industry* (Chicago: Nelson-Hall, 1977), 246.

48. Guralnick, *Last Train to Memphis*, 253.

49. "Relax and Be Yourself," *Ebony*, November 1953; Norman Mailer, "The White Negro: Superficial Reflections on the Hipster," originally published in *Dissent* in 1957, reprinted in *Advertisements for Myself* (1959; New York: Berkeley Publishing, 1966), 311–31, quotes, 314. The first popular account of a "white Negro" was Mezz Mezzrow, *Really the Blues* (New York: Random House, 1946), the autobiography of a white Jewish kid who discovers jazz and the African American men playing it in Chicago in the 1910s and lives the rest of his life acting like he is a black musician.

50. Mailer, "White Negro"; Mailer, September 25, 1957, to Jean Malaquais, in a selection of letters printed in Mailer, "In the Ring: Grappling with the Twentieth Century," *New Yorker*, October 6, 2008, 10.

51. Mailer, "White Negro," quote, 331.

52. Jack Kerouac, *On the Road* (1957; New York: Penguin, 1976), quote, 251; Kerouac, May 28, 1955, to Arabelle Porter, editor of *New World Writing*, in Charters, *Letters I*, quote, 487. I used the following Kerouac sources: Ann Charters, ed., *Selected Letters of Jack Kerouac, 1940–1956* (New York: Penguin Books, 1995), cited as *Letters I*; Charters, *Selected Letters of Jack Kerouac, 1957–1969* (New York: Penguin Books, 1999), cited as *Letters II*; Charters, *Kerouac, A Biography* (New York: Warner Books, 1974); John Tytell, *Naked Angels: The Lives and Literature of the Beat Generation* (New York: McGraw-Hill, 1976); Carolyn Cassady, *Off the Road: My Years with Cassady, Kerouac, and Ginsberg* (New York: William Morrow, 1990); Barry Miles, *Jack Kerouac, King of the Beats: A Portrait* (New York: Henry Holt, 1998); Ellis Amburn, *Subterranean Kerouac: The Hidden Life of Jack Kerouac* (New York: St. Martin's Press, 1998); Gerald Nicosia, *Memory Babe: A Critical Biography of Jack Kerouac* (New York: Grove, 1984); and unpublished Kerouac letters on microfilm at Columbia University Rare Book and Manuscript Library, Columbia University, New York, New York. Unlike J. D. Salinger, Kerouac encouraged critics to read his work autobiographically.

Kerouac wrote *On the Road* about the same time Salinger published *Catcher,* and the novel is set in the same historical period, sometime in the late 1940s. Yet because *On the Road* was not published until 1957, it reached many readers in a different historical moment than *Catcher.*

53. Kerouac, *On the Road,* quotes, 9, 7, 8; Toni Morrison, *Playing in the Dark: Whiteness and the Literary Imagination* (New York: Vintage, 1993). See Kerouac, November 4, 1950, to Ellen Lucey, in Kerouac Collection at Columbia University, on his second novel, which is about "a ten year old Negro boy in his hitch-hiking woes from Carolina to the Coast and back": "I feel like a Negro, and especially a child." This manuscript was published after Kerouac died as *Pic* (New York: Grove, 1971).

54. Kerouac, *On the Road,* 8, 11, 159, 40, 68, 79, 8, 155, 158, 82, 67, 14.

55. Kerouac, *On the Road,* quote, 252; Kerouac, Rocky Mount, N.C., October 2, 1948, to Neal Cassady, in Charters, *Letters I,* 165. See also Kerouac, December 28, 1950, to Neal Cassady, 246–63, quotes, 247, 246, 24, 248, 261; Kerouac, January 8, 1951, to Neal Cassady, 273–81, quote, 274; and Kerouac, [before April 15, 1955], to Neal Cassady, 472–73, all in Charters, *Letters I.*

56. Kerouac, *On the Road,* quotes, 175–77.

57. Kerouac, *On the Road,* quotes, 180.

58. Kerouac, Rocky Mount, NC, October 3, 1948, to Neal Cassady; and Kerouac, Ozone Park, N.J., October 19, 1948, to Hal Chase, in Charters, *Letters I,* 167, 170.

59. Jack Kerouac, "The Essentials of Spontaneous Prose," written in 1953 for Allen Ginsberg and William S. Burroughs, published in *Black Mountain Review* 7 (Autumn 1957) and *Evergreen Review* 8 (Spring 1959) and reprinted in Ann Charters, ed., *The Portable Beat Reader* (New York: Viking, 1992). See also "Belief and Technique for Modern Prose: List of Essentials" (another version of this list), in Kerouac, May 28, 1955, to Arabelle Porter, editor of *New World Writing,* in Charters, *Letters I,* 486–88; and Charters, *Kerouac,* 188.

60. Richard Eberhart, "West Coast Rhythms," *New York Times Book Review* (September 2, 1956); Ginsberg, May 18, 1956, to Eberhart, in *To Eberhart from Ginsberg* (Lincoln, Mass.: Penmaen Press, 1976), quote, 18. On the Beats, see Tytell, *Naked Angels;* Steven Watson, *The Birth of the Beat Generation: Visionaries, Rebels, and Hipsters, 1944–1960* (New York: Pantheon, 1995); Cornelis A. van Minnen, Jaap van der Bent, and Mel van Elteren, eds., *Beat Culture: The 1950s and Beyond* (Amsterdam: VU University Press, 1999); Ann Charters, ed., *The Penguin Book of the Beats* (New York: Penguin, 1992); and George Plimpton, ed., *Beat Writers at Work: The Paris Review* (New York: Modern Library, 1999).

61. "Big Day for Bards at Bay," *Life,* September 9, 1957; "New Test for Obscenity," *Nation,* November 9, 1957; Barry Miles, ed., *Howl: Original Draft Facsimile, Transcript and Variant Versions, Fully Annotated by the Author, With Contemporaneous Correspondence* (New York: Harper and Row, 1986); Bill Morgan and Nancy J. Peters, eds., *Howl on Trial: The Battle for Free Expression* (San Francisco: City Lights Books, 2006); J. W. Ehrlich, *Howl of the Censor* (San Carlos, Calif.: Nourse, 1961); Peter B. Levy, "Beating the Censor: The 'Howl' Trial Revisited," in

van Minnen, van der Bent, and van Elteren, *Beat Culture*, 107–16; Maurice Berger, "Libraries Full of Tears: The Beats and the Law," in *Beat Culture and the New America: 1950–1965*, ed. Lisa Phillips (New York: Whitney Museum of Modern Art, 1995), 123–40; and Edward de Grazia, *Girls Lean Back Everywhere: The Law of Obscenity and the Assault on Genius* (New York: Random House 1992).

62. Jacket copy, first edition of *On the Road*, 1957, in *The Beats: A Literary Reference*, ed. Matt Theado (New York: Carroll and Graf, 2003), 150; "Trade Winds," *Saturday Review*, October 5, 1957, 5–7.

63. Gilbert Millstein, "Books of the Times," *New York Times*, September 5, 1957; Thomas Curley, "Everything Moves, but Nothing Is Alive," *Commonweal*, September 1957; Phoebe Adams, "Reader's Choice," *Atlantic Monthly*, October 1957; Gene Baro, "Restless Rebels in Search of—What?" *New York Herald Tribune*, September 15, 1957; David Dempsey, "In Pursuit of Kicks," *New York Times Book Review*, September 8, 1957. For examples of bad reviews, see Herbert Gold, "Hip, Cool, Beat—and Frantic," *Nation*, November 16, 1957, 349–54, quote, 353, who describes Kerouac and Ginsberg as creating an "ascetics of excess," yearning "for the annihilation of the senses through the abuse of the senses" (354); "Flings of the Frantic," *Newsweek*, September 9, 1957; and "The Ganser Syndrome," *Time*, September 16, 1957, 120. For an early broad review of the Beats that pays special attention to Kerouac and *On the Road*, see Norman Podhoretz, "The Know-Nothing Bohemians," *Partisan Review* 25:2 (Spring 1958): 305–18: "This tremendous emphasis on emotional intensity, this notion that to be hopped-up is the most desirable of all human conditions, lies at the heart of the Beat Generation ethos" (307). On Kerouac's reaction to the publication of *On the Road*, see Jerry Tallmer, "Back to the Village—But Still *On the Road*," *Village Voice*, September 18, 1957; and Joyce Johnson, *Minor Characters* (Boston: Houghton Mifflin, 1983).

64. Kerouac reading from *Visions of Cody* and *On the Road*, *Steve Allen Show*, season 5, episode 7, aired November 16, 1959.

65. Jack Kerouac and Steve Allen, *Poetry for the Beat Generation* (Hanover, 1959); Kerouac, Zoot Sims, and Al Cohn, *Blues and Haikus* (Hanover, 1958); Kerouac, "Aftermath: The Philosophy of the Beat Generation," *Esquire*, March 1958; Kerouac, "The Origins of the Beat Generation," *Playboy*, June 1959. Holmes wrote an earlier piece, "This Is the Beat Generation," *New York Times Magazine*, November 16, 1952. See Charters, *Letters II*, for evidence of his discomfort with the role of Beat Generation spokesman. See also William F. Buckley, "The Hippies," an episode of *Firing Line* (taped September 3, 1968; air date differs among television stations), available online at http://hoohila.stanford.edu/firingline/searchResult.php, accessed July 10, 2009.

66. Paul O'Neil, "The Only Rebellion Around," *Life*, November 30, 1959, 114–32. *The Many Loves of Dobie Gillis* ran on CBS from 1959 to 1963. *The Nervous Set* opened (and closed) at Henry Miller's Theater in May 1959. Bob Hope dressed up like a beatnik in the episode of *The Bob Hope Buick Show* that aired on April 19, 1960. Mr. Magoo was created at the UPA animation studio in 1949. Cool Cat was created by Alex Lovy for Warner Bros. Animation and first appeared in *Cool Cat* (1967).

67. Allen Ginsberg, "Howl," in Miles, *Howl*; Kerouac, *On the Road*, 181.

Chapter 3: Black as Folk

1. Jeff Rosen, liner notes for Murray Lerner, *Festival*, video (1967; reissued, Eagle Rock Entertainment, 2005).
2. Lerner, *Festival*.
3. The lyrics for "We Shall Overcome" are printed in Guy Carawan and Candie Carawan, eds. and comps., *Sing for Freedom: The Story of the Civil Rights Movement Through Its Songs* (Bethlehem, Pa.: Oak Publications, 1990), 15. Many Freedom Song lyrics are also in Folder 26, Freedom Songs, Student Nonviolent Coordinating Committee Records, Martin Luther King Center, Atlanta, Georgia (hereafter cited as SNCC).
4. The 1963 Newport Folk Festival is described in Robert Cantwell, *When We Were Good: The Folk Revival* (Cambridge, Mass.: Harvard University Press, 1996), 293–352, photograph of the famous sing-along, 354; Ronald D. Cohen, *Rainbow Quest: The Folk Music Revival and American Society, 1940–1970* (Amherst: University of Massachusetts Press, 2002); Cohen, *A History of Folk Music Festivals in America* (Lanham, Md.: Scarecrow Press, 2008); Dick Weissman, *Which Side Are You On? An Inside History of the Folk Music Revival in America* (New York: Continuum, 2006); and David Hajdu, *Positively 4th Street: The Life and Times of Joan Baez, Bob Dylan, Mimi Baez Farina, and Richard Farina* (New York: Northpoint Press, 2001), 164–68. Music at the March on Washington is described in Bernice Johnson Reagon, "Songs of the Civil Rights Movement" (PhD diss., Howard University, 1975), 165–67; Taylor Branch, *Parting the Waters: America in the King Years, 1954–1963* (New York: Simon and Schuster, 1988), 877–81; and *We Shall Overcome: Documentary of the March on Washington* (Folkways FH 5592).
5. For the best description of how a person becomes a folk fan and then a revivalist musician, see Jeff Todd Titon, "Reconstructing the Blues: Reflections on the 1960s Blues Revival," in *Transforming Tradition: Folk Music Revivals Examined*, ed. Neil V. Rosenberg (Urbana: University of Illinois Press, 1993), 220–240, esp. 220–22.
6. Barry Shank, "'That Wild Mercury Sound': Bob Dylan and the Illusion of American Culture," *boundary 2* 29:1 (2002): 97–123, helped shape my arguments here.
7. Branch, *Parting the Waters*; Taylor Branch, *Pillar of Fire: America in the King Years, 1963–1965* (New York: Simon and Schuster, 1998); Charles M. Payne, *I've Got the Light of Freedom: The Organizing Tradition and the Mississippi Freedom Struggle* (Berkeley: University of California Press, 1995); Clayborne Carson, *In Struggle: SNCC and the Black Awakening of the 1960s* (Cambridge: Harvard University Press, 1981); Wesley Hogan, *Many Minds, One Heart: SNCC's Dream for a New America* (Chapel Hill: University of North Carolina Press, 2007); Richard H. King, *Civil Rights and the Idea of Freedom* (New York: Oxford University Press, 1982); James Forman, *The Making of Black Revolutionaries* (1972; Seattle: University of Washington Press, 1997). In his narrative approach, Branch uses and extends rather than analyzes the romanticism of civil rights movement that I am examining here.

8. Cantwell, *When We Were Good*.

9. David E. Whisnant, *All That Is Native and Fine: The Politics of Culture in an American Region* (Chapel Hill: University of North Carolina Press, 1983); Benjamin Filene, *Romancing the Folk: Public Memory and American Roots Music* (Chapel Hill: University of North Carolina Press, 2000).

10. See the John Lomax biography, part of "Southern Mosaic: The John and Ruby Lomax 1939 Southern States Recording Trip," Library of Congress American Memory Web site, http://memory.loc.gov/ammem/lohtml/lohome.html, accessed July 10, 2009.

11. On the folk song revival of the Depression era, see Robbie Lieberman, *My Song Is My Weapon: People's Songs, American Communism, and the Politics of Culture, 1930–1950* (Urbana: University of Illinois Press, 1989); William Stott, *Documentary Expression and Thirties America* (New York: Oxford University Press, 1973); Richard H. Pells, *Radical Visions and American Dreams* (New York: Harper and Row, 1973); Michael Denning, *The Cultural Front: The Laboring of American Culture* (New York: Verso, 1996); Jacquelyn Dowd Hall, "Disorderly Women: Gender and Labor Militancy in the Appalachian South," *Journal of American History* 73 (1986): 354–82; Bill C. Malone, *Country Music, USA* (1968; Austin: University of Texas Press, 2000), 129–30; Irwin Silber, "Folk Music and the Success Syndrome," *Sing Out!* 14:4 (September 1964): 2–4; Joe Klein, *Woody Guthrie: A Life* (New York: Knopf, 1980), 142–49.

12. John Lomax and Alan Lomax, *Folk Song U.S.A.* (New York: Duell, Sloan, and Pearce, 1947), preface by Alan Lomax, quotes, ix; Alan Lomax, *The Land Where the Blues Began* (New York: Pantheon, 1993); Klein, *Guthrie*, 142–79.

13. Dave Van Ronk with Elijah Wald, *The Mayor of MacDougal Street* (New York: Da Capo, 2005), 46–47, quote, 46; John Cohen, "A Rare Interview with Harry Smith," *Sing Out!* 19:1 (April/May 1969): 2–11, 41, and 19:2 (July/ August 1969), 23–28, quote, 3; *Folkways Anthology of American Folk Music* (Folkways, 1952).

14. Cohen, "A Rare Interview with Harry Smith," quote, 10; Cantwell, *When We Were Good*, 190; *Folkways Anthology of American Folk Music* (Folkways, 1952); Van Ronk, *Mayor of MacDougal Street*, 49. See Paul Oliver, *Songsters and Saints: Vocal Traditions on Race Records* (Cambridge: Cambridge University Press, 1984), 33–34, for examples of minstrel songs reworked by African Americans. On hillbilly musicians using the blues, see Malone, *Country Music, USA*; John Cohen, "The Folk Music Interchange: Negro and White," *Sing Out!* 14:6 (January 1965): 42–49; Hobart Smith, "I Just Got the Music in My Head," *Sing Out!* 14:6 (January 1965): 10–13; John Cohen, "Roscoe Holcomb: First Person," *Sing Out!* 16:2 (April/May 1966): 3–7; and Charles Wolfe, "A Lighter Shade of Blue: White Country Blues," in Cohn, *Nothing but the Blues*, 233–63.

15. The recording of Lomax's Folksong '59 concert is *Alan Lomax Presents: Folk Song Festival at Carnegie Hall* (United Artists, 1960); Irwin Silber and David Gahr, "Top Performers Highlight First Newport Folk Festival," *Sing Out!* 9:2 (Fall 1959): 21–24; Israel Young, "Frets and Frails," *Sing Out!* 15:2 (May 1965): 75, and 8:4 (Spring 1959): 84; and Ellen Schrecker, *Many Are the Crimes: McCarthyism in America* (New York: Little, Brown, 1998).

16. Susan Montgomery, "The Folk Furor," *Mademoiselle*, December 1960, 98–100, 117–19, quote, 100. Figures like Pete Seeger and Irving Silber, *Sing Out!* editor, linked the left folksong revival to the later folk music revival. See Silber, "Pete Seeger—Voice of Our Democratic Heritage," *Sing Out!* 4:6 (May 1954): 4–7. Silber's annual *Sing Out!* issues devoted to Negro History Week condemned segregation, advocated black rights in Popular Front–era language and reprinted spirituals, black union songs, and other black songs of protest. See, for example, the February 1952 issue (vol. 2, no. 8) with Leadbelly on the cover and a song collected by Lawrence Gellert inside. See also Silber, "Racism, Chauvinism Keynote US Music," *Sing Out!* 2:5 (November 1951): 6–7, 10; Aaron Kramer and Clyde R. Appleton, "Blues for Emmett Till," *Sing Out!* 6:1 (Winter 1956): 3; Lawrence Gellert, *Me and My Captain: Chain Gang Negro Songs of Protest* (New York: Hours Press, 1939); and Gellert, "Negro Songs of Protest in America," *Music Vanguard* 1.1 (March/April 1935): 3–13.

17. Alan Lomax, "Sage of a Folksong Hunter," *Hi/Fi Stereo Review*, May 1960, 40–46; Lomax, "Folk Song Traditions Are All Around Us," *Sing Out!* 11:1 (February/March 1961): 17–18; *Alan Lomax Presents: Folk Song Festival at Carnegie Hall*; Alan Lomax interview on the concert at http://www.alan-lomax. com/links_spitzer.html, accessed May 1, 2008; Harriet Van Horne, "Square Toes Blues," *New York World-Telegram and Sun* (June 17, 1960); Montgomery, "Folk Furor," 99.

18. Titon, "Reconstructing the Blues," quote, 221. On the folk music revival, see David A. De Turk and A. Poulin Jr., *The American Folk Scene: Dimensions of the Folksong Revival* (New York: Dell, 1967); Cantwell, *When We Were Good*; Cohen, *Folk Song Revival*; Filene, *Romancing the Folk*; Rosenberg, *Transforming Tradition*; Irwin Silber, untitled editorial, *Sing Out!* 14:4 (September 1964); Cohen, *Rainbow Quest*; Kingston Trio, *The Kingston Trio* (Capitol Records, 1958), and Harry Belafonte, *Swing Dat Hammer* (RCA, 1960). The version of "Grizzly Bear" collected by Pete Seeger and John Lomax was issued on *Negro Prison Camp Worksongs* (Folkways, 1956). John McPhee, "Folk Singing: Sibyl with Guitar," *Time*, November 23, 1962, 54–60, quote, 54.

19. Alan Lomax, "'The Folkniks'—and the Songs They Sing," *Sing Out!* 9:1 (Summer 1959): 30–31, quotes, 31; "Folk Song as It Is," *Newsweek*, April 14, 1958, 80; B. A. Botkin, "The Folksong Revival: Cult or Culture?" (1964), in De Turk and Poulin, *American Folk Scene*, 95–100, quote, 99; Grace Jan Waldman, "Life Among the Guitars," *Mademoiselle*, May 1959, 88–89, 14, 27, 32, quotes, 88, 89, 14.

20. "Black Is the Color" is on Joan Baez, Ted Alevizos, and Bill Wood, *Folksingers Round Harvard Square* (Veritas, 1959). "All My Trials" is on Joan Baez, *Joan Baez* (Vanguard, 1960). Nat Hentoff, "Folk Finds a Voice," *Reporter*, January 4, 1962, quotes, 40; McPhee, "Sibyl wih Guitar," quotes, 56; Davis, *Blues Legacies*.

21. John Pankake, "Mike Seeger, the Style of Tradition," *Sing Out!* 14:3 (July 1964): 6–9, quotes, 7; Pete Welding, "Crusaders for Old Time Music: The New Lost City Ramblers," *Sing Out!* 11:5 (December 1961/January 1962): 5–7; Mike Seeger, "Mountain Music, Bluegrass Style," *Sing Out!* 11:1 (February/March 1961): 10–13;

Ellen J. Stekert, "Cents and Nonsense in the Urban Folksong Movement: 1930–1966" (1966), reprinted with a new introduction by the author in Rosenberg, *Transforming Tradition*, quotes, 97–98, 87. Field recordings made by Mike Seeger in Baltimore were released as *Mountain Music Bluegrass Style* (Folkways, 1959).

22. Sources on the controversy over white musicians playing the blues include Paul Garon, "Whites Versus Blacks," in *Blues and the Poetic Spirit* (1975; San Francisco: City Lights, 2001); Garon, introduction to special section "Surrealism & Blues," *Living Blues* 25 (January/February 1976); Garon, "White Blues," http://www.bluesworld.com/WHITEBLUES.html, accessed April 2, 2010; and Hollie I. West, "Can White People Sing the Blues?" *Ebony*, July 1979, 14–42.

23. Liner notes to Dave Van Ronk, *Gambler's Blues* (Verve Folkways, 1965), a reissue of his earlier Folkways recordings; Mike Goodwin, "Dave Van Ronk: The Paradox of the Urban Blues Singer," *Sing Out!* 14:6 (January 1965): 26–30; Robert Shelton, "Folk Music Makes Mark on City's Night Life," *New York Times*, November 17, 1960; Newport Folk Festival program, quoted in Cantwell, *When We Were Good*, 300.

24. Nat Hentoff, "The Future of the Folk Renascence," in De Turk and Poulin, *American Folk Scene*, 326–31, quotes, 327; Frederic Ramsey Jr., *Sing Out!* 15: 2 (May 1965): 82; Barbara Dane, "Blues," *Sing Out!* 15:5 (September 1965): 65–71, quote, 70. For a more positive account of white blues singers, see Paul Nelson, "Country Blues Comes to Town," *Sing Out!* 14:3 (July 1964), 14–24. For an optimistic account of whites' ability to sing like blacks, see Waldemar Hille, "Can an All-White Group Sing Songs from Negro Culture?" *Sing Out!* 2:7 (January 1952): 2, 6–7, 14. According to Hille, whites need to capture "the real spirit of the blues"; otherwise, they are guilty of "cultural opportunism." What is interesting about all the discussion of whites singing like blacks is how quickly the sentiment turns after 1965, when it becomes much less acceptable among revivalists. On the Society for the Preservation of Spirituals, see Stephanie Yuhl, *A Golden Haze of Memory: The Making of Historic Charleston* (Chapel Hill: University of North Carolina Press, 2005).

25. Letter to the editor from Joel Fritz, Castro Valley, Calif., *Sing Out!* 15:1 (March 1965): 102.

26. Sam Hinton, "The Singer of Folksongs and His Conscience," *Sing Out* 7:1 (Spring 1957): 24–27, quotes, 24, 25; Hentoff, "Future of the Folk Renascence," 327.

27. Montgomery, "Folk Furor," 118; John Cohen, "A Reply to Alan Lomax: In Defense of City Folksingers," *Sing Out!* 9:1 (Summer 1959): 332–34, quote, 33; Irwin Silber, "They're Still Writing Folksongs Says *Sing Out's* Editor," *Sing Out!* 7:2 (Summer 1957): 30–31.

28. John Cohen and Mike Seeger, eds., *The New Lost City Ramblers Song Book* (New York: Oak Publications, 1964).

29. McPhee, "Sibyl with Guitar," quote, 55; Montgomery, "Folk Furor," 118; Bob Dylan, *Chronicles* (New York: Simon and Schuster, 2004), 236; Schrecker, *Many Are the Crimes*; David Potter, *People of Plenty: Economic Abundance and the American Character* (Chicago: University of Chicago Press, 1954); Daniel Bell,

The End of Ideology: On the Exhaustion of Political Ideas in the Fifties (New York: Free Press, 1960).

30. Leadbelly (Huddie Ledbetter), *Rock Island Line* (Naxos, 1951).
31. Pete Seeger, "Johnny Appleseed Jr.," *Sing Out!* 14:1 (February/ March 1964): 71–73.
32. Nelson, "Country Blues Comes to Town."
33. Ed Badeaux, "Please Don't Tell What Train I'm On," *Sing Out!* 14:4 (September 1964): 6–12; Paul Nelson, "Newport: The Folk Spectacle Comes of Age," *Sing Out!* 14:5 (November 1964): 6–10.
34. Cantwell, *When We Were Good*, 49–80. Shelton, "Singing for Freedom: Music in the Integration Movement," *Sing Out!* 13:1 (December 1962/January 1963), 4–7, 12–17; Theodore Bikel, "We Shall Overcome . . . from Egypt to Mississippi," *Hootenanny*, February 1964, manuscript copy sent by Bikel to James Forman, in Bikel File, Folder 4, Box 11, SNCC; Van Ronk, *Mayor of MacDougal Street*, 131–32, 184. Hobart Smith, for example, played in minstrel shows too. See Smith, "I Just Got the Music in My Head," 13.
35. "Folk Music: They Hear America Singing," *Time*, July 19, 1963, 53; Paul Nelson, "What's Happening," review of 1965 Newport Folk Festival, *Sing Out!* 15:5 (November 1965): 4.
36. Mississippi John Hurt, *Mississippi John Hurt Today!* (Vanguard, 1963); and Hurt, *Avalon Blues: The Complete 1928 Okeh Recordings* (Columbia, 1966); Dock Boggs, *Legendary Singer and Banjo Player* (Folkways, 1963). Hurt's "Spike Driver Blues" and "Frankie" and Boggs's "Sugar Baby" and "Country Blues" appeared on Smith's *Anthology of American Folk Music*; Smith, "I Just Got the Music in My Head;" Cantwell, *When We Were Good*, 290; Robert Cantwell, *Bluegrass Breakdown: The Making of the Old Southern* Sound (Urbana: University of Illinois Press, 1984); Neil V. Rosenberg, *Bluegrass: A History* (Urbana: University of Illinois Press, 1985); Malone, *Country Music, USA*; John Hammond, *From Spirituals to Swing* (Vanguard, 1999) reproduces recordings of this concert in New York City on December 23, 1938, as well as its sequel, a concert with the same name that occurred on December 24, 1939. This set also reproduces the original 1938 program. The McMichen quote is in Nelson, "Newport: The Folk Spectacle Comes of Age," 7.
37. Folk revivalists (fans and musicians) exist on a continuum from the academic scholar and the purist musician like Mike Seeger to the casual fan and most popular adapters of folk songs like the Kingston Trio.
38. Nat Hentoff, "Folk Finds a Voice," *Reporter* (January 4, 1962), 39–42, quotes, 42: Silber, "Folk Music and the Success Syndrome."
39. Cantwell, *When We Were Good*, 51; Michael Rogin, *Blackface, White Noise: Jewish Immigrants in the Hollywood Melting Pot* (Berkeley: University of California Press, 1996); Silber, "Folk Music and the Success Syndrome," quote, 2.
40. The most popular romanticism of the twentieth century—folk revivalism—was in this sense different from the most popular romanticism of the nineteenth century, minstrelsy. In revivalism, the love was right out in the open, but the politics of that love, the theft, the belief that the folk should not change but they might set you free, was denied. Alan Lomax wrote repeatedly of the love. See

"Folk Song Traditions Are All Around Us": "In folklore, more than in any other of the arts, the performer or student must have a devotion to the material which is akin to love" (17).

41. Bernice Reagon, "The Song Culture of the Civil Rights Movement," liner notes to *Voices of the Civil Rights Movement*, 1.

42. Seeger Biographical Material for promoting SNCC benefits. Seeger File, Folder 3, Box 20, SNCC.

43. Len Holt, Norfolk, Va., [sometime in 1962 before June], to Jim Foreman, Atlanta; both in Seeger File, Folder 3, Box 20, SNCC.

44. The first scholar to write about these issues was W. E. B. DuBois, *Souls of Black Folks* (1903). On the Jubilee Singers, see Cohen, *Folk Song America*, 12–14; and *Fisk Jubilee Singers: The Gold and Blue Album* (Folkways records, 1955). Ed Badeaux, "Please Don't Tell What Train I'm On," *Sing Out!* 14:4 (September 1964): 6–12. The politics of folk revivalism at the turn of the century were conservative.

45. Seeger File, Folder 3, Box 20, SNCC; Irwin Silber, "Pete Seeger: Voice of Our Democratic Heritage," in *Sing Out!* 4: 6 (May 1954): 4–7; David King Dunaway, *How Can I Keep From Singing* (New York: McGraw-Hill, 1981), 219–24.

46. Lomax quote in Silber, "Pete Seeger," 7; and Miles College Seeger Concert Promotional Materials and Morehouse College Seeger Concert promotional materials, in Folder 3, Box 20, SNCC.

47. Lee was murdered on Sept. 25. 1962. "We'll Never Turn Back" is in Carawan, *Sing for Freedom*, 93.

48. For the Freedom Song version of "Hold On" see "Keep Your Eyes on the Prize," in Carawan, *Sing for Freedom*, 111; Dunaway, *How Can I Keep From Singing*, quote, 222.

49. Dunaway, *How Can I Keep From Singing*, 219–24.

50. Seeger, [Beacon, N.Y.], May 31, 1963, to Chico, Bob [Moses], and Sam, [Kilby State Prison, Miss.]; and Seeger, Beacon, NY, May 31, 1963, to Jim Forman, [Atlanta]; all in Folder 3, Box 20, SNCC. Seeger also got his manager, Harold Leventhal, involved collecting writer's royalties for three songs copyrighted to SNCC workers, "If You Miss Me At the Back of the Bus," "I Ain't Scared of Your Jail," and "Woke Up This Morning." See Freedom Singers, Folder 6, Box 70, SNCC. The statements from August 1964 show the songs earning almost $800 in the six months ending June 30, 1964. Seeger included Freedom Songs on many of his records in the mid-sixties. See, for example, *We Shall Overcome*, a live recording of Seeger's Carnegie Hall Concert, June 8, 1963 (Columbia, 1963), on which five of the thirteen songs are Freedom Songs.

51. Guy Carawan, La Jolla, Calif., May 15, 1962, to Jim Forman, Atlanta; and Jim Forman, [Atlanta], [November, 1962], to Carawan, La Jolla, Calif.; all in Carawan, Folder 4, SNCC. On Carawan's own troubles in Albany, see Reagon, "Songs of the Civil Rights Movement." On *Freedom in the Air*, see the review in *The Reporter* (December 7, 1963), and SNCC News Release, Freedom Singers File, Folder 10, Box 130, SNCC. For different approaches to the Freedom Singers and the Freedom Songs, see Bradford Martin, *The Theater is in the Street: Politics and Public Performance in Sixties America* (Amherst: University of Massachusetts

Press, 2004), 20–48; and T. V. Reed, *The Art of Protest: Culture and Activism from the Civil Rights Movement to the Streets of Seattle* (Minneapolis: University of Minnesota Press, 2005), 1–39.

52. Carson, *In Struggle*, 64; Reagon, "Songs of the Civil Rights Movement," 39–40.

53. Reagon, "In Our Hands," and "Songs of the Civil Rights Movement." Dunaway, *How Can I Keep from Singing*, 224–25; Toshi Seeger File, Folder 4, Box 20, SNCC. See also the Freedom Singers Folders scattered throughout SNCC.

54. Dorothy Zellner interview, June 7, 2006, and Mary King interview, June 7, 2006, both in the author's possession; Seeger, *Everybody Says Freedom*, 88–89. On SNCC's office, see Forman, *Making of Black Revolutionaries*, 272. Press materials, Freedom Singers File, Folder 10, Box 130, SNCC; Robert Shelton, "Negro Songs Here Aid Rights Drive," *New York Times* (June 23, 1963); Ralph Gleason, "The Voice of Freedom," *San Francisco Chronicle* (April 25, 1965), clipping in Freedom Singers File, Folder 7, Box 70; Fundraising-Freedom Singers File, Folder 8, Box 70, SNCC. The 1964 lineup was all men—James Peacock, Marshall Jones, Charles Neblett, and Emory Harris.

55. Freedom Singers, *We Shall Overcome* (Mercury Records, 1962); Mercury Records File, Folder 5, Box 71; SNCC.

56. See the schedule notes for 1963 in Freedom Singers File, Folder 10, Box 130, SNCC.

57. Neblett is quoted in Clipping, "Out of Southern Jails: Freedom Singers Present Story," *Carltonian* (May 8, 1963), [no author listed in the part that survives]; in freedom Singers, Folder 6, Box 70, SNCC. See the fund-raising folders, confusingly separated into New York, Atlanta, and other offices' files, in SNCC. SNCC used the Freedom Singers, concerts by Pete Seeger and other folk singers (see the Chicago Second City benefit in 1964, which used Theodore Bikel, the Greenbriar Boys, and the Even Dozen Jug Band, among other musicians—see Benefits, Folder 2, Box 121, SNCC) to raise a significant proportion of its annual budgets in 1963, 1964, and 1965. With SNCC's problematic record keeping, exact figures are hard to come by. But in 1963, the year the Freedom Singers began touring, SNCC raised $309,000, up from the $50,000 it raised the year before; $142,000 came from institutions and $74,000 from individuals, but most of the remaining $93,000 came from musical benefits and concerts, many of them featuring the Freedom Singers. Freedom Singer Receipts for concerts between October 3-December 31, 1964 (at which only the Singers performed) account for income of $6,000.79. See Freedom Singers, Folder 7, Box 70, SNCC. The large benefits, at which the Freedom Singers often joined more famous entertainers, did bring in a lot more money per event than the Freedom Singers' college concerts. It is impossible to calculate, however, how many of the increasing number of individuals who sent money to SNCC's national office from all over the country had heard the Freedom Singers. The Singers, in this sense, functioned always as an advertisement for the organization. Forman, *Making of Black Revolutionaries*, 293, 307, 430, 449, 454, talks a great deal about SNCC fund-raising and describes the Freedom Singers in these terms. According to Forman, SNCC's funds, between 1963–1966, besides money from foundations for voter registration

efforts, came almost entirely from white liberals, including college students, and black entertainers like Harry Belafonte, Lorraine Hansberry, Diahann Carroll, and Sidney Poitier. See also Carson, *In Struggle*.

Less successfully than SNCC, CORE also formed its own singing group, the CORE Freedom Singers, also called the CORE Singers, to raise money for and awareness of its civil rights work. See CORE Papers, microfilm, Series II, Reel 11 for CORE's attempt to use a group called "Afro-American Folkloric Troupe" for fund-raising in 1964 and 1965.

The Freedom Singers' southern tour of historically black colleges in early 1964 was a part of SNCC's efforts to recruit more black student workers in reaction to the fact that northern white students began joining the organization in increasing numbers in 1963. One third of the participants at the annual conference in the spring of 1963, for example, were white. The tour was not particularly successful, either in fund-raising or recruitment. The schedule is in Freedom Singers, Folder 6, Box 70, SNCC.

58. The quotes are from Freedom Singers, Folder 6, Box 70, SNCC. See all the SNCC Freedom Singer files for scattered responses to concerts, often in letters asking to host the group again, and clippings from college newspapers.

59. Reagon, "In Our Hands," 2. On unsuccessful efforts to raise money by selling the Freedom Singers Mercury Records album *The Freedom Singers Sing of Freedom Now*, see Fundraising-Mercury Records File, Folder 5, Box 71, SNCC.

60. Hate Mail, Folder 11, Box 15; Jim Ryerson, Station Manager, Radio Station WMUU, Bob Jones University, August 19, 1964, to Morrie Diamond, Mercury Records, Chicago, Illinois, in Mercury Records, Folder 5, Box 71, SNCC.

61. "Folk Music: They Hear America Singing," *Time* (July 19, 1963), 53.

62. Reagon, "Songs of the Civil Rights Movement," 165–67. *We Shall Overcome: Documentary of the March on Washington* (Folkways FH 5592); Branch, *Parting the Waters*, 877; Cantwell, *When We Were Good*, 301.

63. *We Shall Overcome: Documentary of the March on Washington* (Folkways FH 5592); Reagon, "Songs of the Civil Rights Movement,"165–7; Branch, *Parting the Waters*, 877.

64. Thomas Sugrue, *Sweet Land of Liberty: The Forgotten Struggle for Civil Rights in the North* (New York: Random House, 2008); Virginia Durr, *Freedom Writer: Virginia Foster Durr, Letters from the Civil Rights Years*, edited by Patricia Sullivan (New York: Routledge, 2003), 334–35.

65. Porter Grainger and Bob Pickett, *How to Play and Sing the Blues Like the Phonograph and Stage Artists*, quoted in Ann Douglas, *Terrible Honesty: Mongrel Manhattan in the 1920s* (New York: Farrar, Straus, and Giroux, 1996), 393–94.

66. This section draws on Jann Weiner, "The Bob Dylan Interview," *Rolling Stone* (November 29, 1969); Robert Shelton, *No Direction Home: The Life and Music of Bob Dylan* (1986; rpt., New York: Da Capo, 2003); Clinton Heylin, *Bob Dylan: Behind the Shades* (New York: Simon and Schuster, 1991); Heylin, *A Life in Stolen Moments: Day by Day: 1941–1995* (New York: Schirmer Books, 1996), and *Bob Dylan: The Recording Sessions 1960–1994* (New York: St. Martin's Press, 1995); Hadju, *Positively 4th Street*; Carl Benson, ed., *The Bob Dylan Companion: Four*

Decades of Commentary (New York: Schirmer Books, 1998); John Nogowski, *Bob Dylan: A Descriptive, Critical Discography and Filmography, 1961-1993* (Jefferson, NC: McFarland & Company, 1995); Bob Dylan, *Lyrics, 1962-1985* (New York: Knopf, 1995); Bob Dylan, *Chronicles, Volume One* (New York: Simon and Schuster, 2004); and all of Dylan's Columbia recordings through 1966 and Bob Dylan, *Live 1966*, recorded in 1966 and released by Sony Music in 1985. The quote is from the interview with Dylan in Gil Turner, "Bob Dylan—A New Voice Singing New Songs," *Sing Out!* (October/ November 1962), 5-10.

Dylan, *Chronicles*, quote, 244; and Klein, *Woody Guthrie*, 255-61. Jack Kerouac called Woody Guthrie "the first white Negro." See John Cohen, "Roscoe Holcomb at Zebriskie Point," *Sing Out!* 9 (September/October 1970), 20-21.

67. Hadju, *Positively 4th Street*, 63-88; Sounes, *Down the Highway*, 43-72; Heylin, *Stolen Moments*, 3-7, includes photos of Dylan in high school; Woody Guthrie, *Bound for Glory* (1943, rpt., New York: E. P. Dutton, 1976). Whitaker is spelled Whittaker in Dylan, *Chronicles*, 245.

68. Hadju, *Positively 4th Street*, 71-88, quote, 71; Heylin, *Stolen Moments*, 12; Steve Turner, *Angelheaded Hipster: A Life of Jack Kerouac* (New York: Viking, 1996), viii. In October 1975 while on his Rolling Thunder tour, Dylan visited Kerouac's grave in Lowell, MA.

69. Turner, "Bob Dylan," 5-10, quote, 5; Hadju, *Positively 4th Street*, 71-88.

70. Izzy Young's diary entries recording his conversations with Dylan, published in 1968 and reprinted in Benson, *Dylan Companion*, 3-10, quotes, 3-4, 4, 5, 6; Turner, "Bob Dylan," 5-6; Hadju, *Positively 4th Street*, 64-75; Dylan, *Chronicles*, 21; Cantwell, *When We Were Good*.

71. Dylan, *Chronicles*, 255.

72. Klein, *Woody Guthrie*, 139-79, quote, 164. Bob Dylan, *Freewheelin' Bob Dylan* (Columbia, 1963); *The Times They Are A-Changin* (Columbia Records, 1964); Dylan, *Lyrics*. Leadbelly faced the same dilemma when he came to NYC in 1934 but approached it from a very different history, from life in the Delta and in southern prisons. He never dropped his deferential-to-whites southern share-cropper demeanor, even in front of white men he knew well. Woody slept on Huddie and Martha Ledbetter's Murphy bed many nights in the early forties and yet Leadbelly still called him Mr. Woody. Leadbelly had learned in Mississippi that there are reasons to perform that are not aesthetic or commercial or psychological. See Klein, *Woody Guthrie*, 157-58.

73. Cantwell, *When We Were Good*, 351; Klein, *Woody Guthrie*, 363-65; Dylan, *Chronicles*, 247, 250-53.

74. Klein, *Woody Guthrie*, 363-65; Dylan, *Chronicles*, 247, 250-53.

75. Robert Shelton, "Bob Dylan: A Distinctive Folksong Stylist," *New York Times*, September 29, 1961, 31.

76. Dylan, *Lyrics*, quotes, 6, 3, 4; Klein, *Woody Guthrie*, 288-89; Nogowski, *Discography*, 20-21; J. R. Goddard, "Records: Bob Dylan" *Village Voice*, April 26, 1962.

77. Paul Nelson and Jon Pankake, "Flat Tire," *Little Sandy Review* (June 1963), reprinted in Benson, ed., *Dylan Companion*, 20-23, quote, 22-23.

78. Review in *Village Voice* 1962, reprinted in Benson, ed., *Dylan Companion*, 12–13; Heylin, *Behind the Shades*, 58–111; Shelton, *No Direction Home*, 116–208.

79. Dylan, *Lyrics*, quotes, 56, 59; Nogowski, *Discography*, 20–25.

80. "Northern Folksingers Help Out at Negro Festival in Mississippi," *New York Times*, July 7, 1963; "Folk Music: They Hear America Singing," *Time*, July 19, 1963, 53; Danny Lyon, *Memories of the Southern Civil Rights Movement* (Chapel Hill: University of North Carolina Press), photograph, 110.

81. Hadju, *Positively 4th Street*, 164–68; Heylin, *Stolen Moments*, quotes, 47, 49–50; Dylan, *Lyrics*, quote, 111.

82. "I am My Words," *Newsweek*, November 4, 1963, 94–95; and Irwin Silber and Paul Nelson, "What's Happening," *Sing Out!* 15: 5 (November 1965), 4–8.

83. Dylan, *Lyrics*, 135, 129, 139.

84. Some of Bruce Springsteen's early work, especially his 1982 album *Nebraska* (Sony, 1982), is another cycle of this revival.

85. "Bob Dylan's Dream." Dylan, *Lyrics*, 62.

86. "Like a Rolling Stone," in Dylan, *Lyrics*, 167–68. The best description of Dylan's performance at Newport is in Hadju, *Positively 4th Street*, 253–63.

87. Dylan, *Lyrics*, 62. In *Chronicles*, Dylan links his own experiences symbolically and historically to an aesthetic, literary, and musical history of the folk rather than claiming that he is of the folk. A perfect example, among many, of how Dylan in *Chronicles* subtly connects himself to a now canonical line of American music is his description of singing the Bessie Smith hit "Nobody Knows You When You're Down and Out" to audition for Dave Van Ronk and a gig at the Greenwich Village folk venue The Gaslight (21–22). All Dylan interviews, autobiographical writings, etc., are self-conscious performances. The real Dylan isn't any one of these self-representations and cannot be found in Dylan's own words any more than anywhere else. The real Dylan is the performing, continually self-inventing Dylan.

88. Irwin Silber, "After Newport—What?" *Sing Out!* 14: 5 (November 1964): 2.

Chapter 4: Rebels on the Right

1. John Judis, *William F. Buckley: Patron Saint of the Conservatives* (New York: Simon and Schuster, 1988); William F. Buckley, *God and Man at Yale* (1951; South Bend, Ind.: Gateway Editions, 1977), quotes, 151; Grace Elizabeth Hale, "Rebels on the Right: Conservatives as Outsiders from William F. Buckley to Operation Rescue," UVA Miller Center of Public Affairs American Political Development Program's Colloquia Series on Politics and History, February 23, 2006, and the Lockmiller Seminar, Emory University, Atlanta, March 23, 2006; Kevin Mattson, *Rebels All!* (New Brunswick, N.J.: Rutgers University, 2008).

2. "Publisher's Statement," *National Review*, November 19, 1955, quote, 5. The Wallace program is quoted in "Mike Wallace Asks William F. Buckley, Jr., Where Is the Right Wing?" *New York Post*, January 15, 1958.

3. Judis, *Buckley*, 264, 269–70, 309–10; Larry King, "God, Man, and William F. Buckley, Jr.," *Harper's*, March 1967, 53–61; "William F. Buckley: Conservatism Can Be Fun," cover article, *Time*, November 3, 1967, 70–80, quotes, 70, 72.

4. Quotes are from "Publisher's Statement," *National Review*, November 19, 1955, 5, except "the Buckley style," in "Conservatism Can Be Fun," 70.

5. Joan Didion, *The White Album* (New York: Noonday, 1979), quote, 98.

6. Gregory L. Schneider, *Cadres for Conservatism: Young Americans for Freedom and the Rise of the Contemporary Right* (New York: New York University Press, 1999); John A. Andrew, *Young Americans for Freedom and the Rise of Conservative Politics* (New Brunswick, N.J.: Rutgers University Press, 1997); Jennifer Burns, *Goddess of the Market: Ayn Rand and the American Right* (New York: Oxford University Press, 2009).

7. Sources on American conservatism in the postwar period that have influenced my thinking here include Michael Kazin, *The Populist Persuasion* (New York: Basic Books, 1995); Chip Berlett and Matthew N. Lyons, *Right-Wing Populism in America: Too Close for Comfort* (New York: Guilford Press, 2000); Jonathan M. Schoenwald, *A Time for Choosing: The Rise of Modern American Conservatism* (New York: Oxford University Press, 2001); Thomas Frank, *What's the Matter with Kansas?* (New York: Metropolitan Books, 2004); Lisa McGirr, *Suburban Warriors: The Origins of the New American Right* (Princeton, N.J.: Princeton University Press, 2001); David Farber and Jeff Roche, eds., *The Conservative Sixties* (New York: Peter Lang, 2003); Bruce J. Schulman and Julian Zelizer, eds., *Rightward Bound: Making America Conservative in the 1970s* (Cambridge, Mass.: Harvard University Press, 2008); Godfrey Hodgson, *The World Turned Right Side Up: A History of the Conservative Ascendancy in America* (Boston: Houghton Mifflin, 1996); Mary C. Brennan, *Turning Right in the Sixties: The Conservative Capture of the GOP* (Chapel Hill: University of North Carolina Press, 1995); Lawrence Grossberg, *We Gotta Get Out of This Place: Popular Conservatism and Postmodern Culture* (New York: Routledge, 1992); Russell Kirk, *The Conservative Mind: From Burke to Eliot* (Chicago: Regnery, 1953); Kirk, *The Portable Conservative Reader* (New York: Penguin, 1982); George M. Marsden, *Fundamentalism and American Culture: The Shaping of Twentieth-Century Evangelicalism, 1870–1925* (New York: Oxford University Press, 1980); R. Laurence Moore, *Religious Outsiders and the Making of Americans* (New York: Oxford University Press, 1986); Carol Flake, *Redemptorama: Culture, Politics, and the New Evangelicalism* (New York: Anchor Books, 1984); William Martin, *With God on Our Side* (New York: Broadway Books, 1996); Martin Anderson, *Revolution: The Reagan Legacy* (New York: Harcourt Brace Jovanovich, 1988). On the growth of conservatism as a backlash against civil rights and feminism, see Cornel West, *Race Matters* (Boston: Beacon Press, 1993); Dan Carter, *The Politics of Rage: George Wallace, the Origins of the New Conservatism, and the Transformation of American Politics* (Baton Rouge: Louisiana State University Press, 1996); and Susan Faludi, *Backlash: The Undeclared War Against American Women* (New York: Crown, 1991).

8. While corporate funding of conservative institution-building, federal government infiltration and harassment of left-wing organizations through the FBI's COINTELPRO, the right-wing political strategizing of figures like Paul Weyrich and Kevin Phillips, and the direct mail genius of Paul Viguerie are all key

elements in the history of the rise of the New Right, not enough attention has been paid to why so many Americans responded to these new conservative institutions, what I would call the cultural history of the rise of the New Right. It is important, however, to remember in any discussion of the right the tremendous power of the financial resources available to conservatives across the twentieth century. See Kim Phillips-Fein, "Right On," *Nation*, September 9, 2009.

9. Dwight Macdonald, "God and Buckley at Yale," and Irving Kristol, "On the Burning Deck," both in *Reporter*, May 27, 1952; Dan Wakefield, "W.F.B. Jr., Portrait of a Complainer," *Esquire*. January 1961, 49–52, quote, 52. On Macdonald, see Gregory D. Sumner, *Dwight Macdonald and the Politics Circle* (Ithaca, N.Y.: Cornell University Press, 1996).

10. King, "God, Man, and William F. Buckley, Jr.," 53; "Conservatism Can Be Fun," quotes, 70, 72; Mailer quote in Judis, *Buckley*, 267. Buckley ran for mayor in 1965, and Mailer ran in 1960 (an attempt cut short) and 1969. See Wakefield, "Portrait of a Complainer," quote, 53.

11. Judis, *Buckley*, quote, 42; King, "God, Man, and William F. Buckley, Jr."; "William F. Buckley, Jr.: A Candid Conversation," *Playboy*, May 5, 1970, 75–88, 180–91; "Conservatism Can Be Fun." Judis disputes the details of these stories and ignores others altogether. Whether they are true or not is less important for my purposes than that Buckley felt compelled to create an autobiography that figured rebelliousness as a trait he had possessed since childhood. Being a rebel, in this figuration, is not a break with his parents and upbringing, an adolescent or young adult transition. It is instead a mark of continuity.

12. "Conservatism Can Be Fun," 72.

13. Buckley, *Cruising Speed: A Documentary* (New York: Putnam, 1971), quote, 142; Judis, *Buckley*, 52–82, quote, 56.

14. Buckley, *God and Man at Yale*, quotes, 151, 150, 148, v; Macdonald, "God and Buckley at Yale."

15. Buckley, *God and Man at Yale*, quotes, 151.

16. Macdonald, "God and Buckley at Yale," quotes, 37 (typo used "ruled" for "rude"); Buckley, *God and Man at Yale*, quote, lix–lx.

17. Judis, *Buckley*, 92–98. Macdonald cites *America* in "God and Buckley at Yale," 36, as well as sales figures, reviews, and the reactions of other conservatives.

18. Macdonald, "God and Buckley at Yale," quotes, 35, 38; Judis, *Buckley*, 97. See also Peter Viereck, "Conservatism Under the Elms," *New York Times Book Review*, November 4, 1951, as accessed July 23, 2010, at http://www.nytimes.com/books/00/07/16/specials/buckley-yale.

19. Buckley and Brent Bozell, *McCarthy and His Enemies: The Record and Its Meaning* (Chicago: Regnery, 1954), quote, 252; William S. White, "What the McCarthy Method Seeks to Establish," *New York Times Book Review*, April 4, 1954, 4; Harry W. Baehr, review of *McCarthy and His Enemies*, *New York Herald Tribune*, April 4, 1954, 12; Francis Coker, review of *McCarthy and His Enemies*, *Journal of Politics* 17:1 (February 1955): 113–22. Buckley and Bozell appeared on the television program *Author Meets the Critics*, aired on WABD in New York City on March 28, 1954.

20. C. Wright Mills, "The Powerless People: The Role of the Intellectual in Society" (*Politics*, 1944), in *The Power of Truth: Selected Writings of C. Wright Mills*, ed. John H. Summers (New York: Oxford University Press, 2008), 13–24; Reinhold Niebuhr, *Moral Man and Immoral Society* (New York: Scribner, 1932); Michael Harrington, *The Other America: Poverty in the United States* (New York: Macmillan, 1962).

21. First quote, Judis, *Buckley*, 133; W. F. Buckley Jr., "Memorandum, RE: *A New Magazine*," September 1954, Henry Regnery Papers, quoted in Schoenwald, *Time for Choosing*, 167; Richard H. Pells, *The Liberal Mind in a Conservative Age: American Intellectuals in the 1940s and 1950s* (New York: Harper and Row, 1985), 183–261, quotes, 185. Buckley indeed aimed for a "manly" style, and very few women wrote for *National Review* in its first decade.

22. *National Review*, November 19, 1955. For the conspiratorial tone, pick up any issue of *National Review* for the first five years.

23. Judis, *Buckley*, 134–47. For Buckley, being a rebel against "the liberal establishment" was paradoxically a way for him to be like his father. Buckley's brand of rebellion was in effect the family tradition. The best expression of Buckley's political philosophy in his words is Buckley, *Up from Liberalism* (New York: McDowell, Obolensky, 1959). Democracy, he argues there, is a means, not an end, to the just, virtuous, and harmonious society. Democracy warps liberals' judgments, Buckley insists, and he offers two examples, the American South and Africa. He also condemns liberals for the "great emptiness of their faith." Liberalism, he argues, has no vision and therefore no passion: "Liberalism cannot care deeply, and so cannot be cared about deeply" (112).

24. Editorial, *National Review*, February 29, 1956; Buckley, "Why the South Must Prevail," *National Review*, August 24, 1957; Buckley, "Can We Desegregate Hesto Presto?" (*Saturday Review*, 1961), in Buckley, *Rumbles Left and Right: A Book About Troublesome People and Ideas* (New York: G. P. Putnam's Sons, 1963); "Candid Conversation"; Judis, *Buckley*, 138–39.

25. Robert Welch, *The Politician: A Look at the Political Forces That Propelled Dwight David Eisenhower into the Presidency* (John Birch Society, 1963); Schoenwald, *Time for Choosing*, 62–99.

26. Buckley, *National Review*, February 3, 1962; Judis, *Buckley*, 200.

27. Buckley saw Ayn Rand's kind of conservatism, expressed most fully in her books *Atlas Shrugged* (New York: Random House, 1957) and *The Fountainhead* (Indianapolis, Ind.: Bobbs-Merrill, 1943), as immoral.

28. William F. Buckley Jr., "A Conservative's View," and Norman Mailer, "A Liberal's View," *Playboy*, January 1963; Mailer and Buckley, "The Right Wing" debate, *Playboy*, February 1963; "Debate: James Baldwin versus William Buckley: Has the American Dream Been Achieved at the Expense of the American Negro," October 26, 1965, at Cambridge University, Cambridge, England, broadcast in the United States on NET, available online at http://sunsite.berkeley.edu/videodir/asx2/2299.asx, accessed March 30, 2010; James Baldwin and Norman Mailer, "The American Dream and the American Negro," *New York Times Magazine*, March 7, 1965, 32–33, 87–89; "An Interview with William F. Buckley, Jr.," *Mademoiselle*, June 1961, 78–79, 120–24; Judis, *Buckley*, 221.

29. *Firing Line* Television Program Collection, Hoover Institution, Stanford University, online at http://hoohila.stanford.edu/firingline/, accessed May 1, 2009. This site includes information about the program as well as a full, chronological listing of episodes, many of which are available online in either a transcript or video format.

30. *Firing Line* episodes: Harrington on "Poverty: Hopeful or Hopeless?" taped on April 4, 1966; Thomas on "Vietnam: Pull Out? Stay In? Escalate?" taped on April 8, 1966; Lynd on "Vietnam—What Next?" taped on May 23, 1966; Farmer on "Where Does the Civil Rights Movement Go Now?" taped on April 18, 1966; McKissick on "Civil Rights and Foreign Policy," taped on August 22, 1966; Gregory on "Civil Disobedience: How Far Can It Go?" taped on May 16, 1966; Leary on "The World of LSD," taped on April 10, 1967; Murray the K on "What to Do with the American Teen-ager," taped on November 14, 1966; Hefner on "The Playboy Philosophy," taped on September 12, 1966; Ginsberg on "The Avant Garde," taped May 7, 1968; Goodman on "Are Public Schools Necessary?" taped on September 12, 1966; Alinsky on "Mobilizing the Poor," taped December 11, 1967; all at http://hoohila.stanford.edu/firingline.

31. Buckley, "How I Came to Rock," *Saturday Evening Post*, August 24, 1968; "William F. Buckley, Jr.: A Candid Conversation," *Playboy*, May 5, 1970, 75–88, 180–91, quotes, 185, 188; Judis, *Buckley*, 263–76.

32. Frederick C. Klein, "Rapier on the Right: Editor-Debater Buckley Gains More Prominence as Conservatives' Voice," *Wall Street Journal*, January 31, 1967, Mailer quote, 1, 16.

33. Tom Hayden, "Who Are the Student Boat-Rockers?" *Mademoiselle*, August 1961, 239, 333–37, quote, 239. Other contemporary sources on conservative students in the sixties include M. Stanton Evans, *Revolt on Campus* (Chicago: Regnery, 1961); Edward Cain, *They'd Rather Be Right* (New York: Macmillan, 1963); and Erik Erickson, ed., "Youth: Change and Challenge Special Issue," *Daedalus* 91 (1962).

34. Alan Dunn, cartoon, *New Yorker*, April 1, 1961; "Campus Conservatives," *Time*, February 3, 1961, quotes, 34, 34, 34, 37, 37; Russell Kirk, "New Direction in the US: Right?" *New York Times Magazine*, August 7, 1966; Harold Taylor, "The New Young Are Now Heard," *New York Times Magazine*, January 29, 1961; Cain, *They'd Rather Be Right*.

35. Young Americans for Freedom, "The Sharon Statement," *National Review*, September 24, 1960, 173; Andrew, *Young Americans for Freedom*, 53–101, call quoted on 55. The estimate of the number of delegates comes from Schneider, *Cadres for Conservatism*, 33.

36. Hayden, "Who Are the Student Boat-Rockers?" 333.

37. Evans, *Revolt on Campus*, 64; and Schneider, *Cadres for Conservatism*, 32–34.

38. William F. Buckley, "The Young Americans for Freedom," *National Review* September 24, 1960, 172; Edward interview quoted in Schneider, *Cadres for Conservatism*, 34.

39. Andrew, *Young Americans for Freedom*, 5; Dan Wakefield, *New York in the Fifties* (Boston: Houghton Mifflin, 1992), 270; Rebecca Klatch, *Women of the New Right* (Philadelphia: Temple University Press, 1987); Lee and Anne Edwards, *Rebels with a Cause* (Washington, D.C.: YAF, 1969); "Campus Conservatives."

40. *New Guard* 1 (April 1961); *New Guard* 1 (March 1961); Andrew, *Young Americans for Freedom*, 53–101.

41. Andrew, *Young Americans for Freedom*, 53–101. He estimates that YAF had as many as thirty thousand members by the summer of 1961 (93).

42. See photographs in "Campus Conservatives;" Taylor, "The New Young Are Now Heard;" Kirk, "New Direction"; Schneider, *Cadres for Conservatism*; Andrew, *Young Americans for Freedom*.

43. Lawrence F. Schiff, "Dynamic Old Fogies: Rebels on the Right," in *Campus Power Struggles*, ed. Howard S. Becker (New Brunswick, N.J.: Transaction Books, 1970), 121–36, quote, 129; George F. Gilder, "God's Right Hand: The Views and Vita of William F. Buckley, Jr.," *Playboy*, May 1969, 130–32, 236–46, quotes, 242. Schiff's article, which I discovered long after I thought I had coined the phrase "rebels on the right," must take credit as the source.

44. Port Huron Statement, in Miller, *Democracy Is in the Streets*, 329–74, quotes, 332, 333, 331; Rebecca E. Klatch, *A Generation Divided: The New Left, the New Right, and the 1960s* (Berkeley: University of California Press, 1999).

45. Wakefield, "Portrait of a Complainer," 49–52, quotes, 52.

46. Sources on libertarianism include Craig Duncan and Tibor Machan, *Libertarianism: For and Against* (Lanhan, Md.: Rowman and Littlefield, 2005); David Boaz, *Libertarianism: A Primer* (New York: Free Press, 1997); and Larry Norman, *On Classic Liberalism and Libertarianism* (New York: St. Martin's, 1987).

47. Many of Thompson's letters are published in Hunter S. Thompson, *Proud Highway: Saga of a Desperate Southern Gentleman, 1955–1967* (New York: Ballantine Books, 1997), and *Fear and Loathing in America: The Brutal Odyssey of an Outlaw Journalist, 1968–1976* (New York: Touchstone, 2000). Much like populism, the politics of a turn-of-the-century vision of individualism anchored in the political economy, the postwar politics of expressive individualism disrupted earlier political categories.

48. Albert Camus, *The Rebel* (New York: Knopf, 1954); Colin Wilson, *The Outsider* (Boston: Houghton Mifflin, 1956); Jean-Paul Sartre, *Being and Nothingness: An Essay on Phenomenological Ontology* (New York: Philosophical Library, 1956). Thompson is like Kerouac and Ginsberg in his saving of his letters and papers.

49. This news release appeared in the *Command Courier* on November 8, 1957, and is reprinted in Thompson, *Proud Highway*, 74–75, quote, 74; quotes from letters, *Proud Highway*, 71, 68, 69, 70–71, 73.

50. Thompson, *Proud Highway*, 110.

51. Thompson, *Proud Highway*, 118, 119, 121, 101–2, 159, 165, 128, 176.

52. Thompson, *Proud Highway*, 109, 137, 420, 452, 492, 496, 509, 492. See especially Thompson's letter to Johnson, 495–97.

53. Thompson, *Proud Highway*, quotes, 507, 509, 496.

54. Thompson, *Proud Highway*, quote, 110; references to the beatniks include 109, 120, 127–29, 139–40; Thompson, *Fear and Loathing in America*, quotes, 7–11, and see the reprinted article, 5–11.

Chapter 5: New White Negroes in Action

1. Tom Hayden, *Reunion: A Memoir* (New York: Random House, 1988), 39–41; Virginia Durr, *Freedom Writer: Virginia Foster Durr, Letters from the Civil Rights Years*, ed. Patricia Sullivan (New York: Routledge, 2003), 175; James Miller, *Democracy Is in the Streets: From Port Huron to the Siege of Chicago* (Cambridge, Mass.: Harvard University Press, 1994), 33–34, 185–87; Bob Zellner with Constance Curry, *The Wrong Side of Murder Creek: A White Southerner in the Freedom Movement* (Montgomery, Ala.: New South Books, 2008), 61.

2. Scholars have thoroughly explored the intellectual, theoretical, political, and economic origins of the New Left. See Miller, *Democracy Is in the Streets*; Todd Gitlin, *The Sixties: Years of Hope, Days of Rage* (New York: Bantam, 1987); Wini Breines, *Community and Organization in the New Left, 1962–1968: The Great Refusal* (New York: Praeger, 1982); Maurice Isserman, *The Death of the Old Left and the Birth of the New Left* (New York: Basic Books, 1987); Sohnya Sayres, Anders Stephanson, Stanley Aronowitz, and Fredric Jameson, *The 60s Without Apology* (Minneapolis: University of Minnesota Press, 1984); Arthur Marwick, *The Sixties: Cultural Revolution in Britain, France, Italy, and the United States* (New York: Oxford University Press, 1998); and Van Gosse, *Rethinking the New Left: An Interpretative History* (New York: Palgrave, 2005). Scholars have also examined questions of cultural origins in the increasingly popular images of rebellion circulating in rock and roll, movies, and literature in the postwar period. See Steven Watson, *The Birth of the Beat Generation: Visionaries, Rebels, and Hipsters, 1944–1960* (New York: Pantheon, 1995); George Lipsitz, "Against the Wind: Dialogic Aspects of Rock and Roll," in *Time Passages: Collective Memory and American Popular Culture* (Minneapolis: University of Minnesota, 1990), 99–132; George Gillett, *The Sound of the City: The Rise of Rock and Roll* (New York: Da Capo, 1995); and Leerom Medovoi, *Rebels: Youth and the Cold War Origins of Identity* (Durham, N.C.: Duke University Press, 2005). What is missing in this scholarship is an account of what the romance of the rebel does, not for the political economy, but for the people who embrace it—the history of the emotional origins of the New Left.

3. Hayden, Albany City Jail, Albany, Georgia, December 11, [1961], to SDS, Folder 18, Box 9, Student Nonviolent Coordinating Committee Records, Martin Luther King Center, Atlanta, Georgia (hereafter cited as SNCC). Sources on SDS include the 1977 microfilm edition of the Students for a Democratic Society Papers, State Historical Society of Wisconsin, Madison (hereafter cited as SDS microfilm); Miller, *Democracy Is in the Streets*; Kirkpatrick Sale, *SDS* (New York: Random House, 1973); G. Louis Heath, *Vandals in the Bomb Factory: The History and Literature of the Students for a Democratic Society* (Metuchen, N.J.: Scarecrow Press, 1976); and Gitlin, *Sixties*. Sources on Hayden include Tim Findley, "Tom Hayden: *Rolling Stone* Interview Parts I and II," *Rolling Stone*, October 26, 1972, 36–50, and November 9, 1972, 28–36; Steven V. Roberts, "Will Tom Hayden Overcome?" *Esquire*, December 1968, 176–79, 207–9; and Hayden, *Reunion*.

4. Hayden, Albany City Jail, Albany, Georgia, December 11, [1961], to SDS, Folder 18, Box 9, SNCC.

5. "Student Riots in San Francisco—A Communist Coup," *U.S. News and World Report*, July 25, 1960, 68–71; Carl Werthman, "The Student Organization of Protest," *New University Thought*, Autumn 1960, 15–18; Jerold Simmons, *Operation Abolition: The Campaign to Abolish the House Un-American Activities Committee, 1938–1975* (New York: Garland, 1986), 179–97; W. J. Rorabaugh, *Berkeley at War: The 1960s* (New York: Oxford University Press, 1989), 15–16; Walter Goodman, *The Committee: The Extraordinary Career of the House Committee on Un-American Activities* (New York: Farrar, Straus, and Giroux, 1968).

6. Northern Student Movement, *Building a New Reality*, 1963 pamphlet, quoted in Miller, *Democracy Is in the Streets*, 48–50, 186–87; James Brook, "Ghetto Students," *Common Sense*, February 1962, 8–10; Doug McAdam, *Freedom Summer* (New York: Oxford University Press, 1988).

7. Miller, *Democracy Is in the Streets*, 28–40; Sale, *SDS*; Findley, "Hayden Interview II," 38.

8. SDS Conference on Human Rights in the North, May 1, 1960, SDS File, Folder 18, Box 9, SNCC; Miller, *Democracy Is in the Streets*, 28–40. Massimo Teodori, ed., *The New Left: A Documentary History* (New York: Bobbs-Merrill, 1969), provides useful estimates of New Left numbers (35) and a good overview of the broad variety of New Left organizing across the decade.

9. SNCC letters to SDS members thanking them for support; Haber letter to supporters about the integration of the University of Georgia; Haber, SDS, NYC, September 27, 1960, to Tim Jenkins, Philadelphia, all in SDS File, Folder 18, Box 9, SNCC.

10. Hayden, *Reunion*, quote, 18; Findley, "Hayden Interview I, II," quote, I-38; Roberts, "Will Tom Hayden Overcome?" Hayden had a very different background than other earlier SDS members. On Sharon Jeffrey's path into politics, see Miller, *Democracy Is in the Streets*, 31–34, 184–87.

11. Hayden, *Reunion*, 33–52, quotes, including Cason's, 33, 39–41. Only a few students at the time knew that the National Student Association was funded and controlled by the CIA. Hayden, like other radicals, was unaware of the connection and saw NSA as a convenient forum for airing ideas and winning converts. Haber was there in 1960 too, looking for student leaders to recruit into SDS. The NSA-CIA connection was exposed in 1967. See Sol Stern, "A Short Account of International Student Politics and the Cold War with Particular Reference to the NSA, CIA, Etc.," *Ramparts*, March 1967, 29–39.

12. Hayden, *Reunion*, 42–43, 46–47; Clayborne Carson, *In Struggle: SNCC and the Black Awakening of the 1960s* (Cambridge, Mass.: Harvard University Press, 1981), quote, 27. Hayden's *Daily* article quoted in Miller, *Democracy Is in the Streets*, 57; Roberts, "Will Tom Hayden Overcome?" quote, 179.

13. Hayden, Atlanta, November 10, 1961, to Robb [Burlage], SDS microfilm.

14. "Southern Report #2," October 7, 1961, SDS File, Folder 18, Box 9, SNCC. See all the SDS Southern Reports, Series 1, Reel 1, Folders 11, 13, SDS microfilm.

15. Hayden memo to Haber, NYC, "SNCC Meeting; Jackson, Mississippi, September 14–17, 1961," SDS File, Folder 18, Box 9, SNCC. Somehow, a memo marked confidential ended up in SNCC's files.

16. Findley, "Hayden Interview I," 42; Miller, *Democracy Is in the Streets*, 150.

17. Tom Hayden, *Revolution in Mississippi* (SDS Publication, 1962), Series 4B, Reel 37, Folder 159, SDS microfilm, quotes, 22. See also A. L. Hopkins, "Investigation of Negro Student Demonstrators, and Adult Negro Agitators, McComb, Mississippi, October 20, 1961"; September 6, 1962, letter to Mississippi State Sovereignty Commission members; and memo on *Revolution in Mississippi*, n.d.; all in Mississippi State Sovereignty Commission Papers, http://www.mdah.state. ms.us. The memo states: "This booklet (not meant for the eyes of white people) fell into the hands of white officials." In fact, Hayden's intended audience was white students.

    The beating incident received a great deal of newspaper coverage. See, for example, "Miss. Plumber Beats Two Men," *New Orleans Times-Picayune*, October 12, 1961; "Plumber Charged in Attack on Two," *Jackson Clarion-Ledger*, October 12, 1961; and "54 Burglund Students State Second Walkout," *McComb Enterprise-Journal*, October 11, 1961: "Hayes told the police the incident did not involve the race issue." The UPI and AP wire services picked up the story and the photo.

18. Findley, "Hayden Interview I," 42; Hayden, *Reunion*, 64–72. This photograph is reproduced in Hayden, *Reunion*, between 236 and 237, and in Guy Carawan and Candie Carawan, eds. and comps., *Sing for Freedom: The Story of the Civil Rights Movement Through Its Songs* (Bethlehem, Pa.: Oak Publications, 1990), 91.

19. Hayden, *Revolution in Mississippi*, quotes, 5.

20. Sale, *SDS*, 36–37, 663.

21. Hayden quoted in Miller, *Democracy Is in the Streets*, 59; Tom Hayden, "Who Are the Student Boat-Rockers?" *Mademoiselle*, August 1961.

22. Haber, NYC, to Nash, Atlanta, n.d. [late September–early October 1961]; Haber, memo to "Supporters of the SNCC fund raising program," October 26, 1961, both in SDS File, Folder 18. Box 9, SNCC. SNCC remained broke through 1963. James Forman, *The Making of Black Revolutionaries* (1972; Seattle: University of Washington Press, 1985) argues that SNCC counted on SDS and NSA to raise money for them in 1961 and 1962 and that the effort largely failed.

23. "Southern Report #2," October 7, 1961; Hayden memo to Haber, NYC, "SNCC Meeting: Jackson, Mississippi, September 14–17, 1961"; Haber memo, October 26, 1961, all in SDS File, Folder 18, Box 9, SNCC.

24. Sale, *SDS*, 38–41, quotes, 39, 41.

25. On civil rights organizing outside the South, see Thomas J. Sugrue, *Sweet Land of Liberty: The Forgotten Struggle for Civil Rights in the North* (New York: Random House, 2008).

26. Tom Hayden, "Student Social Action: From Liberation to Community," in Mitchell Cohen and Dennis Hale, *The New Student Left: An Anthology* (Boston: Beacon Press, 1966), 270–88; Sale, *SDS*, 43; Hayden, *Reunion*, quotes, 77, 78.

27. Mills, "The Powerless People: The Role of the Intellectual in Society," *Politics* 1 (April 1944), reprinted as "The Social Role of the Intellectual" in Mills, *Power, Politics, and People: The Collected Essays of C. Wright Mills* (New York: Oxford

University Press, 1963), 292–304, quote, 299. Hayden wrote his MA thesis at Michigan on Mills. See Hayden, *Reunion*, 81.

28. Hayden, "Student Social Action."

29. Sale, *SDS*, 42–70; Miller, *Democracy Is in the Streets*, 141–54.

30. All quotes are from SDS, "The Port Huron Statement," 1962, in *"Takin' It to the Streets": A Sixties Reader*, ed. Alexander Bloom and Wini Breines (New York: Oxford University Press, 2003), 51–61.

31. Miller, *Democracy Is in the Streets*, 143–51; Breines, *Community and Organization*. SDS continues this emphasis on both the material and psychological aspects of oppression in its 1963 manifesto, "America and the New Era."

32. Miller, *Democracy Is in the Streets*, quote, 103; Findley, "Hayden Interview I, II;" Roberts, "Will Tom Hayden Overcome;" Herbert J. Gans, "The New Radicalism: Sect or Political Action Movement?" *Studies on the Left* 5 (Summer 1965): 126–40, which includes replies by Tom Hayden, Staughton Lynd, and James Weinstein.

33. Hayden's quote is in *SDS Bulletin*, March–April 1963, Series 4A, Reel 35, Folder 19, SDS microfilm; Miller, *Democracy Is in the Streets*, 187; Sale, *SDS*; Findley, "Hayden Interview I," 42.

34. Tom Hayden and Carl Wittman, "An Interracial Movement of the Poor," Series 4B, Reel 37, Folder 151, SDS microfilm. See also "Prospectus for ERAP Project in Chester, Pennsylvania, During the Summer of 1964," Series 4B, Reel 39, Folder 371, SDS microfilm; Sale, *SDS*, 95–115; and Miller, *Democracy Is in the Streets*, 184–217.

35. Miller, *Democracy Is in the Streets*, 103. This was the argument liberals and labor leaders made in the 1930s as they dedicated resources to civil rights issues like fighting the poll tax. See Patricia Sullivan, *Days of Hope: Race and Democracy in the New Deal Era* (Chapel Hill: University of North Carolina Press, 1996).

36. Al Haber, "A Reply to the President's Report," *SDS Bulletin*, March 1964, Series 4A, Reel 35, Folder 19, SDS, 1, 23–25; Sale, *SDS*, 106–50

37. On the ERAP project, see the copies of the *ERAP Newsletter* in Economic Research and Action Report File, Folder 1, Box 123; ERAP file, Folder 10, Box 55; and Economic Research and Action Project File, Folder 4, Box 13, all in SNCC; and Series 2B, ERAP Papers, SDS microfilm. See also Rennie Davis, "The War on Poverty: Notes on Insurgent Response," Series 4B, Reel 36, Folder 68; Kim Moody, "Organizing Poor Whites," Series 4B, Reel 38, No. 250; "Philadelphia Research and Action Project Prospectus," Series 4B, Reel 36, Folder 82; "Chester, PA: A Case Study in Community Organization," Series 4B, Reel 38, Folder 273; and "Trenton, New Jersey: Report of the ERAP Summer Project, 1964," Series 4B, Reel 39, Folder 373, all in SDS microfilm.

Writings about ERAP projects by participants and observers at the time include Norm Fruchter and Robert Kramer, "An Approach to Community Organizing Projects," *Studies on the Left* 6 (1966): 31–61; Connie Brown, "Cleveland: Conference of the Poor," in Bloom and Breines, *"Takin' It to the Streets,"* 77–81; Richard Flacks, "Organizing the Unemployed: The Chicago Project," in Cohen and Hale, *New Student Left*, 132–46; "Chicago: JOIN Project," an interview with JOIN members Richie Rothstein, Judy Bernstein, Casey Hayden, Rennie Davis, and David Palmer, *Studies on the Left* 5 (Summer 1965): 107–25; and Todd Gitlin and Nanci Hollander, *Uptown: Poor Whites in Chicago* (New York: Harper and Row, 1970). Writings on community organizing include Stanley Aronowitz, "Poverty, Politics and Community Organizing," *Studies on the Left* 4 (Summer 1964): 102–5; and Robert Fisher, *Let the People Decide: Neighborhood Organizing in America* (Boston: Twayne, 1984). Participants' comments years later include Gitlin, *Sixties*, 165–92, 223–26; and Hayden, *Reunion*, 123–72. Secondary sources on ERAP include Miller, *Democracy Is in the Streets*, 184–217; Breines, *Community and Organization*, 123–49; Sale, *SDS*, 95–150; and Jennifer Frost, *"An Interracial Movement of the Poor": Community Organizing and the New Left* (New York: New York University Press, 2001).

38. *ERAP Newsletters*; Sale, *SDS*, 95–115, 131–50; Miller, *Democracy Is in the Streets*, 184–217; Gitlin, *Sixties*, 105–26.

39. Andrew Kopkind, "Of, By and For the Poor: The New Generation of Student Organizers," *New Republic* 152 (June 19, 1965): 15–19, quotes, 18; *ERAP Newsletters*.

40. *SDS Bulletins* for 1964 FIX; and *ERAP Newsletters*. For discussions of methods, see Hayden and Wittman, "Interracial Movement of the Poor."

41. Roberts, "Will Tom Hayden Overcome?"; Hayden, "Open Letter to ERAP Supporters and New Organizers," Series 4B, Reel 39, Folder 369, SDS microfilm.

42. *ERAP Newsletters*. On the welfare rights movement, see Francis Fox Piven and Richard Cloward, *Poor People's Movements: Why They Succeed and How They Fail* (New York: Pantheon, 1977); and Premilla Nadasen, *Welfare Warriors: The Welfare Rights Movement in the United States* (New York: Routledge, 2005).

43. Fruchter and Kramer, "Approach to Community Organizing Projects," quote, 45; Miller, *Democracy Is in the Streets*, 212, and note 59, 398; Forman, *Making of Black Revolutionaries*, 413–19.

44. Richard Rothstein, "A Short History of ERAP," Series 4A, Reel 33, Folder 1, SDS microfilm; Hayden, "Open Letter to ERAP Supporters and New Organizers"; Michael Harrington, "The Mystical Militants" (*New Republic*, 1966), in *Thoughts of the Young Radicals, and Four Critical Comments on Their Views of America*, ed. Andrew Kopkind (New York: Pitman, 1966), 65–73, quote, 67; Tom Hayden, "The Politics of 'The Movement,'" in *The Radical Papers*, ed. Irving Howe (Garden City, N.Y.: Doubleday, 1996), quotes, 374–75; Fruchter and Kramer, "Approach to Community Organizing Projects," 60–61; Findley, "Hayden Interview I, II"; Hayden, *Reunion*, 103–50.

Hayden admitted that it was a mistake to turn away from organizing students: "I think it was a misapplication of the lesson of the South, where black students dropped out of college and became the organizers of people in the communities through SNCC. And they established a line, or a mood, even in the North, that students had no business being in school, that they should be the revolutionary inspiration and catalyst to community movements . . . Not that the work was irrelevant, the work actually produced some results. But I think it came more from trying to follow the SNCC motto than from disillusionment with campus activities." Findley, "Hayden Interview I," 42.

45. Miller, *Democracy Is in the Streets*, 239–40; the speech is described but the speaker is not named in Paul Jacobs and Saul Landau, *The New Radicals: A Report with Documents* (New York: Random House, 1966), 31.

46. SDS Recruiting Pamphlet for summer 1965, *a movement of many voices*, SDS microfilm; Miller, *Democracy Is in the Streets*, 214–15.

47. Harrington, "Mystical Militants," quote, 67–68.

48. SDS, *movement of many voices*; Findley, "Hayden Interview I," 42.

49. Hayden, "Open Letter to ERAP Supporters and New Organizers," Series 4B, Reel 39, Folder 369, SDS microfilm.

50. Tom Hayden, "The Ability to Face Whatever Comes," in Kopkind, *Thoughts of the Young Radicals*, 41. Hayden includes here the clearest expression of the New Left idea of a community of rebels: "Instead of workers driven into motion by class dynamics, the 'proletarians' spawned in the paralyzed society are the various outcasts whose sense of reality cannot be adjusted completely to the dominant myths and given roles. Many Negroes are outcasts in white society. Many working people are outcasts from business society, and most from union society as well. Many young people are outcasts because, if they are poor, they have no future within the existing system; and, if they are affluent, they cannot be fulfilled by endless striving for more of what they inherited at birth. Many professionals are outcasts because their talents are wasted by the Great Society. Housewives too. These outcasts do not form an economic class; they share a common status . . . The strain upon them comes from living with what they cannot accept but cannot change" (38–39).

51. "Memorandum on the SNCC Mississippi Summer Project," Civil Rights in Mississippi Digital Archive, McCain Library and Archives, University of Southern Mississippi, http://anna.lib.usm/%7Espcol/crda/ellin/ellino62.html, accessed November 1, 2009. On the Mississippi Summer Project, see Doug McAdam, *Freedom Summer* (New York: Oxford University Press, 1988); Kathy Emery, Linda Reid Gold, and Sylvia Braselmann, *Lessons of Freedom Summer: Ordinary People Building Extraordinary Movements* (Monroe, Me.: Common Courage Press, 2008); Carson, *In Struggle*, 96–129; Forman, *Making of Black Revolutionaries*, 371–86; Branch, *Pillar*, 341–509; Payne, *Organizing Tradition*; and Eric Burner, *And Gently He Shall Lead Them: Robert Parris Moses and Civil Rights in Mississippi* (New York: New York University Press, 1994). Comedian Dick Gregory went on tour with the new lineup of the Freedom Singers in the spring of 1964. A partial schedule is in Freedom Singers, Folder 6, Box 123, SNCC.

52. Carson, *In Struggle*, 51–53, 100–101. The $5,000 a year SCEF gave SNCC in 1961, 1962, and 1963, supposedly for Zellner and his successor's salary, actually was used to pay for essential organizational expenses. SNCC Executive Committee Meeting Minutes, December 29, 1963, Reel 3, Student Nonviolent Coordinating

Committee Papers, 1959–1972 (Sanford Microfilming, 1982, hereafter cited as SNCC microfilm).

53. Minutes from June 10, 1964, SNCC staff meeting, Reel 3, SNCC microfilm; Danny Lyon, *Memories of the Southern Civil Rights Movement* (Chapel Hill: University of North Carolina Press, 1992), 144–47.

54. Forman, *Making of Black Revolutionaries*, 371–87, quote, 371; Carson, *In Struggle*; Julius Lester, *Look Out, Whitey! Black Power's Gon' Get Your Mama* (New York: Dial Press, 1968).

55. Ralph Allen's letter is quoted in Howard Zinn, *SNCC: The New Abolitionists* (1965; Westport, Conn.: Greenwood Press, 1985), 184.

56. M. S. Handler, "Rustin Sees Losses," *New York Times*, December 2, 1963, 1, 40; Danny Lyon's letter to his parents, February 12, 1964, in Lyon, *Memories of the Southern Civil Rights Movement*, 13. Lyon erroneously describes the Rustin interview as a letter to the *New York Times* written by Rustin. Rustin did write a letter to the *New York Times* that the newspaper published December 28, 1963: "In the Civil Rights Fight: Attack on Political Alignments Now Blocking Reform Urged," 22.

57. SNCC Executive Committee Meeting Minutes, December 29, 1963, Reel 3, SNCC microfilm; Carson, *In Struggle*, 101; Gregg Michel, *Struggle for a Better South: The Southern Student Organizing Committee* (New York: Palgrave, 2004); Constance Curry documents, online at Civil Rights Digital Library, http://crdl.usg.edu/people/c/curry_constance_1933/, accessed July 10, 2009.

58. William H. Chafe, *Never Stop Running: Allard Lowenstein and the Struggle to Save American Liberalism* (New York: Basic Books, 1993); Burner, *Robert Parris Moses*, 115, 252–53; Carson, *In Struggle*; Branch, *Pillar*, 122–23, Lowenstein quote, 23.

59. Minutes from June 10, 1964, SNCC staff meeting, Reel 3, SNCC microfilm.

60. Minutes from June 10, 1964, SNCC staff meeting, Reel 3, SNCC microfilm.

61. For a description of the COFO Mississippi staff meeting in November in which the plan for the summer project was debated and ambiguously approved, as well as the quote from Moses, see Zinn, *SNCC*, 187–88; the other Moses quote is in *Mississippi Free Press* 3:6 (January 18, 1964): 2; Lewis is quoted in Bob Robertson, "Militant Plan to Create Crisis in Mississippi," *San Francisco Chronicle*, December 7, 1963, 4; Carson, *In Struggle*, 99; Burner, *Robert Parris Moses*, 134–37.

62. Lowenstein quoted in Branch, *Pillar*, 123: Chafe, *Allard Lowenstein*; Sally Belfrage, *Freedom Summer* (1965; Charlottesville: University of Virginia Press, 1990), quote, 82; Kenneth Kipnis Mississippi Summer Project Application Form, Mississippi Sovereignty Commission Papers Online, SCR ID # 2–166–1–8–1–1, http://www.mdah.state.ms.us/arlib/contents/er/sovcom/result/php; Paul Cowan, *The Making of an Un-American* (New York: Viking, 1970); all other quotes, Freedom Summer Applications, Box 31, SNCC.

63. Estimates of the number of student or "nonprofessional" volunteers vary widely. McAdam, *Freedom Summer*, 35, 292–93, estimates 900. Elizabeth Sutherland Martinez, ed., *Letters from Mississippi* (Brookline, Mass.: Zephyr Press, 2002), 3, estimates 650. This is a revised edition of Elizabeth Sutherland, *Letters from Mississippi* (New York: McGraw-Hill, 1965).

64. Moses quote in Burner, *Robert Parris Moses*, 155; Martinez, *Letters from Mississippi*, quote, 19; Sara Evans, *Personal Politics: The Roots of Women's Liberation in the Civil Rights Movement and the New Left* (New York: Vintage, 1980), quotes, 70; Carson, *In Struggle*; Branch, *Pillar*.

65. Martinez, *Letters from Mississippi*, quote, 13; Tracy Sugarman, *Stranger at the Gates: A Summer in Mississippi* (New York: Hill and Wang, 1966), 13–14; Burner, *Robert Parris Moses*.

66. Martinez, *Letters from Mississippi*, 3–4, 10, 18. On white women's sense of connection with the black women they met in the movement, see Evans, *Personal Politics*, 25–82. On the power of southern blacks' religious faith and its importance in the movement, see David L. Chappell, *A Stone of Hope: Prophetic Religion and the Death of Jim Crow* (Chapel Hill: University of North Carolina Press, 2004); and Charles Marsh, *God's Long Summer: Stories of Faith and Civil Rights* (Princeton, N.J.: Princeton University Press, 1997).

67. Vincent Harding is quoted in Belfrage, *Freedom Summer*, 7; Elizabeth Sutherland, "The Cat and Mouse Game," *Nation*, September 14, 1964: 105–8; Martinez, *Letters from Mississippi*, 12, 25, 268; Evans, *Personal Politics*, 60–82.

68. Julius Lester, "The Angry Children of Malcolm X," *Sing Out!* 16:5 (October–November 1966): 21–25, quote, 23; John Herbers, "Quiet Saturday in Ruleville, Miss., Ends as Rights Workers Arrive," *New York Times*, June 29, 1964, 17; "Students Set to Open Mississippi Campaign," *Los Angeles Times*, June 20, 1964, 5. Some coverage quotes volunteers leaving for Mississippi as quite articulate about why they want to go and help. Still, even their tone suggests elite whites saving blacks. See David Kraslow, "Civil Rights Volunteers to Expand Dixie Project," *Los Angeles Times*, August 2, 1964, C; and Susana McBee, "800 Youths Gird for Mission to South," *Washington Post*, June 21, 1964, E1.

69. Sherrod quoted in Forman, *Making of Black Revolutionaries*, 276; Martinez, *Letters from Mississippi*, quotes, 57, 59; Evans, *Personal Politics*, 60–82; Constance Curry et al., *Deep in Our Hearts: Nine White Women in the Freedom Movement* (Athens: University of Georgia Press, 2000).

70. Martinez, *Letters from Mississippi*, 6, quotes, 24, 23, 58, 23.

71. Martinez, *Letters from Mississippi*, quotes, 13, 200–201. On SNCC workers' changing dress, see Forman, *Making of Black Revolutionaries*, 349, 365.

72. Martinez, *Letters from Mississippi*, photo, 240, quote, 172.

73. Martinez, *Letters from Mississippi*, 5, 13, 17, 36, 66–70, 251–52, quote, 230–31. "We'll Never Turn Back" is printed in Carawan and Carawan, *Sing for Freedom*.

74. Martinez, *Letters from Mississippi*, quote, 56.

75. Martinez, *Letters from Mississippi*, 21–22, 235–38; Belfrage, *Freedom Summer*, quote, 81; SNCC internal documents reprinted in Kathy Emery et al., *Lessons from Freedom Summer* (Monroe, Me.: Common Courage Press, 2008), 216–24; SNCC Executive Committee Meeting Minutes, December 29, 1963, and SNCC Staff Meeting Minutes, June 9–11, 1964, Reel 3, SNCC microfilm.

76. "They Won't Have a Chance," headline of SNCC advertisements with photo of integrated training session for the summer project, *New York Times*, June 29, 1964, 14, and *Washington Post*, July 12, 1964, B5; Van Gosse, "A Movement of

Movements: The Definition and Periodization of the New Left," in *Companion to Post-1945 America*, ed. Jean-Christophe Agnew and Roy Rosenzweig (Malden, Mass.: Blackwell, 2002), 277–302.

Chapter 6: Too Much Love

1. Thomas J. Sugrue, *Sweet Land of Liberty: The Forgotten Struggle for Civil Rights in the North* (New York: Random House, 2008); Malcolm X, *The Autobiography of Malcolm X*, ed. Alex Haley (New York: Grove, 1965); Guy Carawan and Candie Carawan, eds. and comps., *Sing for Freedom: The Story of the Civil Rights Movement Through Its Songs* (Bethlehem, Pa.: Oak Publications, 1990), 115. See also Don L. Lee (Haki Madhubuti), "No More Marching," in *Directionscore: Selected and New Poems* (Detroit: Broadside, 1971).

2. Jon Pankake, "Pete's Children: The American Folk Song Revival, Pro and Con," *Little Sandy Review* 29 (March–April 1964): 25–31, in *The American Folk Scene: Dimensions of the Folksong Revival*, ed. David A. De Turk and A. Poulin Jr. (New York: Dell, 1967), 280–86; Julius Lester, "The Angry Children of Malcolm X," *Sing Out!* 16:5 (October–November 1966): 21–25. See also Julius Lester, "Beep! Beep! Bang! Bang! Umgawa! BLACK POWER!" 97–107 (which overlaps with "The Angry Children") and "We Shall Overcome," 1–30, both in *Look Out, Whitey! Black Power's Gon' Get Your Mama* (New York: Dial Press, 1968). On Lester, see Carawan and Carawan, *Sing for Freedom*, 27; Lester, *Lovesong* (New York: Henry Holt, 1988); and James Forman, *The Making of Black Revolutionaries* (1972; Seattle: University of Washington Press, 1985), 481. See also Malcolm X's criticism of moderate civil rights organizations: "The harder you kick my ass the more I love you," in *The End of White Supremacy: Four Speeches by Malcolm X*, ed. Iman Benjamin Karin (New York: Seaver, 1971), 147.

3. Lester, "Angry Children of Malcolm X."

4. Lester, "Angry Children of Malcolm X."

5. For an early account of the growing "Black Fury," see Lerone Bennett Jr., *The Negro Mood* (Chicago: Johnson, 1964). For descriptions of the New Left written at the time, see R. David Myers, ed., *Toward a History of the New Left: Essays from Within the Movement* (Brooklyn, N.Y.: Carlson, 1989).

   For criticism of the New Left of the 1960s and 1970s by scholars who do not see themselves as conservatives, see Christopher Lasch, *The Culture of Narcissism: American Life in an Age of Diminishing Expectations* (New York: Norton, 1979); Russell Jacoby, *The Last Intellectuals: American Culture in the Age of Academe* (New York: Basic Books, 1987); Richard Rorty, *Achieving Our Country: Leftist Thought in Twentieth-Century America* (Cambridge, Mass.: Harvard University Press, 1998); and most recently, Sean McCann and Michael Szalay, guest eds., "Countercultural Capital: Essays on the Sixties from Some Who Weren't There," special issue, *Yale Journal of Criticism* 18:2 (Fall 2005), and their contribution "Do You Believe in Magic: Literary Thinking after the New Left," 435–68. For much more sympathetic coverage, see the pioneering Wini Breines, *Community and Organization in the New Left: The Great Refusal* (New

York: Praeger, 1982); and James Farrell, *The Spirit of the Sixties: Making Postwar Radicalism* (New York: Routledge, 1987).

For different versions of the narrative of good sixties/bad sixties, see James Miller, *Democracy Is in the Streets: From Port Huron to the Siege of Chicago* (Cambridge, Mass.: Harvard University Press, 1994); Todd Gitlin, *The Sixties: Years of Hope, Days of Rage* (New York: Bantam, 1987); and Allen J. Matusow, *The Unraveling of America: A History of Liberalism in the 1960s* (New York: Harper and Row, 1984). For analyses and criticism of these narratives, see Sohnya Sayres, Anders Stephanson, Stanley Aronowitz, and Fredric Jameson, eds., *The 60s Without Apology* (Minneapolis: University of Minnesota Press, 1984); Wini Briones, "Whose New Left?" *JAH* 75:2 (1988): 528–45; Van Gosse, "A Movement of Movements: The Definition and Periodization of the New Left," in Jean-Christophe Agnew and Roy Rosensweig, *A Companion to Post-1945 America* (New York: Wiley-Blackwell, 2006); and Gosse, *Rethinking the New Left: An Interpretative History* (New York: Palgrave, 2005); David Farber, "The 60s: Myth and Reality," *Chronicle of Higher Education*, December 7, 1994, B1; and Rick Perlstein, "Who Owns the Sixties? The Opening of a Scholarly Generation Gap," *Lingua Franca*, May/June 1996, 30–37.

Scholars have long debated the reasons for the New Left's shift away from the South after 1965. Crucial victories (the passage of the 1964 Civil Rights Act and the 1965 Voting Rights Act) and failures (the Democratic Party's failure to seat the Mississippi Freedom Democratic Party at the 1964 Atlantic City convention) certainly had an effect. Local movements' demands for more political power and on-the-ground equality than national civil rights leaders and their liberal allies could produce also played a role. External to the movement, growing American involvement in Vietnam also contributed. On the anti-war movement, see Thomas Powers, *The War at Home: Vietnam and the American People, 1964–1968* (New York: Grossman, 1973); Fred Halstead, *Out Now! A Participant's Account of the American Movement Against the Vietnam War* (New York: Monad, 1978); Nancy Zaroulis and Gerald Sullivan, *Who Spoke Up? American Protest Against the War in Vietnam, 1963–1975* (New York: Doubleday, 1984); Charles DeBenedetti and Charles Chatfield, *An American Ordeal: The Antiwar Movement of the Vietnam Era* (Syracuse, N.Y.: Syracuse University Press, 1990); Tom Wells, *The War Within: America's Battle over Vietnam* (Berkeley: University of California Press, 1994); Richard Moser, *The New Winter Soldiers: GI and Veteran Dissent During the Vietnam Era* (New Brunswick, N.J.: Rutgers University Press, 1996); and Andrew Hunt, *The Turning: A History of the Vietnam Veterans Against the War* (New York: New York University Press, 1999).

6. Angela Davis, "Black Nationalism: The Sixties and the Nineties," in *Black Popular Culture*, ed. Gina Dent (Seattle: Bay Press, 1992), 320.

7. Clayborne Carson, *In Struggle: SNCC and the Black Awakening of the 1960s* (Cambridge, Mass.: Harvard University Press, 1981), 134–36, 156–57; Fannie Lou Hamer et al., *To Praise Our Bridges: An Autobiography* (Jackson, Miss.: KIPCO, 1967); Forman, *Making of Black Revolutionaries*, 407–11.

Standard accounts of this period trace a shift of activism from the southern civil rights movement, nonviolence, and integration to the national Black Power movement, armed resistance, and separation. What this narrative actually describes is not the history of black organizing but the history of white middle-class interest in black organizing. As a new generation of historians has argued, civil rights organizing outside the South surged at the end of World War II and continued through the 1950s and into the 1960s. Most of the test cases combined to make the *Brown* case, for example, grew out of attempts to desegregate schools outside the South. The sit-in movement did not stop at the old borders of Dixie. And in 1963 and 1964, as SNCC increasingly became the focus of white liberal and left attention, African American activists worked Philadelphia, New York, Detroit, and elsewhere to end racial discrimination in education, housing, employment, and policing. See Jacquelyn Jones, "The Long Civil Rights Movement and the Political Uses of the Past," *Journal of American History* 91:4 (March 2005), http://www.historycooperative.org/journals/jah/91.4/hall.html, accessed April 8, 2010; and Sugrue, *Sweet Land of Liberty*.

8. For the history of Black Power, see Malcolm X, *Autobiography of Malcolm X*; Malcolm X, *By Any Means Necessary*, ed. George Breitman (New York: Pathfinder Press, 1970), 63–64; Peniel E. Joseph, *Waiting 'til the Midnight Hour: A Narrative History of Black Power in America* (New York: Henry Holt, 2006); Joseph, ed., *The Black Power Movement: Rethinking the Civil Rights–Black Power Era* (New York: Routledge, 2006); William L. Van Deburg, *New Day in Babylon: The Black Power Movement and American Culture, 1965–1975* (Chicago: University of Chicago Press, 1993); Jeffrey Ogbar, *Black Power: Radical Politics and African American Identity* (Baltimore: Johns Hopkins University Press, 2004); Komozi Woodard, *Nation Within Nation: Amiri Baraka (LeRoi Jones) and Black Power Politics* (Chapel Hill: University of North Carolina Press, 1999); Jerry Gafio Watts, *Amiri Baraka: The Politics and Art of a Black Intellectual* (New York: New York University Press, 2001); Patricia Hill Collins, *From Black Power to Hip Hop: Racism Nationalism, and Feminism* (Philadelphia: Temple University Press, 2006).

9. Stokely Carmichael and Charles V. Hamilton, *Black Power: The Politics of Liberation in America* (New York: Random House, 1967), quotes, 208–10; Carson, *In Struggle*, 191–228; Forman, *Making of Black Revolutionaries*, 456–60. Carmichael's major writings in this period include "What We Want," *New York Review of Books*, September 22, 1966; "Toward Black Liberation," *Massachusetts Review* 7:4 (Autumn 1966): 637–51; and *Stokely Speaks: Black Power back to Pan-Africanism* (New York: Random House, 1971). See also Carmichael with Ekwueme Michael Thelwell, *Ready for Revolution: The Life and Struggles of Stokely Carmichael (Kwame Ture)* (New York: Scribner, 2003).

10. "Negroes Divided by 'Black Power' Cry," *Chicago Tribune*, July 8, 1966, A5; "Black Power Is Black Death," *New York Times*, July 7, 1966, 35; "Black Power," *New York Times*, July 10, 1966, 143; Jack Nelson, "Ex-Chairman of SNCC Quits over Militancy," *Los Angeles Times*, July 1, 1966, 6; Gene Roberts, "Why the Cry for 'Black Power,'" *New York Times*, July 2, 1966; Roberts, "Black Power Idea Long in Planning," *New York Times*, August 5, 1966; I. F. Stone, "Why They Cry Black

Power," *I. F. Stone's Weekly*, September 19, 1966; Jack Nelson, "Ousted Chairman Tells of New Setup in SNCC," *Los Angeles Times*, July 29, 1966, 5; Nelson, "Black Power Bid Hurt March, Dr. King Says," *Los Angeles Times*, June 29, 1966, 4; Nelson, "The 'Color' Line Closes on King," *Los Angeles Times*, July 3, 1966, B5, B1; " 'Black Power': Negro Leaders Split over Policy," *New York Times*, July 10, 1966, 143; "Distorted Cry?" *Newsweek*, August 8, 1966, 54.

11. "Uses of Black Power," *Los Angeles Times*, June 24, 1966, A4; "Militancy on the March," *Wall Street Journal*, June 24, 1966, 8; Rowland Evans and Robert Novak, "The Tragedy of Black Power," *Los Angeles Times*, July 8, 1966, A5; Nelson, "The 'Color' Line Closes on King;" Robert Lewis Shayon, "The Real Stokely Carmichael," *Saturday Review*, July 9, 1966, 42; "The Politics of Frustration," *New York Times*, August 7, 1966; William S. White, "Rights Crossroads," *Washington Post*, July 9, 1966, A15.

12. " 'Black Power': Negro Leaders Split over Policy," 143; " 'Black Power' Labeled Damaging to the Country," *Los Angeles Times*, July 1, 1966, 6; Tom Wicker, "White Moderates and Black Power," *New York Times*, July 21, 1966, 25; John D. Pomfret, "President Warns Negroes of Peril to Their Advance," *New York Times*, July 21, 1966; Paul Good, "A White Look at Black Power," *Nation*, August 8, 1966, 112–17.

13. "Black Power—How Powerful?" *Christian Science Monitor*, July 11, 1966; "Distorted Cry?" 54; Wicker, "White Moderates and Black Power;" Good, "White Look at Black Power," 112.

14. Malcolm X, *Malcolm X Speaks* (New York: Grove, 1965); and Malcolm X, *By Any Means Necessary*.

15. Lerone Bennett Jr., "Stokely Carmichael: Architect of Black Power," *Ebony*, September 1966, 25–32; "A 'Black Power' Speech That Has Congress Aroused," *U.S. News and World Report*, August 22, 1966, 6; Peter Goldman, "Black Power: Politics of Frustration," *Newsweek*, July 11, 1966; Gene Roberts, "Black Power Idea Long in Planning,"; Roberts, "Black Power Prophet: Stokely Carmichael," *New York Times*, August 5, 1966, 1, 10; Carmichael, *Ready for the Revolution*. For the speech Carmichael gave at UC Berkeley in October 1966, see Carmichael, "Black Power," audio recording and text, online at American Rhetoric, http://www.americanrhetoric.com/speeches/stokelycarmichaelblackpower.html, accessed April 1, 2010.

16. Carmichael and Hamilton, *Black Power*; Carmichael, "What We Want."

17. Abbie Hoffman, "SNCC: The Desecration of a Delayed Dream," *Village Voice*, December 15, 1966; Carson, *In Struggle*, 295.

18. Lester, "Angry Children of Malcolm X," 21; Good, "White Look at Black Power," 114; Vincent Harding, "Black Power and the American Christ," *Christian Century*, January 4, 1967, 10–13, quote, 12; June Meyer, "Spokesman for the Blacks," *Nation*, December 4, 1967, 597–99. Losing white liberal support, however unrealistic, unreliable, and coated with romance it had always been, hurt more than the group's finances. It also destroyed the small brake white liberals could apply to attempts by conservatives to use federal resources against the

movement. Facing down racist sheriffs and police officers in the South was difficult enough. But challenging local law enforcement officials able to access active FBI and other federal support was suicidal. The FBI had received reports about SNCC since the fall of 1960, and after 1964, FBI field offices began investigating whether Communists had successfully infiltrated the organization. By 1965, FBI director J. Edgar Hoover had ordered wiretaps on SNCC phones. The FBI did not begin active surveillance, infiltration, and sabotage tactics against SNCC, however, until the summer of 1967, when Hoover placed the group in the Counterintelligence Program (COINTELPRO). There, SNCC joined a growing list of other black organizations the FBI and other law enforcement agencies were actively working to subvert, including the Black Panthers and US, a black nationalist organization led by Ron Karenga. COINTELPRO damaged all these organizations. A more structured and disciplined SNCC, however, would have been less vulnerable to government subversion and more able to strategize about the risks and benefits of proposed SNCC actions. See Carson, *In Struggle*, 257–64; David Cunningham, *There's Something Happening Here: The New Left, the Klan, and FBI Counterintelligence* (Berkeley: University of California Press, 2004); Kenneth O'Reilly, *"Racial Matters": The FBI's Secret File on Black America, 1960–1972* (New York: Free Press, 1989); and Ward Churchill and Jim Vander Wall, *Agents of Repression: The FBI's Secret Wars Against the Black Panther Party and the American Indian Movement* (Boston: South End Press, 1988).

19. I. F. Stone, "SNCC Does Not Wish to Become a New Version of the White Man's Burden," *I. F. Stone's Weekly*, June 6, 1966, 3; Andrew Kopkind, "The Future of Black Power: A Movement in Search of a Program," *New Republic*, January 7, 1967, 16–18, quotes, 18.

20. Alvin Poussaint, "A Negro Psychiatrist Explains the Negro Psyche," *New York Times Magazine*, August 20, 1967; Poussaint, "How the 'White Problem' Spawned 'Black Power,'" *Ebony*, August 1967, 88–90. 92, 94, quotes, 90, 92; Charles Hamilton, panel celebrating the fortieth anniversary of the publication of *Black Power*, American Historical Association Meeting, Atlanta, Georgia, January 4, 2007. Poussaint is much more critical of whites in *Ebony*.

21. James Baldwin, *Nobody Knows My Name* (1961; New York: Vintage, 1993), 79; Van Deburg, *New Day in Babylon*, quotes, 5, 11; "Lester, "Beep! Beep! Bang! Bang! Umgawa! BLACK POWER!" 100, 102; "Black Power and Black Pride," *Time*, December 1, 1967; Harold Cruise, *Rebellion or Revolution* (New York: William Morrow, 1968), 95.

22. Lester, *Look Out, Whitey*, 23, 113; Carawan and Carawan, *Sing for Freedom*, 115; 113; National Advisory Commission on Civil Disorders (the Kerner Commission), *Report of the National Advisory Committee on Civil Disorders* (New York: Dutton, 1968); Zaroulis and Sullivan, *Who Spoke Up?* 128–29. The Kerner Commission, appointed by Congress to study the unrest, counted forty-one serious episodes of violence in the first nine months of 1967 alone.

23. Sources on the Black Panther Party include Charles E. Jones, ed., *The Black Panther Party [Reconsidered]* (Baltimore: Black Classic Press, 1998); Jama

Lazerow and Yohuru Williams, eds., *In Search of the Black Panther Party: New Perspectives on a Revolutionary Movement* (Durham, N.C.: Duke University Press, 2006); Joseph, *Wait 'til the Midnight Hour*.

24. Sol Stern, "A Short Account of International Student Politics and the Cold War with Particular Reference to the NSA, CIA, etc.," *Ramparts*, March 1967, 29–38. For Malcolm's use of the phrase "by any means necessary," see Malcolm X, *By Any Means Necessary*. The phrase first appeared as a translation of a line in Jean-Paul Sartre's 1948 play *Dirty Hands*.

25. Sources on the 1967 National Conference for a New Politics include Simon Hall, "On the Tail of the Panther: Black Power and the 1967 Convention of the National Conference for New Politics," *Journal of American* Studies 37 (2003): 59–78; "Symposium: Chicago's 'Black Caucus,'" *Ramparts*, November 1967, 99; Renata Adler, "Letter from the Palmer House," *New Yorker*, September 23, 1967, 58; Richard Blumenthal, "New Politics at Chicago," *Nation*, September 25, 1967, 274; Andrew Ridgeway, "Freak-Out in Chicago: The National Conference of New Politics," *New Republic,* September 16, 1967, 10; Walter Goodman, "Yessir, Boss, Said the White Radicals: When Black Power Runs the New Left," *New York Times Magazine*, September 24, 1967, 28–9, 124–26; Kirkpatrick Sale, *SDS* (New York: Random House, 1973), 269, 277, 347; Miller, *Democracy Is in the Streets*, 258. On the Free Huey movement, see "Backers Pack Court for Huey," *Berkeley Barb*, December 8–14, 1967, 1, 3; and Joel Wilson, "'Free Huey': The Black Panther Party, the Peace and Freedom Party, and the Politics of Race in 1968" (PhD diss., University of California, Santa Cruz, 2002).

26. Simon Hall, *Peace and Freedom: The Civil Rights and Anti-war Movements in the 1960s* (Philadelphia: University of Pennsylvania Press, 2006); Joel Wilson, "Invisible Cages: Racialized Politics and the Alliance between the Panthers and the Peace and Freedom Party," in Lazerow and Williams, *In Search of the Black Panther Party*, 191–222; W. J. Rorabaugh, *Berkeley at War: The 1960s* (New York: Oxford University Press, 1989); *Berkeley Gazette*, February 12, 1968.

27. Karin Asbley, Bill Ayers, Bernardine Dohrn, John Jacob, Jeff Jones, Gerry Long, Home Machtinger, Jim Mellen, Terry Robbins, Mark Rudd, and Steve Tappis, "You Don't Need a Weatherman to Know Which Way the Wind Blows," *New Left Notes*, June 18, 1969; Bob Dylan, "Subterranean Homesick Blues," in Dylan, *Lyrics: 1962–2001* (New York: Simon and Schuster, 2004). On the Weather Underground, see G. Louis Heath, *Vandals in the Bomb Factory* (New York: Scarecrow Press, 1976); Jeremy Varon, *Bringing the War Home: The Weather Underground, The Red Army Faction, and Revolutionary Violence in the Sixties and Seventies* (Berkeley: University of California Press, 2004); Ron Jacobs, *The Way the Wind Blew: A History of the Weather Underground* (New York: Verso, 1997); Dan Berger, *Outlaws of America: The Weather Underground and the Politics of Solidarity* (San Francisco: AK Press, 2006); Bernardine Dohrn, Bill Ayers, and Jeff Jones, eds., *Sing a Battle Song: The Revolutionary Poetry, Statements, and Communiqués of the Weather Underground, 1970–1974* (New York: Seven Stories, 2006); and David Barber, *A Hard Rain Fell: SDS and Why It Failed* (Jackson: University of Mississippi Press, 2008).

28. Sale, *SDS*; Varon, *Bringing the War Home*.
29. Dohrn, Ayers, and Jones, *Sing a Battle Song*.
30. "You Don't Need a Weatherman"; Van Deburg, *New Day in Babylon*.
31. Dohrn, Ayers, and Jones, *Sing a Battle Song*.
32. "You Don't Need a Weatherman"; Dohrn, Ayers, and Jones, *Sing a Battle Song*.
33. Laura Browder, *Slippery Characters: Ethnic Impersonators and American Identities* (Chapel Hill: University of North Carolina Press, 2000).
34. White Panther Party Founding Document, online at http://makemyday.free.fr/wp6.htm, accessed July 1, 2009; Jeff A. Hale, "The White Panthers' 'Total Assault on the Culture,'" in *Imagine Nation: The American Counter Culture of the 1960s and 70s*, ed. Peter Braunstein and Michael William Doyle (New York: Routledge, 2002); John Sinclair, *Guitar Army: Rock and Revolution with the MC-5 and the White Panther Party* (1972; New York: Process, 2007); David A. Carson, *Grit, Noise, and Revolution: The Birth of Detroit Rock 'n' Roll* (Ann Arbor: University of Michigan Press, 2006).
35. Hale, "White Panthers' 'Total Assault on the Culture.'"
36. Hale, "White Panthers' 'Total Assault on the Culture'"; Sinclair, *Guitar Army*; Carson, *Grit, Noise, and Revolution*.
37. Hale, "White Panthers' 'Total Assault on the Culture'"; Sinclair, *Guitar Army*; Carson, *Grit, Noise, and Revolution*.
38. Hale, "White Panthers' 'Total Assault on the Culture'"; Pun Plamondon, *Lost from the Ottawa: The Journey Back* (Victoria, B.C.: Trafford, 2005).
39. In his memoir, Plamondon describes discovering his Native American heritage later in his life. At the time of the White Panthers, however, he thought of himself as a white man. Plamondon, *Lost from the Ottawa*.
40. Patrician Campbell Hearst, *Every Secret Thing* (Garden City, N.Y.: Doubleday, 1982); Vin McLellan and Paul Avery, *The Voices of Guns* (New York: Putnam, 1977); Les Payne and Tim Findley, *The Life and Death of the SLA* (New York: Ballantine Books, 1976); James Feron, "Shouting of Slogans Disrupts a Hearing on Brink's Holdup," *New York Times*, September 16, 1982; Robert Hanley, "State Jury Finds 3 Radicals Guilty in Brink's Killings," *New York Times*, September 15, 1983; Elizabeth Kolbert, "The Prisoner," *New Yorker*, July 16, 2001; Susan Braudy, *The Boudins and the Aristocracy of the Left* (New York: Knopf, 2003); Ayers, *Fugitive Days*.
41. Wells, *War Within*; Michael S. Foley, *Confronting the War Machine: Draft Resistance During the Vietnam War* (Chapel Hill: University of North Carolina Press, 2003).
42. Hayden quoted in Miller, *Democracy Is in the Streets*, 238–313; Andrew Kopkind, "Looking Backward," *Ramparts*, February 1973, 32.
43. "Draft Resistance," project file, Series 3, Section 5, Reel 26, SDS Papers, State Historical Society of Wisconsin, microfilm edition (hereafter cited as SDS microfilm); and Carl Oglesby, *Ravens in the Storm: A Personal History of the Anti-War Movement* (New York: Scribner, 2008).
44. Gregory Calvert's January 1967 report in *New Left Notes*, quoted in Sale, *SDS*, 315–16.

45. Gregory Calvert, "In White America: Radical Consciousness and Social Change," in *The New Left: A Documentary History*, ed. Massimo Teodori (New York: Bobbs-Merrill, 1969), 412–18.

46. Calvert, "In White America."

47. Wells, *War Within*; Zaroulis and Sullivan, *Who Spoke Up?*; Hall, *Peace and Freedom*; Van Gosse, *Where the Boys Are: Cuba, Cold War America, and the Making of the New Left* (New York: Verso, 1993); Carol Brightman and Sandra Levinson, eds., *The Venceremos Brigade: Young Americans Sharing the Life and Work of Revolutionary Cuba* (New York: Simon and Schuster, 1971); Jon Lee Anderson, *Che Guevara: A Revolutionary Life* (New York: Grove, 1997); Craig J. Jenkins, *The Politics of Insurgency: The Farm Workers Movement in the 1960s* (New York: Columbia University Press, 1985); Kirkpatrick Sale, *The Green Revolution: The American Environmental Movement, 1962–1992* (New York: Hill and Wang, 1993); Philip Shabecoff, *A Fierce Green Fire: the American Environmental Movement* (Washington, D.C.: Island Press, 2003). Professors too got in on this act. Historians invented social history, the study of history from "the bottom up," and English professors challenged a literary canon that celebrated the work of "dead white males." My comments about miners and middle-class activists' alliances with the labor movement draw on my current research, "Shooting in Harlan: Documentary Work, the Labor Reform Movement, and New Left Activism."

48. Foley, *Confronting the War Machine*; Carlos Muñoz, *Youth, Identity, and Power: The Chicano Movement* (New York: Verso, 1989); Francisco Arturo Rosales, *Chicano! The History of the Mexican American Civil Rights Movement* (Houston: Arte Publico Press, 1997); Sara Evans, *Personal Politics: The Roots of Women's Liberation in the Civil Rights Movement and the New Left* (New York: Vintage, 1979); Ruth Rosen, *The World Split Open: How the Modern Women's Movement Changed America* (New York: Penguin, 2000); Rachel Blau DuPlessis and Ann Snitow, eds., *The Feminist Memoir Project: Voices from Women's Liberation* (New York: Three Rivers Press, 1998); Maxine Williams and Pamela Newman, *Black Women's Liberation* (New York: Pathfinder Press, 1970); Gloria T. Hull, Patricia Bell-Scott, and Barbara Smith, *All the Women Are White, All the Blacks Are Men, but Some of Us Are Brave: Black Women's Studies* (New York: Feminist Press, 1982); Ernesto Chávez, *"¡Mi raza primero!" (My people first!): Nationalism, Identity, and Insurgency in the Chicano Movement in Los Angeles, 1966–1978* (Berkeley: University of California Press, 2002); William Wei, *The Asian American Movement* (Philadelphia: Temple University Press, 1993).

49. On the hippies, see "The Hippies," cover story, *Time*, July 7, 1967, 18–21; Richard Goldstein, "Love: A Groovy Idea While He Lasted," *Village Voice*, October 19, 1967, 1, 12–13; Hans Toch, "Last Word on the Hippies," *Nation*, December 4, 1967, 582–88; Warren Hinckle, "The Social History of the Hippies," *Ramparts*, March 1967, 5–26; Lewis Yablonsky, *The Hippie Trip* (New York: Pegasus, 1968); Tom Wolfe, *The Electric Kool-Aid Acid Test* (New York: Farrar, Straus, and Giroux, 1968); Paul Perry, *On the Bus* (New York: Thunder's Mouth Press, 1990); Charles A. Reich, *The Greening of America* (New York: Crown, 1970); Timothy Miller,

The 60's Communes: Hippies and Beyond (Syracuse, N.Y.: Syracuse University Press, 1999); and the excellent Carol Brightman, Sweet Chaos: The Grateful Dead's American Adventure (New York: Clarkson Potter, 1998).

50. The quotes are from Goldstein, "Love"; Toch, "Last Word;" and Time's "Hippies."

51. Wolfe, Electric Kool-Aid Acid Test, 9, 112–13, quote, 9.

52. Paul Potter, A Name for Ourselves: Feelings About Authenticity, Love, Intuitive Politics, Us (New York: Little, Brown, 1971); Timothy Leary's 1968 Playboy interview is reprinted as "She Comes in Colors" in The Politics of Ecstasy (1972; Berkeley, Calif.: Ronin, 1998), 118–59; Yablonsky, Hippie Trip.

53. Godfrey Hodgson, America in Our Time: From World War II to Nixon—What Happened and Why (New York: Doubleday, 1976), 337–38; Jon Landau's early Rolling Stone pieces are collected in Landau, It's Too Late to Stop Now: A Rock and Roll Journal (New York: Straight Arrow Press, 1972), quote, 24.

54. Andrew Kopkind, "Woodstock Nation" (Hard Times, 1969), in The Age of Rock 2: Sights and Sounds of the American Cultural Revolution, ed. Jonathan Eisen (New York: Vintage, 1970), 312–18; "A Fleeting, Wonderful Moment of 'Community' " (New Yorker, 1969), in "Takin' It to the Streets": A Sixties Reader, ed. Alexander Bloom and Wini Breines (New York: Oxford University Press, 2003), 508–11.

55. Tom Smucker, "The Politics of Rock: Movement vs. Groovement," 83–91, quotes, 84, 85, 87; and T. Procter Lippincott, "The Culture Vultures," 124–32, both in Eisen, Age of Rock 2. "The Culture Vultures" examines the contradiction within the counterculture between the goal of "revolutionary" change and the fact that many people were making money off the counterculture: "The growing momentum of our groovy 'alternative' subculture . . . continues to be dampened by a fundamental conflict: the attempt to develop a truly human, revolutionary lifestyle within the confines of an exploitative commercial system. Profit motive is robbing us of our thing, especially our music." For the history of how corporate exploitation of the counterculture evolved right along with the cultural rebellion itself, see Thomas Frank, The Conquest of Cool: Business Culture, Counterculture, and the Rise of Hip Consumerism (Chicago: University of Chicago Press, 1997).

56. Kopkind, "Woodstock Nation," 317.

57. Michael Lydon, "The Rolling Stones—At Play in the Apocalypse" (Ramparts, 1970), in Bloom and Breines, "Takin' It to the Streets," 516–20; "California Rock Bash Leaves 4 Dead and 2 Born," New York Daily News, and George Paul Csicery, "Altamont, California, December 6, 1969," in The Age of Rock: Sounds of the American Cultural Revolution: A Reader, ed. Jonathan Eisen (New York: Random House, 1969), 143–48; Hunter S. Thompson, Hell's Angels: A Strange and Terrible Saga (New York: Ballantine, 1967); Albert Maysles and David Maysles, Gimme Shelter (Maysles Films, 1970).

58. Keith Melville, Communes in the Counter Culture: Origins, Theories, Styles of Life (New York: William Morrow, 1972); Richard Fairfield, Communes USA: A Personal Tour (New York: Penguin, 1972); Michael Schumacher, Dharma Lion: A Critical Biography of Allen Ginsberg (New York: St. Martin's, 1994), 508. On the romanticization of Indians, a white fantasy that rivaled white Negroism, see Gary

Snyder, "Why Tribe," in *Earth House Hold: Technical Notes & Queries to Fellow Dharma Revolutionaries* (New York: New Directions, 1969).

59. Melville, *Communes,* quotes, 152; Schumacher, *Dharma Lion,* 508; Raymond Mungo, *Total Loss Farm: A Year in the Life* (New York: Dutton, 1970), quotes, 11–16; Andrew Kopkind, "The New Left Looks East," *Ramparts,* July 1973.

60. Melville, *Communes,* 133–67. On counterculture primitivism, see Reich, *Greening,* 284, 414–24.

61. On Gestalt, see Frederick Perls, Paul Goodman, and Ralph Hefferline, *Gestalt Therapy: Excitement and Growth in the Human Personality* (1951; New York: Julian Press, 1969); and Richard King, *The Party of Eros: Radical Social Thought and the Realm of Freedom* (Chapel Hill: University of North Carolina Press, 1972), 94–100. On the human potential movement, see Abraham Maslow, *Toward a Psychology of Being* (New York: Van Nostrand, 1968); and Carl Rogers, *On Becoming a Person: A Therapist's View of Psychotherapy* (Boston: Houghton Mifflin, 1961). On Esalen, see Hodgson, *America in Our Time,* 329–30; Wolfe, *Electric Kool-Aid Acid Test,* 106–7. Henry Miller, *Tropic of Capricorn* (1938; New York: Grove, 1994), 12. On the Beatles, see John Lennon, Paul McCartney, George Harrison, and Ringo Starr, *The Beatles Anthology* (New York: Chronicle Books, 2000).

62. Ralph Larkin and Daniel Foss, "Lexicon of Folk Etymology," in Sayres et al., *60s Without Apology,* 360–77; Jerry Faber, "The Student as Nigger," *Los Angeles Free Press,* March 3, 1967, reprinted by SDS as a pamphlet, Series 4B, Reel 36, Folders 85, 87, SDS microfilm, and expanded as *The Student as Nigger* (New York: Pocket Books, 1969); Goldstein, "Love"; Naomi Weisstein, "Woman as Nigger," *Psychology Today,* October 1969. "Woman Is the Nigger of the World" was recorded by John Lennon and Yoko Ono's Plastic Ono Band in April 1972 and released as a single in May and on the album *Some Time in New York City* (1972). See Philip Norman, *John Lennon: The Life* (New York: Ecco, 2008); and *The Dick Cavett Show: John and Yoko Collection* (Shout Factory, 2005) which contains this episode, aired on May 12, 1972.

63. Ayers, *Fugitive Days,* quotes, 89–90, 218.

Chapter 7: The Making of Christian Countercultures

1. This section draws on Edward Plowman, "Witnessing to Hippies," *Christianity Today* [hereafter *CT*], June 7, 1968, 905–6; Plowman, "The Battle for Berkeley," *CT,* May 8, 1970, 752; Plowman, "The Jesus Presses are Rolling," *CT,* April 9, 1971, 664; Plowman, "Shore to Shore: Wave of Witness," *CT,* May 7, 1971, 762–63; Plowman, "Demonstrating for Jesus," *CT,* May 21, 1971, 41–42; Plowman, "The Jesus Movement: Now It's in the Hamlets," *CT,* June 18, 1971, 903–4; Plowman, "Jesus Saves: Our Alienated Youth," *Eternity,* August 1971, 8–11, 31; Maurice Allan, "God's Thing in Hippieville," *Christian Life* 29 (1968): 20–23, 35–38; "The New Rebel Cry: Jesus is Coming!" *Time,* June 21, 1971, 56–63; "The Jesus People," *U.S. News and World Report,* March 22, 1971: 97; "The Jesus Movement: Impact on Youth and Culture," *U.S. News and World Report,* March 20, 1972, 59–64; "The Jesus Craze," *Life,* December 31, 1971; Jess Moody, *The Jesus Freaks* (Waco, Tex.:

Word Books, 1971; includes a list of "liberated churches"); "Street Christians: Jesus as the Ultimate Trip," *Time*, August 3, 1970; Phil Tracy, "The Jesus Freaks: Savagery and Salvation on Sunset Strip," *Commonweal*, October 1970; Brian Vachon, "The Jesus Movement Is Upon Us," *Look*, February 9, 1971, 15–21; James Nolan, "Jesus Now: Hogwash and Holy Water," *Ramparts*, August 1971, 20–26; Ronald M. Enroth, Edward E. Ericson Jr., and C. Breckinridge Peters, *The Jesus People: Old-Time Religion in the Age of Aquarius* (Grand Rapids, Mich.: Eerdmans, 1972); Jeannette Struchen, *Zapped by Jesus* (New York: A. J. Holman, 1972); *The Street People: Selections from* Right On! *Berkeley's Christian Underground Student* Newspaper (Valley Forge, Pa.: Judson Press, 1971); Michael Zeik, ed., *New Christian Communities* (New York: Roth Publishing, 1973); Stephen Prothero, *American Jesus: How the Son of God Became a National Icon* (New York: Farrar, Straus, and Giroux, 2003), 142–57; and Tom Wolfe, "The Me Decade and the Third Great Awakening," *New York Magazine*, August 23, 1976. For the larger religious and cultural context, see "The Guru Game: The Peace Which Passeth All Understanding," a special issue of *Ramparts*, July 1973, 26–35, 47–57; Robert S. Ellwood, *The Sixties Spiritual Awakening: American Religion Moving from Modern to Postmodern* (New Brunswick, N.J.: Rutgers University Press, 1994); Donald E. Miller, *Reinventing American Protestantism: Christianity in the New Millennium* (Berkeley: University of California Press, 1997); and Steven Tipton, *Getting Saved from the Sixties* (Berkeley: University of California Press, 1982).

2. "New Rebel Cry," 56; "The Jesus Revolution," *Time*, June 21, 1975, issue includes Jesus cover image.

3. Michael Shamberg, *Guerrilla Television* (New York: Holt, Rinehart, and Winston, 1971): "No alternative cultural vision is going to succeed in Media-America unless it has its own alternative structures, not just alternative content pumped across existing ones." He was writing about the left, but the Christian right in particular seems to have actually built its own structures. Jim Montgomery, "The Electric Church," *Wall Street Journal*, May 19, 1978, 1, 7. On evangelicals' and fundamentalists' creation of their own countercultures, see Carol Flake, *Redemptorama: Culture, Politics, and the New Evangelicalism* (New York: Anchor Books, 1984); and William Martin, *With God on Our Side* (New York: Broadway Books, 1996), Rodgers quote, 320. Nineteenth-century evangelicals had their own institutions, but the nature of this institution-building changed dramatically in the postwar period. See R. Laurence Moore, *Selling God: American Religion in the Marketplace of Culture* (New York: Oxford University Press, 1994).

4. Howard Phillips's account of the meeting that set up Moral Majority is in Dinesh D'Souza, *Falwell: Before the Millennium* (Chicago: Regnery, 1984), 110.

5. Enroth, Erickson, and Peters, *Jesus People*, quote, 103; Keith Melville, *Communes in the Counter Culture: Origins, Theories, Styles of Life* (New York: Morrow, 1972), quotes, 210.

6. Allan, "God's Thing in Hippieville."

7. Jack Sparks, "Letters to Street Christians," *Campus Life*, April 1972, 52–54; Sara Diamond, *Spiritual Warfare: The Politics of the Christian Right* (Cambridge,

Mass.: South End Press, 1989) argues that Bill Bright and Campus Crusade for Christ always covertly funded CWLF as a way to thwart the anti-war movement. Carol Flake, *Redemptorama*, argues that the CWLF, which became the Berkley Christian Coalition, became genuinely radicalized.

8. "New Rebel Cry," quote, 59; Plowman, "Jesus Saves: Our Alienated Youth."

9. Arthur Blessitt, *Turned On to Jesus* (New York: Hawthorn Books, 1971), 143; Sparks, "Letters to Street Christians;" Enroth, Erickson, and Peters, *Jesus People*, quote from *Hollywood Free Paper*, 42. Robert Rogers focused two episodes of his NBC show *First Tuesday* on the Jesus People. Films about the Jesus People include "The Son Worshipers" (1971); George Landow, *Thank You Jesus for the Eternal Present* (1973) and *A Film of Their Spring Tour Commissioned by CWLF of Berkeley, California* (1974); and *The Devout Young* (1970).

10. Plowman, "Jesus Presses are Rolling"; Enroth, Erickson, and Peters, *Jesus People*, 105. The cheer is in Prothero, *American Jesus*, 125–26.

11. Plowman, "Demonstrating for Jesus": Enroth, Erickson, and Peters, *Jesus People*, quotes, 102–5. On the business side of the Jesus movement, see Melville, *Communes in the Counter Culture*; Moore, *Selling God*, 5; and Prothero, *American Jesus*. Like the other counterculture, the Jesus People's counter counterculture became a business. For example, the *Hollywood Free Paper*'s store, mostly a mail order operation, sold bumper stickers, T-shirts, and other Jesus paraphernalia. On the Christian counterculture, see Doug Bandou, "Christianity's Parallel Universe," *American Enterprise*, November–December 1995, 58–61.

12. Enroth, Erickson, and Peters, *Jesus People*. Don Wilkerson, *Coffeehouse Manuel* (Minneapolis, Minn.: Bethany Fellowship, 1973) is a how-to guide for starting a Christian coffeehouse. On Jesus music, see Paul Baker, *Why Should the Devil Have All the Good Music?* (Waco, Tex.: Word Books, 1979); David L. C. Anderson, ed., *The New Jesus Style Songs, Vol. 1* (Minneapolis, Minn.: Augsburg Publishing House, 1972); and Plowman, "Taking Stock of Jesus Rock," *CT*, February 26, 1971, 512–13.

13. Jane Howard, "The Groovy Christians of Rye," *Life*, May 14, 1971; Enroth, Erickson, and Peters, *Jesus People*, 79–83, 91, quote, 80; Philip Yancey, "The Norman Sound of Jesus Music," *Campus Life*, August–September 1971, 58–61; Larry Norman, "Right Here in America," on *Street Level* (One Way, 1970), transcription mine.

14. Nolan, "Hogwash and Holy Water," quote, 23; Bob Hollister, "Christian Communes: A New Way of Living," *Christian Life* 35 (June 1973): 16–18, 66–71; Melville, *Communes in the Counter Culture*.

15. Howard, "Groovy Christians of Rye," quotes, 80, 84; "Guru Game"; Nolan, "Hogwash and Holy Water;" Tipton, *Getting Saved from the Sixties*.

16. "Guru Game"; Nolan, "Hogwash and Holy Water;" Melville, *Communes in the Counter Culture*; Ellwood, *Sixties Spiritual Awakening*; Tipton, *Saved from the Sixties*.

17. Prothero, *American Jesus*, 26–27, quote, 79; George Marsden, *Fundamentalism and American Culture: The Shaping of Twentieth-Century Evangelicalism, 1870–1925* (New York: Oxford University Press, 1980).

18. John G. Turner, *Bill Bright and Campus Crusade for Christ: The Renewal of Evangelicalism in Postwar America* (Chapel Hill: University of North Carolina Press, 2008); Jon R. Stone, *On the Boundaries of American Evangelicalism: The Postwar Evangelical Coalition* (New York: St. Martin's, 1997); Steven P. Miller, *Billy Graham and the Rise of the Republican South* (Philadelphia: University of Pennsylvania Press, 2009).

19. "New Rebel Cry," 36.

20. Enroth, Erickson, and Peters, *Jesus People*, 179–93; Larry Norman, *Upon This Rock* (Capitol, 1970) and *Street Level* (One Way, 1970). The transcription is mine. The most important Bible verse for the idea of the Rapture is 1 Thessalonians 4:16–17. Belief in the Rapture, in this sense, is part of many Americans' intense interest during the late sixties and early seventies in ways of escaping death. Other examples are reincarnation and interest in aliens that are imagined as having ways to prolong life.

21. Prothero, *American Jesus*, 130, 142; Paul Boyer, *When Time Shall Be No More: Prophecy Belief in Modern American Culture* (Cambridge, Mass.: Harvard University Press, 1992), 5–7, where he cites the figure nine million copies sold between 1970 and 1978; Martin, *With God on Our Side*, 92. This work has been continued in the hugely successful *Left Behind* series of novels published by Tim LaHaye and Jerry B. Jenkins beginning in 1995.

22. Linda Meissner, founder and leader of the Jesus People's Army, headquartered in Seattle, is the notable exception. She got her start with Don Wilkerson's Teen Challenge. Wilkerson started a ministry that targeted drug addicts on the streets of New York City in the fifties. See Enroth, Erickson, and Peters, *Jesus People*, 116–23.

23. Craig Yoe and Joseph Hopkins, "Farm Fellowship," *CT*, August 30, 1974, 298–300.

24. Marsden, *Fundamentalism and American Culture*; George Marsden, *Understanding Fundamentalism and Evangelicalism* (Grand Rapids, Mich.: Eerdmans, 1991); Martin, *With God on Our Side*.

25. Marsden, *Fundamentalism and American Culture*.

26. Enroth, Erickson, and Peters, *Jesus People*, 194–206; Howard, "Groovy Christians of Rye," quote, 81; James W. L. Hill, "The New Charismatics 1973," *Eternity*, March 1973, 23–25; Morton Kelsey, *Tongue Speaking: An Experiment in Spiritual Experience* (Garden City, N.Y.: Doubleday, 1964).

27. Edward E. Plowman, "Whatever Happened to the Jesus Movement?" *CT*, October 24, 1975, 102–4; Timothy Jones, "Jesus' People," *CT*, September 14, 1992, 20–25.

28. As I discovered after writing this section, Miller, *Reinventing American Protestantism*, makes a similar argument working from a different set of evidence. His focus is on institution-building and theology, while I am focusing here on cultural style.

29. Kenneth L. Woodward, "Born Again," *Newsweek*, October 25, 1976, 68–78. See also Allan J. Mayer, "Born-again Politics," *Newsweek*, September 15, 1980, 28–36, which estimates thirty million to sixty-five million evangelical Christians in 1980. This section draws heavily on Martin, *With God on Our Side*; Marsden,

Fundamentalism and American Culture; Perry Deane Young, *God's Bullies: Native Reflections on Preachers and Politics* (New York: Holt, Rinehart, and Winston, 1982); William R. Goodman and James H. Price, *Jerry Falwell, an Unauthorized Profile* (Lynchburg, Va.: Paris and Associates, 1981); Susan Friend Harding, *The Book of Jerry Falwell: Fundamentalist Language and Politics* (Princeton, N.J.: Princeton University Press, 2000); Diamond, *Spiritual Warfare*; Frances FitzGerald, "A Disciplined, Charging Army," *New Yorker*, May 18, 1981, 53–69; FitzGerald, *Cities on a Hill: A Journey Through Contemporary American Cultures* (New York: Simon and Schuster, 1981); and Flake, *Redemptorama*. See also Falwell's own publications: Falwell (ed.), *The Fundamentalist Phenomenon: The Resurgence of Conservative Christianity* (Garden City, N.Y.: Doubleday/Galilee, 1981); *Capturing a Town for Christ* (Old Tappan, N.J.: Revell, 1973); *Listen, America!* (Garden City, N.Y.: Doubleday, 1980); *Strength for the Journey: An Autobiography* (New York: Simon and Schuster, 1987); and *Falwell: An Autobiography* (Lynchburg, Va.: Liberty House, 1997). Gallup's estimate of fifty million evangelicals in 1976 was a gross overstatement, and yet the perception that there were so many conservative Christians fueled the rise of the religious right. In 1979, Gallup completed a poll for *Christianity Today* that estimated thirty-one million evangelicals: "The *Christianity Today*–Gallup Poll," *CT*, December 21, 1979, 13. On the controversy over the number of evangelicals and the size of the audience for evangelical television programs in particular, see Diamond, *Spiritual Warfare*, vi, 35–38, 251. Diamond estimates twenty million to forty million evangelicals in 1989. She cites her own interview with George Gallup Jr., who told Diamond that he had revised his early findings. Not one-third to one-quarter but about 10 percent of the population is "actively evangelical" (251).

30. Falwell, "Seven Things Corrupting America," 39–59, quote, 44; see also Falwell, "I Love America!" 21–37, both in Jerry Falwell, *America Can Be Saved* (Murfreesboro, Tenn.: Sword of the Lord Publishers, 1979). This book is hard to find, and the copy I used was located at the Lancaster Bible College in Lancaster, Pa.

31. Martin, *With God on Our Side*, 149–50; Falwell, "The Establishment," in *America Can Be Saved*, 137–49, quote, 148–49. Another version of the sermon, given in Atlanta in 1976, is on audiotape, BR256.F3 E855, in Liberty University Archives, Liberty University, Lynchburg, Va., hereafter LUV. Falwell, "Abortion-on-Demand: Is It Murder?" February 26, 1978, Sermon ID Code: SE-126, typed transcript, quote, 21, LUV.

32. Falwell, "Let's Reach the World Together," 9–19, quotes, 16, in *America Can Be Saved*.

33. Falwell, *Strength for the Journey*, quotes, 102–3.

34. Both cultural forms also came of age as the commercial recording industry developed, and both used recordings in various changing formats to extend the reach of life performances.

35. Falwell's sermons and autobiographical writing on his conversion include Falwell, *Strength for the Journey*, 102–9; Elmer Towns and Jerry Falwell, *Church Aflame* (Nashville: Impact Books, 1971), 22–23; Falwell, "The Divine Mandate for All Christians," 75–76, and "Capture America For God," 98–99, in *America Can*

Be Saved; and "*Penthouse* Interview: Reverend Jerry Falwell," *Penthouse*, March 1981, 59–60, 66, 150–56, quote, 156.

36. Falwell, *Strength for the Journey*, 104, 105, 108.

37. Falwell, *Strength for the Journey*, 110.

38. Falwell, "Abortion-on Demand: Is It Murder?" quotes, 11- 12. See also "Legalized Abortion-on-Demand: Is It Murder?" April 30, 1978, Sermon ID Code OTGH-292, tape, LUV; and Marsden, *Fundamentalism and American Culture*. The converted person often thanks a minister or church community and says they are key, but the accounts almost always foreground the agency of the individual.

39. Martin, *With God on Our Side*, Carter quotes, 150; "*Playboy* Interview: Jimmy Carter," *Playboy*, November 1976, 63–86; Charles Colson, *Born Again* (Old Tappan, N.J.: Revell, 1976), quotes, 115–17.

40. Woodward, "Born Again," 75; Eldridge Cleaver, *Soul on Ice* (New York: Dell, 1968), 44; Cleaver, *Soul on Fire* (Waco, Tex.: Word Books, 1978), 224. On Cleaver, see also James S. Tinney, " "Views of a Regenerate Radical," *CT*, June 8, 1977, 14–15.

41. Graham founded *Christianity Today* magazine in 1956. George Marsden, *Reforming Fundamentalism: Fuller Seminary and the New Evangelicalism* (Grand Rapids, Mich.: Eerdmans, 1987); Martin, *With God on Our Side*, 27–46. On Falwell's position on terms, see "*Penthouse* Interview: Reverend Jerry Falwell," 150–51. Moore, *Religious Outsiders*, argues that a conservative theological perspective has had a continuous appeal for many Americans, but that fundamentalist ministers have taught their followers to see themselves as outsiders. Nineteenth-century evangelicals saw themselves as outsiders too (155–60).

42. On building the Thomas Road Baptist Church and its ministries, see all the sermons in Falwell, *America Can Be Saved*, especially 27, 69, 76, 104, and quote, 161; Falwell, *Strength for the Journey*; and Martin, *With God on Our Side*, 56, 197. Towns and Falwell, *Church Aflame*, claims that TRBC is the fastest-growing church in the nation, and Falwell wants it to be the largest. Falwell's programming was heard daily on 280 radio stations and weekly on 300 television stations (56).

43. Falwell, "Ministers and Marches," transcript of the sermon delivered at Thomas Road Baptist Church on Sunday night, March 21, 1965, as published in Young, *God's Bullies*, 310–17, quotes, 310–12. Someone seems to have culled all copies (written transcripts and tapes) of this sermon—which is often referred to as "Ministers and Marchers"—from the Liberty University archives as of June 2006. See also Falwell, "America's Lawlessness," *America Can Be Saved*, 90–91.

44. Falwell, "Ministers and Marches," quotes, 315–16.

45. Falwell, "Let's Reach the World Together," *America Can Be Saved*, quote, 17; Falwell, "Wide Open Door, but Many Enemies," *America Can Be Saved*, quote, 62; Falwell, "Segregation or Integration, Which?" a 1958 sermon cited and quoted in Martin, *With God on Our Side*, 55–58; Goodman and Price, *Jerry Falwell*; Young, *God's Bullies*; Harding, *Book of Jerry Falwell*. For Falwell's own account, see Falwell, *Strength for the Journey*, 288–99.

46. Young, *God's Bullies*, 199–201, quotes Robert Scheer's interview with Falwell for the *Los Angeles Times*, 199; Falwell, *Strength for the Journey*, 288–99, quote, 296; FitzGerald, *Cities on a Hill*; Harding, *Book of Jerry Falwell*, 21–28. Observers at the time, from African Americans angry at white parents' avoidance of integration to white southerners who embraced the new so-called seg academies certainly connected the openings of these schools to integration. See Joseph Crespino, "Civil Rights and the Religious Right," in *Rightward Bound: Making America Conservative in the 1970s*, ed. Bruce Schulman and Julian Zelizer (Cambridge, Mass.: Harvard University Press, 2008), 90–105.

47. Falwell, "America Back to God," a 1976 sermon cited in Harding, *Book of Jerry Falwell*, that no longer exists in the archive. There is a sermon called "America Must Come Back to God," April 27, 1975, Sermon ID Code: OTGH-133, tape, LUV, but it does not mention politics at all, an indication of just how much Falwell changes in 1976. Falwell, "Conditions Corrupting America," May 16, 1976, Sermon ID Code: OTGH-192, transcript, 16, LUV. On the size of Falwell's church in the late seventies, see Falwell, "Whatever Happened to the Family," December 2, 1979, Sermon Code: OTGH-377. See also Joe Ledlie, "Abortion Became Catalyst for Bible-Belt Politics," *Atlanta Journal*, March 18, 1980; Ledlie, "Politics from the Pulpit," *Atlanta Constitution*, March 16, 1980; and Ledlie, "Christian Voter Drive Wants to Influence Politicians," *Atlanta Journal*, March 17, 1980.

48. Crespino, "Civil Rights and the Religious Right"; Martin, *With God on Our Side*, Weyrich quote, 173.

49. Martin, *With God on Our Side*, 25–73.

50. Martin, *With God on Our Side*.

51. Falwell, "America's Lawlessness," *America Can Be Saved*, quotes, 90, 91, 86–87.

52. Falwell, "The Biblical Answer to Women's Lib," May 11, 1975, Sermon ID Code: OTGH-135, tape, LUV; "Abortion-on-Demand: Is It Murder?" February 26, 1978, quote, 9; "Whatever Happened to the Family?" December 2, 1979, Sermon ID Code: OTGH-377, transcript, LUV, quotes, 17, 18, 19.

53. Martin, *With God on Our Side*, 173–74, Towns and Dobson quotes, 210, 217; D'Souza, *Falwell Before the Millennium*, Marty quote, 116; direct mail reproduced in Young, *God's Bullies*, 309; Falwell, "A Day of Many Solomons," *America Can Be Saved*, 109–21, quote, 120.

54. "American Back to God," February 3, 1980, Sermon ID Code: OTGH-386, transcript, quote, 17, LUV; Martin, *With God on Our Side*, quote, 202; FitzGerald, *Cities on a Hill*.

55. Falwell, "The Biblical Answer to Women's Lib," May 11, 1975; "America Must Come Back to God," April 27, 1975; "Conditions Corrupting Politics," May 16, 1976; "The Establishment," 1976; "Home: Ten Major Threats," May 27, 1979, Sermon ID Code: OTGH-352, tape, LUV; "America Back to God," February 3, 1980, Sermon ID Code: OTGH-386, transcript; LUV; Patricia Pingry, *Jerry Falwell: Man of Vision* (Milwaukee: Ideals Publishing, 1980), quote, 6.

56. D'Souza, *Falwell Before the Millennium*, 111.

57. Falwell, *Strength for the Journey*, 334–47; Falwell, *If I Should Die Before I Wake* (New York: Thomas Nelson, 1986), 31–47; Francis Schaeffer, *How Should We Then*

Live? The Rise and Decline of Western Thought and Culture (Old Tappan, N.J.: Revell, 1976); Martin, *With God on Our Side*, 160; Schaeffer and C. Everett Koop, *Whatever Happened to the Human Race?* (Grand Rapids, Mich.: Revell, 1977). Interestingly, Falwell does not mention Koop at all in his autobiography. Many fundamentalists turned against Koop for his role, as the surgeon general, in fighting AIDS during the later years of the Reagan administration.

58. Mel White (ghostwriter and script doctor for both Schaeffer and Falwell), interview, cited in Martin, *With God on Our Side*, 197. Scholars and journalists have repeatedly questioned Falwell's and his organization's figures for the size of his audience, the number of church members, the number of radio listeners, and the number of television viewers.

59. Falwell, *Strength for the Journey*, quotes, 336–37. Martin, *With God on Our Side*, gives the 1978 date and cites an interview with Elmer Towns. My own research has turned up no existing copies of sermons preached before "Abortion-on-Demand: Is It Murder?" (February 26, 1978) and "Legalized Abortion-on-Demand: Is It Murder?" (April 30, 1978). On the range of Christian perspectives on abortion, see Jeffery L. Sheler, "The Theology of Abortion," *U.S. News and World Report* (March 9, 1992).

60. Falwell, *Strength for the Journey*, quote, 338.

61. Falwell, *Strength for the Journey*, 339–40.

62. Martin, *With God on Our Side*, 172–73, 197–202, quote, 199. Pat Robertson, Jim Bakker, and James Dobson also pushed opposition to the IRS decision issue on their radio and television programs. D'Souza, *Falwell Before the Millenium*, 109–11, argues that Paul Weyrich's strategy was to protest abortion in order to split the Democratic Party coalition by pushing ethnic Catholics and southern white conservative Christians to vote Republican.

63. Joe Ledlie, "Politics from the Pulpit," *Atlanta Constitution*, March 16, 1980, quote, Harding, *Book of Jerry Falwell*, quote, 9; Myra MacPherson, "The Genesis and Gospel of the Reverend of the Right," *Washington Post*, September 26, 1984, quote, D9; MacPherson, "Falwell: Big-Time Politics from the Pulpit of Old-Time Religion," *Washington Post*, September 27, 1984.

64. Falwell, "Abortion-on-Demand: Is It Murder?" quote, 2.

65. Jerrold Seigel, *Bohemian Paris: Culture, Politics, and the Boundaries of Bourgeoisie Life, 1830–1930* (New York: Viking, 1986).

Chapter 8: Rescue

1. Martin Oppenheimer and George Lakey, *A Manual for Direct Action* (Chicago: Quadrangle Books, 1965), xiii.

2. Randall Terry, *Accessory to Murder: The Enemies, Allies, and Accomplices to the Death of Our Culture* (Brentwood, Tenn.: Wolgemuth and Hyatt, 1990); Terry direct mail letter, 1990, Randall Terry file, Political Research Associates. This section draws heavily, with the generous help of Chip Berlet, from the archives of Political Research Associates, Somerville, Massachusetts (hereafter cited as PRA). PRA is one of the few places that have collected the direct mail appeals and other literature of the anti-abortion movement, including the rare *Army of*

God Manual: When Life Hurts, We Can Help. The date of the founding of Operation Rescue is in dispute, with Terry claiming 1986 but other participants and scholars arguing for 1987, the year Terry claims Operation Rescue set up its national office.

3. Sources on American conservatism in the postwar period and the rise of the Religious Right that have influenced my thinking here include Chip Berlet and Matthew N. Lyons, *Right-Wing Populism in America: Too Close for Comfort* (New York: Guilford Press, 2000); Jonathan M. Schoenwald, *A Time for Choosing: The Rise of Modern American Conservatism* (New York: Oxford University Press, 2001: Lisa McGirr, *Suburban Warriors: The Origins of the New American Right* (Princeton, N.J.: Princeton University Press, 2001); David Farber and Jeff Roche, eds., *The Conservative Sixties* (New York: Peter Lang, 2003); Bruce J. Schulman and Julian E. Zelizer, eds., *Rightward Bound: Making America Conservative in the 1970s* (Cambridge, Mass.: Harvard University Press, 2008); Godfrey Hodgson, *The World Turned Right Side Up: A History of the Conservative Ascendancy in America* (Boston: Houghton Mifflin, 1996); Mary C. Brennan, *Turning Right in the Sixties: The Conservative Capture of the GOP* (Chapel Hill: University of North Carolina Press, 1995); Lawrence Grossberg, *We Gotta Get Out of This Place: Popular Conservatism and Postmodern Culture* (New York: Routledge, 1992); Russell Kirk, *The Conservative Mind: From Burke to Eliot* (Chicago: Regnery, 1953); Kirk, *The Portable Conservative Reader* (New York: Penguin, 1982); George M. Marsden, *Fundamentalism and American Culture: The Shaping of Twentieth-Century Evangelicalism, 1870–1925* (New York: Oxford University Press, 1980); R. Laurence Moore, *Religious Outsiders and the Making of Americans* (New York: Oxford University Press, 1986); and Martin Anderson, *Revolution: The Reagan Legacy* (New York: Harcourt, Brace, Jovanovich, 1988);

4. The alternative to politics, in this sense, is war, which mobilizes bodies too, corpses and the maimed bodies of the injured. See Elaine Scarry, *The Body in Pain* (New York: Oxford University Press, 1985). Terrorism, a form of warfare in which small groups kill and injure people, using the bodies to create a spectacle and to provoke a violent response from their opponents, is in this sense violent direct action.

5. On the history of direct action and civil disobedience, see Frances Fox Piven, *Challenging Authority: How Ordinary People Change America* (Lanham, Md.: Rowman and Littlefield, 2006); and Roland Bleiker, *Popular Dissent, Human Agency, and Global Politics* (New York: Cambridge University Press, 2000). On civil disobedience and anti-abortion activism, from the perspective of an activist, see Randy C. Alcorn, *Is Rescuing Right? Breaking the Law to Save the Unborn* (Downers Grove, Ill.: InterVarsity Press, 1990).

6. Ronald Formisano, *Boston Against Busing* (Chapel Hill: University of North Carolina Press, 1991); J. Anthony Lukas, *Common Ground* (New York: Knopf, 1985); Dan Carter, *The Politics of Rage: George Wallace, the Origins of the New Conservatism, and the Transformation of American Politics* (New York: Simon and Schuster, 1995). Pro-choice supporters often argue that there is no nonviolent direct action anti-abortion movement and that Terry and Operation Rescue in particular encourage violent attacks on clinics and abortion providers. It is

true that Terry is on record praying for abortion doctors to die, that former Terry associates and OR members have attacked and killed clinics and doctors, and that Terry has never condemned convicted murderers of abortion providers like Paul Hill. Still, evidence suggests that most people who participated in OR's rescues in the late eighties and early nineties were attracted to the group's public position as nonviolent. All of OR's literature on protesting, often called rescuing, demanded that protesters behave nonviolently and sign a pledge to this effect. On the violent wing of anti-abortion protest and its long history of sabotage, bombings, attacks on people, and murders, and Terry's and other OR leaders' connections to this violence, see Dudley Clendinen, "Abortion Clinic Bombings Have Caused Disruption for Many," *New York Times*, February 6, 1985, A14; and especially Eleanor J. Bader and Patricia Baird-Windle, *Targets of Hatred: Anti-Abortion Terrorism* (New York: Palgrave Macmillan, 2001). Thinking seriously about anti-abortionists' use of the civil rights movement as a model changes the history of postwar protest movements and the use of direct action. In this new story, the eighties look less like a break with a postwar tradition of protest than yet another adaptation of those protest methods by a group— conservative Christians opposed to abortion—who saw themselves as marginalized and oppressed by American society. Nonviolent direct action, and particularly its use in the church-based, Deep South civil rights movement, looks more radical and religious, based in faith in God and a moral commitment to do what is right regardless of the outcome, and much less like political liberalism with its faith in human progress. And alienation—a feeling of psychological, cultural, and moral estrangement from what a person sees as her society—looks a lot more politically promiscuous than most participants in the New Left wanted to believe at the time. On faith and theology and its role in motivating African American Christians in the South, see David L. Chappell, *A Stone of Hope: Prophetic Religion and the Death of Jim Crow* (Chapel Hill: University of North Carolina Press, 2004). For a terrific summary of the historiography of the New Right, see Kim Phillips-Fein, "Right On," *Nation*, September 9, 2009.

7. Terry direct mail, n.d. [attributed by author, 1990], Randall Terry file, PRA, emphasis in the original. Direct mailers often use italics, boldface, and varied fonts.

8. Thomas Hilgers and Dennis Horan, *Abortion and Social Justice* (N.p.: Sun Life, 1980), 105, i.

9. James Risen and Judy Thomas, *Wrath of Angels: The American Abortion War* (New York: Basic Books, 1999), 60.

10. Oppenheimer and Lakey, *Manual for Direct Action*, quotes, xi, 73, 78, 80.

11. Risen and Thomas, *Wrath of Angels*, 61.

12. On the struggle over abortion, see Cynthia Gorney, *Articles of Faith: A Frontline History of the Abortion Wars* (New York: Simon and Schuster, 1998); Kristin Luker, *Abortion and the Politics of Motherhood* (Berkeley: University of California Press, 1984); Rickie Solinger, *Abortion Wars: A Half Century of Struggle, 1950–2000* (Berkeley: University of California Press, 1998); Risen and Thomas, *Wrath of Angels*; Michele McKeegan, *Abortion Politics: Mutiny in the Ranks of the*

Right (New York: Free Press, 1992); Carol J. C. Maxwell, *Pro-Life Activists in America: Meaning, Motivation, and Direct Action* (New York: Cambridge University Press, 2002); and Carol Mason, *Killing for Life: The Apocalyptic Narrative of Pro-Life Politics* (Ithaca, N.Y.: Cornell University Press, 2002); Garry Wills, "Evangels of Abortion," *New York Review of Books*, June 15, 1989, 15–21; James Davison Hunter, *Before the Shooting Begins: Searching for American Democracy in America's Culture Wars* (New York: Simon and Schuster, 1994); Celia Farber, "Mixed Emotions," *Spin*, December 1991, 79–86; and Susan Faludi, "Where Did Randy Go Wrong?" *Mother Jones*, November 1989, 22–28, 61–64. Books that cover the issue of abortion from the anti-abortion perspective include William Brennan, *The Abortion Holocaust: Today's Final Solution* (St. Louis: Landmark Press, 1983); George Grant, *Grand Illusions: The Legacy of Planned Parenthood* (Brentwood, Tenn.: Wolgemuth and Hyatt, 1988); Robert H. Ruff, *Aborting Planned Parenthood* (Lewiston, N.Y.: Life Cycle Books, 1988); Dave Andrusko, *To Rescue the Future: The Pro-Life Movement in the 1980s* (Toronto: Life Cycle Books, 1983); and Hilgers and Horan, *Abortion and Social Justice*. Randall Terry's own books include *Accessory to Murder*; *Operation Rescue* (Binghamton, N.Y.: Operation Rescue, 1988); *To Rescue the Children* (N.p.: Project Life, 1992), an instruction manual for starting an anti-choice ministry; and *Why Does a Nice Guy Like Me Keep Getting Thrown in Jail?* (Lafayette, La.: Huntington House, 1993).

13. John O'Keefe, *A Peaceful Presence* (1978), a self-published pamphlet, in available in PRA.

14. Joseph Scheidler, *Closed: 90 Ways to Stop Abortion* (San Francisco: Ignatius Press, 1985); Joan Andrews with J. Cavanaugh-O'Keefe, *I Will Never Forget You: The Rescue Movement in the Life of Joan Andrews* (San Francisco: Ignatius Press, 1989); Richard Cowden-Guido, ed., *You Reject Them, You Reject Me: The Prison Letters of Joan Andrews* (Brentwood, Tenn.: Wolgemuth and Hyatt, 1989); Maxwell, *Pro-Life Activists in America*; and Kathy Rudy, *Beyond Pro-Life and Pro-Choice: Moral Diversity in the Abortion Debate* (Boston: Beacon, 1996). *Closed* is still the how-to book for anti-abortionists, though the ideas in the book have been copied and adapted and circulate most commonly today on the Web and in pamphlet form. For examples of a pamphlet adapted from the ideas in *Closed*, see California Coalition for Life and Operation Rescue of California, *How to Stop Abortion in Your Community*, in the Operation Rescue—California file, PRA. See also a typed excerpt from the pamphlet *52 Simple Things You Can Do To Be Pro-Life*, by Anne Person and Carol Risser (Minneapolis, Minn.: Bethany Publishers, n.d.), itself an adaptation of the ideas in *Closed*, in Operation Rescue file, PRA. Kevin Sherlock's self-published *Abortion Buster's Manual* also came out in 1985, but it focused on driving abortion doctors out of business by researching and publishing their professional histories and malpractice cases, a tactic that has not been very successful.

15. William Martin, *With God on Our Side: The Rise of the Religious Right in America* (New York: Broadway Books, 1996); Risen and Thomas, *Wrath of Angels*; Wills, "Evangels of Abortion."

16. "Part of the Rescue Operation," *America*, May 21, 1988, 524–26, quote, 524; see also quote from Richard Traynor, attorney and president of New Jersey Right to Life: "Philosophically, blowing up an abortion machine can't be wrong, because it's a machine used for killing innocent human beings. However, I would not do it myself. Instead, I choose to put my body between the machine and the innocent victim."

17. Martin, *With God on Our Side*, 321; Faludi, "Where Did Randy Go Wrong?" 25; Howard Kurtz, "Operation Rescue: Aggressively Antiabortion," *Washington Post*, March 6, 1989.

18. Faludi, "Where Did Randy Go Wrong?" 28; Martin, *With God on Our Side*, 321; Risen and Thomas, *Wrath of Angels*, 219, 223; C. Everett Koop and Francis A. Schaeffer, *Whatever Happened to the Human Race?* (Westchester, Ill.: Crossway Books, 1983); Franky Schaeffer, *Whatever Happened to the Human Race?* (Muskegon, Mich.: Gospel Films, 1984), a multipart film version of the book; Rosalind Pollack Petchesky, "Fetal Images: The Power of Visual Culture in the Politics of Reproduction," *Feminist Studies* 13:2 (Summer 1987): 263–329; Mason, *Killing for Life.*

19. Wills, "Evangels of Abortion;" Faludi, "Where Did Randy Go Wrong;" Francis Schaeffer, *A Christian Manifesto* (1981; Wheaton, Ill.: Crossway Books, 2005).

20. Faludi, "Where Did Randy Go Wrong?"

21. Faludi, "Where Did Randy Go Wrong?" quote, 62.

22. Randall Terry, "Operation Rescue: The Civil Rights Movement of the Nineties," *Policy Review* 47 (Winter 1989): 82–83; Kurtz, "Operation Rescue: Aggressively Antiabortion;" Ronald Smothers, "Atlanta Protests Prove Magnet for Abortion Foes," *New York Times*, August 13, 1988, 6.

23. Martin, *With God on Our Side*, 321; David Treadwell, "Escalating Protests at Abortion Clinics Turning Atlanta into Key Battleground," *Los Angeles Times*, August 13, 1988, 2; Kurtz, "Operation Rescue: Aggressively Antiabortion"; Faludi, "Where Did Randy Go Wrong?"' Lyn Cryderman, "A Movement Divided," *Christianity Today*, August 12, 1988, 48–49; "Witnesses for Human Rights," *America*, May 21, 1988, 523, which compares New York City protests in May 1988, the week preceding Mother's Day, to the Solidarity strike in May 1988 in Gdansk, Poland: "Each group was testifying to the innate dignity and rights of every human being"; Terry, "Operation Rescue: The Civil Rights Movement of the Nineties," and Richard John Neuhaus's letter in response to the piece, *Policy Review* 48 (Spring 1989): 95.

24. Randall Terry, *Operation Rescue* (Binghamton, N.Y.: Operation Rescue, 1988). The verse is from a paraphrase of the Bible into contemporary language, *The Living Bible* (Wheaton, Ill.: Tyndale House, 1971).

25. Terry, "Operation Rescue: The Civil Rights Movement of the Nineties."

26. The best account of the violence committed by anti-abortion activists is Bader and Baird-Windle, *Targets of Hatred.*

27. Nat Hentoff, "Civil Rights and Anti-Abortion Protests," *Washington Post*, February 6, 1989, A11; Julian Bond, 'Dr. King's Unwelcome Heirs," *New York Times*, November 2, 1988, A27. The U.S. Civil Rights Commission refused to investigate police brutality against anti-abortion activists even when urged by

one of its own members, conservative William B. Allen. But, as the ACLU and a few other liberal and leftist groups have argued in the last decade, allowing the police and the courts to shut down nonviolent protest on the part of anti-abortion activists severely limits everyone's right to protest. See William B. Allen, "Police Brutality—but No Outrage," *Wall Street Journal*, August 18, 1989.

28. "Enemy of Abortions Is Also Taking Issue with Protest Tactics," *New York Times*, August 31, 1988, A14; Marshall Ingwerson, "Antiabortion Protestors Try a Tougher Strategy," *Christian Science Monitor*, October 7, 1988, 5–6.

29. Faludi, "Where Did Randy Go Wrong?"; "The National Rescuer Resources," Operation Rescue file, PRA.

30. "The OR National Newsletter," November 1994, Operation Rescue file, PRA; Risen and Thomas, *Wrath of Angels*, 217–338.

31. On the protests in Atlanta, see Smothers, "Atlanta Protests Prove Magnet for Abortion Foes"; Cryderman, "Movement Divided"; "Protests in Atlanta," *Christianity Today*, November 4, 1988, 34; Michelle Hiskey, "Thousands Join 'Rescue Movement' Around the Nation," *Christianity Today*, December 9, 1988, 52; Charlotte Low Allen, "Anti-Abortion Movement's Anti-Establishment Face," *Wall Street Journal*, December 8, 1988, A22; and Ingwerson, "Antiabortion Protestors Try a Tougher Strategy."

32. Terry, "Letter from the Atlanta Jail," October 10, 1989, in Terry, *Accessory to Murder*; Martin Luther King Jr., "Letter from a Birmingham Jail," 1963, in *Testament of Hope: The Essential Writings of Martin Luther King, Jr.* (New York: Harper and Row, 1986).

33. Tamar Lewin, "With Thin Staff and Thick Debt, Anti-Abortion Group Faces Struggle," *New York Times*, June 11, 1990, A16; Smothers, "Atlanta Protests Prove Magnet for Abortion Foes"; Hiskey, "Thousands Join 'Rescue Movement' Around the Nation."

34. Allen, "Anti-Abortion Movement's Anti-Establishment Face."

35. Quotes are from undated Operation Rescue materials in PRA: from the Operation Rescue file, "Everything you ever wanted to know about how to rescue preborn children," "Spring of Life Rescue in Buffalo, New York [1992]," and "Operation Rescue: Boston: The power of prayer and nonviolence"; and from the Operation Rescue-California file, "Rescuer's Check List," "Legal Considerations," and "How to Stop Abortion in Your Community."

36. "Rescuer's Check List"; "Everything you ever wanted to know about how to rescue preborn children."

37. "Legal Considerations"; "Everything you ever wanted to know about how to rescue preborn children"; letters from jail include Keith Tucci, "To Pro-life Christians in America," April 26, 1993, and Bob Jewitt, no title, handwritten on plain paper, both in Operation Rescue file, PRA; Randall Terry, "Ready . . . Aim . . . Backfire," January 3, 1995, in Randall Terry file, PRA.

38. Dorothee Benz, "Inside Operation Rescue," *Sojourner: The Women's Forum*, December 1992, 10; "Pastor Keith Tucci to Judge Eileen O'Neil, Contempt of Court Hearing, Houston, Tex., August 20, 1992," as distributed by Operation Rescue National, Operation Rescue file; Letter to "Dear Friend of the Unborn,"

October 1992, Operation Rescue—California file; *What Does One Abortion Cost?* Operation Rescue file; "Everything you ever wanted to know about how to rescue preborn children," which also includes the Cowgill poem; *Cities of Refuge* pamphlet for protests in seven cities in July 1993, Operation Rescue file; all in PRA.

39. *National Rescue Update*, Summer of Purpose Edition, July 6–11, 1992, Operation Rescue File, PRA. This sporadically produced newsletter is full of photographs and is also a good example of anti-abortion activists' use of the Holocaust analogy—across the font beside images of abortion clinics are the words "Auschwitz, USA."

40. On the rising class status of many evangelicals in the postwar period, see John G. Turner, *Bill Bright and Campus Crusade for Christ: The Renewal of Evangelicalism in Postwar America* (Chapel Hill: University of North Carolina Press, 2008); Jon R. Stone, *On the Boundaries of American Evangelicalism: The Postwar Evangelical Coalition* (New York: St. Martin's, 1997); and Steven Miller, *Billy Graham and the Rise of the Republican South* (Philadelphia: University of Pennsylvania Press, 2009).

41. "Enemy of Abortions Is Also Taking Issue with Protest Tactics"; Ingwerson, "Antiabortion Protestors Try a Tougher Strategy."

42. "The power of prayer and nonviolence: Turning the tide against abortion," Operation Rescue file, PRA; and AOG manual, *When Life Hurts, We Can Help* (n.p., n.d.). My copy is copied from a not very good copy at PRA, and the page numbers are illegible.

43. For the text and history of the bill, see http://www.justice.gov/crt/crim/248fin.php, accessed April 2, 2009.

44. Footage compiled by the research division of Planned Parenthood in the 1990s, videotapes at PRA; Montana Human Rights Network memo, "Missionaries to the Preborn: Combining Anti-Choice Rhetoric and the Militia Movement," PRA; Berlet and Lyons, *Right-Wing Populism in America*; Leonard Zeskind, "Armed and Dangerous: The NRA, Militias, and White Supremacists Are Fostering a Network of Right-Wing Warriors," *Rolling Stone*, November 2, 1995.

45. Terry, "Ready . . . Aim . . . Backfire"; Risen and Thomas, *Wrath of Angels*.

46. Baird-Windle and Bader, *Targets of Hatred*.

47. *Army of God*, part of HBO series *America Undercover*, 2000; transcribed by author.

48. Berlet and Lyons, *Right-Wing Populism in America*; Diamond, *Spiritual Warfare*; footage compiled by the research division of Planned Parenthood in the 1990s, videotapes at PRA.

Conclusion: The Cost of Rebellion

1. Jon Krakauer, "Death of an Innocent: How Christopher McCandless Lost His Way in the Wilds," *Outside*, January 1993, accessed on July 24, 2010, at http://outsideonline.com/outside/features/1993/1993_into_the_wild_1.html. Late in his stay in the bus, a desperate McCandless—in his words, "near death"—signed his real name to an SOS note he pinned beside the bus door.

2. Ned Zeman, "The Man Who Loved Grizzlies: For Timothy Treadwell, the Grizzlies of Alaska Weren't Just the World's Largest Terrestrial Predators," *Vanity Fair*, May 2004, accessed on July 24, 2010, at http://www.vanityfair.com/culture/features/2004/05/timothy-treadwell200405; Werner Herzog, *Grizzly Man* (Lionsgate and Discovery Docs, 2005).

3. The Discovery Channel used Treadwell's footage to make the multiple episodes of *The Grizzly Diaries*, first aired in 2006. After his death, Animal Planet edited more of his film footage into the eight-episode series *The Grizzly Man Diaries*, first broadcast in 2008.

4. Zeman, "Man Who Loved Grizzlies," 3, 5.

5. In fact, no contemporary critique of the outsider romance has yet surpassed those offered by some Black Power advocates in the late 1960s and 1970s, most notably the commentary of Julius Lester.

Index

Note: Page numbers in *italics* indicate photographs.

The Farm, 250
Farmer, James, 144
Father Knows Best (television), 42
Faulkner, William, 157
Federal Bureau on Investigation (FBI), 92, 172, 193, 222–23, 352n18
feminism: and the anti-abortion movement, 282–83, 285; and bohemian culture, 47; and Buckley, 134; and Christian fundamentalism, 256, 268, 270, 274; and cultural separatism, 228; and Falwell, 238; and Jesus People, 250; and "the movement," 206–7
Ferlinghetti, Lawrence, 79–80
Festival (1967), 84–85, 87
Festival of Life, 221
Fiedler, Leslie, 40
field recordings, 91–92, 99
film industry, 16–17, 26–27, 35, 37, 79
Firing Line, 82, 133, 136, 144, 146
Fisk University, 108
Folklore Center, 99, 120, 129
folklore studies, 4
folk music: and Black Power, 214; and the civil rights movement, 8, 87, 88–107, 107–18, 118–32; and Dylan, 86, 96–97, 100, 116, 118–31, *130*, 334n87; and folk revivalism, 88–107, *94*; and the Mississippi Summer Project, 196; and race issues, 86, 88, 91–92, 107, 115–18; and romance of the outsider, 2
Folksong 59 (concert), 92
Folk Song U.S.A., 89–90
Folkways Anthology of American Folk Music, 86, 91, 93, 99
Folkways Records, 90–91, 103, 111
Ford, Gerald, 273
foreign policy, 141, 218–19
Forman, James: and community organizing, 190; dedication to civil rights movement, 192; and the Freedom Singers, 111, 116; and Freedom Village, 170; and Holt, 108; marriage, 164; and SNCC successes, 202
The Fountainhead (Rand), 39, 134, 155
Frank, Thomas, 7
Frankfurt School, 37
Franny and Zooey (Salinger), 43
Freed, Alan, 63, 73
Freedom House, 202
Freedom in the Air, 111
Freedom of Access to Clinic Entrances Act, 299–300
Freedom Rally, 150
Freedom Riders, 109, 166, 173, 176, 199–200
Freedom Schools, 193, 197, *197*, 199, 201
Freedom Singers, 85–87, 110–17, 125, 175–76, 189, 331–32n57
Freedom Songs, 108, 110, 111, 205, 206
Freedom Summer. *See* Mississippi Summer Project
Freedom Village, 170
Freedom Vote experiments, 193, 225
"Free Huey" campaign, 216
free lunch programs, 185
free market economics, 135, 138, 141, 147, 153
The Freewheelin' Bob Dylan (album), 124
"Freight Train," 103
Freudian theory, 27, 31–32, 41
Friends of SNCC, 113–14, 202, 215
Frisbee, Lonnie, 240, 244–45, 248
Fuller, Charles, 257
Fuller Seminary, 261
fundamentalism: and anti-abortion movement, 266, 277;

and the civil rights movement, 265, 267; and conversion experiences, 257; and Falwell, 254–75; and the Jesus People movement, 247, 250–52, 254; Marty on, 237; and romance of the outsider, 3, 303; theology of, 248–50
The Fundamentals, 5
fusionism, 142

Gaede, Marnie, 307
Gallup, 255
Gandhi, Mohandas, 281
Garmen, Betty, 113–14
Gavitt's Original Ethiopian Serenaders, 53
gay rights/liberation movement, 206, 228, 268, 270, 277, 290
gender issues: and anti-abortion movement, 282–83, 288, 298; and beatniks, 45–46, 82; and blackface minstrelsy, 54; and blues music, 59–60; and bohemian culture, 43–48; and *Catcher in the Rye*, 15, 43–44, 46; and the Jesus People movement, 250; mass culture, 47–48; and Presley, 64, 67–68; and romance of the outsider, 308; and the women's liberation movement, 7, 43–48, 267–68. *See also* feminism
Georgia, 190–91, 289
Gestalt therapy, 234
Gidget (1959), 44
Gilbert, Ronnie, 90
Gillespie, Dizzy, 42
Ginsberg, Allen: and the Beat Generation, 45, 79–80; and bohemian culture, 47; and Buckley, 144, 145; and communes, 232; and Dylan, 119; and hippie culture, 230; and the Jesus People movement, 242, 246; and Kerouac, 78; and mass culture, 43; and the new consciousness, 18; and *On the Road*, 76
"Girl of the North Country," 125
Gitlin, Todd, 182
Glass, Franny (character), 43
Glazer, Nathan, 146
Gleason, Ralph, 81, 112
glossolalia, 252–53
Goad, 243
Gober, Bertha, 109, 111
God and Man at Yale (Buckley), 132, 135, 137–38
"God Bless America," 89
Goethe, Johann Wolfgang von, 27
Goldwater, Barry, 147
Good, Paul, 210
Goodman, Andrew, 198, 282
Goodman, Paul, 18, 145, 234
"Goodnight, Irene," 90
Gorman, Betty, 202
gospel music, 50, 258
Gospel Songs from the Old Fashioned Revival Hour, 258
Graham, Billy, 248, 261–62, 266
Grateful Dead, 230
Gray, Arvella, 120
Great Depression, 17, 18
Great Elm estate, 148
Greenberg, Clement, 37, 38
Greensboro Four, 166
Greenwich Village: and bohemian culture, 45–46; and Dylan, 123; and the folk music revival, 90, 99–100, 103; and Thompson, 156
Greenwood, Esther, 44–45, 214
Gregory, Dick, 144

Griffiin, Michael, 299
"Grizzly Bear," 93
Guillard, Slim, 77
Gulf of Tonkin Resolution, 224
Gunn, David, 299
Guthrie, Woody: and the civil rights movement, 111, 112; and Dylan, 118, 120–25, 127; and the folk music revival, 90; and folk music revivalism, 89–90, 100–101; and the Newport Folk Festival, 85

Haber, Al: and civil disobedience, 169–71; and ERAP, 182; and *Revolution in Mississippi*, 174–75; and rise of SDS, 172, 174–77; and student activism, 167; and Students for a Democratic Society, 167–68
Haight-Ashbury, 228, 243
Hair (musical), 145
Haley, Bill, 79
Hall, Prathia, 193
Hamer, Fannie Lou, 185, 197, 201
Hamilton, Charles, 214
Hamlett, Ed, 192
Hammond, John, Jr., 96–97, 100
Hampton, Fred, 219
Hancock Village, 5
Harding, Vincent, 198, 213
"A Hard Rain's A-Gonna Fall," 125
Harper's, 1, 190
Harrington, Michael, 140, 144, 163, 186, 187–88
Harris, Rutha, 85, 111, 112
Harvard University, 152
Harvest House, 245
Hayden, Casey, 171
Hayden, Tom: background, 163–64; and Buckley, 134; and Calvert, 226–27; and ERAP, 180–82, 184–87, 189; and Mailer's writings, 2; and the National Student Association, 341n11; on outsider status, 345n50; and *Revolution in Mississippi*, 174–75;
and romance of the outsider, 6; and student conservatism, 147–48, 152; and student organizing, 344–45n44; and Students for a Democratic Society, 148, 165–80; and the Vietnam War, 225
Hayes, Carl, 174
Hays, Lee, 90
"Hear Me Talking to You," 59
Heefner, Steve, 248, 253
Hefner, Hugh, 42, 144
Hellerman, Fred, 90
Hell's Angels, 158, 231–32
Hell's Angels (Thompson), 158
Hemingway, Ernest, 80
Hentoff, Nat, 98
Heritage Foundation, 290
Hill, King Solomon, 96
Hill, Paul, 366n6
hillbilly music: and Dylan, 120, 121–22, 123–24; and the folk music revival, 90–91, 95–96, 101, 104; and origins of rock and roll, 50; and Presley, 64–66
Hinton, Sam, 97–98
hip-hop music, 303
hippies: and counterculture, 229; and evangelical Christianity, 238, 239; and Falwell, 256; and the Jesus People movement, 239–54; and religious revivalism, 255; and rock festivals, 230; and romance of the outsider, 3; and Thompson, 158; and Vietnam, 225

His Place, 241
historically black colleges (HBCs), 109, 110, 332n57
Hoboken, New Jersey, 187
Hoffman, Abbie, 221, 230
Hog Farm commune, 231
Holcomb, Roscoe, 2
"Hold On," 110
Holiday, Billie, 96
Hollywood Free Paper, 241, 243
Holmes, John Clellon, 81
Holt, Len, 108
"Honkies for Huey," 216
"Hoochie Coochie Man," 92
hootenannies, 90, 93, 119–20
Hoover, J. Edgar, 222, 352n18
Hope, Bob, 82
Horkheimer, Max, 37
Horsley, Neal, 300–301
Hoskins, Tom, 104
"Hound Dog," 67
House, Son, 2–3, 103, 116
House Un-American Activities Committee (HUAC), 149–50, 166, 169
Howe, Irving, 37, 136
Howl and Other Poems (Ginsburg), 79–80
"Howl" (Ginsberg), 43, 47, 80, 82
How Should We Then Live? (1976), 272
How to Sing and Play the Blues like the Phonograph and Stage Artists, 118
How to Survive an Atomic Bomb, 17
Hughes, Langston, 61
Huguenard, Amie, 307
Humphrey, Hubert, 210
Hunke, Herbert, 47
Hunter, Meredith, 231–32
Hurt, Mississippi John, 86, 92, 99, 103, 116

Ichthus, 243
"Ida Blue," 50
"If I Had a Hammer," 109, 110
If I Should Die Before I Wake (Falwell), 271
"I Got a Woman," 67
"I Love America" rallies, 269, 273
imperialism, 218–19, 221, 222
individualism: and Buckley, 138; and the folk music revival, 106; and mass culture, 16–17, 38, 39, 41, 140; and Thompson, 156; and Young Americans for Freedom, 149
integration: and Buckley, 142–43; and Christian fundamentalism, 261, 265–66; and crossover music, 50; and the folk music revival, 92; and the Freedom Singers, 115
Internal Revenue Service (IRS), 265–66, 268, 274
International Workers of the World (IWW), 153, 157
"An Interracial Movement of the Poor?" (Wittman), 181
interventionism, 141, 153
involvementism, 147
"I Shall Be Free," 125
"I Shall Be Free No. 10," 126
isolationism, 141
Israel, 249
"I Wish We'd All Been Ready," 249

Jackson, George, 218, 219, 221
Jackson, Jesse, 291

Little Richard (Richard Wayne Penniman), 71
Little Sandy Review, 105, 124
Living Bible, 290, 292
The Living Room, 243
Logan, Katherine, 198
Lomax, Alan, 89–95, 98, 102, 109
Lomax, John, 88–89, 91, 93, 102
Los Angeles Free Press, 234
Los Angeles Times, 209, 264, 289
The Lost Generation, 80
Lott, Eric, 51, 53–54
Louisiana Hayride, 64
Louvin, Charlie, 72
Louvin, Ira, 72
Love Me Tender (1956), 79
Love Song, 244–45
Lowenstein, Allard, 192–94, 196
LSD, 228, 230
Luce, Carl, 27, 29, 31
lullabies, 100
Lyman, Mel, 85
Lynchburg Baptist College, 268
Lynchburg Christian Academy, 264, 265
Lynchburg Ministerial Association, 264
Lynchburg News, 271
Lynd, Staughton, 144, 145
Lyon, Danny, 125, 191
Lyrical Ballads (Wordsworth and Coleridge), 27–28

Maccoby, Michael, 152–53
Macdonald, Dwight, 37, 38, 40, 135, 138–39
Machtinger, Howard, 220
Maddox, Lester, 263
Mademoiselle, 95, 144, 176
"Maggie's Farm," 128
Mailer, Norman, 75; and black culture, 73–74, 78–79; and Buckley, 136, 144, 146; influence of, 2; and the new consciousness, 18; Salinger on, 26; and transformation, 258
Malcolm X: and Black Power, 204–5, 207, 210, 214; and militancy, 215, 217–18; Thompson on, 157–58
"Man, We're Beat," 82
The Man in the Gray Flannel Suit (Wilson), 39
A *Manual for Direct Action* (Oppenheimer and Lakey), 278, 282–84
The Many Loves of Dobie Gillis (television), 82
Maoism, 228
Mao Tse-tung, 215, 222
March Against Fear, 208
March on Washington, 88, 181, 192, 224
marijuana, 76–77, 81, 119, 133, 146, 221–22, 301
Marjorie Morningstar (Wouk), 43–44
Marty, Martin, 237, 268
Marxism: and alienation, 30; and black militancy, 178; and Buckley, 141, 145; and *Catcher in the Rye*, 27; and Guthrie, 89; and mass culture, 35; and militancy, 216
masks, 101
mass culture: and bohemian culture, 47–48; and Buckley, 140; and *Catcher in the Rye*, 16, 24–25; and the folk music revival, 105; and rebel figures, 34–43; and romance of the outsider, 5–6. *See also* news and media; popular culture
"massification" of life, 39
"Masters of War," 124, 129
Max, Steve, 182

"Maybelline," 50
McCall's, 41–42
McCandless, Christopher, 303–4, 304–5
McCann, Sean, 7
McCarthy, Eugene, 157
McCarthy, Joseph, 139
McCarthy, Mary, 37
McCarthy and His Enemies (Buckley and Bozell), 139, 141
McCarthyism, 34, 99, 139, 149–50
McComb, Mississippi, 86, 170–71, 173–74, 181, 193
McDew, Chuck, 169, 174–75
MC-5, 221
McGhee, Brownie, 121
McGovern, George, 157
McKissick, Floyd, 144
McLaurin, Charles, 193–94
McMichen, Clayton, 104
media. *See* news and media
medicine shows, 57
meditation, 246
Medovoi, Leerom, 7, 44
mega-churches, 253, 254
Memoirs of a Beatnik (Di Prima), 45
Memphis, Tennessee, 63
Memphis Minnie (Lizzie Douglass), 61, 120
Memphis Slim (John Len Chatman), 92
Mercury, 139
Mercury Records, 115
Meredith, James, 208
Merry Pranksters, 228, 230
Meyer, Frank, 142, 149
Meyer, June, 213
Michelman, Kate, 291
Michigan Daily, 147, 170
militancy, 214–24, 349–50n7
militia movement, 299, 301
Miller, Dottie, 190
Miller, Henry, 119, 234
Miller, James, 187
Mills, C. Wright, 18–19, 135, 140, 152, 177–79
The Milton Berle Show, 67–69
"Ministers and Marches" (Falwell), 262, 264, 267
minstrelsy: and authenticity, 102; and Black Power, 208; and the civil rights movement, 108; and Dylan, 121–22, 126; and the folk music revival, 87, 88, 95; and Mailer, 73, 74; and Presley, 62, 63, 67, 69, 71; and rebellion, 83; and "revolutionary blackface," 221; and romance of the outsider, 4; and roots of rock and roll, 51, 52–61; and self-transformation, 102; and "The White Negro," 73
Missionaries to the Preborn, 299
Mississippi Freedom Democratic Party (MFDP), 193, 201, 349n5
Mississippi Sovereignty Commission, 174
Mississippi Summer Project, 8, 189–203, 195, 200, 224, 282
Monk, Thelonious, 42
Monroe, Bill, 104
Monroe, Marilyn, 42
Montgomery Improvement Association, 109
The Moondog Rock and Roll House Party, 73
Mooney, Chris, 281, 282
Mooney, Tom, 281, 282
Moore, Alice, 278
Moore, Scotty, 63, 64
Moral Government Fund, 268